Model and Allied Publicaˈ
Argus Books Ltd,
14 St. James Road,
Watford, Herts.,
England.

First published by Percival Marshall Ltd 1931-32

This facsimile edition 1977

ISBN 0 85242 526 0

SHIPS AND SHIP MODELS was one of the shorter-lived of the Percival
Marshall hobby journals, appearing first in September 1931 and ceasing publication during the run of Volume 9 with the April 1940 edition. It was a victim of the
paper rationing imposed at that time which forced many other publications to
cease. The *Ships and Ship Models* title was then incorporated with *Model Engineer*
and is still featured in the masthead of the latter journal. The April 1940 farewell
editorial talked of resuming publication after the war; it never appeared in exactly
this style, but another Percival Marshall magazine did deal with marine
models for a time in post-war years. In best Percival Marshall tradition, *Ships and
Ship Models* is packed with a fascinating mixture of modelling ideas, prototype
information, model projects and information, and the 'lore' of the sea. Virtually
all the contents of this collector's edition of Volume 1 are of interest and reference
value to the present day ship lover and modelling enthusiast. Contents range from
the useful 'Ship Modeller's Scrapbook' to model steamer design, early notice of
the immortal work of the late Norman Ough, a series on notable ships, and a
lively discussion on the oldest ships afloat in 1931-32. In short a most interesting
addition to the present day ship lover's library, which is, in any case, very rare in
its original edition. Missing from this facsimile reprint are the loose supplement
sheets which have long since 'disappeared' from the file copy used for this
reprint. We have, however, incorporated two of the original loose supplements
as pages 121 and 122 of this volume. We wish to thank Mr David R. MacGregor
for kindly providing the original bound copy from which this edition has been
produced.

Reproduced, printed, and bound by
The Garden City Press Limited, Letchworth, Herts. SG6 1JS

SHIPS AND SHIP MODELS

A Magazine for all Lovers of Ships and the Sea

Single Copies, post free, 7½d.
Annual Subscription 7s. 6d.

Editorial and Publishing Offices:
66 FARRINGDON STREET
LONDON :: E. C. 4

Vol. I. No. 1.   SEPTEMBER, 1931.   Price 6d.

All Hands on Deck

THIS is a magazine for lovers of ships and the sea, for people of all ages who build and sail model ships and boats of all kinds, and for those who, though they do not build, are at least interested for historical or other reasons in ship models and small craft. It comes into being mainly because during my many years' editorship of *The Model Engineer* I have experienced a greater demand for information on model marine subjects than I have been able to supply in the limited amount of space at my disposal in that journal. Although *The Model Engineer* has always been extremely sympathetic towards model ship and boat builders, it has many other interests to serve. The wide range of engineering, electrical, and general model making problems which occupy its pages have imposed limits on the space available for purely marine matters, and sometimes my model ship and boat readers have found their hunger for appropriate nautical matter remain unsatisfied. I recently asked the readers of that journal to write me about their model shipbuilding interests. The surprising enthusiasm of their response has induced me to launch SHIPS AND SHIP MODELS to provide them with a little specialised journal of their own. I now present the first number in the confident hope that it will meet with a wide approval.

The course steered by SHIPS AND SHIP MODELS will largely depend on the response it evokes from its readers. I believe there are thousands of people who will be glad to have a paper of this kind. I want them to regard it as something in the welfare of which they have a personal interest. I want them, in fact, to feel members of a large family of fellow-readers who are united by a common interest in everything relating to ships, and boats, and models. They may be lonely and unattached in their hobby ; the little paper will give them a common meeting ground for the exchange of information, experience, and ideas. I invite them to write to me to tell me what they think of the paper, whether the articles are the kind they need, and in what directions the interest and usefulness of the paper can be extended. I want something more than that. I want them to send me photographs and descriptions of ships they know or models they have made ; I want them to help their fellow-readers by sending helpful hints on model making methods, and I want them to use the correspondence columns for the recording and discussion of all matters of common interest. In short, SHIPS AND SHIP MODELS is to sail on a voyage of good-will and helpful service throughout the model marine world, and I want my readers to be not merely saloon passengers but members of the crew, ready to pull on a rope whenever needed. I shall take my trick at the wheel and hold her to her course, but our ship will need a crew of friendly contributors and correspondents to keep the sails filled.

I would like to say a word or two to the members of model sailing and power-boat clubs. I have many friends in the club world, and I hope this little paper will be of interest to them. I shall be glad at any time to have details of either power or sailing boats of special merit, but I do not propose to publish any extended club domestic news or reports of meetings and regattas. The racing men already have a magazine of their own for this news service and SHIPS AND SHIP MODELS does not enter the publishing field in any competitive spirit. It is rather the organ of the unattached enthusiast who is unfettered by any standardised rules and regulations, and who builds and sails his boats for his own pleasure. There are many such who would be glad of practical hints on design and construction, but are not particularly interested to know which boat won this or that club or inter-club event. The unattached model builder who desires to test his boat against other boats, or who is interested in racing as a sport would do well to join a club. He will find good companionship and

good sportsmanship at its best, and plenty of trophies to be raced for.

From September the 3rd to the 12th, the annual *Model Engineer* Exhibition will be held at the Royal Horticultural Hall, Westminster. For some years past a strong model ship section has been developing at this show, and this year there will be the best display of the kind yet held. There are several valuable prizes offered for ship models, and the exhibition itself will afford a friendly rallying point for ship-model enthusiasts from all parts of the country. I shall be happy to extend a special welcome to all readers of SHIPS AND SHIP MODELS who can attend the show.

My plan for launching SHIPS AND SHIP MODELS has been received with great interest by the leaders of the ship-loving and ship-modelling world. I should not like to close these introductory notes without recording my grateful thanks to the many kind friends who have promised their support. In particular, I am indebted to Mr. G. S. Laird Clowes, Mr. Frank C. Bowen, Mr. R. H. Penton, Mr. Basil Lavis, Mr. T. R. Thomas, Mr. Howard Marshall, Mr. Jeffrey Leighton, Mr. Victor B. Harrison and Mr. F. C. Poyser for their encouragement and practical help.

Our little ship is now launched and I hope it will make many friends. If you like it you can help to make the voyage successful by becoming a regular subscriber, or by placing a standing order for the Magazine with your newsagent. You can help by making it known to your friends and enlisting their support. You can buy an extra copy and send it to someone abroad who will be interested. Finally, as I have already explained, you can help by sending me a useful contribution for our pages, or an interesting letter for our correspondence columns. I want you to become a real member of our crew. Will you sign on now ?

PERCIVAL MARSHALL.

Why I Love the Sea

By HOWARD MARSHALL

Sketch by]   **" Outward Bound "**   *[R. H. Penton*

ONCE—for a brief but happy period, I was assistant steward in a cargo-boat. Not that I claim any knowledge of the sea on that score : my job was as near a sinecure as may be, though it was certainly interesting enough. But I mention it because of a saying of the mate's, a variation of the old " Who'd sell a farm and go to sea ? " plaint which we have heard so often. It was as we plugged up the Elbe, that monotonous river which leads to Hamburg, that the mate first remarked vehemently, " When I pack up, I'm goin' to put an oar over me shoulder an' walk straight inland. An' when somebody points at it, an' says ' What's that ? ' I'll stop right there, an' build me a house."

He was a cheerful enough fellow in the ordinary way, but sometimes the sea was too much for him. And yet, when it comes to the point, I'm willing to bet that he will find his house somewhere on the coast, so that he may watch the ships passing by.

I doubt, too, whether the seaman in Masefield's " Cape Horn Gospel " would ever have carried out his intention, though he had every reason for saying :—

" I'm bound for home in the *Oronook,*
    in a suit of looted duds,
A D.B.S. a-earnin' a stake by
    helpin' peelin' spuds,
An' if ever I fetch to Prince's stage
    an' sets my feet ashore,
You bet your hide that there I
    stay, an' foller the sea no more."

It is an odd business, this fascination of the sea, especially from the sailor's point of view. Perhaps it is easy to understand why those of us who have humdrum work to do in London should wish to escape, why we rush away on every available opportunity to some sort of ship ; why we are only really happy when we feel the deck under our feet again. It is, as I say, an escape from routine, a method of reassuring ourselves that we can still put up with a certain amount of hardship, that civilisation has, in fact, not entirely softened us. And I can think of no better summing-up of the matter than Hilaire Belloc's words, which occur in the dedication to that enchanting book of his "The Cruise of the *Nova*."

" Indeed," says Mr. Belloc, " the cruising of a boat here and there is very much what happens to the soul of a man in a larger way. We set out for places which we do not reach, or reach too late ; and, on the way, there befall us all manner of things which we could never have awaited. We are granted great visions, we suffer intolerable tediums, we come to no end of the business, we are lonely out of sight of England, we make astonishing landfalls—and the whole rigmarole leads us along no whither, and yet is alive with discovery, emotion, adventure, peril and repose."

There you have it : undoubtedly there are tediums ; I remember once drifting off the inhospitable coast of Spain in a dead calm, with the sun blazing down insufferably, and no hope of whistling up a breeze. Our time was short, and our desire to make progress great, but there we lay, helpless and alone. But if there are tediums, there are the golden moments, too, as I was reminded later in that same cruise. We happened at the time to be in one of those small lateen-rigged fishing boats so common in the Mediterranean, and we were making what seemed to be the simple crossing from Spezia over the gulf to Lerici. The great harbour was guileless enough, and a gentle slant of wind sent us skimming over the placid surface with astonishing ease. We had been warned that it was unwise to hug the shore, so we stood out towards the wide opening of the channel. There was broken water ahead, and with a rude abruptness we found ourselves suddenly beset by little hungry waves which grew rapidly larger. The wind had shifted, but we had been given a mark, and there was nothing for it but to hold to our course as best we could. It was magnificent. The little boat behaved like a thoroughbred. It was evening, and the sun hung low on the horizon, turning the heavy spray into clouds of diamonds, and somehow enriching a peculiarly vivid emerald green in the sea. The colour, the freshness of the wind, the exhilaration of having a responsive boat beneath us all blended into an experience which still remains in my memory as something singularly enthralling. We heard, afterwards, that it would have been wiser not to have attempted the passage at all, but as, at last, we quietly slid into shelter behind the long Lerici breakwater, and had leisure to look at the little town with the olive slopes rising sharply behind it, we knew that it should be approached only in this way, through a smother of spray and tumbling green water.

No, there is really nothing surprising in the landsman's love of the sea ; after all, he can leave it when he pleases, and return to the security of a house if things go wrong. And he can talk of ships and the sea as comfortably by the warmth of his own fireside as he can in the cabin of his cruising-yacht. I often wonder— indeed, when I am reading or talking of the days of sail—whether my enthusiasm is not possibly a little artificial. After all, I might think differently if I had to go aloft in a Cape Horn snorter : such names as *Lightning* and *Marco Polo* and *Cutty Sark* might then have a considerably less romantic significance. It is so easy to write sentimental nonsense about sailing ships, and the modern craze for ship models and old prints and stories of windjammer experiences is open to suspicion. At any rate, that is how it strikes me in pessimistic moments, but, on the whole, I am convinced that this enthusiasm is both worthy and justified. When all is said and done, the men who write most lovingly about ships are the men who have suffered with them—David Bone, for example, and Conrad and Basil Lubbock.

However much I may feel that to enjoy their books thoroughly, it is necessary to have known the life they describe, I shall always count those

September, 1931   **Ships and Ship Models**   5

Photo by]   **" These Splendid Ships "**   *[Nautical Photo Agency*

shelves which contain " The Brass-bounder," " The Mirror of the Sea," and " The China Clippers," to name but three favourites, as the most precious corner of my small library. All Lubbock's volumes are there, with their photographs, plans and reproductions, and the straightforward accounts of great ships, which are so much better than some high-falutin' literary stories I have come across. Do you remember the race of *Ariel* and *Taeping* home with the tea from China—how they actually arrived off Dungeness together, and how Captain Keay of *Ariel* bore up athwart *Taeping's* hawse, and so prevented Captain M'Kinnon from nicking in and getting the first pilot ? That and dozens of other incidents spring into the memory, and it is right that they should not be forgotten. Perhaps I may end by once more quoting Masefield : a familiar quotation, I know, but one which retains its truth, and seems peculiarly suitable to the first issue of a magazine of this description. In " Ships," Masefield wrote :—

These splendid ships, each with her grace, her glory,
Her memory of old song or comrade's story,
Still in my mind the image of life's need,
Beauty in hardest action, beauty indeed.
" They built great ships and sailed them," sounds most brave,
Whatever arts we have or fail to have ;
I touch my country's mind, I come to grips
With half her purpose thinking of these ships.

*   *   *

They mark our passage as a race of men,
Earth will not see such ships as those agen.

That, I think, justifies even a landsman's interest in the sea.

Notable Ships of To-day

No. 1.—THE NEW C.P.R. LINER " EMPRESS OF BRITAIN "

THIS magnificent new vessel, put into service at the beginning of June, has earned the highest appreciation of Atlantic travellers during the past three months. The flag-ship of the Canadian Pacific Fleet in Atlantic waters, she has more than fulfilled the expectations of her designers and builders, and has quickly earned the courtesy title of " Empress of the Atlantic." We think the accompanying fine photograph and details of this vessel will appeal to all our readers who are interested in steamship progress.

A 24-knot Ship

She is a vessel of 42,500 tons, 758′ long and 97′ 6″ beam. Her speed of 24 knots enables her to make the passage between Southampton and Quebec in five days, the actual open-Atlantic stretch of the voyage being 3½ days. The ship has an ample reserve of power so that she can maintain her regular speed steadily even under extremely adverse conditions.

She was built to the requirements of the highest class of Lloyd's Registry under special survey, 100 A1, subdivided by water-tight bulkheads and fully equipped with all life-saving appliances to comply with latest requirements of the International Convention for the Safety of Life at Sea.

The Machinery

The *Empress of Britain* has quadruple screws, single reduction turbines and high pressure water-tube boilers, and possesses the largest and most important installation yet constructed with high pressure steam machinery as the motive power. Her immense power gives her speed without vibration.

Oil fuel is used to fire the boilers, and their reserve capacity is more than ample to meet all contingencies. As oil fuel is practically smokeless, two only of the ship's handsome streamline funnels serve the engine-rooms ; the third forms part of the vessel's very perfect ventilation system, for the *Empress of Britain* is essentially a fresh-air and sunshine ship, ideally devised for luxurious world-cruising as well as for her Atlantic service.

Electrical Service Throughout

Electric energy is used on a very large scale throughout the vessel, not only for lighting and for driving auxiliary machinery, but also for all cooking and kitchen services, and in countless less prominent but essential and convenient departments of ship-service for passenger comfort. Electric ray baths for instance, and beauty treatments under expert control, are among the vessel's modern " vanities," and points for electric service are fitted in her spacious cabin apartments. For all this the electric power is provided by both Diesel and steam generators which are fitted in water-tight and separate compartments, thus reducing to a minimum the possibility of any disorganisation of these services.

In addition, there are emergency storage batteries of sufficient capacity to maintain all essential lighting services in the remote eventuality of any cessation of all six main generating sets, and of the emergency paraffin sets with which the ship is also provided.

The Spacious Engine Rooms

Spaciousness characterises this ship, not only as regards her passenger appointments and accommodation, but also in every other department of her being. Her engine and boiler rooms are a model in this respect. All four engines driving her propellers are controlled from one starting platform, a feature of immense advantage in manoeuvring the vessel, and one of the noteworthy special features of her design. Two large engines are

The New Canadian Pacific Liner "Empress of Britain."

placed in the forward engine-room, and two smaller engines in the after engine-room, with water-tight compartments separating these units for complete and effective independent action if required. Engine and propeller arrangements for handling the ship in confined or crowded waterways give great facility of control.

Masts, Funnels, and Decks

The *Empress of Britain* has a straight stem raking well forward, and a cruiser stern, and has three funnels and two pole masts. The funnels are of the pear-shaped section, and measure about 27′ across the widest part and 35′ fore and aft. They are about 68′ high above the sun deck. The masts measure about 208′ above the load water line, and are the longest masts yet constructed at the Clydebank Yard.

There is a continuous shelter deck over the upper deck, a bridge deck over shelter deck extending the full length of the vessel, a promenade deck over the shelter deck for more than three-fourths the length of the vessel, a boat deck over the promenade deck for over half the length of the ship, and a sun deck over this boat deck.

Scientifically Complete

The ship is fully equipped with wireless telegraphy and direction-finding apparatus, wireless telephony, submarine signalling apparatus, gyro compass equipment, electric submerged log, echo-sounding machine, electric loudspeaking telephones, intercommunicating telephones, electric bells, alarm hooters, fire alarms, semaphores and morse lamps, clearview screens, and many other electric appliances.

The First Sea Tests

A new world's record for economy in oil fuel consumption while developing great power and speed at sea was made during her exacting tests on the Clyde measured mile, and in the open sea. Using only 0.57 lbs. of fuel per shaft horse-power per hour, the liner developed a speed of 25.52 knots, and 22.6 knots under cruising conditions with only two of her four engines working.

A Welcome to "Ships & Ship Models"

By G. S. LAIRD CLOWES

TO men like myself, who come daily into contact with enthusiasts on the subject of Ships and Ship Models, it has long been a puzzle why there has been, until now, no English publication which caters directly for their needs.

In spite of our glorious naval history and the keen interest in all maritime matters which is innate in so large a number of Englishmen, it has been almost impossible to provide a novice with any publication which will tell him how to start making a reasonably accurate model of one of our famous ships of the past.

Both in Museums and in Libraries much information is available, but it exists only in such a form as is useful to the man who already knows a good deal about ship-building, besides something of model-making. In America, much has been done for the enthusiastic amateur, but naturally this is mainly concerned with American craft, while for serious research into the details of ships prior to the War of Independence, the American can only draw his data from England.

I therefore welcome the appearance of SHIPS AND SHIP MODELS and look forward to the time when a large proportion of the enquiries which reach me from those who wish to make models, whether of the little sailing ships of the great explorers, the great three-deckers of our victorious fleets, or the more modern steamships of commerce, may be safely referred to SHIPS AND SHIP MODELS.

The Romance of the Figurehead

By FRANK C. BOWEN

A S far as material is concerned, quite a lot of the romance of the old-timers is contained in the figureheads which are now coming into their own in the shape of a good deal of specialised study. The practice of decorating the prow of a vessel with a device which from its position would naturally be carved, goes back to the earliest days, religion and the idea of terrorising enemies combining as a purpose. In Europe every type of warship, from Roman galley to Viking long-ship, carried its figurehead, possibly many of the merchantmen as well, and there is every evidence that infinite care and skill was devoted to carving them.

As the design of the fighting ship was improved and the forecastle became a definite feature, the figurehead for a period became crowded out, the fighting platform taking the place where it would normally have been, and decoration being satisfied by the shields of the knights who were fighting on board. But by that time it had a firm hold on the imagination of seamen and builders, and although it was eclipsed for a time, opportunity was soon found to bring it back again, first in the form of a rather insignificant serpent placed awkwardly under the forecastle platform, but gradually in better form and position.

Then the fighting ships in Northern waters started to come under the influence of the Mediterranean galley, which influence lasted for many years and which gave us the beak bow surmounted by a square bulkhead which lasted until after Trafalgar. This form was absolutely ideal for the purposes of the figurehead which was improved out of all recognition. As a strongly decorative period followed the introduction of the beak bow, the heads became very elaborate, and although they have only survived in picture and model those that were fitted to some of the Tudor and Stuart ships, were of remarkable beauty and richness. The French were passing through a period of the same tendencies, and there was keen rivalry between the designers of the two nations which found expression not only in the figureheads but also in stern galleries, port wreaths and the like, until in some extreme instances the decoration of a line-of-battleship ran up to one-sixth of her total cost.

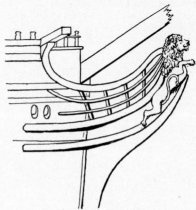

The " Sweep of the Lion "

The beak-head bow gave the opportunity for the designer to give a beautiful sweep of the trail board which supported the figurehead, which in those days was generally a lion standing bolt upright. The " Sweep of the Lion," in fact, became a technical term and gave the opportunity of some very decorative effects, although when a human figure was substituted for the animal the attitude was apt to be strained. The trail boards and bulkhead were also often very elaborately decorated.

After the British Navy had passed through its lion craze, which was much ridiculed in France, there came the period of flattery, when princes, politicians and courtesans were honoured by being made the subject of the figureheads of King's ships. There was a tendency to make them more and more elaborate with an eye for favours to come, so that the Admiralty not only became seriously alarmed at the cost but the bows of the ships were badly over-weighted ; it must be remembered that the foremast and all its gear was already right up in the eyes.

Therefore many attempts were made to abolish the figurehead, but they were always defeated by public interest and the superstition of the seamen. As an alternative, standardisation was tried to reduce the cost, but this gradually broke down and the figurehead remained despite all efforts. Some were heavily gilded, some were painted white, but the seamen's favourites were those painted in " natural " colours, and many captains took it upon their own shoulders to

re-paint the figureheads in this fashion. The gaudier they were the better the seamen liked them, and the painting of most figureheads was striking rather than artistic.

Gradually the Navy began to take a rather more serious view of its job, and considerations of seamanship outweighed the desire for elaborate decoration which was so conspicuous in Stuart days. The men who handled the ships fully realised that the weight of the figurehead, placed where it was, was a very serious factor, and although they would not have it abolished, they fully appreciated the reasons for having it light. Therefore it became usual to carve figureheads out of soft wood, which also meant a saving in weight but which meant a very short life for them. Many ships had several figureheads during their careers, while attempts to preserve

Photo by]   The Figurehead of the " Virgo "   *[Nautical Photo Agency*

Photo by]   [*Nautical Photo Agency*
The Figurehead of the " Kobenhavn "

unusually fine specimens failed for
many years owing to the soft wood
rotting and letting them fall to pieces.

In the Merchant Service the use of
figureheads was not nearly so general
as in the Navy until the beginning of
the 19th century. The exception to
this rule was the case of the East
Indiamen, which invariably carried a
figurehead, and a few West Indiamen.
Most merchant ships, however, had a
straight stem which was sometimes
surrounded by rather a mean " fiddle "
head.

Merchant ship figureheads came into
prominence in the Blackwall frigate
and clipper ship era, when carving them
became a special profession, and some
remarkably fine ones were turned out.
Unfortunately, most of these also
were of soft wood and comparatively
few have survived, although some are
still to be seen and a good many have
found representation in models or
pictures. The old *Seringapatam*, with
her Hindu warrior drawing his sword,

and the *Cutty Sark*, with her figurehead of the witch with her hair and
robe streaming and arm outstretched
to seize the tail of Tam o' Shanter's
horse, are famous examples. It may
be mentioned that where a sailing
ship was given a figurehead with an
outstretched arm in this way, it was
quite usual to unship the arm when
they got to sea, saving the carving
from damage but giving it a very lop-
sided appearance. Even small sailing
coasters and steamers at this time
carried figureheads, some of them
really excellent work, but most of
them crude.

The 19th century Navy also had
some very fine heads, that of H.M.S.
Warrior, whose clipper stem gave an
excellent opportunity to the designer,
being famous. Then the ram bow
came into fashion, which limited the
designers' opportunity to the Union
Jack or Royal Arms with a long scroll
abaft them. Even this was abolished
by Admiralty Order in the 'nineties,

although when we bought the battle-ships *Swiftsure* and *Triumph* from the Chileans in 1903, they had very beautiful bow scrolls, and although they had to be painted over with uniform Admiralty grey, the seamen were very proud of them. The last naval figurehead to be borne at sea was that of the sloop *Odin* on the East Indies station.

An attempt to revive the figure-head was made when the Hamburg-American Line built the *Imperator*, which is now the Cunard *Berengaria*, and whose bow was surmounted by a huge eagle. The experiment was not a success and the head was soon removed, so that now, except for a a very occasional clipper stemmed steamer, figureheads are only built into yachts where happily the clipper stem is replacing the utilitarian post-war straight stem. There is, however, talk about reviving the figurehead in the new ships of the French Navy, whose bows are so curved that they closely approach the old clipper stem.

Ship Models at the Royal United Services Museum

Model of a 64-gun Ship of the Line, 1720

SHIP LOVERS will be interested to know that the Royal United Services Museum, in Whitehall, London, have issued an excellent set of eight post-card photographs of some of the finest models in their collection. The price 1s. per set. By courtesy of the Museum authorities we are able to reproduce one of these pictures. It shows a model of a 64-gun ship of the period 1720. This model was originally in Windsor Castle, and was presented to the Museum by King Edward VII.

Small Scale Steamship Modelling
The Realistic Work of Mr. Victor B. Harrison

Mr. Victor B. Harrison with some of his Models

THE art of making and running as a hobby, small model steamers, which has been steadily developed during several recent years by Mr. Victor B. Harrison, shows much originality, ingenuity and persistence of effort. He may fairly be termed a pioneer and one who has rendered valuable service and encouragement both to the amateur and professional sides of a delightful and instructive recreation. He has established a world of his own in which he devotes leisure hours to follow the occupations of ship designer and builder, marine engineer and master mariner. In business he is a director of a large and old established printing business; discuss model steamers and one might for the moment regard him as manager of a Clyde shipyard, so intense is the enthusiasm with which he will propound his model steamer plans and explain the difficulties he has met and overcome or intends to surmount. He exemplifies the value of a hobby to

relieve the toil and anxieties of business and other cares.

Usually, working model steamships are 30″ to 36″ overall in length as a minimum; excepting tin toys, which are really not models, and launches. A model which might be fairly classed as a ship is generally 3′ to 6′ or more in overall length. In many instances the external appearance is not representative, to much extent, of that of a full-size ship. The salient feature of Mr. Harrison's design and work is construction of realistic looking models, true in proportions, having small overall length and worked by steam. Two of his ships represent L.N.E.R. Hook of Holland passenger steamers, and two others are free lance model cargo steamers, all being 20″ length. Another cargo boat has a length of 30″.

A difficult problem was to propel these vessels by steam power, so that the plant would give a reasonable duration of run, be reliable and ensure that the heat would not cause damage and warping to the deck, the fittings and upper structure. He made extensive experiments before obtaining satisfactory results.

His first attempt was to utilise the hot tube jet system of propulsion; this requires neither a boiler, an engine or a propeller, and therefore appeared to be very adaptable for use in small models. In its simplest form a metal tube bent to hairpin shape is fixed in the hull so that the open ends of the tube project from the stern. The bent portion of the tube is heated by means of a lamp. The heat causes water to be drawn into, and propelled out of, each leg of the tube, thus producing a reaction effect on the ship and causing it to travel forward. The working of this system is obscure but it does give propulsion, and has been known and used for many years. The first models to which Mr. Harrison fitted this

system were 14″ length by 3½″ beam and 1¾″ draught. He used it in the two Hook of Holland steamers and proved that it can be quite successful in a painted and finished scale model.

Mr. Harrison found, however, that plant giving more power would be a desirable improvement and he has evolved compact outfits consisting of a boiler, lamp and reciprocating engine driving a screw propeller. These have been installed in the 20″ and 30″ cargo steamers, and a similar but twin-screw outfit in a 30″ cross-Channel steamer.

Another problem which he has solved, after numerous experiments, is the preservation of the paint of the funnels and upper works from blistering by heat from the lamp. So that he may conveniently experiment with and enjoy running trips with the models, he has constructed a small lake situated in his garden, and a containing wall raises the level of

Mr. Harrison's Model Fleet on the Garden Lake

Another view of the Model Fleet at Anchor

the water to a height at which manipulation of the boats can be effected conveniently.

That Mr. V. B. Harrison could build working models of large size, if he pleased to do so, is evidenced by the one 6′ in length which he made of the s.s. *Mauretania* and exhibited at the *Model Engineer* Exhibition of 1911, and for which he was awarded a bronze medal. But he has preferred, since then, to obtain his enjoyment in making small-size working steamers. At the Exhibition of 1926 he was awarded silver medals for the Hook of Holland and the two cargo boats, and at the Exhibition of 1929 a silver medal also for a small-size cargo boat. The medals are only awarded to models of high degree of excellence. He adopts methylated spirit firing with all his models and considers that scale models to work on open water require to have more than scale power and speed. At the Seafarers' Exhibition, held at Hertford

last May, he had the honour of being presented to H.R.H. Prince George who was greatly interested and pleased by the performance of his models.

Although so devoted to model ship-building, Mr. Harrison also finds time for real sailing in his schooner yacht *Elver*, from West Mersea. He knows every buoy and sand-bank in the Thames Estuary and on the East Coast, and has on several occasions crossed to Holland, Germany, Denmark, and the Baltic. The *Elver* is an unusually pretty ship ; she is 17 tons, Thames measurement, 42′ overall and 39′ water-line.

Mr. Harrison belongs to the Royal Corinthian and Royal Burnham Yacht Clubs, and is equally at home when racing or cruising. One of his model steamers was built as the result of observations of a type of tramp

The hot tube jet system is illustrated in *Simple Mechanical Working Models*, price 10d. post free. An illustrated account of Mr.Harrison's experimental work, written by himself, is published in *The Model Engineer* of June 21st, 1928, price 6d. post free.

steamer frequenting the North Sea. With no plans or drawings or photographs to guide him, he memorised the salient features of this type of boat, and reproduced in miniature a modern

Mr. Harrison's Schooner Yacht " Elver "

tramp which any East Coast skipper would recognise at once. Going smaller still in size, he has now set his heart on building a miniature tug to attend the berthing of his model ships.

Choosing a Prototype

THE ship-lover who is about to build his first model may be inspired by one of two ideas. He may, by his interest in, or his admiration for, some particular ship, be desirous of reproducing her in model form, or he may be enthused with the beauty of ship models generally, and feel anxious to try his hand at this most fascinating hobby. The former type of enthusiast needs no advice—he knows definitely what he wants to do, and only his access to accurate information about his favourite ship, and his skill as a craftsman, stand between him and the accomplishment of his desire. But the novice with a

bent for ship modelling generally may well be embarrassed by the multitude of choice open to him. He will no doubt have a leaning towards a particular type of vessel ; he will, for example, know whether he wants to model a steamer or a sailing ship, and if his choice lies in the latter direction he will probably know whether he wants to build a comparatively modern clipper ship, or whether he wants to dip into history and produce a replica of the *Golden Hind*, or of a ship of a similar period.

The best piece of advice the beginner can have is to choose a prototype of which reasonably full plans and reliable information are available. The true modeller likes his work to be accurate, and a correct representation of a particular ship, even if only passably well made, is better than a beautifully built model which is like unto nothing which ever sailed the seas. Moreover, a simple model well made is better than an elaborate model badly made. It is better to start modelling a small ship rather than a big ship ; the scale can be kept larger and the necessity for minute detail will be avoided. A Thames barge or a small coasting schooner would be easier, from the point of view of detail, than the *Archibald Russell* or the *Cutty Sark*. Similarly, a 2,000-ton tramp steamer would have simpler detail than the *Mauretania* or *The Empress of Britain*. Study drawings or photographs of the prototype carefully before a tool is taken up. Decide which are the important characteristics of the vessel which make her recognisable at a glance for what she is. Reproduce this feature faithfully and do not worry at first about loading her up with too much detail. Above all, be exact to scale in every measurement. A full-size drawing of the model made in advance would help enormously. Having built a comparatively simple type of model with success, the novice may turn this experience to useful account in attempting with confidence one of the more impressive triumphs of the ship designer's art.

A Ship Lover's Library

By "MAIN ROYAL"

Mr. Frank C. Bowen

PICTURE to yourself a room in a tall building overlooking the Thames at Gravesend. In this room there is a desk by a window, and through that window there is a magnificent view of the river stretching seaward from the town. A telescope stands on the desk, and, on the wall behind, there hangs a chart of the house flags of the ships of all nations. Can you imagine a more perfect setting for a ship-lover to do his daily work? That is where I found Mr. Frank C. Bowen, the writer and historian of ships and shipping.

Everybody who is interested in ships knows Mr. Bowen, or at least knows his writings and his books. Ship-lovers will always be grateful to him for that gorgeously illustrated volume *The Golden Age of Sail,* and for his delightful book, *From Carrack to Clipper,* while the general reader and the younger generation of ship enthusiasts are bountifully supplied with fascinating material in his first volume entitled quite simply, *Ships.* I had been lured to Gravesend by stories I had heard about the wonders of the Bowen library of nautical books and records. It used to be housed in London, but a few years ago the spell of London River enticed Mr. Bowen to settle in Gravesend, and with him went the library.

I tried to get Mr. Bowen to talk about himself. I wanted to know the secret of his sea enthusiasm, and I wanted to start him spinning yarns about his own experiences. But I failed miserably ; he always returned to his favorite topic—ships. I asked him for his portrait, and again I failed ; he showed me pictures of ships instead. Here and there he relaxed for a moment ; a twinkle in his eye revealed some passing memory of a sea story, and he related little bits of the human side of a sailorman's life. He even reminded me of the master of the old-time coaster who messed with the crew, and groused wholeheartedly when the biscuits were buttered on the side with the holes ! Then I mentioned the famous library, and Mr. Bowen said : " You shall see. it for yourself." I wandered through room after room. Here on one set of shelves was a complete set of *Lloyds Register* dating back to 1838; another shelf housed the *Bureau Veritas,* and yet another the *Navy List.* Volume upon volume of books on ships and the sea loomed before my eyes ; Mr. Bowen, by his passing comments, seemed to know their contents all by heart. There were rows and rows of scrap-books containing thousands of press-cuttings relating to every possible kind of ship. On the walls were prints, and photographs, and drawings, all of ships and each with a history. There were even ship models, including one of the time-honoured *Santa Maria* and the other a half-model of the *Port Jackson.* But of all the treasures, two stood out alone in their significance. One was a diary in manuscript form of the births, lives, and deaths of the ships of many, many years. Compiled in a series of large note-books, this diary recorded month by month over a very long period the essential facts in the lives of a thousand ships. Where and when a ship was built, who owned her, the name of the master, a record of her voyages and her cargoes, and finally, when her days were done, how and where she died. A work of monumental patience and industry, and a wonderful book of reference, this diary had been compiled by a well-known barrister for his own edification, and he recently passed it into the appreciative care of Mr. Bowen. One other feature of this remarkable library was a card-index of people, places, ships, and things about which information was likely to be wanted. Through this index, containing nearly half-a-million references, Mr. Bowen can immediately locate any item or record in his vast collection, and verify or expand his facts when writing or replying to one of the numerous inquiries he so helpfully and sympathetically deals with in the interests of his fellow members of the Ship Lovers' Association.

I doubt if there is another such library in the whole wide world, and yet Mr. Bowen is generous indeed with his great possession. Serious seekers after knowledge may have free access to his books. He even provides a table, a chair, and an ashtray for their convenience when making notes or extracts. Perhaps that is why he moved to Gravesend; the journey is a test of the visitor's sincerity.

By the way, I got that portrait, and here it is. I think it ought to be inscribed " Frank C. Bowen, the Shiplover's Friend."

The Thames Barge Race, 1931

BY ONE WHO FOLLOWED IT.

THE Thames barge is a familiar sight all round the coast of the British Isles and at many Continental ports. She is a very ancient craft, and up to the present has succeeded in holding her own against the onslaughts of the mechanical age. But it is to be feared that as the vessels come to the end of their useful service they will be replaced by motor barges. The Annual " Thames Sailing Barge Match," to use the official title, was started in 1863, and until 1913 was a most popular fixture, attracting steamers full of excursionists from London, and being watched with intense interest by the inhabitants of the riverside towns and villages. Owing to the War it was allowed to relapse, but its revival in 1927 was attended with such success that it seems probable that it will be an annual event so long as that picturesque craft survives.

The race is open to all spritsail barges, and in order that the smaller types may have equal chances of winning a prize, they are divided up into three classes. First comes the " Coasting Sailing Barge," measuring from 75 tons up to the 145 tons of the *Alf Everard*. This vessel would pass more readily for a private yacht than a cargo carrier, with her white painted hull and trim brown sails. Second class, similar in appearance to the Coasters, are the Bowsprit Class, which measure from 50 to 75 tons. Last comes the Staysail Class, without bowsprit, including all of the small craft of 50 tons and under.

Before the event all the barges are thoroughly refitted, their hulls scraped, painted and polished, and sails and rigging overhauled. Each fly a distinguishing racing flag from the mizen mast. Their crews, for the most part, dress in white ducks, blue guernseys and red-stocking caps. Spick and span with their tanned sails, treated with fish oil and ochre, these little craft, as they come gliding gracefully through the water on a sunny day, make one of the most picturesque sights to be seen on the river.

Conditions on the day of the race were ideal. There was a fine fresh breeze from the West. At 10.15 a.m. the stand-by gun was fired, followed five minutes later by the starting gun. First to get away were the *Reminder* (winner in 1930), *Imperial*, *Cambria*, *Redoubtable* and *Sara*. These were followed by 15 others, the last of all being the old *Goshawk*.

Under the rules governing the race, ordinary working canvas must be used, namely, two jibs, staysail, spritsail, topsail, and mizen. When running before the wind the majority set their large jib as a spinaker.

On reaching the Nore, course was altered to the Northward, jibs were set normally, and all efforts were concentrated on gaining the best position for rounding the mark boat. This provided the most thrilling sight of the race. It calls for keen judgment and skilful seamanship. The *Reminder* was first on the mark, followed by *Redoubtable*, *Imperial*, *Sara*, and *Phoenician*. Then a roar of cheering broke from the onlookers in the pleasure-steamer *Crested Eagle*, chartered by the Race Committee, as the Skipper of the *Phoenician* manoeuvred his vessel close in between the mark boat and the next barge with barely two feet on either side, and so placed himself in line with the *Reminder*. For this smart piece of work the *Phoenician's* Skipper received Commodore Millett's prize for " the master showing the best seamanship in rounding the mark."

All the 19 barges rounded within 20 minutes, and it is interesting to note that 10 knots was the average speed from the start to this point, a distance of 23 miles.

The course home was practically dead against the wind. Most of the craft made a long tack to the Maplin Sands, but the *Fortis* sixth, and the *Nelson* eighth, after a little while went about, and made for the South bank of the river. Their skippers, knowing local conditions, had observed signs of a change in the wind. In a short time it shifted to the South'ard, and in their new position were the first to feel the advantage of it. This, with the stronger tide inshore, enabled them to creep up stream ahead of the others, who were by now well in on the opposite shore. This lead the *Fortis* retained and ended the race just three seconds ahead of the *Sara*, with the *Nelson* a close third. Thus the *Fortis* had the honour of winning two prizes, one as the first barge home, and the other as the first of her class, the 50-ton Staysail barges.

An hour later the *Goshawk* crept in !

But she had finished the course, a gallant effort for which she was duly rewarded, since masters and crews of all barges, other than the actual prize-winners, receive a sum varying from £4 10s. to £3, according to class, for completing the race. B. H. LAVIS.

Some of the River Class Barges--" Sara " nearest

How to Build a Model of a Dutch Admiralty Yacht

By JEFFREY LEIGHTON

I HAVE chosen a Dutch Admiralty yacht of the early 18th century as a suitable model for an article for several reasons. The size of the model enables detail and decoration to be carried out very accurately, while, though the model is highly decorative, there is not the tremendous amount of repetition work on carving, rigging and fittings as in a model of a full-

The Hull

This is built in three sections on a system which allows greater ease of handling, shaping and finishing than cutting from a single block of wood. The hull sections (see sketch, Fig. 1) are cut from straight-grained pine or deal, using card templates made from scale sections AA, BB, CC, and from the stern transom. The two

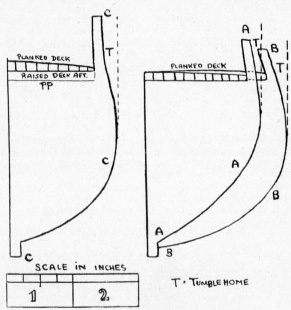

Fig. 1. Hull Sections for Making Templates

rigged ship of the same period. The vessel, while showing many of the characteristics of larger vessels of the same period, has that peculiar charm of Dutch sailing ships of all time. I am dealing with the hull construction of the model in as simple a manner as possible, for the benefit of the model maker with but little equipment. The scale of the model shown is one-sixtieth of actual size of the prototype.

halves, roughly shaped outside, should next be hollowed down to deck level, leaving bulwarks 1" high and $\frac{3}{8}$" thick (to allow for tumble home). A portion of the bulwarks aft should be left $\frac{1}{2}$" thicker than the rest, and $3\frac{1}{2}$" long (see XX sketch, Fig. 2). The decks should be perfectly level for planking later. Now cut down the bulwarks to the proper sheer curve with a small spokeshave or chisel, shape in the

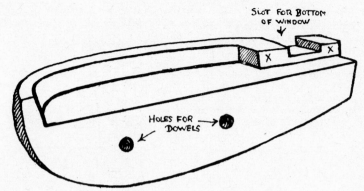

Fig. 2. Half Section of Hull showing Bulwarks

" tumble home " (see sections), and rub down both halves with coarse sandpaper, finishing off with medium. Cut the two slots shown in XX for the quarter badge windows $\frac{3}{16}''$ deep, the width being slightly less than that of the windows. Next mark and drill the gunports, three to a side, using a $\frac{3}{16}''$ drill, taking care not to split the bulwarks. Now shape the keel section (Fig. 3). This piece serves several purposes, the top is level with the deck, cut-in side sections, the projection at the bow forms the stem head and the next forms forefoot, keel, deadwood, sternpost, etc.

The shape should be taken from the sheer elevation and should project slightly beyond the stern transom, as in Fig. 4. The edges of the stern, forefoot, and keel should be slightly chamfered before fitting. Next drill holes for the dowels in all three sections, cutting in the holes in the middle section a shade larger to avoid splitting. The three sections should now be dowelled and glued together and left in a carpenter's cramp or tightly bound with tape for at least 24 hours. (Remember to protect the hull from bruising in the cramp, with rags.)

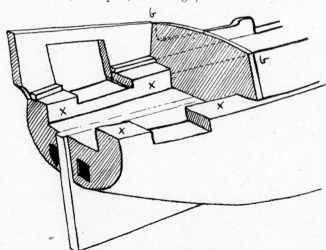

Fig. 4. Constructive Detail of Stern

The Round House

Cut from good ${}^{3}_{16}''$ three-ply the forward bulkhead of the round house (see sketch, Fig. 4). This should fit snugly against deck and bulwarks, the edges inclining inward above the bulwarks at an angle equal to the "tumble home." The top edge should be slightly curved to give a camber to the roof. The whole should now be

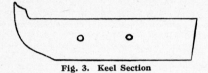

Fig. 3.   Keel Section

glued and pinned to the forward ends of xx. Next cut from the three-ply the sides, each with an extension to form the raised section of bulwark and with apertures for the quarter windows. The edges should be bevelled at the bottom so that the sides lean inwards and make a flush joint with the hull, and the top to take the edge of the roof. Next fit fillets of wood to xx for the sides to back against. Glue them both into position and pin with small veneer nails to the edge of bulkhead and pin down through

Fig. 5.   Two Halves of Hull with Keel Section Between

the extension piece to the bulwark, using long panel pins. When using small nails throughout, always start the hole for them, using a D drill made from a sewing needle held in a pin-vice or hand-chuck ; this prevents splitting.

Finishing the Hull

The hull should now be coated to fill all cracks and grain marks with a mixture of surgical plaster-of-paris stirred into hot glue size until the mixture is of the consistency of cream and free from lumps. Apply quickly

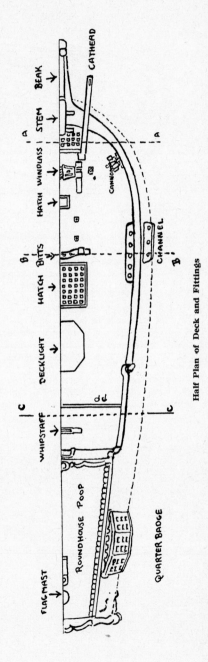

Half Plan of Deck and Fittings

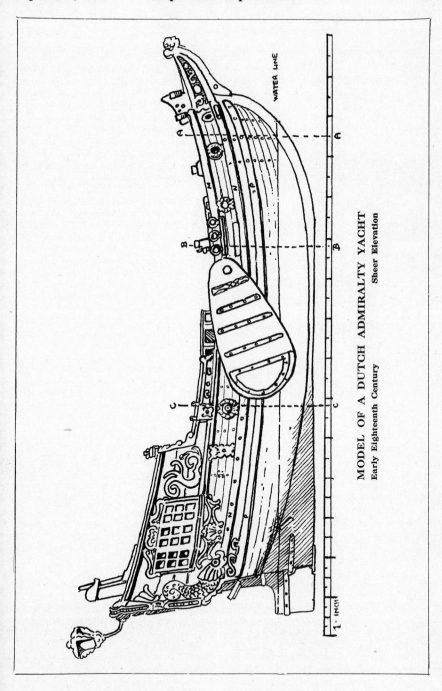

MODEL OF A DUTCH ADMIRALTY YACHT

Early Eighteenth Century   Sheer Elevation

while hot with a broad paintbrush till the whole hull is fairly thickly coated, seeing that all cracks and shakes are filled in. Allow the whole at least 48 hours to dry hard, then rub down, commencing with medium sandpaper

SCALE IN INCHES

1   2

STERN DETAILS.

Stern Details of Model Dutch Admiralty Yacht

and finishing with very fine, so that the whole hull outside presents a smooth flawless surface. Next give two coats of Coverine matt white undercoating, rubbing down after each is dry with fine sandpaper ; the hull is now ready for fitting and decorated work. (*To be continued.*)

It is important to place a definite order with your newsagent or bookstall, or to send a yearly subscription to the publishers, if you wish to ensure a regular supply of SHIPS AND SHIP MODELS. It is probable that the early issues will quickly go out of print, as a limited edition only is printed. Ask your friends also to place a regular order.

Our Rough Log

WE have received a copy of a little publication called *The Ship*, which is issued by Mr. John Anderson, of 41, Adams Street, Falkirk, Scotland. The magazine is in unpretentious manuscript form and contains notes and data relating to famous sailing ships. It is issued by Mr. Anderson to members of his organisation The Ship Club, which is a friendly circle of correspondents and others interested in ships and the sea.

*   *   *

A SAMPLE of a cold-water glue, suitable for ship modellers, has been submitted to us by Mr. J. Trevor, 30, Red Lion Street, Holborn, London, W.C.1. Tests we have made show that it is equally effective with wood, earthenware, and thick felt. Joints made with this glue appear to hold well, and a short immersion in water seemed to have no deleterious effect. We understand the joint also resists oil and acid. The glue is marketed in 6d. tins.

*   *   *

WAR-TIME memories of the sea are vividly aroused by a book entitled " With the Harwich Naval Forces, 1914-1918." The author is Commander Claude L. A. Woollard, R.N. (Ret.), F.R.G.S., and there is an introduction by the Duke of Montrose, Commodore of the R.N.V.R. The narratives related are mainly the personal experiences of the author while serving in the Harwich Naval Force under Commodore Tyrwhitt, in the North Sea. These graphically written reminiscences are supplemented by first-hand stories of the experiences of brother-officers in the same sea and, in the words of the Duke of Montrose, they give " a splendid idea of a phase of the Great War acted away from the lime-light and public applause." The book contains 114 pages, 38 photographs, and two maps. Copies may be obtained from Commander Woollard, c/o The Strand Touring Association, Ltd., 407, Strand, London, W.C., price 5s. 6d.

Elements of Model Steamer Design

By T. R. THOMAS, B.Sc., M.I.Mar.E.

I.—MODEL PROPELLERS

THE title of this series of articles is, strictly speaking, incorrect, because there should be no necessity to design any part of a small ship which is a faithful copy of her larger sister, but as it is quite impossible for the model maker to produce a working model on such a reduced scale, it is sometimes necessary for him to apply the principles which the designer of the full-size ship has used. Fortunately, however, when the model maker follows the correct principles, it usually leads to the maximum efficiency of the particular part of his model which he is designing, as well as to realism, and it is the purpose of these notes to show how the model maker can take advantage of the experience of the designer of the big ship and adapt them to his own ends. Whenever possible, consideration will be given to the owner whose ship is already " sailing the seas," as well as to the designer and builder of a new model. If the latter will keep the articles for reference, he will find that he will soon have sufficient information to enable him to build a model of any particular type of ship which he chooses, with the knowledge that it is at least something like the original.

It may seem that to begin with a discussion on the design of model propellers is starting at the wrong end, but the propeller is one of the things which the model maker is forced to design himself, because the conditions under which it is working are probably very different from those in the full-size ship. It is also a part of the model that can be modified without too much trouble, and it has a very important bearing on its success. Too often, however, the care which has been expended on the hull and machinery is not applied to the propeller, with the result that much power and efficiency is lost.

Unfortunately, when fixing on a suitable propeller for any particular model, we at once come up against considerable difficulty, because of our lack of knowledge, or, at least, of accurate information of the conditions under which the propeller is working. One important point which we have to decide is, at what angle we must set the blades of the propeller, or in other words, what " pitch " we must give it in order that it should drive the model at the desired speed when turned at the maximum revolutions of which our machinery is capable. To make even a rough estimate it is necessary to understand just how the propeller is acting when it drives the model forward, and to do this, we must imagine that the propeller is part of a screw which is working in a nut—the water is the nut in this case and the angle of the blade determines how far the screw will travel through the nut in one revolution. This distance is called the " pitch." It is not difficult to see that if the propeller blade is at right-angles to the shaft it will not travel forward at all, while if it is parallel with the shaft it will only succeed in thrashing the water. Obviously, then, there is an intermediate angle at which we must set the blade so that it will progress through the water as it is turned and the distance which it progresses will depend, not only on the angle, but on the speed of revolution. Therefore, within certain limits and given a certain speed of revolution of the machinery, the greater the angle, the greater the speed at which the ship will move forward. There are, of course, limitations to the increase in the angle, because the water does not act as a solid nut, but we, at least, now understand roughly what the effect of the angle of the propeller blades is, although we cannot fix the amount of the angle in the absence of definite information. We can say, however, that if we are concerned in designing a propeller for a model of moderate speed, say three or four miles per hour, having slow-running machinery, the blade should be set at a big angle to the vertical—as much as 45 degrees. On the other hand, if the same model is driven by an electric motor which develops its full power at much higher revolutions than the steam engine, the angle should be reduced and may be about 30 degrees. The principle which we must adopt in general is, that fast-running machinery will require a much smaller angle of blade than will slow-running machinery, provided that both types develop

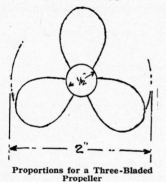

Proportions for a Three-Bladed Propeller

approximately the same power, to ensure that the model will have the maximum speed.

When the " angle " of the blade referred to here, the mean or average angle is meant because the blade must be twisted so that the angle at the " root " or at the boss is greater than at the tip. A little consideration will show that the tip of the blade is moving faster than the root and that, consequently, its angle must be smaller if its forward progress in one revolution is to be the same. Although the angle of the blade at each point can be found quite easily, it will be sufficiently near if, when the blade is made, it is carefully twisted as indicated in the drawing.

Another point we must decide is the

size or diameter of the propeller. In order to exert a certain thrust against the water, we must have a certain area of blade, and we can either make the blade long and narrow, or short and wide. The long narrow blade is not good practice, and if we adopt the shape of blade shown, we will have a more efficient propeller and one which is more in accordance with the practice on the full-size ship. This shape of blade is the same as fitted to the Pacific Steam Navigation Company's T.s.s. *Oroya*, and we will therefore not go far wrong in following the general outline. If we adopt this shape, the diameter of the propeller will regulate approximately the area of the blade, and this will, of course, depend on the amount of power we wish the propeller to exert. For a model about 30″ long and a moderate speed, a three-bladed propeller of 1¾″ to 2″ diameter will give sufficient area if it has blades of this shape to exert the thrust required without loss of efficiency. The section of the blade should be as shown in the figure, and the after or driving surface should be flat. There is no necessity to " spoon " the blade, as many model makers seem to think, and by doing so we decrease the efficiency of the propeller. The blade itself, while being flat on the driving surface, should have the front rounded. Various developments in the direction of making the blades of an aerofoil section are at present taking place, but it is not yet certain that this is an advantage in all types of ships and the section of blade shown is a good one. The boss of the propeller can be made comparatively large with advantage, even as much as one-third of the diameter, but it must be tapered, as shown, in order that the flow of water to and from the propeller should be smooth. The boss on the after side can be made more pointed than that on the fore side. We have not yet decided as to how many blades the propeller should have, and as a matter of fact this is not very important. The two-bladed propeller is not very efficient and its appearance is not good. The three blades is more general in big practice and will, as a rule, suit the model maker, but if he prefers he can distribute the area of the propeller over four or even six blades without great loss of efficiency.

As regards the construction of the propeller, it is more satisfactory to build it up rather than to attempt

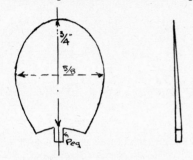

Propeller Blade with Peg Fixing

to make it from a single sheet of brass, but if the model maker prefers this latter method, he should be careful to see that each blade is of the same area and that he twists them to the same angle and makes the twist as sharply as possible. In this case, of course, the cones fore and aft of the propeller should be made separately and can be used to lock the propeller on the shaft. The more satisfactory method is to build the propeller up from a short length of brass rod about ½″ diameter. This should be drilled to fit the shaft and provided with a small set screw, or the shaft screwed and the hole in the boss tapped to suit, locking the propeller on the shaft by means of a small nut. It can be turned to shape, but if a lathe is not available, the same result can easily be attained by filing. The blades themselves may be of sheet brass filed to shape fixed into this boss by cutting three diagonal slots and soldering in, but I prefer to make the blade with a small peg, as shown, and to drill holes in the boss into which this peg fits, soldering the whole together. The method of cutting slots

is inclined to be difficult, because there is no means of holding the blade in the slot while soldering the job, unless each blade is a fairly tight fit. In the second method, it is easier to make the blade firm before soldering, and it also permits of a fairly easy alteration in the angle of the blade without having to renew the boss.

The finished propeller must be balanced so that it runs smoothly without vibration. This is roughly tested by slipping it on to a rod of smaller diameter than the shaft or, more accurately, by fitting a short shaft and balancing on knife edges and filing the back of any blade which is heavy, but it is not so easy to make sure that it is balanced when running on the model. We can only make it as carefully as possible, seeing that the blades are of equal area and properly spaced. The use of a piece

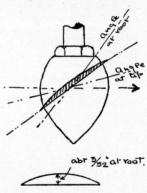

Section of Blade and Shape of Boss

of hexagon rod for the boss makes the spacing simpler, and all blades should be shaped at one time. The angle or pitch of each blade must be the same, and this is probably best done by putting the propeller on a rod and setting each blade by eye. The use of any kind of gauge is difficult and no more satisfactory.

After a trial trip, the owner will almost certainly wish to test the effect of alterations in pitch and he may do so with advantage, but he will probably find that there is little variation in speed if the propeller has been built along these lines, unless his machinery is much slower or faster running than usual. If, however, he finds that the engine slows up too much or the motor " labours " and warms up, he should reduce the angle. If the machinery " races " and the angle of the blades is already about 45 degrees, he must increase the diameter of propeller and therefore blade area.

Certain features of the ship close to the propeller may affect the effi-ciency considerably, but it is only possible to mention these briefly at the moment. The shape of the hull aft is important, but this is a matter for later consideration. The rudder shape and position are also important, but this is also a big subject and it is sufficient to note that the rudder especially, if of the balanced type, should be kept *close* up to the propeller and should be as thin as possible. The presence of a vertical fin, such as the rudder, close to the propeller has an excellent effect.

(To be continued)

Tools for Ship Modelling

O NE of the points in favour of ship modelling as a hobby is that it can be carried on with a minimum of workshop space and equipment. The seat of a taxi-cab might not be regarded as an ideal workshop, yet it is a fact that many of the fittings of a model of the *Santa Maria* were made by a London taxi-driver while sitting on his cab waiting for fares. The model, when completed, was good enough to win a medal at *The Model Engineer* Exhibition.

So much ship-modelling work is minute in character ; the tiny pieces can be made on the corner of the dining-room table, or while sitting in an arm chair. A sharp pocket-knife, a few small files, a pair of cutting pliers, a small pair of round-nosed pliers, one or two fine bradawls, a light hammer, a small soldering outfit, a fret-saw, and some good liquid glue will enable a great deal of the deck-fitting and upper-work to be done. For the decorative work on historic models one or two of the smaller wood-carving tools should be added to the kit. The hull of a ship is a heavier job, and may require something larger in the way of a saw and a plane, a chisel and a gouge or two, and some kind of a bench on which to do this work. A bench indicates a suitable place to fix a small vice which will be found useful for holding work in progress. A hand-drilling brace, with an assortment of small twist-drills, nearly completes a good all-round equipment. Tools must be kept sharp ; neat cutting depends on keen edges, and therefore a small oil-stone must be kept handy for this purpose.

The king of workshop tools is the lathe ; although not essential to the model shipbuilder, unless he intends to make the machinery for a model power boat, a lathe of some kind is a valuable addition to the workshop, if space for it can be found. Although many rounded parts can be shaped by careful hand work, the lathe enables jobs of this kind to be done more expeditiously and more accurately. It is particularly useful where there is much repetition of a single detail to be done, as for example in the making of stanchions, and of small guns. The lathe is also an excellent drilling machine, and many small drilling and boring jobs can be done expeditiously by its aid. For the general run of ship modelling work a very simple type of lathe will serve. Back-gear and screw-cutting gear are unnecessary, but a compound slide-rest will be found of frequent service. A good self-centering chuck is another accessory which is almost essential. Both metal and wood can be turned in the same lathe, though differently shaped tools are necessary. A treadle-drive should be fitted, unless the model shipbuilder is able to install the luxury of a small electric motor.

The Ship Modeller's Scrap Book
A DICTIONARY OF SHIP DETAILS IN ALL PERIODS

Anchor

ANCHORS in some form are of the very greatest antiquity and date back almost as long as the ship, for having discovered that he could move his log through the water by means of skin sails, man soon realised the necessity of stopping it. The earliest anchors were certainly merely stones on a hide cable, but apparently these got quite elaborate in their way, for Ancyra, in Egypt—hence the name

A Roman Anchor

—had a great reputation for the skill of its inhabitants in forming them. Shaped lead was also a very early type of anchor, but quite elaborate ones on modern principles came into being at a very early age.

In China, where they like to have their historical ideas neat and complete, the Emperor Yu is given the credit of inventing the anchor in 2,000 B.C. and, although he may not be the actual inventor, the date is probably not far out. In the Bronze Age we know that there were single-fluked anchors in general use and, in the early Roman days, two-fluked, mostly without stocks but some quite like the modern anchor.

The ordinary stocked anchor was made with very little difference in principle for over 1,000 years, probably very much more than that, and is constantly to be found in mediaeval religious prints and coats-of-arms. The anchor in the famous " Picture by W.A.," might have been fitted in any merchantman of 100 years ago or less. Chain cable has long been invented, but totally discarded in spite

of the obvious disadvantages of hemp.

The stock was designed to cant the anchor so that the flukes were bound to grip the ground and were not simply dragged over the bottom on their flat sides. It was, therefore, always set at an angle to the arms, generally at a right-angle, and as it did not require the same strength as either the shank or the arms, wooden stocks were favoured for centuries, made as big as possible to get the necessary cant and always built up and hooped. Some may still very occasionally be seen in very old Scandinavian or Mediterranean sailing ships, but they are most familiar through the pictures of Cooke and others.

This general type of anchor that was in use for so long was not by any

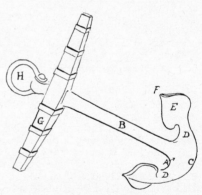

A Wooden Stock Anchor

A—trend ; B—shank . C—crown ; D—arm, E—fluke or palm, F—pea or bill ; G—stock, H—shackle.

means a bad one, its fault being that the shank was liable to break. The traditional sizes for the best bower or principal anchor in the ship were : in the Navy, that the number of hundredweight in its weight should equal the number of guns that the ship carried, and in the Merchant

Service, that the tonnage of the ship should be divided by 20 to find the anchor's weight in hundredweights.

Until the early days of the 19th Century the arms were nearly straight, and the improvement of a careful curve, giving great advantages in holding the ground and also in breaking out, must be credited to an Admiralty clerk named Pering. He made a very big difference and started something of a craze in new anchor forms, culminating in a special section and competition in the Great Exhibition of 1851.

In that competition Trotman's was acknowledged to be the best for holding purposes, an adaptation of the first

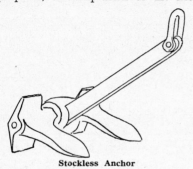

Stockless Anchor

patent anchor. That was the idea of Lieut. Belcher, R.N., who, in 1818, patented his " Tumbling Fluke " anchor, in which the arms were connected to the shank by a pin, so that they were hinged and would naturally adjust themselves to the biggest biting angle. Belcher was the inventor, but it must be admitted that most of this anchor's success came when Mr. Trotman, a landsman, had invented his canting palms to make sure that it rolled into position to get a proper grip.

In 1823 Hawkins invented the first modern stockless anchor, going back to the practice of ancient Rome or the unchanging Chinese. It was far more convenient for stowing, but by far and away the best stockless anchor was patented in 1854 by Martin, a Frenchman, and taken up very gener-

ally from the 'sixties onwards. It occupied a small space, stowed flat, and latterly proved easily adapted for drawing straight up into the hawse-pipe instead of having all the trouble of getting it on deck, a great convenience as long as the order to stop

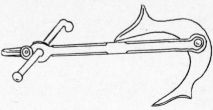

Trotman's Anchor

heaving on the windlass is given quickly enough.

It may be mentioned that the stockless anchor was very bitterly opposed by many practical seamen in its early days on account of its being generally regarded as inferior in holding qualities to the old-fashioned stocked anchor. On the other hand, its convenience in stowing was fully recognised and many types were put forward in which the stock unshipped and could be lashed to the shank. In all such types the stock was iron and not wood.

Modern Stocked Anchor
(Stock Housed)

Chain cables had again come into use for big ships in the early 'thirties and were both convenient and advantageous in every way. Their result was a tendency to give anchors shorter shanks, but their principal effect was in the interior design of the ships, when it was no longer necessary to provide a huge space for the stowing of hemp cables.

In sailing ships the anchors were unshackled from their cables as soon as the ship got out of soundings and was unlikely to use them for a spell. The anchors were secured on the forecastle head, while the hawse pipes, which generally led straight into the forecastle, were plugged and cemented in order to keep the men's quarters as dry as possible. This was seldom very successful and, at the beginning and end of the voyage, the forecastle was simply flooded out every time the ship took a plunge. A steamer's hawes-pipes lead through on to the deck.

There are, of course, numerous other types of anchors that have not been mentioned, some of them pure freaks, like those with divided palms, which were provided for the *Great Eastern* in order to pierce the bottom more readily, and others which have been more or less adopted for a greater or shorter period.

(To be continued)

The Ship Lovers' Association

IT is the intention of the Editor to place this section monthly at the disposal of the Shiplovers' Association for the publication of both questions and answers which are of general interest. The Association was founded in London in 1927 to bring shiplovers into touch with one another by meeting or correspondence, and is divided into the following sections :—

I. Pre-19th Century Ships.
II. Old Warships.
III. Modern Warships.
IV. Sailing Merchantmen.
V. Early Steamers.
VI. Modern Steamers and Motorships.
VII. Packets, Coasters and Paddlers.
VIII. Local Sailing Types.
IX. Yachts and Motor Boats.
X. Life on Shipboard—past and present.
XI. Exploration and Navigation.
XII. General Interest in Anything that Floats.
XIII. Models.
XIV. Painting and Appearance of Ships.
XV. Marine Literature and Art.
XVI. Craft.
XVII. Harbours, Lights, etc.
XVIII. Shipping Business.

Members may join any or all of these sections on their subscription of 5s. per annum ; 2s. 6d. for cadet members still at school. The Hon. Sec., *pro. tem.*, is Mr. Frank C. Bowen, Customs' House Building, Milton Place, Gravesend, Kent.

Regular fortnightly meetings, every other one a dinner, followed by papers, are held in London and some other centres. Since 1927 Shiplovers' Associations have been established in Tasmania, Victoria and New Zealand, and are flourishing. Other associations are in process of formation in other countries.

Members' Recent Queries and Answers

M.M. (Cape Town, now in London) is completing a history of South African steamships and steamship services. Are there other members particularly interested in these ships ?

F.T.W. (London) and a party of friends are making a number of models of the various sailing cargo coaster types before all accurate knowledge of these very interesting, but poorly recorded, vessels passes away. They will be grateful of any co-operation from fellow enthusiasts.

Co - operative model - making by London members is suggested for the coming winter. Will members interested please let the Secretary know.

J. McR. (Wallasey).—The North German-Lloyd record-breakers *Kaiser Wilhelm II* and *Kronprincessin Cecilie* are still afloat in American waters as the *Monticello* and *Mount Vernon*, but they have been laid-up for years, and whether they will ever go to sea again is an open question. The *Von Steuben*, ex *Kronprinz Wilhelm*, was broken up at Philadelphia.

F.S.B. (Bristol).—The steel full-rigged ship *Talus* of 1891 left the Clyde for New York on June 14th, 1919, was sighted passing Kildonan on the same day, and was never heard of again.

P.M.A. (Rotterdam).—The steamer *Nederland en Orange* of 1883 was sold three years later to Hajee Cassum Joosub, of Bombay, who ran her as the *Akbar* until she was scrapped in the spring of 1907.

———

Any members interested in the above can get into touch with the enquirers through the Secretary. All queries are, and will be, answered through the post ; only those of more general interest appear here.

Will the Funnel Disappear ?

MODERN ships are in one respect resembling modern locomotives —the funnel is becoming less and less a prominent feature of the outline. The apparent disappearance of the loco- motive funnel is largely due to the increased diameter of the boiler and to its higher pitch on the engine framing. The funnel is still there, but it is mostly concealed inside the smoke-box, and only a squat affair is visible outside at the top. Similarly, the growing size of the modern liner, and the increasing height of the super-structure, are factors tending to dwarf the amount of funnel to be seen extern- ally. The advent of the marine internal combustion engine disposes of one of the reasons for the existence of the funnel, for no furnace draught is needed. There is also no smoke to be disposed of, other than an almost invisible exhaust. The motor ship funnel, where it is fitted, is mainly a concession to popular expectation. When will the last ship funnel be seen at sea ?

Ship Models at the " Model Engineer " Exhibition

A NUMBER of unusually interesting ship and boat models will be on view at the *Model Engineer* Exhibition at the Royal Horticultural Hall, West- minster, which runs from September 3rd to the 12th. The competition sec- tion will include a Bengal pilot brig, a " Cutty Sark," a " Halloween," a " Llangibby Castle," an " Anne Royal " of 1625, a 50-gun ship of 1730, a scenic model of a war-time convoy, a Thames sailing barge, a 16th century galleon, a " Majestic," a wool clipper " Mary Penhale," a " Santa Maria," a mer- chant ship of the 15th century, and numerous liners, tramps and tugs. A novelty will be a pocket sailing yacht, a real sailing model which can be readily un-rigged and transported in the pocket. There will be a number of other interesting nautical exhibits in the loan section, including some fine examples of ship-modelling from the collection of Messrs. A. Fleming (Southsea), Ltd., and some splendid marine pictures from the Parker Gallery.

*　　*　　*

Another interesting ship model will be the s.s. *Duke of Rothesay*, one of the latest L.M.S. boats serving on the Heysham-Belfast Service. On the club stands will be shown some examples of working model power boats, and fast petrol-driven model hydroplanes. The Exhibition is open from 11 a.m. to 9.30 p.m. each day, and the admission is 1s., tax included. All ship-lovers should make a point of attending this fascinating show.

SHIPS AND SHIP MODELS

A Magazine for all Lovers of Ships and the Sea

Single Copies, post free, 7½d.
Annual Subscription 7s. 6d.

Editorial and Publishing Offices :

66 FARRINGDON STREET
L O N D O N :: E. C. 4

Vol. I. No. 2.   OCTOBER, 1931.   Price 6d.

About Ourselves

OUR little ship has left her moorings and is out at sea. She has found a fair wind, the sails are filled, and she is heading due east for the sun of success. All this means that SHIPS AND SHIP MODELS has made a happy beginning to its voyage. We have received compliments and good wishes from all quarters, and we hope that, with the promised assistance of many kind friends, we shall continue to earn our readers' good opinion. Interest in the sea is naturally world-wide, and it is pleasing to find that in ship models there is a corresponding bond of interest between ship lovers in all countries. Here, for example, are a few indications of this interest from our list of subscribers. The countries from which subscriptions have already been received include the United States, Newfoundland, Canada, the Bahamas, North Africa, France, Holland, Belgium, Denmark, Norway, Finland, Australia, Malta, Italy, India, and China. Even Palestine and Poland appear on our list, and we have no doubt that the South African,

Australian and New Zealand mails will bring forth further geographical distinction to our register in the very near future. All branches of the Naval and Mercantile Marine services are represented, as well as famous museums and public institutions. It is perhaps invidious to mention any names, but we are rather proud to acknowledge subscriptions from Capt. R. G. Malin, R.N.R., the new Commodore of the Cunard Line, and Gustav Erikson, the owner of the *Archibald Russell* and a fleet of fine ships sailing under the Finnish flag. Our little paper has started with a distinguished following ; we hope the number of our friends will continue to grow.

*   *   *

At " The Model Engineer " Exhibition

There was a fine display of ship models at the Royal Horticultural Hall this year, ranging from the river tug and barge to the full-rigged clipper ship and the most modern motor liner. Several fine examples of historic models were in the Competition Section, including the *Anne Royal*, two

Santa Marias, a 15th century merchant ship, and two 18th century men-of-war. The Cup for the best sailing ship model of a prototype prior to 1900 went to Mr. J. D. Attwood for his beautifully-scaled model of the *Mary Penhale* of London, and the " Borneo " Cup, offered for a historical model of a 19th century prototype, was awarded to a realistic model of a Bengal Pilot brig by Mr. J. D. Allison. Mr. T. H. Roberts-Wray contributed two very complete small-scale models of the *Halloween* and *Cutty Sark*, while in steamship modelling an outstanding example was Mr. R. A. Blows' *City of Canterbury*, which secured the " Joy " prize for realistic appearance.

In the Loan Section there were some most interesting ship models from Messrs. A. Fleming (Southsea), Ltd., a Bristol Channel pilot cutter by Mr. A. W. B. Prowse, a 17th century warship by Mr. H. P. Jackson, a sailing model of the *Cutty Sark* by Mr. Roland Oliver, notable for its beautifully-modelled hull, and several other very fine ship and boat models. Mr. Fred C. Poyser lent a glass-bottle model of a full-rigged ship, which is one of the finest examples known of this quaint form of model-making enthusiasm. We shall publish photographs and descriptions of some of the more interesting models in later issues. A feature of the Loan Section which was much admired was a collection of beautiful colour-prints of marine subjects lent by Messrs. Thomas H. Parker, Ltd.

* * *

Ship Modellers Meet

The Exhibition formed a happy meeting-ground for ship modellers. On one evening alone we met Mr. Frank Mason, Mr. Beaufort, Mr. R. H. Penton, Mr. Fred C. Poyser, and Mr. Basil Lavis. Admiral Sir Reginald Bacon came to see us, and Mr. G. S. Laird Clowes, Mr. Norman Robinson, Mr. T. H. Roberts-Wray and his son, Capt. Roberts-Wray, all spent several hours in the show. We had a very interesting chat with Mr. J. D. Allison, the builder of the Bengal Pilot brig model. Mr. Allison has spent many years in the Bengal Pilot Service, and has promised us some reminiscences of his work and some notes on the building of his model.

* * *

Ship Models at Liverpool

Through the courtesy of Lieut.-Commander J. H. Craine, R.N.R. (Ret.), we have received a programme of the recent Liverpool Shipping Week, in which a collection of ship models, instruments and pictures made a very appropriate feature. The models, staged in chronological order, ranged from a funerary boat from the Nile, 2,000 years old, and a Grecian galley of 350 B.C., up to the *Loch Maree* and the *Cassiope* among sailing ships, and the *Empress of Britain* among modern steamships. Over 180 models were on view. We are interested to note that steamers are catalogued under the heading " The Machine Driven Ship," a title we do not remember to have seen before, but which may now come into more general use in view of the arrival of the motor-ship and the marine adaptation of electrical power. The programme runs to 80 pages and contains some most interesting articles on the Port of Liverpool and on the evolution of the ship. The price is 6d., and it is published by the Liverpool Organisation, Ltd., Liverpool.

* * *

Lone Hands

There are doubtless many ship-lovers who would be glad to know of others in their own districts with similar interests. Similarly, there are those who would like to correspond with other enthusiasts at home or abroad for the exchange of photographs or information. We shall be pleased to publish the names and addresses of any readers who would like to get into touch with fellow-readers if they will write us, stating the precise nature of their interest, whether ship modelling, collecting, marine history, or other subject.

A Model of an Elizabethan Galleon

Recently constructed in The Science Museum

By G. S. LAIRD CLOWES

AT the Science Museum, the great bulk of the collection of ship models consists of contemporary dockyard or builder's models, made in the yard in which the ship was built and usually under the superintendence of the shipwright who had charge of her construction. Consequently, it is only under exceptional conditions that it is desirable to undertake the labour and expense involved in building an elaborate model.

There must be, firstly, sufficient exact numerical detail on which to found the model and, secondly, no reasonable chance of a good contemporary model coming to hand.

But the habit of making dockyard models of men-of-war only became general about the time of the Restoration of the Monarchy in 1660. It is true that two scale models of English ships of a slightly earlier date have been found, but no one has yet discovered a good contemporary model of any of the ships of Queen Elizabeth, nor is there any record that such models were made at that period. Consequently, when it was found that one of the MS. in the Pepysian Library at Magdalene College, Cambridge, contained a number of shipwright's plans dating from about 1586, and a sail-plan of a little later, that MS. there—dated 1600—gave the lengths of all the masts and spars of the Royal ships and agreed substantially with the sail-plan just mentioned, while a third—of eleven years later—exhibited the sizes and lengths of all the ropes, it seemed that there was sufficient data on which to construct an accurate model of an Elizabethan galleon of about 1600, and that the work would be well worth doing.

This model has now been completed, and its formal description reads as follows :—

" This model (scale 1 : 48), made in the workshops of the Museum, is based on the only shipwright's draughts of the sixteenth century known to exist in England.

" The draughts are contained in a MS. which Samuel Pepys entitled ' Fragments of Ancient English Shipwrightry,' and which is still preserved in his Library at Magdalene College, Cambridge. It is probably the work of the master-shipwright Matthew Baker and, from internal evidence, appears to date from a little before 1586.

" Photographic transparencies of four of these draughts, which were used in the construction of the model, are exhibited in a desk-case on the west side of the gallery. The draughts, however, show the generalised designs prepared by a shipwright for future use, rather than the individual ships which were actually built. The painting of the model has been copied exactly from the colour-scheme of one of the more brightly decorated draughts, that of a large ship to which a rough sail-plan has been added.

" This sail-plan, sketched by a later hand, has been utilised in rigging the model, for the dimensions of the mast and spars have been found to agree with those recorded for the largest ships in a MS. list of the dimensions of masts and spars for each ship of the Royal Navy, which is dated 1600. The details and sizes of all ropes and rigging have been obtained from a further MS., dated 1611, which, like the others, is preserved in the Pepysian Library.

" For the guns, a naval bronze demi-culverin inscribed ' Richard Phillips, 1601,' and now preserved in the Tower of London, has been taken as a model and the other types of ordnance have been made in true proportion.

" The actual dimensions of the model are those of the *Elizabeth Jonas*, rebuilt in 1597-8 :—Burthen, 684 tons ; ton and tonnage, 855 ; length of keel, 100′ ; rake forward, 36′ ; rake aft, 6′ ; breadth, 38′ ; depth of hold, 18′.

" The period illustrated is that of the last few years of Queen Elizabeth, when the galleon with its comparatively fine lines, a forecastle set well back from the stem and a long beak, was firmly established. The typically Tudor decoration, which relied on simple mouldings and brightly contrasting colours, had not yet given way to the carving and gilding of the Stuart period. The four-masted rig was then normal for the larger men-of-war and while main-mizen and bonaventure-mizen topsails of the lateen type had been discarded as useless, the square topsails for these masts, as well as the spritsail topsail, had not yet been introduced. In this particular only the rigging list of 1611 has not been followed, as it foreshadows the introduction of all these three sails, a change which was not completed till 1618. Top-gallant masts and sails on both main and fore-masts were a recent innovation, and it will be noted that both topsails and topgallant sails were still cut very narrow in the head.

" The armament of the *Elizabeth Jonas* is very variously stated in different lists. That shown in the model, which may be taken as a mean approximation, consists of : 2 Demi-cannon, 2 Cannon-Perier, 18 Culverines, 14 Demi-culverines and 10 Sakers, together with smaller guns. These bronze guns were the equivalent respectively of the short 32 and 24 pounders of the long 18, 9 and 6 pounders of a later date."

For the benefit of the practical model-maker, it may perhaps be worth mentioning a few further points of interest. The whole of the hull below the lower gun-deck was shaped from planks of yellow-pine, secured together in " bread and butter " fashion, while above that the top-sides were properly built up with lance-wood timbers and sycamore planking. The decks of yellow-pine were lined but not laid in individual planks. The lower masts and spars were all made of sycamore, the upper part of lance-wood.

In order to avoid the sticky effect so commonly produced by oil-paints, only water-colours were used in the painting, but these were set by means of french polish.

For the rigging, each rope of which is accurately to scale, use was made of the silk twist supplied by surgical instrument makers. All the blocks and deadeyes had to be made specially, of pear-wood, for none commercially obtainable had either the shape of the period or the necessary finish.

After the sails had been bent and the yards braced up on the port tack, each sail was blown out by means of a powerful electric fan, and then, while the sail was exhibiting the real strains exerted on it by each of its ropes, it was set in place by running over it a dilute solution of celluloid. This is probably the first occasion on which such a method of stiffening the sails of a model has been attempted, and it is generally considered to have met with considerable success.

The flags were made of lithographic paper and were treated with celluloid solution under an air-blast, just as were the sails. It has been found that silk is seldom satisfactory for flags ; for it is either too stiff to look natural or too flimsy to take the colour well.

In consequence of the life-like effect achieved with the sails, it was decided to go further and to attempt to complete the picture by showing the vessel on a sea of glass. The hull was, of course, much too valuable to allow of it being cut through on the water-line, so the glass " sea " had to be very carefully cut and ground to fit round the hull. For the purposes of the Science Museum it was necessary that the form of the under-water body should be visible, just as plainly as the top-sides, and, consequently, it was not possible to close in the sides

The Elizabethan Galleon in the Science Museum

of the " sea," but despite this slight difficulty, the general artistic effect is by no means unpleasing.

(All ship model lovers will join us in an expression of appreciation to Mr. G. S. Laird Clowes for the splendid photograph of the Elizabethan Galleon and for the interesting notes he has kindly added to the official description of this fine piece of model-making craftsmanship. This model is an out-standing example of careful historical research and meticulously accurate construction, and every ship-modeller should make a point of visiting the Science Museum and studying the Galleon in detail. Mr. G. S. Laird Clowes' co-operation is great encouragement from such an acknowledged authority and enthusiast, and we shall endeavour to continue to deserve his good opinion.—ED., S. AND S.M.)

Notable Ships of To-day

No. II.—THE EAST ASIATIC COMPANY'S " EUROPA "

WHEN they decided to put on service the first ocean-going motor ship in 1912, the *Selandia*, which is still running, the East Asiatic Company went to Burmeister and Wain, the Copenhagen shipbuilders and engineers, and these two firms have been working in the closest harmony ever since. Since those days the line has put on service a long series of diesel-engined cargo liners whose design was a direct development of the pioneer *Selandia*, improved in every detail, it is true, and the number of masts increased from three to four, but unmistakably a direct development. All these ships have twin screws, keeping the horse power per cylinder within a very reasonable limit, and one of the most conspicuous features of the company's fleet was the remarkable freedom from accident.

But when the company decided that its secondary service through the Panama Canal to the North Pacific ports should be maintained by diesel driven ships as well, it was felt that a new type was necessary, particularly as all the Eastern ships had been without funnels, while the Pacific ships were to have excellent passenger accommodation, and the passenger is both old-fashioned and illogical in his demand for smoke stacks whether they are necessary or not. Accordingly, a single-screw passenger and cargo liner was planned with two enormous funnels, whose artistic placing was a matter of greater difficulty on account of the economic placing of the engines. The *Amerika*, which was put on service in January, 1930, was such a striking success that she has been joined by the *Europa*, a sister ship with many minor improvements.

The length of the new ship between perpendiculars is 465', overall 484' 3", her beam 62', and her moulded depth 40'. This gives a gross tonnage of rather more than 10,200, the deadweight tonnage being about 12,000 and her nett carrying capacity 615,000 cu. ft. of bales. Although she is primarily a cargo ship one of the *Europa's* main points of difference compared with the *Amerika* is the improved passenger accommodation for 56 people who may prefer the more free and easy and enjoyable life in a liner of this sort to the formality of the giants. All these passengers were accommodated in two-berth rooms, 22 of them being on the bridge deck and 6 on the promenade deck. The fact that she is not primarily a passenger carrier has no effect on the comfort, for 12 of the rooms have their own private bathrooms and all are well fitted. The dining saloon is on the bridge deck forward of the passenger accommodation, and below it there is a large smoking room and ladies' lounge.

Although this passenger accommodation is not by any means negligible, it is second in money-making to the cargo capacity, 91,000 cu. ft. of which is insulated and refrigerated for the carriage of fruit from the North Pacific. Fruit is not like meat as a cargo and its temperature has to be kept down by the cold-air system which calls for very expert handling.

As the ships were designed to run on regular schedule, the hatches and deck machinery have been given special attention in their design, so that there is no chance of their being held up in port. There are five hatches, the biggest 36 ft. in length, and each has its full quota of deck machinery. No. 1 hatch goes up to the forecastle deck, where naturally its securing is a matter for the greatest care, while No. 3 trunks right through from the main deck to the promenade deck, so that there is no interference with the passenger accommodation. The winches on all these hatches are

The East Asiatic Company's New Motor Ship "Europa"

electric, the lifting capacity of the derricks varying from 1 to 30 tons at No. 2 hatch to many with the ordinary capacity of 3 and 5 tons each. The winches are carefully grouped to give easy control.

The introduction of funnels into these ships, after the East Asiatic Company had been the leaders of the

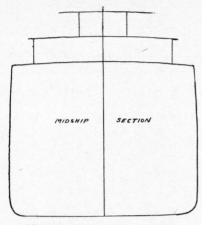

MIDSHIP SECTION

Mid-ship Section of the "Europa"

funnelless motor ship school for many years, has already been mentioned, and it has to be admitted that, outwardly, they are the least desirable feature of the ship's design. The position of the engine room made it very difficult to place them to advantage, only the forward one being used to take the exhaust from the big

diesel. The shape and dimensions are dictated by the desirability of obviating all the troublesome echo of the exhaust, but the long side and top cut-off parallel with the water-line somehow gives them an unreal appearance, which is a pity considering the remarkably beautiful lines of the hull, which are, for a ship designed primarily as a cargo carrier, unusually fine.

The main engine, which exhausts into the foremost funnel, is a double-acting two-stroke diesel by Burmeister and Wain, the new type being introduced for the first time into the *Amerika*. It normally develops, roughly, 7,000 brake horse power at 95 revolutions per minute and is the most up-to-date machine of its kind afloat. Its makers have been building diesel engines now for many years and brought all their experience into its design, obtaining the utmost power with the most compact and economical engine. The *Amerika* claimed to be the most economical diesel ship afloat, and the *Europa* is out to beat her. For her general purposes she is not designed for extreme speed but, on trial, an average of 17.2 knots was obtained with 8,300 brake horse power (9,300 i.h.p.) and excellent economy.

From the model-maker's point of view the *Europa* has many features of interest, a ship of moderate size and not too intricate design, yet so up-to-date that she is well worth a lot of trouble in the portrayal.

Sketch by]   **"Ships, Sea, and Sky"**   *[R. H. Penton*

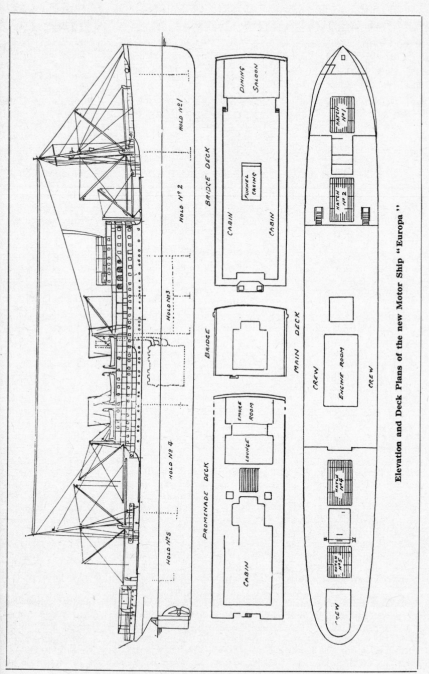

Elevation and Deck Plans of the new Motor Ship "Europa"

A Thousand Ships and More

A Chat with Mr. Fred. C. Poyser of the Nautical Photo Agency

By "MAIN ROYAL"

THE telephone bell rang. A voice said "We want photographs of a thousand sailing ships, all different. Can you supply them?" "That" said Mr. Fred. C. Poyser, of the Nautical Photo Agency, "was, I think, the most remarkable enquiry we have dealt with. We accepted the order and completed it; I doubt if there is another photographic agency in the world who could have done it."

Mr. Fred. C. Poyser

We were seated in the "ship room" at Russell Grove, Mill Hill, where Mr. Poyser finds filling the needs of ship-loving picture collectors a peaceful and pleasant change from the rough and tumble of seafaring days. With pipe alight, I persuaded him to talk. I started with a little experience of my own on the G. S. N. boat *Grive* in the Bordeaux trade. He smiled and said "I was the second mate on that boat. I made the Bordeaux run seventy-seven times." He produced a private log book and showed me every trip he had made methodically noted down. It was a remarkable record; Vancouver, Antofagasta, Lisbon, Panama, The Straits of Magellan, Australia and dozens of other places figuring in the list. Three times round the Horn in his first voyage to sea, which lasted two years, six weeks on end without a dry stitch of clothing or a warm meal, and twice torpedoed during the war. These experiences he passed over with a smile, and then he pointed to one entry and said "I'm rather proud of that." It read thus—"passed for Master in sail"—"I had some difficulty in getting that," he said "for

I was in steam at the time of my examination. Although the law allowed the granting of a certificate, the examiner held the view that candidates for a sailing ship Master's certificate should still be in sail." He explained his attitude to me and questioned me for three and a half hours. Finally he said "Well, I've tried to prevent your getting it, but you've convinced me against my will. You shall have your ticket."

It is a delightful room, that "ship room" at Mill Hill. Ship pictures and ship models abound. Some of the models are unfinished; they are bargains which Mr. Poyser has picked up in the sale room, and some day he is going to finish them. There is one I admired very much; a green and black hull of a full-rigged ship, with the masts and rigging broken down and gone. The hull is a gem of neat craftsmanship, beautifully planked, and bearing the stamp of a master ship-builder in the realism of its constructive detail. Apparently it had fallen into unappreciative hands, and had been the plaything of destructive children until it finally found its way with other discarded possessions to the sale room. Mr. Poyser bid three pounds for it and got it. Whether he completes it or not, it is a treasure and a delight.

There was another model hull of an auxiliary-engined warship of the eighteen-fifties. "I bought that in the Caledonian Market," said Mr. Poyser, "The vendor asked ten shillings for it I offered him five," "Oh! no Sir" said the dealer "you can't beat me down on that, why sir, the curator of the British Museum told me it was a hundred years old." "Well, I said "the next time you see your friend the curator ask him for the names of any ships of that type a hundred years ago which were fitted with propellers."

Then Mr. Poyser showed me some photographs. Not one or two, or a dozen, but hundreds. Sailing ships of all countries, in full sail, at anchor, in harbour; motor ships, liners, trawlers and in fact everything that floats. "I get asked" he said "for every kind of ship and I can usually supply what is wanted. I was even asked for a picture of a Norfolk Wherry. I have many friends and correspondents at sea and abroad with cameras, and when they get an interesting picture they send it along to me. Here for instance are some photographs of the *Panope* in full sail taken from a fisheries protection Cruiser. They are rather good." I saw pictures of the *Preussen*, the *Herzogin Cecile*, the *Kobenhavn*, and dozens of other famous ships and could have spent hours in yarning about the histories of these beauties of the sea, but time did not permit. I made a mental note,

however, that here was a store of delightful material for the pages of SHIPS AND SHIP MODELS, and Mr. Poyser very kindly offered most friendly assistance in this direction.

Mr. Poyser has recently been fortunate in securing the co-operation of Mr. James Randall, of Bristol, who has a remarkable collection of sailing ship photos amounting to 760 names, and these will shortly be all transferred to Mill Hill.

It must not be imagined that Mr. Poyser "hands, reefs, and steers" this fascinating photographic collection single-handed. He doesn't. There is his charming secretary, Miss Mildred Vincent who though she does not hold the ticket of a "master in sail" knows nearly as much about a full-rigged ship as her chief. I am sure many collectors who have rung up "Mill Hill 1969" must have been surprised at the competent response to their enquiries in her delightful voice.

(Readers who are interested in ship photographs may inspect a stock of Nautical Photo Agency pictures at the office of SHIPS AND SHIP MODELS, 66, Farringdon Street, London, E.C.4., where copies may be purchased.)

Photo by]　　　　**The "Panope" in full sail**　　　　[*Nautical Photo Agency*

A Small Model Frigate of 1750

By R. W. PRANCE

The Hull of the Model Frigate

SHIP models, especially those of old wooden warships, have always held a particular fascination for me, and often I had thought how much I should like to try my hand at constructing one myself.

One day I decided to make an attempt, and after a certain amount of preparatory research, a start was made. The little ship shown in the photographs, relative to this article, was the outcome of my endeavours in this direction, and I was more than satisfied with the result. At last year's *Model Engineer* Exhibition she was awarded a silver medal with certificate, which to say the least, gave me still greater satisfaction.

She is built to a scale of $\frac{1}{8}''$ to 1'. The original frigate, on whose lines she was modelled, measured 128' on gun deck, with a beam of 34', her tonnage was 667.

Not possessing a workshop, she had to be built on the sitting-room table, and, for convenience of construction, I kept the scale as low as possible. I might add that I really consider she is quite small enough, measuring only $7\frac{3}{4}''$ from stem to sternpost. I have made some smaller models, but the work is really too finicky, especially when one gets down to the rigging.

The Hull

Of course, drawings were made beforehand, and they were of great assistance in obtaining the correct transverse sections for the frames, of which there are 12 in number. The hull was built up with 18 planks a side, $\frac{1}{16}''$ chestnut being used. This was steamed, bent and pinned into position for each plank. For the waling, false work on head, etc., bamboo was used, purloined from an old Japanese sunshade. This splits very nicely into small sections, but is tricky to work, especially when fixing in position, as it splits rather easily when pierced.

Stern and quarter galleries, with gingerbread work, were all carved from birchwood, and the windows with their miniature sashes of bamboo, are all glazed with thin celluloid.

The figurehead, together with all blocks, deadeyes, cleats, etc. (there are over 300 of them) are all of bone, old toothbrush handles being requisitioned for the job. All guns were made from $\frac{3}{32}''$ brass tubing, and having no lathe, they had to be filed up by hand.

They are run out on small carriages at all gun ports, the port lids being fitted with tiny ring bolts as were used in actual practice, for lashing down.

The Masts and Yards

The masts, yards, stunsail booms, bowsprit, etc., were all made from the old Japanese sunshade, and there was precious little of it left by the time the model was completed. The fore, main, and mizzen tops are properly secured on crosstrees and trestle trees; in fact, she was properly rigged with the shrouds set up and hove taut by means of the usual deadeyes and lanyards. I found it practically impossible to put in everything there should be on so small a scale. For instance, I couldn't get the three holes per deadeye, so had to content myself with one hole with lanyard rove through three times. Likewise the ratlines are stuck across the shrouds, instead of being clove-hitched.

An old sailor, who recently examined the model, was disgusted about this. He said it should have been done properly, as it spoilt the look of her,

and to a certain extent I think he is right. I never object to competent criticism ! However, to satisfy him, I tried rattling down a 3½″ bone model of the *Victory* I have recently completed. Well, I really did it in the approved fashion, but never again ; it took me weeks to do, and incidently, severely strained my eyesight into the bargain.

I merely mention this in passing,. as it shows what can be done if one is determined upon doing it, but I certainly wouldn't encourage any brother ship-modeller to attempt it ; it isn't worth the trouble on such tiny ships.

Rigging Details

However, to carry on with the rigging of the frigate, all cordage and tackling was made from silk ligatures of various grades. This is very strong stuff and can be obtained very fine.

Practically all that should be in was put in, both running and standing rigging. Sheets, tacks, braces, clew

A Model Frigate of 1750, by R. W. Prance

lines, are all there, and could be hauled on and generally manipulated if necessary.

Deck Fittings

As to the decks and fittings, there is a top-gallant forecastle, then the waist, next quarter-deck and, being an early-type frigate, a short poop deck. The forecastle carries a tiny grating, with foremast bitts, galley stove pipe, and belfry. In the waist, on either side, are the 32-pounder guns; her boats should be chocked up here, together with spare spars, but so far these haven't been fitted.

On either side of the grating the deck planking is up, showing transverse beams, around foot of mainmast are the gallows and bitts, together with the pumps. The quarter deck carries a grating with capstan for heaving in cables when getting under way, also 9-pounder guns on either side. The poop deck is fitted with small skylight right aft. With regard to colouring, the model was varnished all over natural colour. The varnish has given the wooden hull a rather nice golden tint; there is a broad black stroke along the waterline, with a light greeny-blue band on the top sides, relieved with gold scrolls.

All carved work on stern also was gilt. Bulwarks inboard, together with underside of gun ports, are all blood-red.

The doors to forecastle and cabins are shown just ajar, also forward are the four wooden stocked anchors catted and fished. Last of all, she carries a golden poop lantern with flag over the stern. The flag, at a glance, looks likes our present Red Ensign, but is shown minus the St. Patrick cross in the upper canton. At the period when the original frigate was in commission it was the custom to divide the fleets into three sections, namely, red, white and blue, hence the red in the ensign, showing she was attached to the Red fleet.

Two Years' Work

The model took something like two years of spare time work. In order not to tire of the job I sometimes put it by for a week or so, but I thoroughly enjoyed every minute that was spent on her construction. For details of rigging, fittings, etc., several visits were made to the various museums in London that exhibit old ship models; I also examined any reproductions of old nautical prints that came my way, and were suitable for the purpose. In conclusion, I trust this description of my little frigate will prove of interest to all lovers of sailing ship models, and give encouragement to those brothers who, like myself, must content themselves with a few tools and a corner of the table for their miniature dockyard.

Sketch by]   **" Traffic "**   *[R. H. Penton*

A Scale Model of the "Santa Maria"

By W. O. K. LEITCH

THIS model is a copy of a larger one now in the Science Museum. I saw the large model in the Museum one day and, on making inquiries, I managed to obtain a blue

Stern view of the "Santa Maria"

print and four very fine detail photographs.

Having started off, I produced a scale drawing of $\frac{1}{8}''$ to $1'$ which gave the following dimensions for the model: tip to tip, 24"; keel to main truck, $17\frac{1}{2}''$; and beam, $5\frac{1}{2}''$.

The hull is solid and was carved out of yellow pine, using templates from the drawing to get the right profile. The gunwales and deck fittings were made from American white wood, since it was easy to work and gave a smooth finish. The hull, with the forecastle and poop, when finished, was then painted, an undercoating of matt white paint and finished with "poster paints." It was finally given two coats of cellulose lacquer. The stanchions for the three decks were

bought, as I had no lathe to turn them on; incidentally, these were the only fittings or parts bought.

The masts and yards were made from ash, shaped and "french polished." Now came the most difficult job of all, the rigging. After searching round for some realistic material to use for the ropes and stays (string was of course no use as it was too coarse), I found the right thing, thanks to Mr. Dowell of the Ship Department of the Science Museum, who also very kindly allowed me to take measurements from the Museum model. He advised me to use "ligature silk." This I got from Messrs. Down Bros., surgical instrument makers, and I found that it was just the stuff. It is made in about a dozen sizes, from $\frac{1}{100}''$ to $\frac{1}{8}''$—this silk looks just like the real thing and some of it was dyed black to represent the tarred ropes.

The larger blocks were carved from cherry and boxwood, while the smaller ones were punched out from hard

Bow view of the "Santa Maria"

leather with a sadler's punch, as also were the deadeyes.

The sails were made from balloon cloth with stitched brown lines to represent the sail cloth. The sails, when bent to the yards, were treated with " Cellon airplane dope," and blown out with an electric fan to give them a bulging appearance.

The flags and pennants are made from silk with the emblems painted on and then treated with the dope as for the sails. The anchors were made from ebonite and the little lantern on the poop from cardboard wire and celluloid.

One of the most ticklish jobs of all was coiling up the loose ends of the silks to represent coils of rope.

The finished model, which had given me many hours of pleasure building it, is, as can be seen from the photographs, quite realistic and looks, as I imagined it looked, when Columbus set off into the unknown eventually to discover America.

A Water-line Model of H.M.S. "Cumberland"

By "HAUSE PIPE"

THE making of water-line models, though by no means such an interesting hobby as the making of working ones, presents a very interesting spare-time occupation to people such as myself, who never have a settled home for more than a few months, and therefore have no opportunity of fitting up a workshop. The model illustrated was made with the aid of very few tools, in fact all the tools and materials used, except of course the wood, were kept in a small cardboard box.

The model is built to a scale of 1″ to 20′ and the overall length comes out at 32½″. The hull, upperworks to the level of the base of the funnels, the turrets and guns, are made of wood, and also the boats and masts. The remaining upperworks are made of

A Water-line Model of H.M.S. "Cumberland"

cardboard. I find cardboard, well painted, is extremely durable and looks very realistic; in fact, I have used it on working models where weight saving is an important factor, and found it quite satisfactory. A good quality cardboard must of course be used.

The funnels are made of rolls of paper (about six thicknesses), the joint being smoothed off with sandpaper. The other upper-deck details are made with the aid of pins, wire, cork, etc.

The rigging, with the exception of the wireless aerials, was made of transformer wire; the insulators in the rigging, which are a distinctive feature of all modern warships, are made by putting little dots of black paint on to the wire from the end of a pin. The shiny end and brass bands on the guns are of course made of silver and gold paper.

I find a very good way of making a planking effect on the decks is as follows: With a sharp knife cut a series of parallel shallow slits in the deck at the required distance apart, then, with the side of a mapping-pen, run indian ink into these slits.

If anyone should think of trying this, I advise them to try it on a piece of wood first, as it requires a little practice.

In conclusion, a word of advice to those who are starting on water-line models for the first time: Start on warships! Although they may not appear so to look at, they are very much easier. There are several features in liners which are exceedingly difficult to reproduce nicely in the larger models; to mention only one, cowl ventilators. I have been trying for years to find a means of making these satisfactory with the tools and materials usually at my disposal.

In case any readers should think that cardboard used on models would soon "rot away," I might mention that the model was three years' old when this photograph was taken and had never seen the inside of a glass case.

Over-Rigged Models

HOW rarely does one see a completely rigged model ship, in which all the masts, spars and rigging details are perfectly in scale with the dimensions of the hull. The novice usually begins with an intense enthusiasm for completeness in his model. He selects his prototype, and models a very nice hull. Having admired some perfect piece of small-scale craftsmanship, or having only a limited accommodation for doing his work, he builds his hull to a very restricted scale. He then proceeds with the masts and spars and rigging, and probably proportions them largely by eye alone. The scale height of the masts and the scale length of the spars may be right, but perhaps with some thought of their strength in mind, or with some difficulty in thinning them down to the required dimensions, they are allowed to pass a trifle over scale. Then come the ropes, and the lashings, and the blocks and the deadeyes. Everything must be put in, but it is perhaps difficult to get exactly the right size in these miniature materials. A trifling departure from scale is accepted, and the rigging is proceeded with. Gradually the model is completed, but at the same time she gradually assumes a clumsy air. As each rope is added, each knot tied, so does the hull become more and more overweighted by the rigging. Final touches of unnecessarily thick paint or varnish complete the spoliation. Every little over-scale item adds to the clumsiness of the whole model, and at the finish the builder is disappointed with his production.

A simple model in which the general character is preserved by perfect scale is far more pleasing to the eye than one in which an endeavour to secure absolute completeness of detail is marred by the over-scaling of many of its component parts.

Testing a Model of a Modern Cunarder

A Model of a new Cunard Liner under test

MOST of the big shipbuilding yards have large tanks, something like an ordinary swimming bath, where models of projected ships are tested before the actual ship is built. These models are usually made of wax, partly for simplicity of preparation, and partly because modifications in the lines of the hull can readily be made as the tests proceed. The models are towed along the tank from a travelling bridge platform, on which are mounted various recording instruments which register the power required to tow the model at given scale speeds. From these records the performance of the real ship can be ascertained in advance with a very close accuracy.

Here is a model being tested in the experimental tank at Messrs. John Brown's Clydebank Shipyard, but in this instance the model is self-propelled. She represents a new Cunarder now under construction, and as yet unnamed. The model is 18' long and is fitted with small motors which drive four propellers. Artificial waves are produced in the water, giving the effect of heavy seas, and the behaviour of the model is carefully observed. The wax models previously referred to are only miniatures of the hull, but in the model illustrated the superstructure has been completed in very full detail, so that the effects of wind-resistance and other points in the behaviour of a ship with extensive upper works may be studied.

This is an interesting example of the utilitarian side of ship-modelling. The great value placed on this method of anticipating the performance of real ships through model tests may be gathered from the fact that the installation and equipment of a suitable testing tank costs many thousands of pounds.

Elements of Model Steamer Design

By T. R. THOMAS, B.Sc., M.I.Mar.E.

II.—HULL DESIGN

BEFORE proceeding to the discussion of the actual design of the hull of the model which we contemplate building there are certain general aspects to be considered—we must determine, as definitely as possible, the type of model to be built, the facilities and skill which we can bring to bear in the building of it and the conditions under which the model is to be sailed. The choice of type is influenced, among other things, by the amount of detail work which we are prepared to put into the model and whether speed is to be an important consideration. We must not make the common mistake of attempting to drive a type of model, the scale speed of which is two miles an hour at six miles an hour. This matter of scale speed is worth a little consideration. The speed of a cargo ship, say four hundred feet in length, may well be in the neighbourhood of twelve knots and by use of the expression $v/\sqrt{L}$ where V is speed in the knots and L the length of the ship, we can arrive at an approximate scale speed for any particular length of model of the ship. The value of $v/\sqrt{L}$ for the big ship is .6, so that if our model is three feet long the scale speed will be .6 multiplied by 1.732 or approximately 1.2 miles per hour. In other words the realistic speed for a model of this character is very small, but the tendency of the average model maker is to try to drive the model at a greater speed. A model travelling at 1.2 miles per hour however, has not sufficient power to overcome the resistance of wind and water, the effects of which, of course, are not reduced in accordance with scale. A greater speed than the scale speed is permissible and the model may be driven at three miles an hour without any great sacrifice in realism. It is usually better, however, to select a type of model in which the scale speed is greater. The cross channel steamer, three feet in length, may, for instance, be driven at four or four and a half miles an hour and the torpedo boat destroyer at about six miles an hour, and yet the scale speed maintained approximately.

Types of Models

Faster speeds still can be properly used if a model of the motor launch type is built and the maximum speed which the model maker is able to obtain will not be out of place. Here it is worth while drawing attention to the essential difference between what is called the displacement type of model and the hydroplane. The hydroplane skims on the surface of the water while the hull of the displacement model must be pushed through the water. The design of the hydroplane hull is, however, too specialised a subject for treatment here and any readers interested are referred to the book Model Power Boats which is supplied by Percival Marshall & Co., Ltd. The various types which we may model offer varying opportunity for our skill in reproducing the original. The cargo ship makes a good model in which there need not be too much detail in order to obtain a reasonably good effect. The ship will probably have a poop bridge and forecastle and the principal deck fittings will be hatches, windlass, and winches, masts and derricks—the fitting of the navigation bridge may be made as elaborate as the skill and patience of the model maker permits. Some notes on fittings and their construction will be given later when this type of ship is discussed in greater detail.

The cross channel steamer presents little more difficulty in the design and construction of the hull, but the deck fittings and arrangements must be much more elaborate to give realistic appearance. The torpedo boat destroyer is fairly simple to arrange and construct in this respect and such fittings as are necessary can be purchased. They are however, rather difficult to make. Probably the simplest proposition for the beginner is a model of a motor launch as the scale is not so extreme and the number of fittings comparatively few.

Hull Construction

Our ability and the facilities for the construction of the hull affect the choice of the type and we must first briefly review the methods which we can adopt. The simplest, of course

of ship-shape form is probably by using the bread and butter system. In this, several planks are screwed and glued together to form the block out of which the model is cut. It is convenient, of course, to do a certain amount of work of shaping of the planks before they are fastened together, but this, in fact, is not necessary. The builder need have no fear of the efficiency of this method of construction as a perfectly sound hull can be made, but it will not be so light as the dug out hull owing to the necessity of leaving a certain thickness to form a joint between the planks.

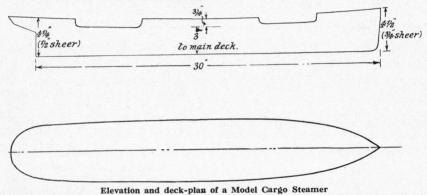

Elevation and deck-plan of a Model Cargo Steamer

is to dig the hull out of a solid wood block—a decision to adopt this course depends on our ability to obtain a fairly good block of pine of the required dimensions. Yellow pine is our first choice, but is not easy to obtain and the cost is considerable. Provided, however, that the wood is sound and free from large knots, its particular character does not matter very much, provided it is fairly soft and reasonably easy to work. This method is the simplest we can adopt, because it requires no elaborate preparation on the drawing board—all that is required is a midship section and profiles of the stem and stern; a fairly good eye; some idea of the general shape required and care and patience. In order of simplicity the next method of constructing a hull

Still having wood construction in mind, we can frame and plank a hull as model yachts are often built, but this is a method of construction which requires considerable skill and a great deal of labour. It is not proposed to describe it in detail because it does not result in a suitable hull to carry anything but electric machinery and it is practically impossible to build some types of models in this fashion, as the curves to be negotiated are more abrupt than those of the model yacht.

During the War when the necessity of producing ships quickly and economically was of great importance an interesting form of hull was adopted which had the advantage of incorporating practically nothing but straight lines. This form of design is quite suitable for certain models and it will be shown later on that with care a model motor launch, for instance, of good appearance can be designed to enable us to use this form of straight line construction.

In the bread and butter method, mentioned previously, it is necessary to have a complete set of lines for the model, but when a straight line form is used, the design is much more simple and does not call for skill on the drawing board. The straight line form also enables us to use ply-wood successfully and is a simple and interesting method of construction, the details of which will be given. It may be that the builder prefers to use metal rather than wood, and if so

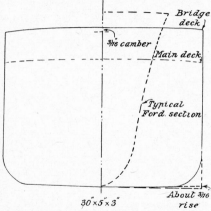

30″×5″×3″

Midship section for Model Cargo Steamer

he can frame and plate the model in the same way as the full sized ship is constructed. This method, however, requires a certain amount of skill in the handling of metal tools. It will be realised that the straight line form can be constructed of metal sheets in place of ply-wood and if a metal boat is contemplated this is the model which the beginner should adopt. The foregoing remarks may have assisted the model maker to decide on both the type of model and the method of construction, and some particulars of each will be given so that the work may be proceeded with with a fair chance of success.

It has already been suggested that the preliminary drawings for a model to be dug out are simple and a midship section stem and stern frame for a cargo vessel are given herewith. We will assume that the model is to be thirty inches long—the breadth may be made 5 inches and the depth to the main deck may be 3 inches. The depth to the top of the poop bridge and forecastle will be about 3¾ inches so that the constructor has to decide whether these are to be cut out of the solid block or treated as additions to be made after the main portion of the hull is completed. The first step is to trace the deck line on the wood block. So long as this conforms generally to the shape shown the exact contour does not matter— the block should now be cut out to this shape, the sides in the meantime being kept vertical. The next step is to shape the block out for its whole length to the midship section shown i.e., to round the bottom corners or " bulges ". If the constructor is afraid to rely on his eye to do this, a template should be made from thin ply-wood. This is best done by making a drawing of one side of the ship and reversing this drawing about a centre line drawn on the ply-wood. Spots on the outline can be pricked through and afterwards joined up, the complete section being cut out by a fretsaw and cleaned up with sandpaper. The block can now be shaped to the template, exercising reasonable care, especially when the correct form is being approached. The big ship very often has what is called a " tumble home " which means that the upper portion of the side falls in a little to the centre line, leaving the maximum breadth at say ⅓ of the depth from the keel. This, however, is so slight that it is hardly noticeable in the model and the extra work involved in its inclusion is not warranted. When the block has been shaped to the midship section, the profile of the stem and stern should be marked out and the ends of the block cut away in accordance. The remainder of the work consists in

shaping the block down to these profiles, and it can best be done by eye
if the constructor is a fair workman.
If the desire is to reproduce an accurate
model of a prototype, the bread and
butter method is the most suitable
and it has been assumed, of course,
that the model makers object is, in
this case, to reproduce a type rather
than a particular ship. In shaping
the hull he should note that a small
length of the hull midships, say six
inches, is probably of the midship
section and after this shapes regularly
and gradually to the ends. There
should be no hollows in the hull except
perhaps at the stern where the shape
of the ship depends very largely on the
form of stern adopted. Two types of
stern are shown—the old fashioned
or elliptical stern. and the new of
cruiser stern. The latter is quite
correct for the modern cargo ship and
is easier to shape. Its effect, however,
is to make the ship look a little shorter
than does the elliptical stern, although
tis appearance can be very effective
if it is properly designed. It should
be noted that the line of the stern

until the hole for the shaft has been
drilled. The shaping of the after
portion of the ship looks more difficult
than it is and it will be found that
given the right profile of the stern, the
proper shape comes naturally. The

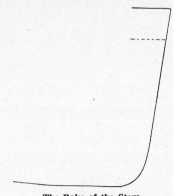

The Rake of the Stem

stern frame, shown in the sketch, is
best made of brass plate about $\frac{1}{8}''$
thick. If it is " built up " a flat can
be provided to screw to the bottom
of the hull and a projection to take

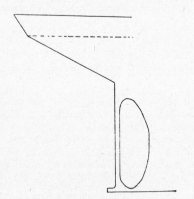

The Elliptical Stern

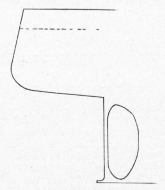

The Cruiser Stern

from the round above the water line
to the deck is straight, or nearly so,
as a curved profile increases the effect
of " stumpiness." A swelling or boss
should be left in the hull where the
propellor shaft is to come out, but
the final finish of this should be left

bearing for the rudder at the top as
well as at the heel.
   The stem is shown " raked " or
sloping away slightly. This slope
should not be overdone for an average
model although in some ships it is
rather extreme. The bows may be

fairly sharp or rounded to a radius of about $\frac{3}{8}''$ at the deck level to $\frac{1}{8}''$ at the turn. This is quite in order and gives a stem less easily damaged when the model comes alongside.

Practically all ships have " sheer " or in other words the deckline slopes up to the stem and stern, the lowest point being amidships. The slope forward is greater than aft. A little sheer is necessary to prevent the ship looking " broken backed " but too much makes her look shorter so that it should not be overdone.

The same may be said about the " camber of the deck—a small camber on all decks looks well but the rise should not be more than $\frac{3}{16}''$

Note that the deck line forward is wider than the water line so that the hull slopes out slightly to the deck edge. A certain amount of curvature as shown in the typical section can be given, but this is rather difficult to achieve satisfactorily and the hull here can be made flat if preferred.

(To be continued)

The Collecting of Ship Models

BY R. H. PENTON

MOST people collect something—stamps, pottery, furniture—the list is endless, and collecting old ship models has claimed the enthusiasm of an increasing number of people in recent years.

Like most other hobbies, it may cost much or little ; much, if the collector wishes for even a few perfect specimens of old models ; little, if he is content to buy " wrecks " and spend many months—perhaps years—mending them.

The types to be found in the shops of the antique dealers range from the contemporary, dockyard-built, scale model—very rare—to the somewhat crude model made by some old sailor or fisherman to while away his leisure hours. The former are beyond the purse of most in these days ; the latter may often be picked up quite cheaply and, although the details may be clumsy and hopelessly out of scale, they have a charm of their own.

Belonging to neither of these classes is the " prisoner-of-war model," made by French prisoners confined in English prisons during the Napoleonic Wars and generally of bone or ivory, but sometimes of wood. According to the skill of the craftsmen—often

expert ivory-carvers or skilled watchmakers—these models are generally extremely beautiful and decorative objects, but they are rarely true models of the ships they purport to represent.

Unless the enthusiast has ample accommodation (and a long-suffering wife, if married) for the storage of large-scale models in glass cases, it is advisable to concentrate on the acquisition of small models. If, however, it is in a bad state of repair, the smaller the model, the more difficult it is to put right, as it involves a very steady hand, small tools, the use of a magnifying-glass and unlimited patience.

Few models to be found nowadays are in perfect condition, and once having been " bitten " by the craze, the temptation is to buy one " wreck " after another in the hope of " getting down to it some day." If these ships all belong to different periods, a vast amount of research is necessary before beginning the work of restoration and, more often than not, the rigging, in attempting to patch it up, will be found to be rotten. The only thing to do in such a case is to scrap it and start from the beginning, but before doing so, careful notes should be made.

Sometimes, of course, an old and rather clumsy model may be improved considerably—that is, if the hull is reasonably true to type. A complete set of new fittings can be made, copied from the original fittings, of course, but much more nearly to scale.

One very common defect in the " sailor made " model is the size of the masts and spars as compared with the hull, which is nearly always too small and with very little under-body. The assumption is that the sailor seldom saw his ship out of water, but he knew all the details of the spars and rigging extremely well and on these he concentrated his work.

One very picturesque type is the " Scenic " model. This sometimes contains several ships in one case, with a crudely painted background, generally supposed to represent some foreign port. These are fairly common but they vary much in quality.

The keen collector's joy is the " built " model. In almost any state, one of these may well be worth all the rest of one's collection, and the repairing of it will mean a high standard of workmanship and much skill only to be obtained by practice, but all well worth while.

After a time, a ship model collector's room, though very overcrowded, may well be a joy to its owner and a source of perpetual romance. A clipper of the 'seventies lies at anchor not far from an early 19th century fruit schooner racing home under a big spread of canvas with her perishable cargo. An early North-East Coast square-rigged steamer is passing a distant lighthouse inward bound, away on the painted horizon are two Geordie brigs outward bound. In another case opposite, is a very large brig-o'-war, bristling with guns and with every stitch set, but this looks like a tragedy, for a serious collision with a rapidly approaching full-rigged ship on the other tack can hardly be avoided. One or two others are in dockyard hands, quite obviously, but the yard is shorthanded and the shipwright and rigger has to go from one to the other—shall it be said—as the inclination of the moment prompts him. But what more fascinating occupation could there be for a winter evening— or even a dull evening in our so-called summer.

(There must be many of our readers who have had interesting experiences as collectors. Stories of unexpected " finds," of re-building or re-rigging, of the histories of authentic models, of buying and selling, and similar matters, would all be of great interest to other readers. Please send your little story along, with, or without, a photograph of the model.—ED., S. & S.M.)

Sketch by]   **" Hove To "**   *[R. H. Penton*

A Model of the East Indiaman "La Hogue"

By J. G. SURTEES

THE photos herewith are of a water-line model of the East Indiaman *La Hogue*, built at Sunderland by James Laing in 1855. Length,

The "La Hogue"—Starboard Side

226', beam 35', depth 22' 9"; 1,331 tons.

I saw a small picture of her in "Blue Peter," and copied the model from it. She is 12" long and 2" wide. As she is so small, only a certain amount of the rigging was possible, but enough to tell what class of vessel she is supposed to represent.

The hull was cut to shape at the deck line, then the forecastle and poop were made by cutting down $\frac{3}{16}$" to form the main deck and a piece $\frac{3}{16}$" added to make the heighth of each. The hull was then cut to shape from figurehead to quarter galleries.

As the shrouds and back stays on this class of vessel come outside the hull, small pieces of triangular wood were drilled with the necessary holes and glued on the sides to form the

channels, as it was too difficult to make dead eyes, the rigging was brought through these holes, pulled tight and fastened to the hull by cutting a groove and pressing the thread into it and glueing a piece of wood in flush with the sides.

Before starting to rig her, the deck house, companion, skylight, hatches, and other deck fittings were made and fixed, also the stanchions (pins) and rail made from wire were fixed. The anchors were also made from brass wire and the cable of an eye-glass chain. Before stepping the masts, the necessary eyes to secure the blocks for halliards, etc., were made from pins by cutting off the heads, making an eye, and then pushing into the deck.

The "La Hogue"—Port Side

A start was then made with the spars, first the bowsprit and jibboom was fitted in place. I then made all the masts; the tops and caps were made of cardboard and glued on, the lower mast painted white, the topmasts, topgallant and royal masts varnished, and the mastheads of each, white. The yards were next made, painted black, the foot ropes and pennants fixed.

The foremast was fixed and the rigging set up, first the fore stays, then the shrouds and back stays; then the yards were crossed and the lifts and halliards brought down to the deck. It is less difficult to do it this way than to fix all the masts and rigging first. The mainmast was rigged next, then the mizzen. The braces were then rove and fixed. Those on the mizzen were the most difficult to fix, for they cross the main braces, and it is astonishing how obstinate a bit of thread can be; it performs all sorts of antics and will go anywhere but where you want it to go.

The boats—there are seven of them —were from a piece of wood the necessary width and thickness but about 8″ long, which gives you something to hold on to while you carve them out. They are 1″ long, the thwarts and stern sheets are of cardboard and glued in place and pins form the ring bolts; they were then fixed to davits from bent pins—two of them lie on the deck-house.

The painting was then finished, and then she was fastened on a board painted to represent water and moored to two buoys. There is also a boat alongside and a tug 4″ long standing by.

I have made everything connected with her, except the chain for cable. It has been an interesting job, but sometimes wearisome. Then it is best left alone for a time and you come back fresh to the job. The great thing is patience; the cost *nil*.

The Shiplovers' Association

IT is the intention of the Editor to place this section monthly at the disposal of the Shiplovers' Association for the publication of both questions and answers which are of general interest. Particulars of the Association are to be had of the Hon. Sec., *pro tem.*, Mr. Frank C. Bowen, Customs House Building, Milton Place, Gravesend, Kent.

Members' Queries and Answers

One of the original objects of the Association was to collect full details of the various local types of fishing craft before they disappeared entirely. P.F.A. (Gravesend) has consented to collect the information; will members who are keen on this side, and willing to help, please communicate with him through the Secretary.

R.M.T. (London).—The height of the main truck of the Italian sail training-ship *Cristoforo Colombo* is

188′ above the deck and her main yard is 92′ long.

A.F.H. (London) is making a collection of ships in bottles of all kinds and is anxious to get into touch with other members who have taken up this particular branch of the hobby.

F.S.B. (Bristol).—The four-masted barque *Invertrossachs* of 1891 was abandoned in the North Atlantic while bound from Philadelphia to Calcutta with case oil, in February, 1892, and the *Gosford*, of 1892, was burned off the Californian coast in the following year. The barque *Criffel*, of 1863, was wrecked as a schooner in 1902 and must not, of course, be confused with the barque *Criffel* of 1891, which became the Norwegian *Bauen* in 1909.

All answers are sent by post; only those of more general interest are summarised here.

The Model Motor Launch "Scout"

By JAMES S. LAWSON, B.E.

THE original intention was to build an 18′ motor launch for river use and the purchase of the necessary materials was in contemplation when it occurred to the writer that, with no previous experience in boat building, it might be advantageous to experiment with the model first. The drawings had been prepared one-sixth the full size and thus were well adapted to use as full-size drawings for a model.

Most of the framework was formed from scrap and odds and ends. The keel and keelson were originally ordinary sawn plasterer's laths. The stem and transome were cut from scrap bits of elm, and the stringers and gunwales from ¼″ square pine. The *Scout* was built over five moulds shaped out of 3-ply, the keelson, stringers and gunwales being notched in flush. The planking was a source of difficulty for a time but eventually a sheet of mahogany veneer was used to form a double diagonal skin fastened with ½″ pins. This proved to be a success and the gunwale capping and rubbing band were formed out of mahogany and pinned on. The capping was rebated round the inner edge to house the decking, which is from ⅛″ mahogany lined to represent planks.

Drilling for the propeller tube presented some difficulty for a time, but was at length satisfactorily performed with the aid of a heavy breast drill clamped to a 3″ × 3″ hardwood block arranged to slide between two similar blocks screwed to a board. The hole was bored with a long centre-bit, the centre block with the drill being fed up carefully by hand, and the result exceeded expectations, for the tube was found to be a perfect fit. After first boring the hole the drill was withdrawn and an oak chock screwed to the keelson inside the boat and the hole then continued through it, so that the oak chock formed a stout support for the tube inside the vessel. The ¼″ steel propeller shaft, brass stern tube, glands and propeller were purchased before the drilling was done. The "Engine" is an electromotor, driven by a 4-volt accumulator, the latter being housed under the front deck, and behind a 3-ply bulkhead in which is a door giving access to the battery.

The floor is from ⅛″ mahogany with pencil lines drawn to represent planks as was done with the decks. There are two thwarts and a stern seat, with side seats at the after end, all made from ordinary deal.

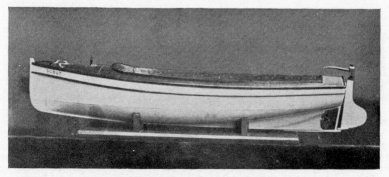

The Model Motor Launch "Scout"

The hull had two coats of white paint, followed by two of enamel— white above and pale blue below the water-line, and the name was added with gold powder made up with boiled oil and turps. The inside of the hull got two coats of lead-coloured paint, and the decks, flooring, rubbing band, coaming, etc., were varnished after the fittings had been screwed on. The " Engine " is covered by a boxing of mahogany with glass roof. On the top is fitted a brass lever which engages with two spring contacts on the motor to complete the circuit and start the boat moving. By pulling back the lever the current is broken and the drive stops. The electric drive was adopted as a temporary measure, and it is hoped to replace it by a miniature petrol engine at some future date.

Books to Read

Ships and Shipping. Edited by EDWIN P. HARNACK. London : Alexander Moring, Ltd. Price 7s. 6d. Postage 5d.

This is the fourth edition of this well-known handbook of popular nautical information. It is pocket-size, and contains over 500 pages, and is packed full of interesting information and data about shipping of all kinds, flags, signals, tides, navigation, rank marks, yachts and yacht clubs, Lloyd's signal stations, docks, ship canals, and lighthouses and lightships. It is well illustrated with line-drawings of various ships, and coloured plates of flags and historic types of ships. To the sea-going traveller, the ship-lover and ship-modeller this informative little volume may be cordially recommended.

* * *

Mariners of Brittany. By PETER F. ANSON. London : J. M. Dent and Sons, Ltd. Price 12s. 6d. Postage 10d.

Mr. Anson deserves well of shipovers for preserving in such an attractive and readable form the traditions and types of the maritime community of Brittany. The Bretons are fishermen from generation to generation, but since their fishing takes them as far afloat as Newfoundland, Iceland and Greenland, they are sailormen as well, and the French Navy finds the fishing ports of Brittany a splendid recruiting-ground. Mr. Anson not only describes the religion and social conditions of the men and their families ; he takes us on tour from port to port, from village to village, and makes us feel that we know these hardy folk and the lives they lead as intimately as we do the fishermen of our own country. But Mr. Anson is more than an interesting chronicler of peoples and of places, he is a delightful artist. The book abounds with admirable line-drawings of fishing vessels and small craft of all kinds. He says that the coast of Brittany is changing ; it is being invaded by the tripper, and he visualises the possibility of the types of fishing craft he illustrates becoming extinct, even in ten years time. This, in itself, is a justification of his careful and informative record. His drawings are so clear, and so full of detail that the building of models of the various types of craft would be a comparatively easy matter. Mr. Anson has achieved the difficult task of conveying the technical details of the boats he illustrates without any sacrifice of a very marked artistic appeal.

TO CORRESPONDENTS.—We have to thank many readers for their interesting and appreciative letters, and for useful suggestions for increasing the utility of our journal. These will all be carefully considered, and suitable use of photographs and descriptions of models enclosed with the correspondence will be made, where possible, in later issues.—ED. S. AND S.M.

The Ship Modeller's Scrap Book
A DICTIONARY OF SHIP DETAILS IN ALL PERIODS
(*Continued from page* 31)

Armstrong's Patent

THE name invariably given by the British sailing ship man to the "dolly" winch of the simplest construction, which was all that the average ship-owner fitted for the working of cargo at a time when German and French sailing ship owners were giving all their vessels steam power which could be used for working the cargo in

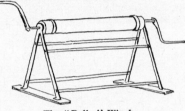

The "Dolly" Winch

port, heaving up the anchor, and on occasions for hoisting and handling the yards. This was at a time when Armstrong's guns and cruisers were a subject of constant discussion, particularly on the West Coast of South America, where the competition with the Continental sailing ships was particularly felt and where the heat made work with the "dolly" winches particularly arduous. The "dolly" winches were succeeded by the portable donkey boiler, and only in a few of the latest ships by proper steam winches. The term was also used for other gadgets with manual power instead of steam.

Balance Reef

A reef band running diagonally across a fore and aft sail from the uppermost reef cringle of the leech to the throat earing. It was a gadget which found some favour in the 19th century, as it permitted half the sail, either upper or lower, to be set, but it never came into very general use in square riggers, and it

was replaced by the numerous types of spanker which came into fashion in later days.

Showing position of a Balance Reef

Beak Bow

Was a highly decorative, but very unpractical, legacy left to the naval architects of Britain and most other maritime countries by the old-time galley. In her case it was unavoidable and useful, for the ram remained one of her most important weapons which encouraged end-on fighting, and the long row of oars along the broadside made the forecastle one of the only places where guns could be mounted. It was maintained in sailing broadside men-of-war as a tradition which persisted long after its

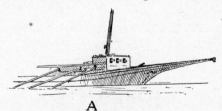

A

The Beak Bow of the Galley

danger had been clearly proved, and hundreds of lives had been unnecessarily sacrificed by its use. Frigates abandoned it about 1760 and took to the " round " bow, and most of the more elaborate merchantmen who copied naval tradition, such as East Indiamen, followed suit about the same time. In line of battleships,

B
The modified 18th Century form of Beak Bow

however, it persisted much later, although without the beautiful decoration of pillar and panel seen in the Tudor and Stuart ships. Although several ships rebuilt in the early days of the 19th century were given built-up round bows, it was not until 1811 that the beak was officially abolished.

(A) Shows the necessary and practical beak of the galley, and (B) the modified 18th Century form, which caused so many casualties at Trafalgar while the British Fleet was approaching the allied line and before it could fire a single shot.

Belfry

The shelter for the ship's bell, often

The Shelter for the Ship's Bell

very elaborate in the old days, when the bell was given so much importance

and frequently very finely carved, particularly in the old men-of-war. Its shape and the details of its design were entirely a matter of taste, but it was almost invariably in the form of a canopy supported by pillars. It disappeared when the excessive ornamentation of the King's ships was reduced for reasons of economy. The finest were those worked into the decoration of the break of the poop or forecastle.

Bentinck Boom

Used to spread the two clews of the foresail, usually in coasting brigs and the like, but also occasionally in whalers, particularly those working in ice. It was boused down in the centre to the deck on the fore side of the foremast and permitted the sheets to be dispensed with, only short tacks, as a rule, to the forecastle

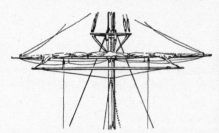

The Bentinck Boom

head. When the Bentinck boom was used the sail was usually cut very much shorter at the foot than at the yard. It was useful in saving men and also permitted the ship to go about very quickly in making short tacks up a river, etc., but it was responsible for many bruised heads.

(*To be continued.*)

Dutch Admiralty Yacht

We regret that, owing to the miscarriage of some drawings in the post, we have been obliged to defer the continuation of this article till our next issue.

The Ship's Mail

Readers are invited to make use of this column for the discussion of matters of mutual interest and the exchange of ideas and information.

Figure Heads

DEAR SIR,—In your article on " The Romance of the Figurehead," in the current issue of your most interesting Magazine, SHIPS AND SHIP MODELS, the author states that the figurehead " has only survived in picture and model." It may interest your readers to know that, in Devonport Dockyard, there is a very large collection of fine figureheads, from the old line-of-battleships and frigates of Nelson's days—and well worth a visit by any of your readers who may happen to be in the neighbourhood.

Yours sincerely,
Scarborough.   CHAS. E. WANLESS.

British Sea Fisheries

SIR,—I have recently been commissioned by a London publisher to write and illustrate a book which will deal as completely and exhaustively as possible with the sea fisheries of the British Isles.

The work approaches the subject, not so much from the industrial point of view, as from the " human " and historical. Special importance will be attached to providing an accurate and detailed record of all the various types of British and Irish fishing craft, many of which are now extinct, and of which the only records available are old drawings, photographs and models. Should any of the readers of SHIPS AND SHIP MODELS be interested in this side of maritime life and happen to possess any information dealing with the history of fishing craft and life of sea fishermen in these Isles, I should be most grateful if they would communicate with me.

Yours truly,
PETER F. ANSON.
12, Park Place, Gravesend.

The " Thermopylae "

DEAR SIR,—I have read with interest the first number of your Magazine, and wish to voice my approval of your action in bringing it into being. I am a keen reader of anything concerning ships and the sea, and this Magazine, I feel sure, will enjoy long life and prosperity. I am now engaged in making a waterline model of the Aberdeen clipper *Thermopylae*, but am somewhat hampered by the absence of deck plans. If any of your readers could help me in this, I should be greatly obliged. Wishing your Magazine every success.

Yours sincerely,
G. C. JOHNSON.
94, Oakleigh Park Drive,
Leigh-on-Sea.

The S.S. " Rugby "

DEAR SIR,—I have recently acquired a half-model of a ship, the s.s. *Rugby*, the only information that I have of her is that contained on a plate, which reads as follows :—

s.s. *Rugby*
John Priestman and Co., Sunderland.

together with the measurements of the ship. She is a single-funnelled cargo-steamer. Colours : Funnel pink, hull black, upper works cream, and cream below the water-line.

Could you let me know anything more about her, or where I could find out her history and obtain some photographs.?

Wishing you and your new paper a very successful maiden voyage, and continued freedom from rocks, shoals, and the perils of uncharted seas.

I am, yours truly,
Yeovil.   S. G. SMITH.

(The *Rugby* was a very ordinary tramp-steamer, built in 1897 by Priestman's of Sunderland for Galbraith, Pembroke and Co., of London, 3,286 tons gross. She was sold to the Greeks in 1913 and re-named *Aspasia*, although still managed by her former owners. In 1917 they got a very heavy price for her from Norwegian owners, who re-named her *Lorna*, but she was torpedoed and sunk by a German submarine in the Atlantic on August 7th, 1918.—ED. S. AND S.M.)

Some Views on Power Boat Modelling

DEAR SIR,—The model " power boat " enthusiast has in the past been somewhat neglected, as far as literature on his hobby is concerned, and the advent of a new journal dealing with this fascinating branch of model engineering should give it a decided impetus.

To my mind, model power boats can be divided into two classes only, the craft built purely for speed work, and the actual model of existing craft, and I must confess that to me the latter has the most appeal. The salient feature of the speed boat is its machinery, the outward appearance of the hull is but a detail, and the interest is purely mechanical.

With the model of actual craft we need to strive after reality of appearance, and many models that I have seen, though of masterly finish and workmanship, from the point of view of reality and truth to type would give the real sailor-man a pain ! I call to mind two craft I saw at an exhibition some time ago : one was an alleged " submarine chaser," full of detail, finished with meticulous care, but alas ! she was no more like a submarine chaser than a cokernut, which indeed her shape resembled. Her beam was about a third of her length and she couldn't in reality have chased a barge ! And then, too, there was a beautifully finished " destroyer," which got worse as you got aft, for on her after deck was mounted an armoured turret with a pair of guns apparently belonging to a battle cruiser ! After that, a model of a famous sailing ship with a huge glass skylight on the foc'sle head seemed quite a mild offence !

Another case was that of a couple of " destroyers " I saw on a pond in the Midlands some time ago. One was of commercial make, and needless to say was of impeccable finish. Oxydised funnels, oxydised and silvered guns, tubes and other fittings galore (some of them decidedly under scale) and glossy sides and polished decks she might have made a pretty ornament for the sideboard, but " at sea " she looked, well—out of place. The other boat was clearly amateur built, but the maker had stuck to realism. If guns and tubes were not full of minor details, they were at least to scale, and were far more " real " in appearance. There was no shiny metal work, no glossy enamel about her, she looked her part, a hard-bitten, serviceable, dare-devil warcraft, not an up-river luxury launch !

Again, in the writer's opinion, more satisfactory results are to be obtained by making a large-scale model of smaller types of craft than small-scale models of larger craft. A $\frac{3}{16}''$ scale model of a 300′ craft would produce more satisfactory results and appearance than a $\frac{1}{10}''$ scale model of a 600′ craft. And whether the constructor desires to build mercantile or naval craft, there are plenty of these smaller types available : in the mercantile section we have tugs, both river and sea, trawlers, coasters, the cargo tramp and even small passenger boats. As regards war craft, we have a very wide range available—destroyers, gunboats, sloops, cruisers of earlier types (graceful craft these) and even battleships of a " pocket " type, including those built by British firms for smaller foreign countries.

These are, of course, the writer's own personal ideas, and they may not probably commend themselves to many, but my view in model ship building—as in model railway work—always has been, more realism and less " spit and polish " in our models.

Yours truly,

London, W.1.   " E.C."

SHIPS AND SHIP MODELS

A Magazine for all Lovers of Ships and the Sea

Single Copies, post free, **7½d.**
Annual Subscription **7s. 6d.**

Editorial and Publishing Offices :
66 FARRINGDON STREET
LONDON :: E.C.4

Vol. I. No. 3.   **NOVEMBER, 1931.**   Price 6d.

The Ship's Log

Ship Modellers' Clubs

LIVERPOOL has the distinction of being the home of the first ship-modellers' club to be established in this country. The Ship Model Makers' Club of America, founded by, and so efficiently steered by, Captain E. Armitage McCann, has been pursuing a successful career for several years, and in its widely distributed membership has acquired something of an international character. In our own country we have a large number of clubs devoted to model sailing yacht and power boat building and racing, but nothing solely concerned with the modelling of ships of all periods and all kinds. There is the admirable Society for Nautical Research, the Shiplovers' Association, the Seven Seas' Club, and the Little Ship Club ; all these are doing excellent work, but their respective spheres of interest go a good way beyond ship modelling. There is no reason why the example of the new Merseyside Ship Model Makers' Club, reported elsewhere in this issue, should not be followed in other centres, particularly in the seaport cities and towns. The organisation of such a club need not be a very difficult business, especially if the programme mapped out for the club's activities is not too ambitious in character. A comfortable central meeting room, preferably where light refreshments can be obtained, and a gathering of a dozen or so enthusiasts once a month or once a fortnight, where over a pipe and a cup of coffee, experiences could be exchanged, models and photographs submitted for inspection, and perhaps simple demonstrations given on the construction of details, are really the elements of an enjoyable club. From these small beginnings such a club might grow considerably. We shall probably have something further to say on this subject in a later issue, but meanwhile we should be glad to hear from any readers who would be willing to take the preliminary steps towards the formation of a club in their own district. One of the initial difficulties in the formation of any club or society is to bring the interested parties together. Now that SHIPS AND SHIP MODELS is in being, this difficulty can readily be solved by a suitable notification in our columns.

Shiplovers in Tasmania

That shiplovers delight in gathering together, even in remote corners of the globe, is indicated by the recent formation of the Shiplovers' Society of Tasmania. We have received a friendly request for copies of SHIPS AND SHIP MODELS from the Society, and we imagine that while the members take a broad view of their mutual interest in maritime matters, ship model making will be one of the things to which considerable attention will be given. The Hon. Secretary is Mr. H. W. Wilson, Box 607E, G.P.O., Hobart, Tasmania. We wish the new association every success and hope at some future date to be able to publish a little account of their model making doings.

*   *   *

A New P. and O. Colour Scheme

With a view to discover which colour gives the coolest ship, the P. and O. Company have recently made tests of both white and their usual buff. They have found that white is four degrees cooler than the buff, and the upperworks of their new liner *Corfu* have accordingly been painted white. The *Corfu* sailed on her maiden voyage to the Straits, China, and Japan on October 16th.

*   *   *

A " Santa Maria " at Sea

The historic voyage of Christopher Columbus across the Atlantic in the *Santa Maria* is to be repeated next month, in a full-size replica of that famous ship. A Spanish naval officer, Captain Don Julio Guillen, who supervised the building of the replica for the Seville Exhibition of 1929, now plans to sail the ship across to the United States. He will carry a crew of twenty-five instead of the fifty-two men who accompanied Columbus, but in other respects the conditions of the crossing are to be the same as in the original voyage. Captain Guillen hopes to spend three years in cruising in American waters, after he has crossed the Atlantic.

The Mis-naming of Ship Models

One day in the future, when Parliament finds itself with nothing to do, it might consider the passing of a law to prevent builders of model ships and boats mis-applying the names of famous ships to their models. The number of models which have been christened *Shamrock*, or *Cutty Sark*, or *Olympic*, merely because the builder admired the prototype, or had heard that there was a famous ship of that name, must be enormous.

*   *   *

To New Readers

We have to thank many new subscribers and readers for kindly messages of encouragement and approval. A few copies of No. 1 and No. 2 are still available, and we would recommend new readers to obtain these to make their sets complete. The early parts and volumes of this journal are bound to increase in value as time goes on and the parts go out of print. SHIPS AND SHIP MODELS covers a very wide field of interest ; every issue will naturally vary in the nature of the subjects treated, and the complete volume at the end of twelve months will contain an exceptional range of fascinating articles and valuable drawings and data. As a reference book of maritime and model making information it will be unique.

Books Received

Motor Boating for Beginners. By GEOFFREY PROUT. Glasgow : Brown, Son and Ferguson, Ltd. Price 3s. 6d. Postage 3d.

The Story of the Liner. By G. G. JACKSON. London : The Sheldon Press. Price 6s. Postage 6d.

Sea Songs and Shanties. Collected by CAPT. W. B. WHALL. Sixth Edition. Glasgow : Brown, Son, and Ferguson, Ltd. Price 5s. Postage 8d.

Small Sailing Craft. By R. THURSTON HOPKINS. London : Philip Allan and Co., Ltd. Price 15s. Postage 8d.

Sailing Ships in the London River

By G. C. JOHNSON

Sketch by]   **With Timber from the Baltic**   *[S. E. Beck*

THOSE of us who are interested in the movements of the windjammers of to-day have missed this year the once familiar sight of the ships of the firewood fleet in the Thames. During recent years their numbers have been steadily decreasing, and now their owners seem to have at last given up their fight with steam. These ships are now nearly all owned in Finland and sail between the Gulf of Bothnia and the Thames with cargoes of split wood. The *Alastor*, *Shakespeare* and *Loch Linnhe* are perhaps the most well known of the "onkers" and all three are real old-timers. The *Alastor* was built at Sunderland in 1875, and at one time sailed under the Shaw Savill and Albion flag, making some good passages in the emigrant trade. She was sold to Norway in 1895, later on going to Finland and the firewood trade. The *Shakespeare* has seen much service in many parts of the world before taking her present place among the "onkers." She was built in Liverpool in 1876, and is an iron barque of 798 tons. Her owners put her into the

Australian trade, and when ousted by the big packets, she was put on the nitrate run, from the West Coast of South America to the Continent. In this trade she lasted for some years, but she could not successfully compete with the big ships of Laeisz's Flying P line, and after a year or two of tramping all over the Seven Seas the *Shakespeare* settled down into the firewood trade in 1923. The famous " P " line of Hamburg numbers among its ships some of the largest and fastest sailing ships in commission, and it is still said that some of these latter-day cargo carriers are as fast as the clippers of the 'seventies. The giant *Preussen*, of 5,081 tons, and the *Potosi*, both five-masted barques, have on many voyages logged average speeds of 11 knots.

The *Oatlands* is reported to be the fastest ship of the " onker " fleet, and when I saw her off the Nore in 1928 it certainly seemed to me she had a very fair turn of speed. She is an iron barque of 999 tons, and was built in Dundee in 1876. The *Lingard*, some weeks ago, left Gravesend in company with the *Alastor*, with every prospect of an interesting race, as they were bound for adjacent ports in the Baltic. Both remained anchored off Southend for some days until the wind came fair, when they left together. The *Alastor* passed Elsinore on September 9th, and the *Lingard* arrived at Norrsundet on the 13th. *Loch Linnhe* was built by J. and G. Thompson, of Glasgow, in 1876, and is an iron barque of 1,323 tons. In 1882 she made a very good run to Port Chalmers. Commanded by Captain Pittenreigh she left London on November 14th, but meeting with adverse winds in the Channel, did not clear Ushant until the 28th. She crossed the Line on December 21st, and arrived in Port Chalmers on February 12th, a run from Ushant of 74 days.

The *Prompt* and the *Plus* are also well known in the London river, and are both products of Hamburg yards. The *Plus* was launched in 1885, and the *Prompt*, a steel barque of 1,400 tons, two years later. The *Prompt* was built for Laeisz, of Hamburg, as an addition to his famous " Flying P " fleet.

The rest of the " onker " fleet is composed of several wooden barques, *Elakoon*, *Warma*, *Carmen* and *Fred*, all Finnish built, of about 700 tons, and the schooners *Palawan*, *Gunn*, *Atlas* and *Valborg*. The *Palawan* and the *Gunn* are both post-war American productions. From time to time, there are other visitors to the Thames, and the *Archibald Russell* created quite a sensation when she arrived in the East India Docks this year. The *Archibald Russell* is a four-masted barque of 2,354 tons, and was built on the Clyde in 1905. There are rumours prevalent that Captain Erikson intends to fit both her and the *Herzogin Cecelie* for passenger carrying. In 1927 two well-known ships appeared together in the Port of London. These were the *Lawhill* and the *Gustav*. The *Lawhill* is still sailing regularly in the Australian grain trade, and this year made a passage of 105 days from Adelaide to Queenstown. She was among the last of the big cargo carriers built for British owners, being built by W. B. Thompson, of Dundee, for a Liverpool firm, preceding by three years the *Archibald Russell*. The *Gustav* was another Scottish-built barque, launched in 1892 for Peter Dennison and Co., of Glasgow, but she has been owned in Germany now for some years.

It is with a deep feeling of regret that we now hear of the loss of the *Shakespeare*, and in a few years the presence of a windjammer in the Thames will be a sight not soon to be forgotten.

" Lingard "   " Alastor "

TWO SURVIVORS OF THE " FIREWOOD FLEET "

How to Build a Model of a Dutch Admiralty Yacht

By JEFFREY LEIGHTON

(Continued from page 24.)

Decorating and Fittings

THE priming thoroughly dry, the next step is to imitate planking on the outside of the hull above the waterline. Sketch in the seams with a pencil and at intervals of approximately three quarters of an inch, measuring from the bows, mark the position of the ribs from the gunwhale down to the waterline. Now, using a sharp knife edged file, score out the seams; it should not be necess-

cut down to three eighths of an inch length, the slightly projecting heads of the pins give a good effect when painted. In fixing wales always begin at the bow. The after end of the round house should now be made ; do not fix this in place before the wales, planks etc., are complete, as the slightly projecting edge will be found greatly in the way. The shape should be taken from the sketch of the stern given in the previous article.

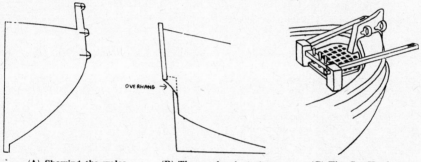

(A) **Showing the wales.**   (B) **The overhang at stern.**   (G) **The Cat-Head**

ary to cut deeply with the file, if carefully done a little deeper than the thickness of the priming will suffice.

Mark out the position of the ribs with small veneer nails, the heads not driven too far home, these should be two to a plank per rib. The planking will, when the hull is painted, amply justify the trouble taken.

Next cut from satin walnut the wales, three to a side (see sketch A) these should be an eighth of an inch thick and one sixth of an inch in width. The end intended to curve round the bows should be notched slightly with a file, on the inside at close intervals to facilitate bending. The wales should be drilled at intervals of half an inch to take the nails, smeared with adhesive, and gently tacked into place using common pins

Those readers who are expert at small carving or who are fortunate enough to possess, as do many model makers nowadays, a dental engine and burrs, will prefer to carve the decoration on the stern, etc., before fitting to the model ; they will have their own methods of doing so. The majority of model enthusiasts will I expect have insufficient facilities for undertaking such tedious work, for tedious it can certainly be, even to the expert. I have kept in mind throughout this little article the model maker who is keen enough to undertake a historical ship model, but has not the facilities or experience of the artists, who made the exquisite pieces in our naval museums.

I shall therefore deal with the carving in a way that can be undertaken by the veriest novice and yet imitate the real thing so successfully as to defy detection. The stern should therefore be cut from three-ply and the two apertures for the stern windows cut out, frames, etc., to be fitted later. Pin and glue the stern into position finishing off with a piece of soft pine to form the overhang (sketch B). To the inside of this stern piece should be fitted a small ledge joining the two sides of the coachhouse and curving slightly up in the middle to give a camber to the roof. The inside of the cabin can now be given a coat of dark stain or paint and a small hole cut, in which to step the post that supports the flagmast. The roof should be made from very thin three-ply and pinned and glued in place, a hole three-eighths of an inch in diameter being cut for the post mentioned above. The deck can now be made from white holly or sycamore, this should be actually planked, cut a rectangular piece just big enough to take the shape of the deck, plane down from the middle to give a slight camber, sandpaper thoroughly, mark out the shape of the deck on it and cut out very slightly larger than the outline with a fretsaw, now cut into strips three-sixteenths of an inch wide, glue the centre planks into position first, working outwards to the bulwarks. When thoroughly stuck pin down with rows of veneer nails which should of course correspond in line to the

ribs on the outside of the hull. The raised section of deck in front of the roundhouse (Do in deck plan) can be very effective in the form of gratings. Gratings are not so difficult as they look, and the following will be found a practical and simple method of making them on a small scale.

Take a piece of hard mahogany or redwood, make saw cuts in both directions with a tenon saw about a sixteenth of an inch deep and one-eighth of an inch apart. Cut tiny slips of holly or sycamore just thick enough to fit the saw cuts tightly and wide enough to project slightly when in place. Smear these with adhesive and tap lightly into place with a hammer (in one direction only of course). When dry trim nearly to level with a sharp knife and finish by sandpapering the whole with fine sandpaper, until absolutely flush, varnish or french polish and the result leaves little to be desired.

The remainder of the fittings can be dealt with in " tabloid " form.

Quarter Badges

These should be built as shown in sketch C using scrap wood. The frames of the windows should be built up with veneer wood or bristol board and glued on a base of celluloid (an old car side screen will provide plenty as it does not matter if it is brittle and discoloured in such small pieces). The whole quarter piece should be glued and pinned into place.

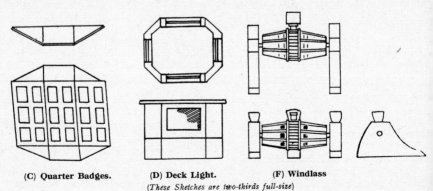

(C) **Quarter Badges.**   (D) **Deck Light.**   (F) **Windlass**

(These Sketches are two-thirds full-size)

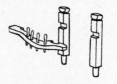

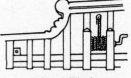

(E) Main Bitts.   **(H) Lee Board Pins.**   **(I) Hand Winch.**   **(J) Tiller**

Stern Windows

These can built up as in the case of quarter badge windows.

Deck Light

Built from this three-ply ard cellulcid as shown in sketch D.

Main Hatch

Built of close grating with a neat mahogany coaming round.

Main Bitts

These should be built up from scrap satin walnut as shown in sketch E.

Pin Rails

Two pin rails are shown in the deck plan, on the inside of the bulwarks. Small shelves made of satin walnut glued and pinned in position and belaying pins either turned from brass wire or made from bootmaker's brass nails with the points cut off and the heads rounded off at the top slightly with a file complete these.

Windlass

This can be made from odd scraps of wood and the barrel shaped with a sharp knife from soft wood, the holes for the bars can be drilled and then squared by gently inserting the tang of a small file (see sketch F).

Catheads

These are comparatively light on this vessel consisting of square spars with the inboard ends stepped in sampson posts as shown in sketch G. A grating fits between them in the bow space and a pin rail (not shown in the plan) connects the two posts. The outboard end of the cathead is slotted and fitted with a sheave.

The Beak Head

The small beak head can be shaped from a piece of the same wood as the keel section mentioned in the previous article, a small head being roughly shaped with a knife at the extremity. The stem head itself should be fitted on the starboard side with two metal hooks for the bowsprit to run through. The bowsprit when run inboard should just clear the top of the starboard side of the windlass barrel.

The ornamentation on the beakhead will be dealt with under Carving.

A small piece may be cut out of the stem to make a snug joint when the head is pinned and glued on.

Lee Boards

These can be shaped from $\frac{3}{16}''$ satin walnut and the metal strips made from brass foil or card stuck in place and the bolt heads simulated with tiny pins (Lillikins) clipped down and tacked lightly in place. A small carved strip of wood glued on near the top completes these. Pivot pins through the bulwarks on which the boards move complete these (see sketch H). A rope from the sternmost end leads through a hole in the bulwark to a tiny hand winch made of scrap (sketch I).

Rudder

Should be cut from the same wood as the keel section tapering towards the stem. Dummy pintleirons, etc., may be made from thin brass or bristol board and the bolt heads from lillikins as in the lee boards. The Rudder should be pinned in position with a short dummy tiller through the top to go into the hole shown in the stern drawing between the two middle brackets (see sketch J).

The forward bulkhead of the round house can be finished off with a dummy door made of veneer wood in the centre and steps running up one side made of slips of wood glued on. The bulwarks may be finished off now with dummy ribs, etc., made from veneer or bristol wood (see sketch I).

Carving

The carving can be represented in the following way :—

Obtain from any artists' colourman a tin of " Barbola " paste which will be supplied with directions for use.

It is extremely simple to handle, and the only tools required are a bundle of orange sticks or wooden spills sharpened at the ends to chisel edges, sharp and blunt points, etc., and a small penknife or manicure knife. A large damp rag, a small bowl of water and a water colour brush.

Coat the parts where carving is to be with a thin even layer of seccotine or other similar adhesive, allow to get tacky and apply a thin layer of Barbola to the part to be dealt with. Barbola is like dough in consistency and can be easily moulded in the fingers.

It should not be more than $\frac{3}{16}$" thick at the maximum anywhere. The edges of the mass applied should be trimmed roughly to the shape of the design with the knife and the surplus removed.

Then proceed to model the design with the sticks, repeated damping and wiping the ends with the damp rag. If the carving looks somewhat rough after modelling do not touch but allow to nearly dry, then work over it with a water colour brush moderately charged with water, until a uniform " roundness " has been imparted.

Barbola should be left at least three days in a dry atmosphere before colour is applied.

All the carving on the hull can be dealt with in this way. Beakhead, wreathports, carving on quarter badges, stern and the brackets under the stern, with but little practice quite large masses of relief ornamentation can be built up with it and it dries hard and strong. No particular artistic ability is needed to handle it. Care and patience are all that is necessary, and if the result is anywhere unsatisfactory it can be remodelled at once with little trouble.

(To be continued).

Notes about Cannons

THESE were first used in Cogs in 1346, but really only came into general use in the 16th Century. Carronades came in 1797, Flintlocks in 1780, the detonating lock and percussion tube in 1842, when also flannel bags were used instead of paper for cartridges. Truck-gun carriages went out in 1865 ; gun quoins were discarded in 1825, when elevating screws came in ; port holes were first used on Tudor ships in 1501.

Types of Cannons

Cannon Royal, 11' long, 8½" bore. with 60-lb. ball.

Demi cannon, 10' long, 6½" bore ; 30-lb. shot, range 1 mile.

Culverin, 17-pounder.

Demi Culverin, 9-pounder.

Saker, 5-pounder.

Minion, 4-pounder.

Falcon, 3-pounder.

Falconet, 1½-pounder.

Robinet, 1-pounder.

The base was a breech-loader with a bore of 1½", 4' long, and 9" chamber for charge and projectile.

The cannon Perier, short range, 24-pounder for firing broken stones ; 32-pounder, 9' 6" long, weighed 55½ cwt., at about 3 tons with carriage ; bore, 6¼" ; diameter of shot, 1/5" less ; powder charge, 10 lbs. 10 oz.; crew, 6 to 18 men ; could fire one round one minute ; range, 1½ miles elevated 10 degrees.

The 32-pounder carronade was 4' long, weighed 17-18 cwt., powder charge of 2 lbs. 10 oz. It could be worked by one man and one boy, if necessary.

Carronades were discarded before the war with Russia and when shells were introduced.

Stone cannon balls went out during the reigns of Charles I and II.

Temperament in Ship Modelling

With some Notes on the Northumbrian Coble
By DEN ENSOMME

A typical Present-day Northumbrian Coble

WHEN the latent, passive enthusiasm for the water which, it may be assumed, resides in most of us who are attracted by the contents of these pages, has matured to a certain degree, it is a common experience to find we have arrived at a parting of the ways. It is at this point in our development—when we are just becoming aware of the vastness of the subject which interests us—that some definite course should be chosen and followed, else we get lost in a maze of possibilities. There are two main roads which can be explored. The one winds its way towards the Dreamland of the visionary, whose ethereal yearning and love for the sea is an abstract thing wrapped up in nebulous memories and associations, pleasant or distressful, but rarely invigorating. The other, straighter, maybe, yet not without its rocks and shallows to make the course interesting, can take us to a land of activity where opportunities for practical achievement are so plentiful that bewilderment is apt to get us by the throat, and the energy and vitality which could have been applied in some definitely absorbing and constructive direction, satisfying and purposeful, are consumed in the fervour of ineffectual contemplation. Let us consider matters carefully. There is, and I think you will agree, a subtle difference between judicious consideration and unwarranted speculation concerning any proposed course of action. Remember what happened to our friend who was possessed of all the virtues, but was tempted one day to think too long and earnestly. With him deliberation bred hesitation, and was the cause of his undoing. He was the owner, designer, skipper, and crew of a jolly little auxiliary; and, knowing marine motors to be what they can be, concluded that by adopting the simple expedient of installing two, and twin screws, starting up one engine one morning and the other the next, what time breakfast was cooking, he would be immune from sudden disaster. All went well for a while. Then, one morning, after putting the last of the kippers on the Primus he went aft to carry out the usual starting-up performance—and became lost in contemplation. Which engine had he run yesterday? What was said upon his eventual return to the galley need not be recorded ; but it is permissible to surmise that he was impressed with the newly acquired knowledge that speculation overdone leads to nothing useful.

The inexperienced craftsman, coming fresh from his books to the bench, may naturally expect to meet many an obstacle on his way to fame as a builder of little ships, but his difficulties will be lightened considerably

Stem to Stern view of Coble

if he uses a modicum of that judicious consideration we have just been talking about, when selecting a subject for his hands to execute. It is as important that the character of the proposed work should harmonise with his temperament as that his tools and general equipment should suit the work.

Many will at a first attempt fall short of the ideal. Some will meet purely mechanical difficulties which

their manual skill is unable to surmount ; others will be stumped by an injudicious selection of material, or maybe they have no choice, and must use what is available. Again, there may be a temptation now and again, to emulate in a minor key and with slight variations, our old friend the pram builder, hopeful that some short cut or improvisation will lead to success. But these difficulties will not recur indefinitely, and so long as we keep an eye on the outstanding characteristics of the job and see to it that they are well and properly developed, the ultimate result will be good to look upon, even as a painter's sketch may, to the discerning, sometimes excel the finished work of which the sketch is but a study.

If you are a real Britisher—that is, a Northumbrian—you may want to build or model the coble of our illustration. It is not a type of craft which the inexperienced craftsman should elect to begin with, but the builder of moderately good practical ability and with an aversion to small fiddling work, could model it successfully. The boats are, on the whole, fairly heavily built ; the timbers are much further apart than in any other craft of similar dimensions, hence there are fewer to cut and fit ; the planks are wide, which again means fewer to cut and shape ; there are no more inside fittings or trimmings than are absolutely essential to the working of the vessel. Fine intricate work, it will be seen, is almost wholly absent, and yet the craftsman with an eye for precision will have scope and to spare in retaining the lines and contours so characteristic of this type of vessel.

It cannot be too greatly stressed that the charm of these little ships lies not only in the beauty of the sheer curve but in the contour given by the bow, midship, and stern sections. Cobles vary in length from 22′ to 28′, and have a beam of about 7′. The height at the bow is as much as 6′. above the keel line, and that at the stern but little more than half that.

The bow sections are sharp and there is a slight tumble-home from a little forward of the midship sections to right aft. The transom is flat and well raked, and the iron-work to carry the deep rudder is extraordinarily hefty. The latter, of course, is not shipped until the boat is away from the shore. It, and the deep forefoot, provide the necessary lateral resistance when under sail. The draft at the stern is, as I said, practically nil. This is desirable both for launching and landing. Launching from the sandy beach is carried out with the help of a pair of wide tread wooden wheels—iron shod—which are easily hauled clear when the boat takes the water. The last man aboard gets in over the stern after he has given a final shove-off when up to his thighs in water. The form of the transom stern lends itself well to this manner of launching—the only possible manner, in fact—but one which can be performed with comparative ease even when a good sea is breaking. I believe some of the boats down south, in Yorkshire, have sharp sterns, so

probably the conditions there are somewhat different from those prevailing along the Northumbrian coast. At any rate the absence of buoyancy, which the full quarters of the Northumbrian boat provides, would seem to be a very obvious disadvantage if working from a gradually shelving beach in all weathers, especially as landing, too, is effected stern first. Both going out and coming in require consummate skill at the oars which, in the two man boats when only one man is pulling are handled cross-arm fashion on account of their length inboard. When three men are aboard two oars are worked from one side and the third from the quarter opposite, reminiscent of the stjornbordi* of the Viking ships, thus making the most effective use of the available man power. The sail commonly used is the dipping lug, which has to be lowered and set again every time one goes about. The halliard does duty as the mast stay and is perfectly effective.

*Stjornbordi (Icelandic) ; Styrbord (Danish and Swedish); Stuurboord (Dutch) = Starboard (English.)

A Sailing Model "Cutty Sark"

With a Novel Winch Gear for Trimming Sail

By CAPTAIN G. S. HUSSEY, M.C., A.M.Inst.T.

I WELCOME the advent of SHIPS AND SHIP MODELS. By chance I saw it on the bookstall and am now a subscriber. With some diffidence, in the hope that it may interest you and your readers, I give below a description of a working sailing model of the Clipper-ship *Cutty Sark*, which occupied my spare time last winter. I always devote a large part of the autumn to thought on what torture I can submit pieces of wood and metal in order to occupy my mind and fingers in model making during the long winter evenings and nights.

After careful deliberation last autumn, assisted by a taunt from an acquaintance that square-rigged model ships that would really sail were not feasible, I decided on a scale model of the most famous of all sailing ships. I enclose a photograph of the result.

The model sails well on all points of sailing, and above all, loves a gale of wind, so that in this, at all events, it is true to its prototype.

Two difficulties had to be overcome :—

(1) A scale model of a square-rigged ship, by reason of the fact that the hull is reduced by the cube of the scale and the sails by the square of the scale, has not sufficient power to carry full sail.

(2) To put the model " about " from one tack to the other meant hauling and adjusting the braces and sheets of 26 sails, if the model were to sail " under all plain sail."

It may, therefore, interest your readers to learn how these two difficulties were overcome. I enclose a diagram showing the answer to No. 1.

The hull on the stand looks, and is,

The model " Cutty Sark " under sail at Southwold.

right, but before the model is sailed, a piece of the keel from (A) to (B) is detached, and in its place is secured a deep plate, carrying enough lead to maintain the model at correct l.w.l. and to give it power to carry full sail in all reasonable winds. My model is

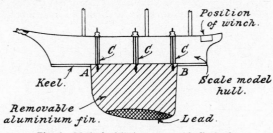

Fig. 1. Method of fitting removable fin-keel

30″ on the water-line, and the detachable fin is an aluminium plate 11″ deep with 3 lbs. of lead at the foot thereof. The method of attachment is clear from the diagram (Fig. 1), but may be briefly described as follows :—

Three copper tubes (C), run through the hull from keel to deck, and through these tubes the three supports (rustless steel screwed rod) of the fin, run, being secured by screws in the shape of capstans on the deck itself.

Item (2) was a bit more troublesome, and I have not got it quite right yet, although the expedient adopted worked with fair success and was as under :—

Hidden under the poop-deck and revealed by the lifting of the saloon skylight is what may be termed a " differential winch," with a turning handle projecting through the side of the model. All the braces of the yards from each mast are run through the blocks in accordance with original practice, but become common leads to the winch in accordance with the width of the yards. The winch is stepped on both sides (see diagram, Fig. 2), so that all braces from yards of the same length come on the port side (P) to the same diameter step and, equally, in the reverse direction, on the starboard side (S). When the winch is turned, one side is paid out

and the other hauled in. A few nice mathematical calculations were necessary, and the device works, with this proviso. When, in stress of weather, the braces got wet, they were inclined to twist round themselves at the blocks and, in the end, as will be seen from the photograph, I left the main mast properly rigged and ran braces in unorthodox fashion from the main yards direct to the fore and mizzen yards. By this means the difficulty was overcome and the model has sailed many times with great success this summer or winter, according to one's view of the season now passing.

I intend, this winter, to re-rig the model true to prototype and overcome the difficulty described in another way, as I dislike makeshifts in model work. Models should be true miniatures of the real thing. If successful in the new theory, I will write again.

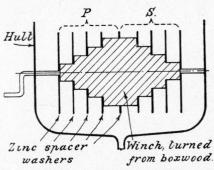

Fig. 2. The differential winch

My model of *Cutty Sark* sails true on all points of sailing and, even dead before wind, it does not deviate from its course. It can point into the wind if not as closely as a fore and aft model, at least nearly so, although I did not expect that it would be successful on anything closer than a beam wind.

I have tried the Braine steering device, and although it may have helped in some degree, I found setting the rudder—only scale size—after one trial run is sufficient to ensure a true course. The Braine steering device was worked by the foresail, jibs, and staysails, all sheets from which are led aft to a common sheet on the port and one on the starboard.

The model is much more interesting to sail than a fore and aft rigged yacht, and infinitely more interesting to make and to watch.

The photo was taken at the model yacht pond, Southwold, and I must express my indebtedness to Mr. E. W. Hobbs' book on "Model Clipper Ships," and to his kindness in correspondence, and to Mr. Lubbock's "Log of the *Cutty Sark*."

The model is at present in dock for rigging repairs due to collisions at sea at Southwold, which were many, as the yacht pond there is crowded with craft in the season.

Modelling a Bristol Pilot Cutter

By A. W. B. PROWSE

THE hull I bought from a second-shop, and is that of a Bristol Channel pilot cutter, to a scale of 1″ to 1′. I have fully and carefully re-rigged her as a cutter of about 30 years ago. The approximate proportions of the sails and spars I have taken from a sketch of the pilot cutter *Faith* in Keble Chatterton's book "Fore and Aft." There are, however, two points on which I have followed an article on these cutters which appeared in *The Yachting Monthly* in about 1927 ; according to

this article they did not carry bob-stays or runners and pendants, so I have omitted these. All riggings and blocks are to scale.

The deck fittings are : raised coach roof over main cabin with dummy sliding hatch and skylight. From the aft end of this raised roof, coamings are carried aft on each side and across the aft end to represent a cockpit. There is a dummy sliding hatch forward for access to the forecastle. Capstan, riding bitt, chain stopper and pipe combined, chain controller, stern-

The Cutter under sail

Out of the water

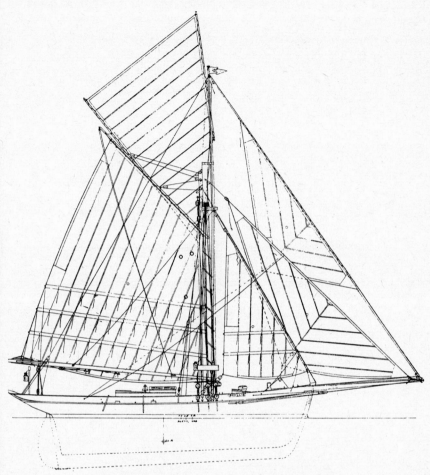

The rigging and sails of a Model Bristol Pilot Cutter

head roller, cat davit, chain and anchor. Bitts just abaft the mast, bowsprit bitts. Covels and cleats as necessary. Buffer for the main-sheet, gallows frame for the main boom when the sail is furled. Sidelights and screens and sternlight, and ship's bell. The sails are properly roped, and are cross-sewn to represent the clothes, strengthening pieces, etc., and are fitted with reef points and cringles as necessary.

She represents a vessel 40′ long over all and 12′ beam. Her overall length, including bowsprit, is 4′ 8″ and maximum beam over channels is 1′ 2″. She is a sailing model I enclose two snaps of her which give some idea of her appearance. Her painting is black above and shrimp-pink colour below water. Inside of bulwarks black, deck varnished and deck fittings brown. All fittings which would be galvanised are painted with aluminium paint. She has new sails and various extra fittings since these photos were taken.

There is one other point about her which I might mention : the hull is

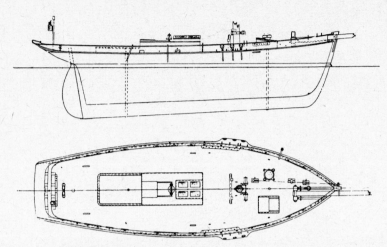

Elevation and Deck-plan of the Model Bristol Pilot Cutter

planked with oak and is rather heavy for the size ; this means she can't carry a heavy-enough lead keel to make her really stable when sailing.

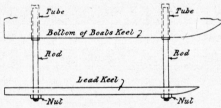

False keel fitted for sailing

To get over this difficulty I have fitted two brass tubes, one forward and one aft, right through her from keel to deck (as shown on the general arrangement elevation). I have two brass rods with a head one end and a nut the other, which I drop through the tubes when sailing ; on the lower ends of these rods I secure the lead keel by means of the nuts. The rods project about 8″ below the bottom of the keel, so giving the extra leverage for the same weight.

I find this is simple, works very well and does not spoil the look of the model when out of the water.

———

Mr. R. C. Stallard, 55, Kedleston Road, Hall Green, Birmingham, would like to get into touch with other readers of "S. & S.M." in his district. He is particularly interested in collecting sea books and photographs.

Sketch by]   **A typical Whale Catcher**   *[S. E. Beck*

The Restoration of H.M.S. "Victory"

By BASIL LAVIS

AMONG ship - model enthusiasts there must be few who have not yearned to build a model of one of the old-time wooden sailing ships of war, being deterred only by the difficulty of obtaining sufficient data. There are a few books which deal with clipper ships, and occasionally one is to be seen in the London Docks or elsewhere. Again, it is possible sometimes to get first-hand information from those who have actually served their time in these nearly extinct sailing vessels. But it is not easy to learn enough about the old wooden walls of a century or more ago, or to get sufficient details for a good model. In museums there are some very fine models to be seen, but suitable books or drawings on the subject are few and far between.

But since the Society for Nautical Research have done such remarkable work in restoring the old *Victory* to her Trafalgar appearance, there is no

longer any reason for the model ship builder to delay.

In selecting an old-time wooden warship, H.M.S. *Victory* seems the obvious choice, if only on account of her long record of successes, concluding with Trafalgar. Moreover, the list of valiant admirals and captains who served in her, culminating in Nelson himself, make her a worthy ornament for any Briton's home. She is the representative of the most powerful type of capital ship, the design of which altered but little until the introduction of steamships and ironclads.

No model of the *Victory* can be considered without reference to the dockyard drawings of 1759. There are no outstanding features in the design of this vessel, the lines laid down by Sir Thomas Slade, at the time Senior Surveyor of the Navy, being common to the majority of 100-gun ships of this period. This

Photo by]   **H.M.S. "Victory" as restored**   *[Basil Lavis*

applies with equal force to the measurements of the masts and spars, and to the practice of rigging.

Wooden ships at this time lasted so much longer than the ironclads which succeeded them, or the steel ships of to-day, that any important changes

service in 1816. At this date the familiar beakhead had been removed and the bows built up, an upper deck was added, and her masts and yards were considerably cut down. In this rig she remained for many years at her moorings in Portsmouth Harbour,

Photo by]   **H.M.S. " Victory "—Bow View**   [Basil Lavis

in design were incorporated in the older vessels as they were sent to the dockyards for refit. This happened to the *Victory*, quite a number of reconstructions taking place between the date of her first commissioning and her being relieved from active

a very different ship from the one Nelson knew.

In 1921 it was discovered that the strain of the tides was becoming too much for the old ship, and unless she was removed immediately to dry dock she might founder at her moorings. Thanks to the untiring efforts of the Society for Nautical Research, who approached the Admiralty and enlisted their Lordships' interest, the *Victory* was placed in No. 2 Drydock at Portsmouth, incidentally the oldest drydock in the world. Thus, after 143 years afloat through storm and

appearance. This entailed much research work among Admiralty, dockyard and private records. It must be a source of the utmost gratification to those responsible in varying degrees for the result, to see the *Victory* as she is to-day in the knowledge that there is no monument which more

Photo by]   **H.M.S. " Victory "—Stern View**   *[Basil Lavis*

battle, a permanent resting place has been provided, where she can still fly the Flag of the Commander-in-Chief at Portsmouth, at the same time serving as an imperishable memorial to the glory of England's sea power.

Once in drydock, the next step was to strip off her misleading disguise, and restore her to her Trafalgar

completely enshrines the spirit of the Nelson era.

One of the most important features of this noteworthy restoration is the closed stern. At the time the *Victory* was built it was the custom to construct stern galleries in all ships-of-the-line—one at the level of the quarter deck, with a second at the level of the main deck in three-deckers, and one only in the case of two-deckers. These galleries were built across the stern and were from two to three feet wide. At the end of the 18th century they were done away with.

Of the carved work decorating these galleries and the figurehead, much for a long time remained obscure. This is particularly the case as regards the figurehead, which was changed on more than one occasion.

In the space of this article it is not possible to go into such details as alterations to the masts and yards, rigging, bulwarks, position of the

channels, hammock nettings, method of painting the vessel, etc. All these are now as they were in the Battle of Trafalgar. To the embryo ship model maker a knowledge of these restorations is of course of the first importance.

I have been fortunate in obtaining very full authentic information and photographs of the restoration of the *Victory*, and I should be pleased to hear from any readers of SHIPS AND SHIP MODELS who may contemplate making a scale model of this fine old ship.

A Miniature " Victory " Under Sail

ALL lovers of the *Victory* will be interested in the accompanying photograph of a remarkable reproduction of the ship to a much reduced scale, which can actually go to sea with a live crew. Our picture shows the little ship under sail during the

Portsmouth Navy Week, where she aroused both curiosity and admiration. The model, for such it really is, though a large one, looks exceptionally well in the water and enables one to visualise something of the appearance of her famous prototype at sea.

A Minature " Victory " under sail at Portsmouth

Elements of Model Steamer Design

By T. R. THOMAS, B.Sc., M.I.Mar.E.

III.—THE EFFECT OF HULL DESIGN ON SPEED

L AST month we dealt with the main points of hull design of a cargo steamer, and before proceeding to discuss types which have developed from the cargo steamer and which are, so to speak, higher up the social scale, it may be interesting to review briefly how the cargo steamer has developed along the lines of economy, and how various features of the design of a modern cargo vessel contribute to the efficiency from the point of view of being able to carry the maximum cargo at the least cost of operation.

Power and Hull Design

Some of the very oldest cargo ships afloat—which are more " aristocratic in appearance " than the modern ones —the first iron and steel vessels, were built on the same lines as the sailing ships of the olden days were built. The old sailing ship under normal conditions had to make the best possible use of the comparatively small power developed by sails, and it was, therefore, necessary that the hull should be what we call " fine " and that the " lines " should be graceful. They had, therefore, considerable " rise of floor," in other words the bottom sloped upwards from the keel, and they also had a large " round of bilge." You will readily understand from the remarks which have been made on the construction of the hull of the cargo ship, shown in the previous article, that this large round of bilge meant that it was only necessary to taper the hull gradually to the stem and stern and that the resulting hull was slender and well shaped.

With the development of steam machinery, however, the cargo ship had a constant and always available source of power. The natural result was a desire on the part of the owner of the vessel to carry as much cargo as possible and, consequently, the mid- ship section was gradually filled out until at one stage it resembled the section of a square box with the lower corners slightly rounded. At the same time, in order to make the ship carry as much cargo as possible, the midship section, which approximated to the box, was carried as far aft and as far forward as possible, so that some twenty years ago we had cargo ships built which were really long boxes shaped in the stem and stern as far forward and aft as possible. As in all matters of this description the tendency was overdone and a ship of this type is very uneconomical to drive at anything but a very slow speed and is seriously held up by bad weather. In the past few years we have returned to a much more shapely form and, nowadays, the average cargo ship is comparatively fast and her hull is designed to attain the maximum speed with the minimum of effort in good and bad weather.

Skin Friction

There are one or two aspects of this question of economical speed which are of interest to the model maker. The resistance of a body such as a ship passing through the water is made up of several parts—there is, first of all, what is called the " skin friction " resistance, which is, of course, the resistance caused by the surface friction of the ship. This is only important at comparatively low speeds, but at the same time the condition of the painted surface of the hull is most important. The resistance of the full-size ship may, for instance, increase very appreciably after the ship has been only a week or two out of dry dock. When we consider the reduction in scale in the case of a model, we have no difficulty in appreciating that the surface should be exceptionally good before it can compare as regards scale with the surface of the big ship. It is, therefore, necessary that the hull should be well finished as far as painting is concerned, and a good practice to adopt is to give the hull two or three coats of good paint well rubbed down and to finish with clear varnish.

Wave Resistance

The most important part of the resistance of a full-size ship being driven through the water at a reasonable speed is what is called the wave-making resistance. Everyone who has been to sea or has noted a model running on a smooth pond, recognises that certain waves are made by the ship form. Generally speaking, two sets of waves are generated, the first the bow wave, which spreads out on either side of the bow at an angle which depends on the fineness of the form, and, secondly, a series of waves which spread outwards from the stern at a slightly greater angle. When these two sets of waves interfere with one another, we get peculiar effects on the resistance of the ship. For instance, when the speed of the ship is very high, the two sets of waves may combine to form a series of bigger waves and the resistance of the ship may be seriously increased. Similarly, at other speeds, these sets of waves may damp themselves out and the resistance of the ship is reduced. Thus we find that a torpedo-boat destroyer travelling at 30 knots may require that the engine should develop a certain horse power. To increase this speed to 32 knots may require a very large increase in power, because at that particular speed the wave resistance may be increasing rapidly, but the power required at 34 knots may not be appreciably greater than at 32 knots, because between 32 and 34 knots the wave-making resistance is hardly increasing at all.

We draw attention to this aspect of hull design, not because it affects the model maker vitally, but to show how important very small variations in the shape of the hull of high-speed models may be.

Yet another form of resistance is that due to sharp edges or square posts, such as stern post, and this is called eddy-making resistance. The resistance of a square stern post drawn through the water is very considerable and care should always be taken to make both the back and front of any post, such as a stern post, well rounded to allow the water to flow smoothly over the surfaces.

Another factor in the total resistance which perhaps is of more importance to the model maker than to the designer of the full-size ship is the wind resistance of the upper portion of the hull and the superstructures. No model with large superstructures is desirable, because the pressure of the wind may have very serious affects on the speed and on the stability.

The Cross-Channel Steamer

Some of the foregoing considerations must be taken into account when we come to consider a type of vessel which has developed out of the cargo ship. The cross-Channel steamer, which, although in some part a cargo ship, is essentially designed for the rapid transport of passengers over short distances. The speed, therefore, is high—a vessel 350' long may have a maximum speed of 30 knots, so that the model may be driven comparatively fast. High speeds in full-size ships cannot economically or practically be attained without the use of more than one propeller, and here a word of warning to the model maker which is necessary. In the full-size ship the propellers are practically identical and the sets of machinery driving them develop almost exactly the same power. If one engine is developing more power than the other, it is a simple matter to reduce the revolutions until they correspond exactly with the other. In the model we are not able to do this. It is true that by the use of gearing we can link up the propellers so that they run at the same speed, but it is extremely difficult to make two propellers which will develop exactly the same power under different conditions of speed of model revolutions, etc. It becomes difficult, then, to get a twin-screw model to steer satisfactorily, apart from the fact that there is considerable loss of efficiency in the gearing or in the duplication of machinery. For simplicity we must consider the single screw, and unless we are careful, this will modify the design of hull.

(To be continued.)

The Schooner 'Enterprise' of Chester

A PRIZE-WINNING MODEL OF THE LIVERPOOL SHIPPING WEEK

THE organisers of the recent Shipping Week at Liverpool adopted a novel idea for the encouragement of ship modelling. Incidentally, this idea emphasised the fact that model making may be a very inexpensive hobby. A prize was offered for the best model ship, not more than 20″ in overall length, and costing not more than 3s. in materials for construction. Over 100 models were entered, and the prize was won by Mr. W. Lewis of Burnley, who exhibited a model of a trading schooner which only cost 1s. 3d. to produce. In spite of this remarkably low cost, Mr. Lewis succeeded in building a model so realistic in character that it has been purchased by the Liverpool Corporation for their Museum. It represents three weeks' hard work.

The prototype selected by Mr. Lewis for his model was the schooner *Enterprise* of Chester. This was a very fast vessel, trading between Woolwich and Chester, and made some record passages, one of them being only 74 hours. Mr. Lewis knew this schooner well, as he used to sail in her. We give a photograph, by courtesy of the *Burnley Express*, of Mr. Lewis with his model. In business Mr. Lewis is a fruiterer, but he builds many models of sailing ships as a spare-time hobby, and we think he may be congratulated on the very excellent little production shown in our photograph.

Photo by]   **Mr. W. Lewis and his prize model Schooner " Enterprise "**   [*" Burnley Express."*

The Story of the "Golden Hind"

THE *Golden Hind*, Sir Francis Drake's flagship on his famous voyage of circumnavigation, started the voyage as the *Pelican*, a little ship of 100 tons burthen mounting 18 guns and built on the combined principles of trader and fighting ship that they so often followed in those days. It was in the Straits of Magellan that Drake decided to re-christen her *Golden Hind*, that being Sir Christopher Hatton's crest, and he having introduced Drake to Queen Elizabeth and obtained for him the financial support that was necessary for his voyage. The manner in which, despite all misfortunes, he contrived to keep her afloat for the entire voyage round the world is one of the epics of the sea, returning to Plymouth and then up to Deptford.

While the Queen's attitude towards his conduct was still in doubt he became the popular hero of London, and the action of the Benchers of the Middle Temple in admitting him *honoris causa* most probably influenced the Queen's decision. When she had visited him at Deptford and knighted him on the deck of the *Golden Hind*, it became a show ship, and the Queen decreed that such a noble vessel must be preserved for the instruction and edification of future ages. A deep trench was dug into the river bank at Deptford and she was hauled in and the entrance sealed, her masts being cut down and a roof put over her. Instead of being used for the edification and instruction of future ages she became rather a disreputable banqueting hall, and ultimately, after a lapse of 40 years, fell to pieces.

Our photograph shows a silver model of this famous vessel recently presented by the town of Plymouth to Viscount and Viscountess Astor on the occasion of their silver wedding.

A Presentation Silver Model of the " Golden Hind "

The Ship Modeller's Scrap Book
A DICTIONARY OF SHIP DETAILS IN ALL PERIODS.

(*Continued from page* 62)

Bill-Boards

IN modern sailing ships (A) merely an extra board on the bulwarks or bow, or a plate of sheet iron, to protect the ship from being damaged by the anchor when being handled. In the old men-of-war (B), where the foremast was stepped well forward,

Modern Bill-Board

Old Man-of-War Bill-Board

they were stout pieces of timber bolted to the ship's side just forward of the fore channels, on which the anchors were stowed, being faced with iron billboard plates both for protection and to enable the anchor to move freely.

Binnacle

Ever since the mariner's compass has been used, it has been necessary to provide a weather-proof casing (binnacle, formerly bittacle) for its use. The design varies greatly, from the simple lighted box (A) which stands on the skylight of the little wooden coaster which has little or

no need to worry about magnetic influences in the ship to the modern binnacle (B), with its elaborate precautions against interference. Ex-

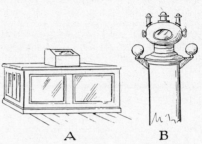

Lighted Box Binnacle   **Modern Binnacle**

ternally, the binnacle of the biggest liner differs little from that of the iron or steel sailing ship.

Bitts

The bitts were any form of upright piece of timber through the deck, generally joined by a horizontal piece or cross-bit. There were various types for various purposes in the old-time sailing ships, but of these the more important were as follow :—

Cable bitts, to which the ends of the anchor cables were attached (hence

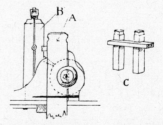

Carrick and Pawl Bitts   **Riding Bitts**

the expression " the bitter end "), were below and would not show on any ordinary model. The carrick bitts (A) supported the windlass and generally had the pawl bitt (B) in the centre of the cross-bit or strongback, with a pawl to prevent the barrel reversing and letting the cable run out. The riding bitts (C) secured the cable when the ship was riding at anchor, often called fore bitts, and giving their name to the " fore-bitters " or sea songs, which were sung round them in the dog watches for amusement, as distinct from the shanties or working songs. Topsail sheet bitts (D) were arranged around the foot of the mast, the cross bitts being the fife-rail with holes for the belaying pins shown originally always of ash but latterly of iron or metal, which were the traditional weapons of the " bucko "

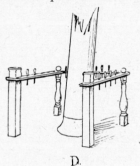

D.
Topsail-Sheet Bitts

mate. Gallows bitts were for the stowage of spare spars, boats, etc., generally between the main and mizzen masts, keeping them clear of the deck.

Blocks

Of all sizes and many shapes according to their various functions. The ordinary block (A) could have any number of sheaves from one to four, according to the purchase required. The sheaves, or wheels inside the blocks, were of metal or hard wood. The gin block (B) was used almost entirely for the single whip for working cargo or for some temporary job about the ship, and the snatch block (C) for taking the bight of a rope when it was inconvenient or impossible to get at the end to reeve through the sheave-hole or swallow. Sister blocks had two sheaves one above the other.

The ordinary block changed remarkably little through the ages.

Bowlines

Designed to hold the weather leach of a square sail as far forward as

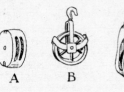

A   B   C

Three types of Blocks

possible, one of the earliest devices to help a ship sail close to the wind and very necessary in the days of baggy, ill-fitting sails. The bowsprit (*q.v.*) was originally designed to take the bowlines. The topsail bowlines went out with single topsails, but the fore bowline on the foresail survived. The bowlines were attached to the leach of the sail by bowline bridles. Another kind of bowline controlled the after edge of a fore-staysail and held it aback to pay off the ship's head in going about.

(*To be continued.*)

A Ship Model Catalogue

THE new edition of the Model Ship Catalogue issued by Messrs. Bassett-Lowke, Ltd., of Northampton, is just to hand. It covers over 90 pages and is a veritable encyclopaedia of model ships and boats of all kinds, ranging from inexpensive model sailing yachts, to speed boats, steam yachts, liners, and battle cruisers of the most completely detailed kind. Engines, boilers, and electric motors for model boats are listed, and there is an excellent section of scale model ships' fittings in great variety. A list of drawings and designs for both historic and modern types of ship model will be of much interest to model builders. This firm have been responsible for the building of many of the beautiful scale models owned by the principal Shipping Companies. The price of the Catalogue is 6d. post free.

The Ship's Mail

Readers are invited to make use of this column for the discussion of matters of mutual interest and the exchange of ideas and information.

The Elizabethan Galleon

DEAR SIR,—I have had a good look over the Elizabethan galleon in the Science Museum, as described in your October issue, and I noticed two important details omitted, unless they have been recently added. The port lids have no port lifts to keep them raised, and the catheads, though slotted for lifting anchors, have no blocks or gear on them, though the anchors are lashed alongside for sea. How did they get them up there ?

Yours truly,

Southsea.   R. WILSON.

Mr. G. S. Laird Clowes kindly sends the following note in reply :—

" Your correspondent seems to have confused accuracy and completeness. What is shown is all right, but it does not follow that there are not further details which might be shown.

" As for example, there should be three boats, but although I have the main dimensions, I am still trying to find a good contemporary reproduction of one of the double-ended type still in use. Similarly, there is no capstan visible, because the main capstan was then housed below the quarter (or half deck) while I have not yet been able to satisfy myself that the jeer capstan has been introduced ; for jeers were still in their infancy and the lower yards were hoisted by means of ties and halyards.

" The reason for the absence of port-lid lanyards is that it was the general convention in the best ship-model making—in the 17th and 18th Centuries—to omit these ; in the one or two examples here which show port-lid lanyards, they certainly look rather clumsy. As, however, the ship is shown under sail, I will consider the possibility of having them added.

" The absence of the cat-block and the cat-falls is, however, quite another matter. After safely stowing the anchor, the old practice was always to unreave the cat-falls and to remove and stow inboard the very cumbersome cat-block. As the ship is under way, no cat-block is shown."

DEAR SIR,—Mr. G. S. Laird Clowes, in his very interesting description of his model of the *Elizabeth Jonas*, gives " Burthen, 684 ; ton and tonnage, 855."

In a list of the names of ships and captains serving under Charles Lord Howard of Effingham, Lord High-Admiral against the Spaniards, A.D. 1588, the *Elizabeth Jonas* is given as 500 tons ; Captain, Sir Robert Southwell ; and a crew of 500 mariners.

In another list of the names of such ships as Her Majesty Queen Elizabeth left at her death on March 24th, 1602-3 : " The *Elizabeth-Jonas*, 900 tons ; men in Harb., 30 ; men at Sea, whereof, 500 ; Marin, 340 ; Gunn., 40 ; Sail, 120."

Yours truly,

London, S.W.   T. R. BEAUFORT.

DEAR SIR,—May I add a few further notes to Mr. Laird Clowes' article in your last issue on the galleon *Elizabeth Jonas* ?

She was originally built as one of the great ships of Henry VIII's Navy, and was known as the *Peter Pomogranate*. In 1558-9 she was rebuilt (a term which seems to have covered anything from a general overhaul to a complete alteration of structure and design) as an 800-900 ton ship at Woolwich, and renamed the *Elizabeth Jonas*.

The year 1587 found her out of commission and laid up in Gillingham Reach below Chatham, and considered unseaworthy for winter cruising. The alarms and rumours of that year, however, caused her to be hastily recommissioned, with Sir Robert

Southwell in command, and posted to
Lord Howard's Squadron. This she
joined in Margate Roads in May, 1588.

Later in the year, after experiencing
much bad weather, she, with the
remainder of the Squadron, joined
Drake in Plymouth Sound, where he
was storm-bound and awaiting a
change of wind. This came in July,
and the Fleet was able to leave the
Sound and commence their search
for, and attacks on, the advancing
Armada. During the running engagements and the chase of the Spaniards
which ensued she was very active, and
no doubt her further rebuilding in
1597-8 was necessitated by the damage
she had received during the operations
both from the enemy and the in-
clement weather.

I have not traced her after 1602.

Yours obediently,
E. E. EGLINTON-BAILEY, Capt.
Putney, S.W.15.

Notable Merseyside Ships

DEAR SIR —I offer no apologies for
sending you the enclosed four photographs, in the hope that they may be
of some interest to other readers.

No. 1 is the *Britannic*, the famous
White Star motor-liner now on the
Liverpool-New York run. The photo
shows her undocking at Gladstone
Dock, Liverpool, prior to taking her
maiden sailing, on June 28th, 1930.

No. 2 is the *Lady Connaught*, of the
British and Irish Steam Packet Co.,
one of the trio of vessels which
maintain the night passenger service
between the Mersey and Dublin.

She was built by Harland and
Wolff, Ltd., Belfast, in 1906, as the
Heroic, for the Belfast Steamship Co.,
Ltd. Length, 320′ 3″; breadth, 41′
3″; depth, 16′ 8″. Twin screw, with
a speed of 18 knots.

In March, 1930, she was transferred
to the B. and I. Line and overhauled
and reconditioned for her new service,
being given an additional funnel;
her sister ships, *Graphic* and *Patriotic*,
were likewise dealt with and renamed
Lady Munster and *Lady Leinster*
respectively.

No. 3, *Mona's Queen*, the last
paddler of the well-known Isle of
Man Steam Packet Co.'s fleet, built at
Barrow in 1885. Length, 320′ 1″;
breadth, 38′ 3″; depth, 14′ 5″; speed,
17½ knots.

Mona's Queen had a long and
honourable career in the famous red-
funnelled fleet, and was a popular
vessel with hundreds of thousands of
holiday-makers.

She was sold to shipbreakers on the
Clyde at the end of the 1929 season,
leaving Douglas for Glasgow on her
last passage, on October 7th, 1929.

No. 4, the last, but by no means the
least in interest, the famous *Royal
Iris*, of the Wallasey Ferry service.
This vessel's exploits in the memorable
attack on Zeebrugge, on St. George's
Day, 1918, are known to shiplovers
everywhere. Now I see she has made
her last trip on the Mersey, and is up
for sale. Built by R. Stephenson and
Co., Ltd., Newcastle, in 1906. Length,
152′; breadth, 40′ 6″; depth, 11′ 2″;
twin screw.

Closing now with all best wishes for
the success of our new magazine.

Yours faithfully,
Preston.   HARRY STEWART.

Making Model Cowl Ventilators

DEAR SIR,—I was very pleased
indeed to receive the second number
of SHIPS AND SHIP MODELS the other
day, and am particularly interested
in the article by " Hause Pipe," as
he seems to deal in work very similar
to my own. Funnily enough, I hit
on the system of making funnels
about a year ago which he mentions
in his article. Mine, however, are
made round a wooden core extending
some way up inside the funnel, and I
notice he does not mention having
one in his.

I wonder whether it would interest
him to know of my system of making
the cowl ventilators which he mentions. For numbers of years I also
tried all kinds of ways and, while I
had to content myself with nails and
pins with the heads bent over, I
experimented with copper wire, lead

The "Mona's Queen"
The "Royal Iris"

NOTABLE MERSEYSIDE SHIPS
Photographs by Harry Stuart

The "Britannic"
The "Lady Connaught"

pipes, tin and all kinds of devices, with absolutely no success.

But, about two years ago, I began making them from wooden knitting-needles, and the result is so successful that I have never changed the method.

All that is required is some sand-

(5) Shape off the top with the knife, roughly, and then finish off with some sandpaper wrapped round a suitable piece of wood, using it like a file.

This is rather a lengthy description, but in reality it is a most simple job,

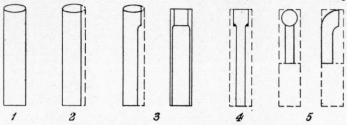

A Simple Method of Making Model Cowl Ventilators

paper, a good sharp pocket-knife, the needles, and a small vice. Mine is a little steel one, and the only one I possess.

Choose a fairly hard wood for the needles. They can be obtained in many different sizes and different woods, but the grain should run as nearly as possible parallel with the needle. The size, of course, depends on the size of the cowl, the diameter of the needle should be slightly greater than the diameter of the mouth of the finished ventilator.

The little sketches above will show best the way to do it :—

(1) Cut the needle into a length a good ½" longer than the length of the ventilator, and fix it upright in the vice, with the grain running towards the side to be cut.

(2) Cut straight down one side with the knife ; the breadth of the flat part is then the breadth or diameter of the cowl mouth.

(3) Cut in still deeper, as shown in Fig. 3, having a square flat piece at the top, which is the square surrounding the cowl mouth.

(4) Cut off the bottom corners of the square and cut the edges off the " shaft " down to the vice. Then get a strip of No. 0 sandpaper and pull it backwards and forwards round the shaft until it is smooth and round.

and I can easily make cowls of any ordinary size in about two or three minutes each.

When removed from the vice, the bottom part can be cut off and the cowl fitted as required.

They lack reality in not being hollow, but since in nearly all cases the inside is a different colour to the outside, this does not matter very much, and they look most realistic when finished.

It is perhaps a somewhat crude method, but I hope " Hause Pipe " may find it useful.

Yours faithfully,
Much Wenlock.   J. H. ISHERWOOD.

———

DEAR SIR,—Your contributor, " Hause Pipe," in the course of his article on a fine waterline model, said he had been searching for years to find a method of making cowl ventilators with the tools and materials at his disposal. I had encountered the same difficulty in building a 30″ tugboat I have in hand at the moment. I have no tools worthy of the name, and less cash. Woolworths are my toolmakers !

While grappling with the ventilator problem I hit on the idea of building them up with plastic wood over a candle-wax former, with remarkable results. The wax former is in two parts—stem and bowl—which are joined by running melted wax in the joint and smoothing over with the fingers.

The plastic wood is not easily applied and will not go over the wax smoothly, but if a good thickness is put on, the roughness is easily taken off with sandpaper when the wood is hard. The main trouble is that the wax gets soft quickly under one's fingers and needs frequent cooling in cold water, or better, a cool room. For the same reason, six or eight hours should elapse before attempting sand-papering. Before quite finishing that, the wax should be removed. Run the point of a penknife round the inside edge of the bowl and the wax will probably fall out. Very little persuasion is needed anyway, as the wood does not adhere to it. The stem wax may be removed by holding it in the hand until it is all soft inside, and gentle persuasion with the knife does the rest.

While putting on the Plastic wood, the fixing flange may be added, but should be thick enough to allow for finishing. Handles of bent wire may

also be fitted before the wood sets. Plastic wood may be obtained in tubes at 6d., or in tins, but that in tubes is much more easily handled and does not harden when not in use as it does in tins. There are several makes. Rawlplug is the best ; " New Discovery " in a blue tube is almost as good. A softening fluid, by Necol Chemical Works, can be had at 5½d. per tin, and is useful where additions to already hardened work have to be made. Most ironmongers and builders' sundriesmen sell these products.

Yours faithfully,
South Harrow.   S. GALLOWAY.

The " Thermopylae "

DEAR SIR,—I enclose a photograph of a model of this ship, which may interest your correspondent, Mr. G. C. Johnson. I also enclose a rough deck-plan of the model, approximately full size, which please send to him.

The details of the original ship were 991 tons, 212′ long, 36′ beam, and 21′ depth. She was built in 1868. My model is plank-built in

A Model of the " Thermopylae "

veneer mahogany, and measures 14″ on the deck-line. The general lay-out of the deck-plan is as follows :—

The poop extends 3″ forrard, with monkey-poop on top ; mizzen-mast is stepped about ½″ forward of monkey-poop ; at break of poop is the flag-locker ; two harness casks just east side of mizzen-mast : No. 3 hatch on main deck, just forrard of break of poop ; two boats on skids just for-ward of hatch ; main deck capstan, main mast, then main hatch ; a spare spar in waterway on port and starboard sides ; deck-house with two boats, bottom up, on skids ; wire reel on forrard end of house ; fore-mast and forrard of that No. 1, or fore-hatch ; windlass on after part of forecastle-head ; companion to crew's quarters ; capstan ; catheads and anchors.

I should be pleased to show my model to your correspondent, by appointment, if he would like to see it.

Yours truly,

London, W.　　　　　　T. EVANS.

Making a Model Sea

DEAR SIR,—I should be pleased to know of some good material for making the sea on scenic models. I have used putty, but it is rather messy and hard to work, and it also takes a week to dry. Perhaps some other reader can advise me ?

Yours faithfully,

PHILIP MADDOCKS.

Streatham Hill, S.W.2.

Correspondence Desired

Mr. Georg Gjersoe, Tollbodgaten 17, Oslo, would like to correspond with collectors with a view to exchanging photographs of sailing vessels, especi-ally wooden and composite ships.

The Merseyside Ship Model Makers' Club

AN auspicious start to the new Merseyside Ship Model Makers' Club was made when Mr. Robert Gladstone presented to them for annual competition a silver challenge cup. This cup is to be held by the member, or members, who make the best ship model of the year. It is believed that this is the first ship model makers' club in the United Kingdom, and it is already in a flourishing state with very ambitious plans for the ensuing twelve months. Members meet fortnightly for dis-cussion, but work at practical model making independently or in groups according to period or type of ship. Among the groups so formed are those of coracles and curraghs, Tudor ships, earliest steamships, modern steam craft, estuary craft, windjammers and clippers, and model sailing yachts. Members have enrolled up to a radius of 40 miles already.

More than half the members have already exhibited in various exhi-bitions, and the birth of this present club is due, primarily, to the great shipping exhibition which was held in St. George's Hall at the end of August this year. The prime mover is Lieut.-Commander Craine, who was so successful in gathering together the unique collection of shipping models in that exhibition.

It is proposed to hold an annual exhibition of members' models, to-gether with other appropriate exhibits in the spring of the year.

One unique feature is the corps of Honorary Members, known as Gentle-men Adventurers, who, although not desirous of partaking of actual model-making exercise, are ship lovers in every sense of the word and form a useful backbone to a young club desirous of extending itself over a wide area.

At the fortnightly meetings a paper is read by one of the members, usually followed by a keen and vigorous discussion.

Particulars of the Club will be sent gladly by the Hon. Secretary, Mr. L. F. Holly, 9, Jasmine Street, Everton. Liverpool.

SHIPS AND SHIP MODELS

A Magazine for all Lovers of Ships and the Sea

Single Copies, post free, **7½d.**
Annual Subscription **7s. 6d.**

Editorial and Publishing Offices:

66 FARRINGDON STREET
LONDON :: E.C. 4

Vol. I. No. 4.   DECEMBER, 1931.   Price 6d.

The Ship's Log

Something You Can Do

UP till now SHIPS AND SHIP MODELS has enjoyed a very happy voyage. It has made friends literally all over the world, for there is now scarcely a country which is not represented on our list of regular subscribers, and dozens of letters have reached us expressing appreciation of the interesting nature of the matter in our pages. In spite of this success we feel that we have only touched the fringe of the enormous public who are ship-lovers at heart, and of the perhaps smaller, but still very extensive, public whose love of a ship is shown by their activities in building models. Our present readers can help us, in a practical way, to make our paper more widely known, if they will give their kind co-operation. They can purchase an extra copy of this issue and send it to some friend at home or abroad whom they know to be interested in ships. They can even please such a friend very much by sending us a year's subscription with instructions to send the paper to him. Imagine the effect of that action. Each month their friend would receive a copy of our paper which would not only interest him very much, but every copy would be a delightful reminder to him of the kindly thought of the sender. A subscription to SHIPS AND SHIP MODELS would be an exceptionally pleasing birthday or a Christmas gift. The cost of such a gift would be very small; its effect would be both pleasing and lasting. But if, in these days of forced economy, the cost is a matter which weighs, there is a simpler method of helping the good cause. Send us a post-card with the names and addresses of any of your friends whom you know to be definitely interested in ships or ship modelling, and we will send them a specimen copy free of charge. We want to get in touch with everybody who will appreciate our paper, and the most direct route is through those who have already joined our crew. So when you read these lines, please make a definite move in one of the directions we have indicated.

Brixham Trawlers

A correspondent who is anxious to build an authentic model of a Brixham trawler asks if any reader can help him to get the genuine lines of one of these famous fishing boats. His inquiries lead him to suppose that these boats are built by tradition rather than from measured drawings, and that no actual " lines " are available.

*   *   *

House Flags at Poplar

The Council of the Borough of Poplar recently arranged a most interesting display of house flags and photographs representing most of the well-known ships using the Docks during the past 100 years. Mr. Daniel R. Bolt, who was largely instrumental in getting this collection together, is an authority on the shipping history of the Thames, and is to be complimented on this instructive contribution to marine records.

*   *   *

An Essex Exhibition

We congratulate the Essex Yacht Club on their enterprise in arranging an exhibition of ship and boat models in their Club House at Leigh-on-Sea, which is the old Tilbury ferry-boat *Carlotta*. This vessel has been converted into a very roomy and comfortable house-boat for the Club ; the main saloon will allow about eighty people to dine in comfort. An excellent show of models was staged for the exhibition week, including racing yachts, ships of war, clippers, and a Thames barge.

*   *   *

Ship Models at the Baltic

If one were asked where in London the greatest interest might be expected in ship models, one would probably reply, " At the Baltic." At any rate, at a recent Exhibition of Arts and Crafts, promoted by the Baltic Mercantile and Shipping Exchange, it is a fact that marine models were one of the most prominent features of the exhibits. Altogether, there were sixteen marine models displayed in the

exhibition recently arranged at the Merchants' Hall, St. Mary Axe, London. These naturally included more than one model of the *Santa Maria*, but we were pleased to notice models of a less spectacular kind representing the *Sinaloa*, the *Royal Albert*, the motor-boat *Gwalia*, and even a model of a collier brig. The model of the s.s. *City of Canterbury*, illustrated elsewhere in this issue, was another notable exhibit. This model is worthy of particular attention, as it recently took the " Joy " prize at the Model Engineer Exhibition. Mr. Basil Joy is a stickler for realism in ship modelling, and he offered a special prize for a model ship which was the most " true to life " in its representation of a real ship. The fact that the *City of Canterbury* passed the scrutiny of the judges, as well as of Mr. Joy himself, as best filling this qualification, lends additional interest to the photograph and description we publish in this month's issue.

*   *   *

The Story of Water Transport

At the mid-November meeting of the Shiplover's Association, Mr. W. J. Bassett-Lowke read a paper on " The Story of Water Transport Through the Ages." He traced the development of the ship from the early Egyptian days of 2000 B.C. up to the present time, indicating all the notable advances from oars to sail, from sail to steam, and from steam to oil power. The lecture was illustrated by a fascinating collection of miniature model ships, some thirty in number. These were all made to the same minute scale of 100ft. to the inch, and each model represented a notable boat or ship. A very interesting discussion followed, in which the subject of modern ship decoration and furnishing provoked some interesting exchanges of opinion. The meeting was held in the Admiral's Cabin, the popular shiplover's restaurant in the Strand, where some unique ship models and pictures form most attractive wall decorations.

The Oldest Vessels Afloat

By G. E. FARR

THERE are several difficulties that beset the seeker after old vessels, the chief of which may fairly be said to be the absence of any absolute definition with which to classify them. Some persons, realising that ancient Viking boats are preserved in the museums of Norway and Denmark, and others of contemporary and even older times than these, are probably to be seen in similar institutions elsewhere, would immediately come down through many centuries and call the famous *Victory* the oldest vessel, as she is by no means kept indoors. Others, however, will say that, being not afloat or in active commission, she is definitely not eligible ; but, if one could find the oldest vessel in Lloyd's or the Board of Trade Register, one would there have the oldest working craft.

However, it is entirely wrong to assume that only those craft which are registered are in active commission, as any sailor would tell the inquirer. On this score, it is claimed that the Port of Bristol harbours the oldest vessel working and afloat. She is the Ketch *Jane*, built at Runcorn in 1800, and now used in the somewhat inglorious capacity of a coal-hulk alongside a brewery. As may be expected, she has had a very chequered career and has been used for piracy and smuggling on many occasions. During the Peninsular, Crimean and Great Wars she was used as a fleet auxiliary, and in this capacity must have met many times what is the second oldest vessel still afloat. She is the *Ceres* of Bude, a ketch built at Salcombe in 1811 and re-built at Bude in 1865. Unlike the *Jane*, she is still used in her original rig and has been fitted with an auxiliary motor to assist her in her voyages along the extremely dangerous Cornish coast. The tonnages of the *Jane* and *Ceres* are, respectively, 40 and 44.

For those who favour the " Lloyd's " definition, the oldest sailing vessel is the *Olivia*, a wooden schooner now registered at Cabo Frio, Brazil. She was, apparently, built in Ueckermunde, Germany, in 1819, and then called the *Martha*, but whether she was lengthened or shortened when re-built

The Oldest Ship Afloat—The Ketch "Jane" built in 1800

The Oldest Steamer Afloat—The " John " of Bristol

in 1852, it is difficult to conjecture, as at the present time she is only of 157 tons, or 86′ × 23′, and she has crossed the Atlantic in the interim.

It is pleasing to note that the second oldest vessel in Lloyd's is British—she is the Schooner *Perthshire* of Dundee, of 126 tons, built in 1836 at Perth by J. Young.

These, then, are the oldest sailing vessels ; what of the steamships ?

By a strange coincidence, those who favour either the Lloyd's definition or the other, will both be satisfied on this score, as the oldest steam-vessel is still registered. She is the *John*, now owned in Bristol and used as a coal-carrier between that port and South Wales. She was built in 1849 at Neath Abbey and is of 72 nett and 140 gross tons, with dimensions of 90′ × 19′ and has 24 h.p. engines. A companion vessel, the *Collier*, built in 1848, and also registered at Bristol, was wrecked only a few years ago off Ilfracombe.

The Ketch "Ceres" of Bude, built in 1811

A Scale Model of the s.s. "City of Canterbury"

By R. A. BLOWS

A FEW words regarding the prototype of this model may be of interest to readers, as she is not in the public eye very much.

She was built in 1923 by Swan, Hunter and Wigham Richardson, Ltd., and has a registered tonnage of about 8,500, and a displacement of 15,500 tons. Her dimensions are : Length 466' 11", breadth 56' 4", and moulded depth 34' 1". The propelling machinery consists of a quadruple expansion engine and auxiliary turbo-electric drive, giving her a service speed of about 13 knots. She has accommodation for about 175 passengers.

The building of the model has taken just over a year and has provided me with a very congenial change from my usual occupation as a clerk. Very few tools were used in its construction, such things as manicure files, razor blades, drills made from needles, a penknife and a sewing machine doing most of the work. Materials included meat skewers, parts of old braces, air-gun slugs, shoe eyelets, and thousands of pins. It is very surprising the variety of scrap which can be used in ship models. The overall dimensions of the model are : Length 3' 7¾", breadth 5½", height to top of masts 1' 5".

The Hull

This was built up on the " bread and butter " system from mahogany planks, 6" × ⅞". Each layer was prepared from a separate template, and the inside cut right out with a keyhole saw, leaving the sides about ¼" thick. The layers were then screwed together with a thick coat of paint between, instead of being glued and pegged. Old paint which is too thick for ordinary use is ideal for this purpose. All screws were well countersunk and driven ight home while the paint was still tacky, pressing it well into the grain and making a good water-tight joint. A groove was cut in the stern of the second layer to take the propeller shaft tube, the tube laid in and the groove filled in with plastic wood, this method being easier and more accurate than drilling the hole when the hull was finished. The after end of the tube had previously been tapped to take a small packing gland. When roughly finished, the hull was marked off into 2" sections from stern to bow, and a separate template cut for each section. The hull was then finished with plane and gouge until each template was a good fit. A three-sixteenth hole was drilled through the cruiser stern and a length of brass tube pushed in to take the rudder post, which is a piece of Meccano rod with the rudder soldered into a slit down the centre. A friction tiller, consisting of a flanged bush and spring arm, is screwed to the top of the post, keeping the rudder stiff. The superstructure was the next job. (See Fig. 1.) The sides of the hull were recessed to a depth of one-sixteenth of an inch, and the sides of the superstructure cut from one-sixteenth three-ply wood, and glued and pinned into the hull. Bow and well deck bulwarks were treated in the same way. The motor was purchased from the Economic Electric Co., and is eight-pole with a disc commutator. A 2" Meccano gear-wheel was fitted to the propeller shaft and meshed with a ½" pinion on the motor shaft, giving a speed reduction of 4 to 1. This reduces the motor speed of 3,500 revolutions to about 600, which drops to about 450 in the water. In the stern of the hull, the sides had not been finished smooth, but were left with the layers forming steps. These steps were very useful for fixing the bearings, as it saved drilling the bottom. The packing gland is a wireless terminal drilled out half way through to ¼″ with a small washer soldered over. It is packed with string and keeps very water-tight. The boss of the propeller started life as a football adaptor, the bulbous end being turned right off in a twist drill, and blades of sheet brass soldered into the boss. An ⅛″ thread was put on both shaft and boss and the propeller locked on with a small nut. The accumulator is 6-volt and just goes through the

camber, and fitted into slots in the side of the hull. The deck in the forward well is removable, so as to get at the accumulator and batteries.

The painting of the hull took over a month, as each coat had to be allowed to dry before applying the next. Good enamel was used, and as there were two coats of each colour, this meant that some parts of the hull had eight coats altogether. I shall never use enamel again, as it

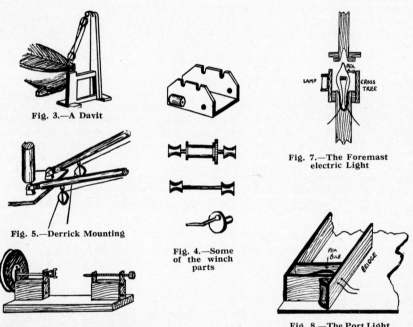

Fig. 3.—A Davit

Fig. 5.—Derrick Mounting

Fig. 4.—Some of the winch parts

Fig. 6.—My home-made Lathe

Fig. 7.—The Foremast electric Light

Fig. 8.—The Port Light

forward well. To prevent the boat getting tender, a lead keel, weighing 2 lbs., was cast and let into the bottom of the hull.

The deck was cut from one-sixteenth mahogany ply and planked with a blunt penknife, taking care only to cut through the top layer. The holes to take the various deck buildings and hatches were cut out before fitting, and the deck fastened down with ½″ brass lills. Cross-beams were cut from three-sixteenth plywood, the tops being curved to give the necessary

is inclined to run where it is not wanted. A good flat paint, rubbed down with powdered pumice and afterwards varnished or polished, gives the best results.

The Upperworks

I was just beginning to realise what a handy tool a penknife can be for work of a rather delicate nature, such as davits, lifeboats and ventilators The penknife, which cost the modest sum of 6d., had lost over half an inch in length since work was started. All the deck buildings and

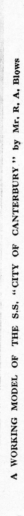

A WORKING MODEL OF THE S.S. "CITY OF CANTERBURY" by Mr. R. A. Blows

most of the hatches were made
removable so as to get at the interior.
Most of them are cardboard, built
on a framework of wood, the windows
being glazed with adhesive paper, well
varnished to keep out the water.
Shoe eyelets were used for port-
lights, there being over two hundred
in all, and were stuck in the holes
while the paint was still tacky.
Doors were cut from mahogany veneer
with small pin-heads as handles. The
stanchions were purchased and represented over a third of the cost of the
whole model. Ten amp. fuse wire
was used for threading them. Imitation hatch tarpaulins were made
from black blind holland and glued
on. The funnel is a length of $1\frac{1}{2}''$
diameter brass tubing, wire bands
being soldered round and a base
flange. Pins soldered across a small
brass framework made a good fiddley
grating. The davits are of the semi-
automatic type, cut from one-sixteenth
plywood. (See Fig. 3.) The 13
winches presented some difficulty, as
I had no lathe to turn the drums and
cogs and, after trying various ways
and means, I made a little lathe to
work on the sewing-machine. (See
Fig. 6.) It had two interchangeable
chucks made from Meccano pinions
to take $\frac{3}{8}''$ and $\frac{3}{16}''$ rod. Axles, drums
and cogs were turned up intact, using
a small wood chisel and a round file,
the teeth in the cogs being filed in.
Pins with the heads flattened and
soldered to the cranks made quite
good pistons and connection rods.
The winch frames were built up from
plywood with wooden cylinders. (See
Fig. 4.) There are 17 derricks cut
from wooden knitting-needles, the ends
being forked and bound with fuse
wire to prevent splitting. (See Fig. 5).

Electric Light Fittings

At this stage it was decided to
light the model with flash-lamp bulbs,
and four 2-volt bulbs wired in series
were used to light the saloons. The
current for these is supplied from a
grid bias battery. The navigation
lights were a little more difficult to
fit. Fig. 7 shows how the foremast

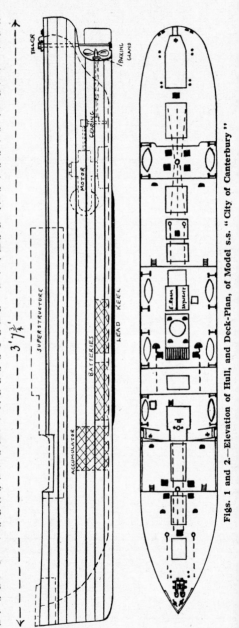

Figs. 1 and 2.—Elevation of Hull, and Deck-Plan, of Model s.s. "City of Canterbury"

riding light was fitted. The light shines through a hole in the front of the cross-tree and illuminates the tiny lamp in front, which is glazed with a piece of an old photo negative. The current is taken up to the lamp *via* the shrouds. Tiny boxes with tight-fitting lids were made at each end of the bridge to take the port and star-board lights, and the current carried to them through the funnel stays. A lamp has not yet been fitted to the mainmast, but a hollow metal mast is now being made to take a pea bulb. The model is quite a pretty sight with all the lamps alight in a darkened room.

General Fittings

There now only remained to make small fittings, such as lifeboats, derrick and davit blocks, engine-room tele-graphs, ventilators, bollards, fair-leads, etc. Lifeboats were carved out with the penknife and provided with covers of black blind holland. Two air-gun slugs soldered to a small piece of brass sheet and pinned down to the deck make good bollards. Engine-room telegraphs, binnacle and steering wheel posts were turned up on the little lathe. Ventilators were cut from firewood, the hole in the mouth being first drilled with a countersink bit. The stems of the larger ventilators are old pencil stumps. Samson posts are meat-skewers. The reels for the fair-leads in the forward bulwarks came from an old pair of elastic braces. Derrick blocks, of which there are seven dozen, were made by glueing three pieces of veneer together and binding with fuse wire. Blocks for the lifeboats were cut from an old boxwood ruler. Letters for the name and registry port were cut from 'bus tickets, the punch-hole being very useful for the O's, C's and G's. Two strands of 5-amp. fuse wire twisted together were used for stays and shrouds. Switches for motor and lights are under the two after hatches, which are removable. Small pearl beads, painted black, with a bent pin pushed through the hole and bound to the ends of the lines, made hooks and weights for the derricks.

When all the fittings were finished, it took over a fortnight to put them on and generally finish things off.

The model behaves very well in the water and attains a speed of about $2\frac{1}{2}$ m.p.h., the accumulator lasting nearly an hour.

(This model was awarded a Diploma and the " Joy " prize for realistic steamship modelling at the recent *Model Engineer* Exhibition.—ED., S. and S.M.)

Drawing by] **" The Old Shipyard "** *[R. H. Penton*

A Maker of Miniature Models

Some Notes on the Work of Mr. Charles Hampshire

By "MAIN ROYAL"

IT is not every ship-modeller who has the patience and delicacy of touch possessed by Mr. Charles Hampshire, whose hobby is the building of very realistic models to a very small scale. His work is well known to visitors to the *Model Engineer* Exhibition, where he has on more than one occasion obtained a high award ; some examples of his models were also shown at the recent Engineering and Shipping Exhibition, and he has also achieved distinction in other quarters. He works to a scale of 64 feet to the inch ; what this means will be understood when I point out that the model of a 300′ ship would be less than 5″ long. Yet, in spite of this minute scale, his models are remarkably complete, and in perfect proportion throughout. I recently examined his model of the *Golden Hind*, one of the daintiest pieces of miniature model making I have ever seen. So delicate is the workmanship and so beautiful the lines of the model, that when I saw it, I thought of a golden butterfly. The photograph shows the model about *twice* its actual size, so that its minute scale will be readily appre-

Mr. Charles Hampshire

ciated. Unfortunately, the sails do not come out well in the picture, so that the picturesque beauty of the model itself is not apparent.

Mr. Hampshire spent some years at sea as a marine engineer ; this is largely responsible for his love of ship models and for his competent knowledge of what both a ship and the sea should look like. But how the hands which could build and control the massive machinery of a sea-going steamship can perform work of the extraordinary delicacy shown in his models is a standing mystery to me.

Although I have known Mr. Hampshire for several years, it is only since the advent of SHIPS AND SHIP MODELS that I have attempted to extract from him some of the secrets of his work. I discovered, in course of conversation, that we had both worked in the same engineering shop in our younger days. That made things easier ; not that Mr. Hampshire is reluctant to talk about ship models, but from reminiscences of old times, we got down to present-day interests, and so the story came out. This is what he told me :—

" I have made a special feature of

Model of the " Viceroy of India " with the 100-year old " William Fawcett " alongside

A Miniature Model of the " Golden Hind " (twice full size of model)

this method of modelling for many years. I always wanted to portray a ship as though one was looking through the wrong end of a telescope, and I practiced with many different materials and tried many methods. I use cedar wood for the hull up the the main deck, then build up the different decks, and finish each one off before the next one is in position. I then am able to correctly complete each one as I go. I use human hair and very fine horse-hair for all ropes and hand-railing. For wireless I use the fine strands which are on the drum of condensers in a wireless set. The plans I always either get from the builders or the shipping firm, so as to be quite correct. My scale has always been 64' to the inch, which I think just makes a nice portable model which can be taken around

comfortably. The ship yard is a roll-top desk, and my tools are a very fine knife and needles for assembling the parts together. A steady hand, a good light, and a very large amount of patience. I always make my flags appear as though the wind is fluttering them, so as to be as realistic as possible. The seas I shape of plasticine and shape the bow waists correctly, having been about 14 years at sea. I have studied waves carefully, also I have aerial photos of ships. The *Viceroy of India* and the *William Fawcett* I made to illustrate a 100 years' progress in shipbuilding. The *Golden Hind* I made for Sir Neville Wilkinson to commemorate the visit of the Prince of Wales, and Titania's Palace, to South America recently. This model, I believe, is the smallest detailed scale model of an Elizabethan

The " Empress of Japan " with two tugs

warship ever made.   I got particulars and drawings from South Kensington Museum through the courtesy of Mr. Laird Clowes.   The *Golden Hind* was I think, about 95′ long.

"The C.P.R. *Empress of Japan* is the largest and most luxurious British liner in the Pacific.   I have made two tugs belonging to the Liverpool Towing Co., and are perfectly to scale and complete in all details.

"Sir George W. Sam Brown, of the C.P.R., had a number of photos taken of this model and had her exhibited in the Cockspur Street Offices for some time.

"One of my models I like best is on the base of the Engineers' Memorial in the Institute of Marine Engineers, Minories.   It is of the *Titanic*, which was lost on her maiden voyage."

If any of my readers have the good fortune to come across Mr. Hampshire's work, I advise them to study it. Moreover, I would advise them to bring out a magnifying glass; the work will stand it.   If, by particular good fortune, they see his model of the *Golden Hind*, they will experience a thrill of pleasure which I am sure they will long remember.   I only hope it won't induce them to go home and put their own models under a heavy hammer.

Sketch by]   **" Out with the Drifters "**   [*W. M. Birchall*

How to Build a Model of a Dutch Admiralty Yacht

By **JEFFREY LEIGHTON**

(Concluded from page 72.)

Painting

I have found " manufactured " paints unsatisfactory for models for various reasons, and should recommend that the model-maker makes his own. I have found the following satisfactory on over a hundred models of various types. It dries quickly, has an " eggshell " finish, and can be altered either in thickness or tone very easily. I might add, I have also found it very effective in interior decoration. It can be easily made up with little mess, the ingredients are cheap and it may be made up in small quantities at a time. Obtain from any painters' colourman 2 oz. of each of the following dry colours, burnt sienna, raw sienna, ultra-marine blue, chrome yellow or any bright yellow, yellow ochre, crimson and chinese red. These should cost but a matter of a few pence per ounce. Obtain also a pint bottle of white (shellac) polish and a pint of methylated spirits. Also a few student's quality water-colour brushes in three sizes—fine, medium and large —these latter should be tightly bound for a little way down the bristles to prevent " moulting." The powders should be kept in airtight tins or jars until required, as they are liable to become lumpy if exposed to damp air. A small tin of eggshell black will also be required for touching in " ironwork," e.g., ringbolts, guns, etc. Carefully break down all lumps in the dry colour required (an old tooth brush handle does this admirably), and, having shaken the bottle well, mix with white polish in a small jar until of a fairly thick consistency. If too thick, a spot or two of methylated spirits can be added to thin. When thoroughly mixed, strain off into a jar which can be corked or sealed. Muslin or a gauze petrol funnel does

for straining. When separate colours have to be mixed together, it is best to mix the solutions and not the powders.

The hull of the model below the waterline should be left in white coverine. From the waterline to the top of the bulwarks should be a deep warm brown, a mixture of burnt sienna and raw sienna, with a little ultramarine blue added until dark enough. A thinned-out solution of this brown may be used for staining the bitts, windlass, etc. The inside of the bulwarks a deep red, chinese red and crimson lake in equal parts should do. The flat background between the carved work on the stern, the sides of the poop, the raised portion of the bulwarks just forward of the roundhouse and the dummy boltheads on the sides can be painted in eggshell black. The carving should next be painted with a mixture of ochre and a little burnt sienna, giving a warm brownish-yellow colour, when dry, apply bright yellow to the relief portions of the carving only with a fine brush prior to gilding. To obtain the best effect, only the high relief portion of the carved work should be gilt. The lee-boards should be the same red as the bulwarks, the ironwork picked out in black. The decks and fittings may be varnished, using the clear white polish, and if the finish of the hull be too dull for the taste of the builder, it may be varnished, allowing a clear 24 hours to elapse between the times of painting and varnishing. The poop lantern I have purposely left until last, as it is liable, if fitted before painting, to be continually in the way when turning the model about, and is likely, if caught in one's sleeve, to either split the carving or loosen in its socket.

The lantern should be made of soft wood covered with " barbola " and modelled to shape, and mounted on a stout copper wire arm, the hull end of which may be easily hammered or filed into a four-sided taper spike, which, pushed firmly home into a small hole drilled in the stern, will prevent the lantern " boxing the compass " when touched. The two guns, shown in the deck plan, are of perfectly standard type, truck-mounted and fitted with four wheels. The other gun ports apparently served mainly as wash ports on the type of yacht I have in mind, though doubtless on review days, and during sham fights, they were used for very small-calibre signal guns, of the type known, I believe, to the English of that period as " poppers." The anchors are also the old " Admiralty " pattern—a drawing is therefore hardly necessary if the dimensions are given. The shank should be 2″ long by ¼″ diameter, the flukes should be 1¾″ apart from tip to tip, and the stock, of wood, 2″ long by a ¼″ square in the middle, tapering to ⅛″ square at the ends. The most satisfactory method of making these would be to purchase two good-quality cast-brass anchors of the approximate size, remove the metal stock and file down to shape and size, afterwards fitting wooden stocks and wire shackles. Such anchors are stocked by most good toy-shops for model yachts. The anchors should be lashed just abaft the catheads on either side, the shanks lying on top of the bulwarks, stocks in a vertical position overside, the flukes, of course, being in an horizontal position athwartships. The hawsers of stout cord, whipped for ¼″ above the shackles with stout cotton, led through the hawsehole, and led aft round the windlass barrel ; they can then be " faked " to seem to lead down the hatch immediately abaft the windlass.

Masts and Spars

The mast and spars should be made from straight-grained deal or, better

still, the soft yellow wood which American canned goods are often packed in. I have found several model-makers using these boxes recently, none knowing the name of the wood ; it is soft, free from grain marks and shakes, has a smell suggestive of vanilla, and takes a beautiful polish. The mast and spars should be stained with a thinned solution of the brown used for the hull and wax-polished (even common boot-polish, applied briskly with a rag, does very well). The mast has a topmast fished to it. The mast and topmast should each be flatted for 2½″ and glued together, securing at the top and bottom with " hoops of fish " (find cord invisible bindings). The lower yard for the topsail is necked at the ends and is slung by a yard tackle and secured to the mast with a bead parrel ; the upper yard is merely shipped like a lugsail, the hoist being led from the truck through a single block in the centre of the yard, and from thence through a sheaved hole in the topmast and down to the foot of the mast, which should be fitted with a spider hoop or fine cleats, and belayed. Please note, that the lower yard only has topping lifts. The bowsprit is shipped through the iron hoops on the stem head and has a small wooden chock on the outboard end to carry a flagmast with small Dutch tricolour flag. The gaff is fitted with jaws and bead parrel round the mast. It may be inquired how the spanker could be lowered, without also lowering the mainyard, the answer being that the spanker was furled by means of brails and not lowered. A flagmast on the coach-house completes the list of spars. The ornamental trucks on flagmasts and topmast can be either carved or modelled in barbola.

Rigging

The standing rigging is very simple, consisting of three shrouds to a side, secured to the channels in the ordinary way, the deadeyes or the channels being shackled thereto. Ratlins

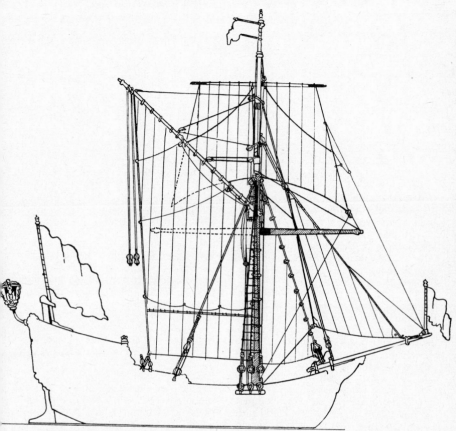

The Masts, Sails and Rigging of Model Dutch Admiralty Yacht. (¼ full size)

should be set up on these shrouds. The forestay, leading to the after end of the sternhead terminating in a deadeye, the lanyard of which is rove through three holes in the actual sternhead. A single shroud just forrard of this, terminating in two wooden cringles and lanyard, the lower cringle being made fast to the extreme forward end of the sternhead. Two backstays, leading well aft and terminating in a stay tackle, complete the standing rigging.

Sails and Running Gear

The sails should be made of thick canvas-coloured tussore, machine-stitched to imitate seams, and edged with fine cord. The best way of getting out of a lot of hard work is to hand over the sailmaking to the ladies of the household.

Taking the sails one by one :—

The Jib

The foot is hooked to a traveller on the bowsprit, the outhaul leading through a sheave near the end of the bowsprit. The sheet on the lee-side is made fast to the pinrail amidships, the weather-side being coiled down on the deck (seccotine coiled-rope ends to the deck, holding in shape with pins until dry). The jib halliards are belayed at the foot of the mast.

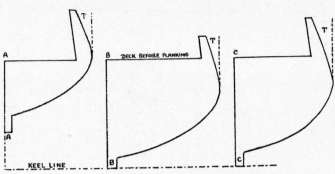

Corrected Sections for Building the Hull   (half size)

Fore Staysail

This runs on rings on the forestay, and the sheet is led to a cleat on the bulwarks half-way between the backstay and the rungs, the weather sheet being coiled down at the foot of the mast.

Spanker

The spanker, or mainsail, is laced to the gaff, and to the mast with rope grummets, a bonnet will be noticed in the plan ; this can be simulated with a double row of machine stitching in brown cotton. Peak and throat halliards are belayed to the fife-rail on the bitts, on the port side of the sail. The vangs, two to a side, from the peak, are shown incomplete in the drawing, in order to allow the leads of the sail to show clearly. The runner should be spliced to the tail of the single block on the bulwarks up through the lower half of the sister block, down through the lower block, up again through the top of the sister block and down to a cleat on the inside of the bulwarks. The main sheet is belayed to cleats on the bulwarks on either side, first passing through small cringles on the bulwark immediately above the cleats. The brails pass through small metal eyes on the leads of the sail, the top pair leading through blocks on the gaff, down through double blocks on either side of the throat to the fife rail amidships via a fairlead on the shrouds. The lower one leads, through eyes on the sail, to a small single

block on the mast, thence to the fife-rail between the bitts.

The Square Topsail

This is laced to the upper yard, the lower one being merely to take the sheets, these latter being led from the yard through a single block on the sail and down to the midship pinrail on the bulwarks. *There are no braces to the yards*, the toprail being set in the same way as a lagsail. Bowlines lead from the leach of the topsail to blocks on either side of the bowsprit flagment step, thence aft to the forward pinrail.

Flags

The two flags and the vane should be made of red, white and blue ribbons, stitched edge to edge, and laced to the poles, the van being stiffened for part of its length with little slips of cane.

I hope, one day, Mr. Editor permitting, to give a little article on making blocks, without a lathe or elaborate tools. Unless the reader has experience of making these, I should advise buying them ready-made, though not quite correct shape for models prior to the 19th Century. Rigging cords may be obtained in every size and variety from the leading model dockyards, or good fishing-tackle dealers. Running rigging should be thoroughly beeswaxed before use. Knots should be lightly touched with white polish or thin gum before cutting off the tails ; this enables a clean cut to be made, close to the knot without fear of the knot "springing." If rigging is to be painted, use thin eggshell black ; this does not hide the lay of the cord, or give the heavy overbearing effect which makes some of our finest sailors' models look so crude. Paint not only covers a multitude of sins, but also a lot of fine rigging. Use fine-pointed tweezers for rattling down ; they halve the difficulties. In conclusion, I have tried to keep the model within certain bounds as far as construction goes, in the hope that it may be of some use to model-makers with but few tools and small workshop facilities. I have myself constructed, within the last few weeks, an Admiralty yacht of similar design, on exactly the lines laid down in this little article.

A Correction

I am sorry that, in the first instalment of this article, I inadvertently included the drawings of the hull sections of another similar model, in place of the sections belonging to this design. I now give the correct section drawings (half-size), which I hope will clear up the queries raised by some of my correspondents. The reference to these drawings on page 20, second column, should read : " leaving bulwarks $1\frac{1}{4}''$ high and $\frac{1}{4}''$ thick," instead of " $1''$ high and $\frac{3}{8}''$ thick."

Two Sailing Ship Models

Mr. F. Prowse, of Wallasey, writes :—In my office at the dock I keep a stock of scale plans of sailing ships, and any of the company's people or dock officials who want to make a model, can have one. A good

The "Drumcraig"

many plans go out, but not many models come back. They seem to get on all right till it comes to making sail, and then get disheartened and take to making models in bottles.

The half-model of the ship *Thalatta*, in which I served my time, was exhibited at the Great Fair in St. George's Hall last October, and at the Shipping Week Exhibition last September. The only paint used was

for the side light screen, as I could not get a piece of wood red enough. She is 27″ overall. The hull is of white pine plated with ebony, half round and figure-head, and boats ivory, masts and spars cedar, deck fittings teak, and the sails are of New Zealand pine. The case is of oak, ebony, teak, walnut, red gum and golden wood.

The model of the four-masted barque *Drumcraig*, which I was second of in the early 'nineties, is 22″ overall and constructed of similar materials. She is now in the Liverpool Museum.

The "Thalatta"

The Model Sailing Brig
"Golden Vanity"
By S. A. P.

Two views of the Model Sailing Brig "Golden Vanity"

IT all began on account of that incomparable tome, " Treasure Island," the reading of which led us by natural ways to that picture-book, the Atlas, and so on by easy stages to the Doldrums and those Grand Old Roaring 'Forties.

Arriving here, we must needs search high and low to find the pictures of the ships that dealt with such forces. An old (1907) Motor Boat Manual provided the necessary on various rigs and how to recognise ; so that it was at once decided that a square rig should join the present fleet consisting of two Bermuda-rigged yachts, both owned by the one " director."

Now since the other " director " had no boat, but an almost bursting money-box, it was only natural, after a hurriedly called and conducted board meeting, that one boat should change hands at the rate of 2s. 6d., leaving as it did a reserve capital to the rattling value of 3½d., sounding thus sufficient to the new yachtsman.

The new ship selected was the brig, the builder having been emphatic in limiting the masts to two, so with slide-rule set at 1.5 to 18, the sketch having scaled 1½″, and our ship to be 18″, we proceeded to lay out a full-size drawing. All this was on the Thursday ; on the Friday we were seen returning from the local builders, a pre-motor wheelwright, with his best piece of pine measuring 4″ × 4″ × 18½″, plus another piece 2″ × 4″ × 18½″, planed up by the son ready for glueing.

Tools and Materials

Going up to our workshop, a large upturned packing-case round the back, and reviewing the tools, we produced one 8″ second cut half-round, one 4″ three-cornered, ditto flat, and ditto half-round, all not new, together with one bradawl, one screwdriver, ⅛″ twist drill, a hacksaw with the last remaining blade, an almost new pair of tinman's snips, and the not-to-be-forgotten Woolworth grinder, 1s. To which we

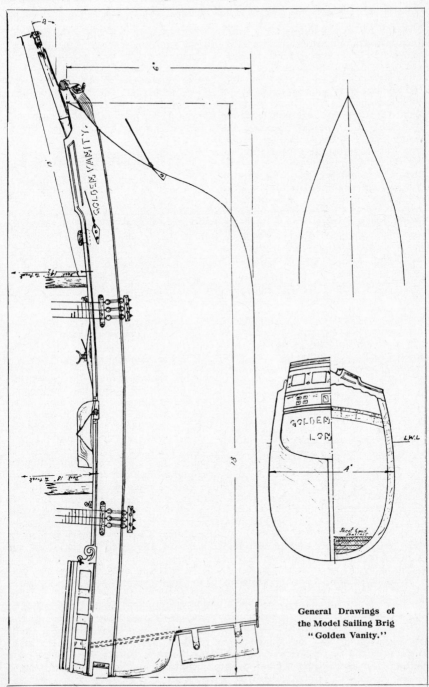

General Drawings of
the Model Sailing Brig
"Golden Vanity."

must add the Woolworth pliers, a " Gift " smoker's penknife, very worn, and a torch and soldering iron combined. To the existing funds already voted was added sufficient to buy one 1″ carpenter's chisel and a ⅝″ gouge, thus equipped a start was made.

The wood, having been received planed, the glueing was our first job, being left to set under pressure, one heavy box of odds and ends per square lot. Starting to take the rough off the block of timber, it was soon found that the hacksaw could not do the job and the pruning saw proved even worse, so once again the ex-wheel-wright's son was consulted, even to the suggestion that a spot of brace and bit might make the gouging much easier ; so willing was he that a mortising machine was unearthed and 'ollowing proceeded apace.

Either the tool was a little blunt or the planing not of the best or even our pressure glueing lacking in cohesion, for, at the last cut 'ee come away in me 'and and we were, as we were, with two pieces of wood instead of the united whole. Not wishing to appear overbearing, we

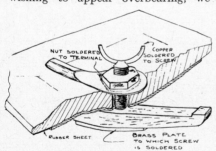

Sectional view of Hatch fitting

did not call for re-planing, but returned somewhat saddened to our bench amid the trees and things.

It is an ill wind . . . for we soon found that it would have been next to impossible to gouge out 5½″ in so short a length.

Having finished the hollowing to our satisfaction, we " re-planed " the surfaces of the two pieces of wood by finding the most level table-top in

the house on which to lay the sheet of sandpaper, so that rubbing-down might be fairly true. This time the glueing together was assisted by the addition of one good and proper long screw in the stem, one short one on each under-side of the counter and one on either side amidships. One of these last-named chose to run out and would not reverse out of its

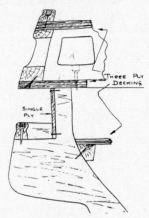

Construction of the Admiral's Walk

counter-sink, forcing us to the expedient of undermining the delinquent from the side and forcing him back ; not, however, before first trying to unglue the whole job and re-set the screw properly. Our ways had left their mark and we were forced to call in the plastic wood, this being the first and last illegitimate use of same.

Four templates were used in the shaping of the outside of the hull for the most part, the eye being expected to serve the best purpose, combined with very short immersion spells in the bath to ascertain the balance.

It was the original intention that the lights on the admiral's walk should be real, so that with a sky-lighted hatch it would be possible to see within, not just merely into an ill-carved hold, but down a well-planked deck through which carried the mighty masts. We were not " thinking in scale," the lights were not to be real, although the deck was there.

Fitting the Decks

With this type of ship the hulls are usually set inwards above the water-line, and, when we came to fit in the first deck, the idea of springing it into its place did not work well. Mahogany timbers duly cambered, were fitted and fixed in, and although the three-ply deck was steamed over the best existing steam supply, a pan of home-made beer in the making, it proved very troublesome, for once in, or half in, it would lock and be the devil to move. We should have made it in two pieces, divided down the longitudinal centre line.

Nevertheless, fixed it was, as also the main deck, hatches having been cut in both, one over the other. Before this fixing, it should be noted that a trial floatation showed that 1 lb. 10 oz. of keel would do the trick ; incidentally, the hull with decks weighed 1 lb. 11 oz., for the readers, and perhaps constructors', benefit we subsequently found that 2 lb. 10 oz. to be the correct amount. Our keel was constructed of sheet lead, $8'' \times 8''$, folded into four, bent out to conform to the hull's interior and fixed by trial ; and screwed. The later addition, being cast up separately in a wooden mould, using the after or main mast as a centralising point against the V notch in the lead and one screw directly under the hatch.

The admiral's walk was cut out of the main hull timber, faced with a single layer off some three-ply, glued, and fixed with pin brads after being steamed to take the curve, the walk was railed with mahogany cut to suit, made up of four pieces, the canopy being the projection of the main deck. The lights, being cut out of the ply facing, whereas the door was outlined by the red-hot wire process.

The poop-deck supports were cut out of mahogany, the port holes being made with the " Gift " knife, its point ground off and an edge ground on to

something like a narrow chisel edge, the tool being used after that fashion.

As this wood was $\frac{3}{8}'' \times \frac{1}{4}''$ and the knife had lost the pipe-stopper end, the hand that worked it was carved out almost as hollow. Where the side pieces break into the ordinary taff-rail, a little fancy work was indulged in, having by that time become quite natty with the weapon.

The Rudder Gear

Before the poop-deck proper could be fitted, the rudder gear had to be attended to ; this consisted of a piece of mahogany fixed to the rudder post of galvanised wire, by means of copper clamps sweated to the post, and held to the rudder with screws, the rudder post being carried up to the main deck through a copper tube fitted with a copper-sheet flange sweated thereto, which in turn is held to the hull with screws, the top end being held to the deck by a brass plate screwed down to the deck. The sheet copper is a remnant from the Copper-mending days and was drilled and countersunk by means of the tang-end of the small flat file, ground up to be a diamond-pointed drill, whilst its other end, ground up likewise, made a counter sink. The sheet brass first did service as a wireless dial plate and carries its fantastic embossing to this day hidden shamefacedly downwards whilst in such stern service. The hole for the rudder tube was first burnt through with a pilot red-hot knitting-needle enlarged with other rods and finally sized with a length of the same copper tube, given a cutting edge of sorts.

The tiller was a piece of brass fixed with a blob of solder, the weight of the rudder being taken on a loose nut under the tiller. The poop decking could then be fixed, and was provided with a taff-rail and a gangway, allowing for the ladder, made of one-ply, carefully recessed for each step and braced with copper wire under two steps, to which were sweated angle brackets of aerial copper strip forming holding-down brackets.

(To be concluded)

The New Flotilla-Leader
"Dubrovnik"
Launched at Scotstoun on October 12th, 1931.

The launch of the new Flotilla Leader " Dubrovnik "

THE Flotilla-Leader *Dubrovnik*, which Messrs. Yarrow and Co. are constructing for the Royal Yugoslav Government, is a most modern high-speed vessel 371′ 6″ length over-all, 35′ breadth moulded, and 22′ 9″ depth moulded. The displacement is 2,400 tons and the shaft horse-power 42,000. Its hull has been specially designed with a view to securing the greatest possible combination of strength, speed and manoeuvring power, together with good sea-going qualities. The bow is of improved form, with a raised forecastle and good flare forward. Experience has shown this form of bow to give the best results as regards seaworthiness and fighting qualities in a head sea. The stern, of the special flat type developed by Yarrow and Co., for high speed, is of sufficient width to protect the propellers when coming alongside, and the rudder is below the water-line

for protection from shot. High tensile steel is used for all parts of the hull upon which longitudinal strength depends, and the whole construction is in accordance with latest up-to-date naval practice. The accommodation is roomy, comfortable and well-ventilated.

The armament comprises four 5.5″ breach-loading guns, anti-aircraft guns and two triple 21″ torpedo tubes. A very complete electrical installation is provided, with wireless and fire control.

The vessel is twin-screw and propelled by geared turbines. Each set consists of a high-pressure and a low-pressure turbine driving, through pinions, a gear-wheel mounted on the propeller shaft. Special cruising turbines are coupled through a clutch to each H.P. turbine and ensure maximum economy at low cruising speeds. The astern turbines are incorporated in the low-pressure cylinders. The main engines will develop sufficient power to give the vessel a speed of 37 knots. A very complete equipment of auxiliary machinery is installed in accordance with first-class naval practice.

A feature of the vessel is the boiler plant consisting of three Yarrow patent water-tube boilers arranged for oil-firing. Each boiler is situated in a separate stokehold and is capable of being worked independently. Yarrow superheaters and Yarrow air-heaters are arranged in conjunction with the boilers, which will return high efficiencies for cruising and be capable of heavy forcing.

This Flotilla-Leader is the largest and most powerful of its kind ever built in this country for the British or any other Navy and represents a radical advance on anything hitherto accomplished for this class of service.

Notes on Carronades

By THOS. R. BEAUFORT

CARRONADES, established by an Admiralty Order on November 19th, 1794, were short guns, capable of carrying a large ball, and useful in close engagements at sea. They take their name from the iron foundry on the banks of the Carron, near Falkirk, in Scotland, where this sort of ordnance was first made, or the principle applied to, an improved construction. Shorter and lighter than the common cannon, and having a chamber for the gunpowder like a mortar, they are generally of large calibre, and carried on the upper works, as the poop and forecastle.

The 112-gun ship carried two 32-pounders on the forecastle and six 24-pounders on the poop ; the 100-gun ship had a similar complement ; the 98-gun ship two 32-pounders on the forecastle and six 18-pounders on the poop ; the 90-gun ship two 32-pounders on the forecastle and six 18-pounders on the poop ; the 80-ton ship two 32-pounders on the forecastle and six 18-pounders on the poop ; the 74-gun ship two 32-pounders on the forecastle and six 18-pounders on the poop ; the 64-ton ship two 24-pounders on the forecastle and six 18-pounders on the poop ; the 50-gun ship four 24-pounders on quarter-deck, two 24-pounders on the forecastle and six 12-pounders on the poop ; the 44-gun fifth-rate two-decker had six 18-pounders on the quarter-deck and two 18-pounders on the forecastle.

Soon after the commencement of the year 1793, carronades became so extensively employed, sometimes in lieu of, and sometimes in addition to, the quarter-deck and forecastle guns, that an exact enumeration of the ship's long guns, the alleged ground-work of the classification would have multiplied without end the number of classes, besides subjecting them to repeated fluctuations ; in short, the object of any classification at all would thereby have been defeated. One instance, and that a real one, may suffice. A frigate receives on board as her equipment 38 long guns and 8 carronades, and becomes, in consequence, a 38. She afterwards exchanges her 28 main-deck long guns for carronades, and is then or, in strictness ought to be, a 10-gun frigate. She subsequently receives back her long 18's, and is restored to a 38, but presently parts with six of her long 9's for an equal number of carronades, and, in obedience to the rule laid down, ought then to be a 32. An enumeration of the carronades, as well as the long guns, would have continued her as a 46 through all these changes ; but not only were carronades not considered as *guns*, but they were, as yet, too partially mounted to be of any great use in classification.

Books to Read

Small Sailing Craft. By R.
THURSTON HOPKINS. London :
Philip Allan and Co., Ltd. Price
15s. Postage 8d.

Mr. Thurston Hopkins has done
many of us a good service. Some of
us know as much as there is to be
known about some small craft, and
some of us have a superficial knowledge of a wide variety of small craft,
but few of us, I think, have made it
our business to inquire so thoroughly
into the history and development of
so many types as the contents of this
volume indicate the author has done.
The book is not merely a catalogue
of types ranging from the simple
coracle to the coasting barge and the
Lowestoft smack ; it is rather a
series of character sketches of the
craft themselves and of the race
of fine old seamen who sailed them.
The author's pilgrimage to gather
and verify the information he presents
us with, appears to have extended
from our north-east seaboard down
and along the south, and so far up
the west coast. A reference is made
to some of the Irish small craft, but
the south and east coast types receive
most attention. The chapter on the
Yorkshire (including scme of the
Northumbrian) cobles, is particularly
interesting, and naturally so, for the
coble—both the large and the small—
possesses the most striking indi-
viduality of any British small craft.
From the very first it seems to have
fulfilled its purpose, and consequently
to have suffered little or no modification. Some of the illustrations are
capital. We should have liked to
have seen some mention of the
Scotch herring boats, which, next
perhaps to the cobles, are as distinctive
a class and have as much beauty and
practical ability as any around our
coast ; and they undoubtedly man a
class of seafarer whose skill is not
surpassed even by the crews of the
North Sea trawlers. It is indeed as
thrilling and invigorating a sight to
watch a fleet of these heavy-masted
fishers putting out from Dunbar as
anyone may experience in watching
the smacks from the pier-heads at
Lowestoft or Gorleston.

Reminiscence, anecdote, and breezy
comment are blended in admirable
fashion. This, together with the pen-
and-ink drawings by Capt. Irvine
Bately, and some hitherto unpublished
drawings by E. W. Cooke, R.A.,
combine to make the volume one
which should be a part of every little
ship lover's library.

Motor Boating for Beginners. By
GEOFFREY PROUT. Glasgow: Brown,
Son and Ferguson, Ltd. Price
3s. 6d. Postage 3d.

The owner of a motor boat needs
to know something more than how
to keep his engine running. He must
be navigator, deck-hand, and engineer
all in one, and Mr. Prout, in his advice
to beginners, wisely gives some sound
instruction in elementary seamanship
and management afloat, as well as
on the technical details of the power
plant and boat equipment. The chapters on buying a boat, on " safety
first," and on upkeep and repairs,
are full of useful practical hints, and
help to make this book an admirable
introduction to a branch of smooth-
water cruising which is rapidly growing
in popularity.

Sea Songs and Shanties. Collected
by Capt. W. B. WHALL. Glasgow :
Brown, Son and Ferguson, Ltd.
Price 5s. Postage 4d.

This is the sixth edition of Capt.
Whall's well-known collection of songs
of the sea, with their correct musical
settings. Very few, if any, of us
may hear the real Shantyman again
in song, but there is ample reason for
the preservation of these inspiriting
verses which have helped so many
thousands of sailormen to pull their
weight. They could not be presented
in a more complete or more authentic
form.

THE THREE-MASTED SCHOONER, "KATHLEEN AND MAY,"
of Youghall, in Dry Dock at Appledore, Devon.

Drawing by R. H. Penton.

THE P. & O. TURBO-ELECTRIC LINER, "STRATHNAVER."   H.P., 28,000.
Gross Tonnage, 22,547.

Two New Ships

A New White Star Motor Liner

MESSRS. Harland and Wolff have just launched from their Belfast shipyard their second motor vessel for the White Star Line—the twin-screw cabin class motor liner *Georgic*. Officially, the *Georgic* and the *Britannic* are duplicate, but actually, as is so often the case with so-called " twin " ships, the *Georgic* differs from her sister ship in a number of important respects. In her design it will be found that the developments which were incorporated in the *Britannic* with such marked success have been carried a step further. The *Georgic* has accommodation for 1,632 passengers in cabin, tourist and third class, and this accommodation, slightly greater than in the *Britannic*, will be. on the lines of the high standard already set in that vessel.

The *Georgic*, like the *Britannic*, has been built under the survey of Lloyd's and the Board of Trade. Designed by Harland and Wolff on modern lines, the vessel has a straight stem, cruiser stern, two low broad-type funnels, and a curved bridge front. In the latter she differs somewhat from the *Britannic*. The principal dimensions are as follows :—

Length, b.p. .. 680′ 0″.
Breadth, moulded 82′ 0″.
Depth, moulded 43′ 9″.
Gross tonnage .. 28,000 approx.
Load draft .. 34′ 3½″.
Total power .. 20,000 h.p.

She has nine complete decks and eight cargo holds for the carriage of dry and refrigerated cargo. The hatchways are served by 16 electric winches and derricks capable of dealing with loads up to 10 tons. The deck machinery includes, in all, 18 silent electrically-driven winches for cargo handling and warping, and 20 for handling the lifeboats, steering gear, four large capstans and two large windlasses.

The propelling machinery consists of two 10-cylinder double-acting four-cycle motor engines of Harland-B. and W. type. The cylinders are cooled by fresh water and the pistons are oil-cooled, while all the auxiliary machinery is electrically driven. The two main engines are of air-injection type but have not attached compressors, these being arranged in the compartment forward of the main engine room, which contains also the four generators, which supply the necessary electric power for engine room and ship's purposes, and are driven by six cylinder trunk engines of the same general type as the air compressors.

The *Georgic* is technically a " Cabin " ship and will sail from Liverpool, but her passengers, as on the *Britannic*, will have surroundings and comforts equal to any *de luxe* liner from Southampton. The *Britannic* has proved most successful in the Liverpool-New York trade and in cruising, and the completion of her sister ship is eagerly awaited.

The first *Georgic* was sunk on December 10th, 1916, off the south of Ireland by the German Raider *Moewe*.

A New L.M.S. Pleasure Steamer

ONE of the most important contracts secured by a British shipyard during the past few months is that which has been entrusted by the Midland and Scottish Railway Company to Harland and Wolff, Ltd., who are to build a sister ship to the Clyde Pleasure-Steamer *Duchess of Montrose*. This ship will be built in the firm's Govan Yard, as it is only natural that the ship which will spend the whole of her life carrying Clyde-siders on their native river should be built on this river. The new Clyde vessel will have triple screws driven by direct turbines, taking steam from Scotch boilers. The machinery will be built at the firm's Belfast Works.

The Ship's Mail

Ship Models for Table Decoration

DEAR SIR,—The enclosed snapshot shows (not very clearly, I am sorry to say) an arrangement for a Christmas dinner-table decoration which I adopted last year when I was in China. The idea is subject to individual treatment, but the main facts are that ship models may be used very effectively as a table centre. What I did was to put down a mirror about 3′ long by 20″ wide, in the centre of the table. Thereon I placed two of my model ships and surrounded the edges

A Model Ship Table Centre

of the mirror with cotton-wool. Powder, imitating snow, as used for Christmas trees, was sprinkled over ships, rigging and mirror surface. With the fingers, or a dry paint-brush, the " snow " was swept away astern of the ships to represent the wake or open water. On the larger surface, between the ships, the " snow " was " swept " away with the finger-tip in the form of writing. I wrote : " A Merry 'Xmas."

The snow (cotton-wool) banks, representing icebergs, etc., were suitably decorated with holly, crackers, etc.

The whole scheme was very effective, and I suggest that your readers may like to adopt the idea this year.

Afterwards, all traces of " snow " from the rigging, spars, decks, etc.,

was removed by blowing it away. Care should be taken that the ships are not recently made, as should any varnish or paint be present in a " tacky " state, it might be very difficult to remove all traces of the powder used.

I am only home on furlough, and am sorry to say that I shall be returning to China in two months' time, but I can assure you that your publication, SHIPS AND SHIP MODELS, will be sent out to me regularly. It will be a link with the " Old Country."

Yours faithfully,

Pocklington.   P. A. TRAVERS-SMITH.

Making a Model Sea

DEAR SIR,—Your correspondent, Philip Maddocks, wished to know of some materials for making the sea on scenic models. I have so far only made three scenic models. The first time, I used " Glitter wax "—a streaky mixture of green, blue and white. It was easy to work, and the effect was not so bad as it sounds.

The second time, I used " Barbola" —a soft of artificial clay. This was very satisfactory and took water-colour and varnish very well. The third time I used Poly Roly plastic wood. It is, in reality, a form of slow-drying plaster. It always seems to be either so wet that it will not stay put, or so dry that it cracks when moulded. However, I shaped it with a knife when it was hard and, when painted and varnished, it was quite effective.

In making small models, 6″-10″ long, I have found cotton very useful for finishing-off deck fittings and for building-up small rails or gratings. The thin gold lines, which are so often seen round the hulls of clipper ships, can be very effectively done by sticking a piece of cotton, rolled in gold paint, parallel to the bulwarks, which I find much easier to do and neater than painting them on. On very small models the stanchions, or any other small rails, may be very effectively built up by gumming pieces of cotton on top of one another. It is advisable not to varnish these, or to do so very carefully, as the varnish makes the cotton shrink until it dries.

Yours faithfully,

Harpsden.   K. DUNBAR KILBURN.

Information Wanted

DEAR SIR,—Can any of your readers help me regarding a model of an early war vessel I have. I have had the enclosed photo taken of her. The upper portion of the stern is missing, and I would like to restore it, if I knew what kind of decoration would conform with the lower and sides of stern. I do not think the stern is intended to be risen very much above the level of the rails, as some of the old-time vessels were built. As you will see, she is a single-deck craft, with poop and low forecastle-head and has ports for seven guns a-side. These

The vessel has an exceptionally long curved tiller, and appears to be a two-masted craft only, unless the hole in the deck and sheathed round, just before the hatch at break of poop, is intended for the stepping of a mizzen-mast. It seems to me to be rather too close to the main-mast, although, from the point of sailing, it seems she should have some sail further aft than the main mast. Planks are taken up from her decks to show the cross-beams, which are beautifully made and fitted, and the hatch combings are covered with gratings (not hatches). The entrance to the cabin is on port side of poop and by a round-topped companion, and ladder down to cabin floor, which is lower than the main deck.

She is built and planked and fastened throughout and altogether splendidly constructed, red bulwarks inside and red gun-carriages, combings, bitts, etc., and gilt ornamentations of quarter galleries and round the stern. There

Can you identify this Model ?

cannons are beautifully made in brass, turned, bored and ribbed, and are 1½″ long. They are mounted on wooden gun-carriages on four wheels, with ring bolts and staples fitted for bowsing them about, and there are also turrets fitted all along the bulwarks (as shown), 11 each side. These carry brass guns, similar to the deck guns, but smaller. (1″ long), which ship into the top of the turrets, being attached to a brass forked and swivelled stanchion.

are no signs of masts, or rigging of any sort, so whether the builder intended her to be rigged and it was not completed, or whether it is only meant for a model of the hull, I cannot say, and I cannot find out. The original owner is dead, and it does not seem possible to get any information regarding it from anyone. However, if I can get the stern completed to conform with the rest of it, it is all I desire now, as I have repaired all that was damaged and missing.

If your readers can let me know, from the description and the photograph, what period she represents, and whether she's a sloop, barge or ketch, or merchant vessel, I should be pleased to know ; any other information would be greatly appreciated.

Yours truly,

Penarth.   R. LENG.

Making Cowl Ventilators

DEAR SIR,—Your correspondents, Mr. J. H. Isherwood and Mr. S. Galloway, in their advice to " Hawsepipe," have fairly good ideas, but I think that I have one that is more realistic, in that the ventilators are hollow. My method of making is as follows :—

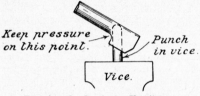

Keep pressure on this point. *Punch in vice.* *Vice.*

Forming the Cowl of a Ventilator

Take a piece of annealed copper tube, the same diameter as the stem of ventilator, and drill a hole not more than one-third diameter of tube through one side, about 1¼ diameters away from end of tube. Put a fine hacksaw (or metal cutting fretsaw) 'through from end to hole, taking care not to cut back edge of hole. Open out to form of a U and cut off outer corners of metal.

Now get an iron, or mild steel punch with a round end about ½ diameter of tube ; grip it in a vice, place tube over end, as in sketch, and hammer lightly, keeping back edge of hole pressed hard up against the bar so as to form lip on bottom of the ventilator. Keep the tube working from side to side, and work gradually out towards the end ; lower the left hand all the time so as to throw the end of tube over and thus form the mouth. The proportions should be, I think, mouth = 1½ tube. It is an advantage to use a larger diameter punch as mouth grows larger.

To produce a bell mouth, take a thin washer, with the hole a little less than the mouth of the ventilator you are making, place the washer over the hole, which should be about half outside diameter of the washer ; put a round bar a little larger in diameter than the hole in the washer in the centre and give the bar a blow with a hammer. This will force centre down and outside up. Then solder into the mouth of ventilator. It will now only need a little trimming up to be a really presentable job.

I have devised this method as a result of last month's notes on the subject, and I think that if " Hawsepipe " uses this method, with a few inches of ⅜″ or ½″ copper tube and a half an hour's spare time, he will produce exactly what he requires.

Yours truly,

Somerset.   J. E. LANG.

TO CORRESPONDENTS.—We have to acknowledge several interesting letters which are unavoidably held over through pressure on our space this month. We hope to use them in our next issue.—ED. S. AND S. M.

Model Galleon Building

READERS who are interested in decorative ship modelling will appreciate the facilities for this class of work offered by Beverley Crafts (Dept. S), 27 Albert Street, Birmingham. They supply three complete outfits for building the *Santa Maria*, *La Bona Esperanza*, and the *Golden Hind* respectively. The sets include the hull completely assembled with fittings, and all the materials and details necessary for rigging and finishing. Even paints and brushes and an instructive handbook are included. Beverley Crafts also supply outfits for modelling a 17th century cannon, and a 17th century Sedan chair. Model ship fittings and materials are separately catalogued in their list of outfits and supplies, which may be obtained post free for 1½d. stamp.

The Ship Lovers' Association

PARTICULARS of membership were given in full in the September issue of SHIPS AND SHIP MODELS.

Regular fortnightly meetings of members in London and the home counties, every other one a dinner, followed by papers, have been held every winter, and it is now suggested that these shall be on the first and third Tuesdays of every month, so that visiting members from the country or abroad may know and make their arrangements in advance. The rendezvous is the Admiral's Cabin Restaurant, 167, Strand, where a remarkable collection of ship models has long attracted a number of ship enthusiasts.

Hon. Secretary, *pro tem.* : Mr. Frank C. Bowen, Customs' House Buildings, Milton Place, Gravesend.

Members' Queries and Answers

H.M. (Felixstowe).—The Cunard *Asia* and *Africa* were sisters, built in 1850, wooden paddlers of 2,226 tons, both from R. Steele's yard at Greenock. Their speed was in the neighbourhood of 12 knots and they burned about 76 tons of coal per day, which worked out at nearly 4 lbs. per i.h.p. per hour. The *Asia* held the Blue Riband with 9 days 14 hours between Boston and Liverpool, and also with 10 days 11 hours 30 minutes from Liverpool to New York. They were both taken off the Cunard Service in 1867, after which the *Africa* became a floating barracks at Liverpool during the Fenian trouble, and the *Asia* was converted into a sailing ship, to be burned at Bombay in 1878.

C.G. (London).—The Ducal Line was officially the Eastern Steamship Co. of London, and was founded in the early 'seventies with a fleet all named after Dukes. The *Duke of Devonshire* (1873) was the first liner built by Messrs. Vickers under contract. Finally, the company was taken over by J. B. Westray and Co.,

and its last ship, the *Duke of Norfolk,* of 1889, was sold in 1905 to become the German *Marellus*.

R.S.M. (Newfoundland).—The *Isabella Ridley* was a barque built at Greenock in 1858 for Ridley, Son and Co., 233 tons. Under Captain R. Bulley she traded between the Clyde and Liverpool and Newfoundland until 1870. She was sold to M. Jones, of London, about 1871, W. Tod and Co. in 1873, and W. Guthrie, of Dunedin, New Zealand, in 1875, being wrecked two years later. The *Kelpie* was originally another Ridley vessel, a 176-ton brig, built at Bridport in 1851. She was sold to Quebec in 1863 for the transatlantic trade and drops out of the 1870 Lloyd's Register.

G.N. (London).—You will probably find all you want in " Ships and Shipping," by E. P. Harnack, published last year by Alexander Moring, Ltd. Another book of the same name was published in two shilling volumes by Nelsons' before the War. It contained a mass of information, some of which is still current, and copies ought to be obtainable on the second-hand market.

Home-made Castings for Model Ship Fittings.

A CORRESPONDENT asks for information on making whitemetal castings for small-scale ships' fittings. He writes :—

" I am desirous of producing whitemetal castings in reasonable quantity, consisting of such items as model cannon, anchors, fairleads, bollards, etc., and shall be glad of information which will enable me to do this. I have already experimented with plaster of paris moulds and " printers' pie," but I find that after three or four castings have been made in a mould, the mould begins to break away at the edges and the castings are very rough. What is the best white-metal alloy to use, and where can it be obtained ? "

Northern Notes

By "JASON"

This column has been allocated by the Editor to model-making notes of interest to all in the English Northern Counties, Scotland and Ireland. It will be conducted by "Jason," who at all times is eager to help model makers generally and particularly in club formation, queries on Northern craft, exhibitions, and competitions.

To Northern Readers

WHEN I was first invited to conduct "Northern Notes" by the Editor I was already aware that there are hundreds of enthusiastic model makers in the North working individually with all the handicaps to be found in such circumstances.

What model shall I make? is a problem not easily answered. Where shall I find my details? very often means that the conscientious worker gives up in despair. Even if this obstacle be surmounted it is seldom indeed that one person is equally at ease in fashioning the hull, making the sails, rigging the model and making the deck fittings. Only recently I was the means of bringing together two men who for years lived within a few hundred yards of each other. Both were model makers, but their models suffered in finish. One was clever at hull and deck fittings, and the other was quite expert in rigging. Now they are joyfully working on each other's models. Their joint work is a delight. It may be that only a few streets away there is someone just as keen as you are on model making. Obviously you should know each other. It will be mutually advantageous to discuss your work and your problems.

At the Mersey-side Club

I had the privilege of attending a meeting of the Merseyside Ship Model Makers' Club recently. Nearly 30 members were present. No sooner had I entered than the Secretary introduced himself. A few pleasant questions and I was introduced to a group of members who specialise in my chosen "period of ships." In conversation with the Chairman later, I found out that plans are well advanced for the formation of ship model makers' clubs in Manchester and Hull. In this, I was invited to co-operate. Accordingly, I shall be glad to hear from anyone in the Manchester and Hull districts who would lend their support to the formation of a club in their own district. Letters should be addressed to " Jason," c/o The Editor, SHIPS AND SHIP MODELS. It is not without interest to note that on the occasion of my visit to the Liverpool Club there were several members present who had journeyed from Manchester.

Bury (Lancs.) Model Competition

A three-shilling model competition forms one of the items in the Great Sailor Exhibition and Fair, to be held in the Drill Hall, Bury, December 3rd to 8th, 1931. Unfortunately this issue will not be out in time to give readers an opportunity of entering, but the conditions are similar to the Shipping Week Model Competition, which was such a successful part of the Shipping Week Exhibition held in St. George's Hall, Liverpool, last August. My impressions of this coming Exhibition, which is being organised by the Missions to Seamen, will appear in our next issue.

To my correspondents

Will readers please note that any questions to be dealt with in this column must reach the Editor of SHIPS AND SHIP MODELS not later than the 10th of the previous month. A stamped and addressed envelope must be enclosed where a reply by post is required.

SHIPS AND SHIP MODELS

A Magazine for all Lovers of Ships and the Sea

Editorial and Publishing Offices:

Single Copies, post free, **7½d.**
Annual Subscription **7s. 6d.**

66 FARRINGDON STREET
L O N D O N :: E. C. 4

Vol. I. No. 5.   JANUARY, 1932.   Price 6d.

The Ship's Log

Clipper Ship Modelling

CAPTAIN E. Armitage McCann is known to every American ship-modeller, and to many in our own country, not only as a great enthusiast for authentic models, but as an authority on their detail. He has now completed Volume II of his series of works on Ship Model Making, and this has just been published by The Norman W. Henley Publishing Co. of New York. It is entitled " How to Make a Model of an American Clipper Ship," the prototype selected for description being the *Sovereign of the Seas*. This famous clipper was launched in 1852, and at that time was the largest sailing ship afloat. She is reputed to have been one of the most beautiful vessels built by Donald McKay. Her story is told at some length in one of the early chapters of the book, and the builder of the model will doubtless take a keener interest in his work, with his imagination fired by the adventurous record of this fine ship. Captain McCann has written this book for the beginner in the sense that no previous knowledge of ship construction or of ship modelling is

assumed, but, at the same time, the model described is sufficiently accurate and complete to be worth the attention of the advanced craftsman. It is important to observe that the whole of the book is devoted to the building of this one model. After some general hints and definitions, and some notes on tools and materials, the reader is taken step by step through the work of building and rigging, starting with setting out the lines of the hull and finishing with the hoisting of the flag. Each detail is separately described and illustrated, and the work of assembling carefully explained. Two full-size plates are included with the book, one giving the lines of the hull very clearly and fully set out, and the other the arrangement of the masts, yards, and rigging. This is an ideal book for the beginner who desires to model a clipper ship, but feels some doubt about his ability to master the intricate detail of such a craft. He need hesitate no longer with such a guide before him. Captain McCann is to be congratulated on the thorough manner in which his very practical lesson in ship-modelling is presented.

Realising that this book would make a strong appeal to many of our readers, we have obtained a small stock of copies from the publishers, and can supply them at 15s. each, the present exchange equivalent of the published price of 2 dols. 50 cts. Sixpence extra should be enclosed for copies ordered by post.

*   *   *

The Oldest Vessels Afloat

We are sure our readers will be interested in the further notes on this subject, which we are able to give this month through the courtesy of several correspondents. When we hear of big Atlantic and other liners being scrapped, almost in the prime of life, because modern developments in speed, and tonnage, and luxury equipment, have rendered them obsolete according to present-day standards, it is refreshing to hear of some of the smaller veterans of the sea which are still running and still apparently managing to pay their way. Indeed, some of the records revealed in our notes are really amazing. Mr. T. R. Beaufort, who kindly sent us the picture of the *Good Intent*, also sent for our inspection an advertisement of the sailings of this old vessel. She

is therein described as " The first Hoy for Dover," and is announced to take in goods and passengers for Dover and other places along the South Coast as far as Romney and Barham. She lay at Brewer's and Chester's Quay, Custom House. The master was James Shuttle, and the owner Thomas Chester. Several correspondents have called our attention to the claims of the paddle-steamer *Premier* of Weymouth. Some data are given elsewhere in this issue, but we are glad to be able to reproduce the accompanying photograph of this vessel through the courtesy of Mr. H. A. Allen, of Brighton. The picture was taken as recently as September last.   *   *   *

Royal United Service Models

The Museum at the Royal United Service Institution contains some of the finest examples of ship modelling we have in this country. We are pleased to inform our readers that Captain E. Altham, R.N., the Secretary of the Institution, has very kindly sent us some excellent photographs of the principal sailing-ship models in the Museum, together with an informative article on the history of the models. We hope to publish this interesting matter in our next issue.

The oldest Steamboat afloat—The " Premier " of Weymouth

The "Charles W. Morgan"

THE LAST OF THE NEW ENGLAND WHALERS

By DOUGLAS DIXON

The New England Whaler " Charles W. Morgan "

AMONG the many pleasant days spent in New England before the start of the Trans-Atlantic race, it is difficult to differentiate, but the two of most interest were undoubtedly those spent in a really fully-rigged and fully-found ship through the kindness of Mr. Grinnel, of South Dartmouth. Such is the *Charles W. Morgan*, although admittedly her hull is never likely to be waterborne again, for though the Atlantic may sometimes wash her water-line, her underbody is secure in concrete on the sandy shore.

Last of the famous New Bedford whalers, she was enshrined by the forethought of Colonel Green on the shores of what is now the Colonel's private air-port. A very modern and efficiently-equipped station in strange contrast to the old timbers of a past age, be they never so smartly kept. Hetty Green, mother of the Colonel, is reputed to have strictly economised in all and everything, including laundry, for she would only pander to the second of the virtues in allowing the hem of her petticoat to be washed.

To cleanse the remainder would, to her, have been an extravagance. May she rest the better for the fortune she amassed, allowing of the preservation of this fine old ship, and all she means to those whose eyes are gladdened by the sight of sticks and string.

The Nantucket industry for the capture of the ocean mammals, particularly the sperm or cachalot, opened in 1712, and the *Morgan* was built in 1841, when the game was at its height and there were well over seven hundred vessels employed. One hundred and eight feet overall, about three hundred tons burthen, bluff bowed, and ship rigged, she followed the way of the whale for more than the allotted span of man before she was saved from the usual " knacker's way " with old ships in 1926.

When the wind is light and fair she still sets the canvas, which may be seen bent in the photographs. Full-rigged to royals with old-time single tops'ls, the great hoist of the tops'l yard is worth noting, every halyard, clew and bunt lin', brace and sheet, is ready rove and kept to its own pin. Whale boats, gripped to, but otherwise already " for to lower." Oars, irons, whale line in its tubs and " foregoer " (the first light part of the line which is thrown by the harpoon hand), even the knife in its sheath on the little foredeck is in its place handy to the bowman in case " he sounds "

The " Charles W. Morgan "—Bow view

beyond the 600-fathcm limit of the line and would tow the hunter under. Between the main and fore, under the spar deck is the blubber cauldron with rousing irons and dippers. From the starboard main top the heavy " cant purchase " can be seen already rove as it would be when turning over the huge carcass brought alongside for " flensing."

Below, her main body is open from focsle to cabin flat and galley, while under the main deck the space is filled with hogsheads waiting oil. In the saloon her last " Articles " are framed. Under Captain Filton she carried 37 souls all told, including the master and his assistant pilot, Mrs. Filton, as she was then signed on.

Starboard aft is the master's berth, and contains a very homely double-bed, all made and slung from gymbals. A cumbrous piece of furniture, which it would be ungracious to grudge the master and his good lady when it is remembered that these ships rarely kept the sea for less than three years to a voyage.

Though the crow's nest on her fore to'-gallant mast may never again resound with the cry of " thar she blows ! " her main truck daily flies the

The " Charles W. Morgan "—Stern view

House Flag of one or other of the Whaling Companies. Long may she live in rest, and may it prove true that the *Cutty Sark*, in Falmouth Harbour, will be seen again with cloths aloft to delight the visiting Yankee's eye, as much as *Charles W. Morgan* delighted mine.

Mr. J. Sagar, 16, Liley Street, Higher Crumpsall, Manchester, would like to get in touch with other readers in his neighbonrhood who are interested in ships.

The " Mary Penhale "

A Model of an Australian Wool Clipper Ship

By J. D. ATTWOOD

THE *Mary Penhale* represents a type of iron clipper-ship built about 1875 for the Australian wool trade. Of such were the " Bens " and " Lochs " and many others. As I had no deck plan of any of these ships, I cannot claim her to be an exact model of any special vessel. The scale is 24' to 1", so she would be 240' long, 38' beam and 21' deep. She is full-rigged, with double topgallants on all masts. I had a sail and rigging plan of the *Ben Voirlich* (built 1873), with length of yards and masts given, in Mr. Basil Lubbock's " Colonial Clippers," and these I used, reducing them proportionately, as the *Mary Penhale* is 240' long and the *Ben Voirlich* 255'.

I am a marine engineer ; so much of the model has been made at sea. I started in 1928, and have worked on and off ever since. The scale was decided by the thickness of the piece of teak I found (?) from which to construct the hull. She measures 10¼" from figurehead to taffrail. I shaped the hull mostly by filing. The topgallant forecastle and poop are screwed on separately, and the bulwarks are cut from strips of teak and let into the forecastle and poop and secured by screws and liquid glue. I then marked off the position of masts and where all the shrouds and backstays would come, giving her the same number as the *Ben Voirlich*. I then made the lower masts out of a piece of ash and stepped them, also the bowsprit. Then set up the shrouds and fore and aft stays ; these were of gut, part of a fishing-line. I then put the ratlines on, a tedious job ; it took ages ; they are made of cotton stranded out as thin as I could manage. Afterwards I made topmasts and topgallant masts, and set them up. Then came the yards, also made of ash. The mast caps and crosstrees are cut out of brass ; the iron bands of the yards, jackstays, and yard trusses are made of thin wire, as also are the foot ropes under the yards.

The details of the rigging I found out from looking at sailing ships, also from the South Kensington Museum models, and from Kipping's " Masting and Rigging."

Next, I started making deck fittings and painted them with Joy's cellulose enamel, and put them on. But I had an awful job getting them in, because of all the rigging ; I ought to have put the deck fitting in first. The deckhouses, boats and skylights, etc., are made of boxwood. There are two deckhouses, the forward one would contain the petty officers' cabins and the galley ; the after one for the apprentices. Four boats, which I hollowed with drills and a knife and files, shaping the outside afterwards. They are easier to hold in a vice if unfinished outside while the hollowing is in progress. The handrail stanchions are of banjo string, very thin, but hard steel wire, with still finer copper wire stretched across them. When painted this wire sticks to the stanchions very well. The anchors and pump wheels are cut out of brass. The boss of the steering wheel is boxwood ; the rim is a section cut from a vulcanite fountain pen-holder. Holes are drilled through and wire forms the spokes. The scroll work is twisted brass wire.

The figurehead is Mary Penhale, a character from the late Crosbie Garstin's book, " The West Wind," and was filed out, being part of the forecastle. The anchor cables are of copper wire, in which are a series of hitches which look like the links of a chain.

The lower braces are of insulated copper wire, which is just about the colour of rope. The topgallant and royal braces are of the same wire with the insulation off, as they have to be finer than the lower ones. The blocks are of sections of lead wire with holes pushed through with a needle. They were difficult to make, especially the smaller ones. Rigging the braces needed patience, especially the mizzen ones, which came forward to the main mast and became all muddled up with the main braces which lead to the mizzen.

The flags are of paper—painted.

Then I painted the hull with Joy's cellulose enamel—black topsides with painted ports, and grey under them to the waterline ; from the waterline to the keel, dark green. I made a wooden pattern for the sea, which was cut out of green glass for me by the firm from which I bought it. Putting her in a sea shows up the sheer, I think, and gives the model life.

The later stages have been done at home. On the main mast, the flag, which is divided diagonally, the upper portion yellow, the lower blue, is a copy of the one flown by my great-grandfather, who was a sea captain, commanding Guernsey vessels in the foreign trade.

In my last ship, an oil-tanker, the cook said the model looked a little lady, and as ladies were held by him in high esteem, I took it as a great compliment. He wanted me to carve out a figure of the cook sitting outside the galley, peeling potatoes. But I had had such a struggle trying to make the figurehead the shape of a human being, that I decided not to attempt carving a representation of a sailing ship's cook.

(This model was awarded the special Cup for the best sailing ship model at the recent *Model Engineer* Exhibition.—ED., S. and S.M.)

Did You Know ?

Beakheads were discarded in favour of rounded bows in 1811 ?

Compass or sailing needle was used in the 16th century ?

Chain cables date from 1811, but hemp cables are still carried ?

Chain plates were on a level with main deck until 1705, when they were removed to upper deck by the French and Dutch ?

Lion figureheads which were used in the 16th and 17th centuries were, in 1703, made official M.O.W. Badge for 1st Rates, which hitherto had borne an equestrian statue of reigning monarch. Near the end of the 18th century full-length figures emblematic of ship names were used until Nelson mode of painting came in, when plain white bust or three-quarter length figure was used ?

Great ship, or galleon, was three beams to length ?

Hammocks were issued at the end of the 16th century ?

The old round top for masts went out at the beginning of the 18th century ?

Nelson's ships were painted black, with wide streak of bright yellow along gun-tiers, with port lids painted black; after peace was declared the yellow band gave way to white ?

Rudders came into use during the Plantagenet period, the 13th-14th centuries ?

Round sterns were introduced by Sir Robert Seppings in place of square transom stern in 1820.

Stern galleries were universal during the 18th century ; triple tier in 1st Rates in 90-gun ships, and single tier for 74- and 64-gun ships ?

Decorated sails went out at the close of Elizabeth's reign ?

Steering wheel first used not earlier than 1703, not later than 1747 ? The Science Museum Handbook gives 1715.

Yard-arms were provided with iron hooks or sickles for cutting rigging in the Elizabethan period ?

The Model Australian Wool Clipper " Mary Penhale "

Ship Models in Bottles

A Curious Branch of the Shipmodeller's Art

HISTORY does not record who first conceived the idea of putting a model ship into a bottle, but for many years this ingenious trick has found both followers and admirers, particularly among sailor-men. Its experiments vary very much in their imagination and their skill. The great majority of bottle models are rather crude in their conception and execution, and possibly this is not to be wondered at in view of the forecastle conditions under which many of them have been made. The horny hands of " limejuice Jack " and the crude tools and materials at his disposal, are not conducive to the delicacy of craftsmanship which the real shipmodeller likes to see. He has probably been more concerned with the amusement of making a freak model which will excite wonderment in the eyes of the beholder, and bring him a few shillings at the end of the voyage.

Here and there, however, one may come across a real gem of craftsmanship among these bottle models, and when such an example is discovered, it is worth acquiring. Mr. Fred C. Poyser is fortunate enough to own two particularly good models of this kind and has kindly supplied us with the following details.

A French Five-masted Barque

This model, shown in the accompanying photograph, was on view at the recent *Model Engineer* Exhibition.

It was evidently made by a Frenchman, as she is flying the French flag under full sail, in that she has six square sails on each of the four forward masts, two staysails between each mast, three jibs, spanker and gaff topsail. These sails are made of a kind of cartridge paper and are well set and not crumpled. The hull is about 6″ long overall, and in addition, the jib-boom is another ¾″ or so ; it is a spike boom and carries no dolphin striker. She is set in a slight putty sea, but so made that the tops of the masts are hard up against the bottle, so that she cannot get adrift. The masts are all in one piece, no pretension to topmasts or top-gallant masts, neither are there any tops or cross trees, but the lower rigging and backstays are very complete, though no ratlines on the former.

The hull is painted black, the upper part being covered with yellow silk, white water-line and red boot-topping. Taking the deck from forward, she has cat-heads but no anchors, and on the forecastle head she has a capstan, skylight, and two lighthouse towers,

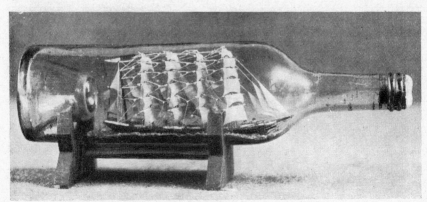

A Model French Five-Masted Barque in a bottle

whilst the rail round is made of silk. Next comes the foremast and then a house, abaft this the main-mast and another house with skylight on top, then the midship section with the mizzen-mast in the middle of it, also a skylight and two donkey boilers with funnels on the after end ; running the length of it, on both sides, is a rail worked in silk, similar to that on the forecastle head and also round the poop. Next comes the jiggermast and then a house with two boats on top, and then the aftermast, set in the fore end of the poop, with skylight and wheelbox abaft it. Every brace, even the royal and topgallant, which seems a pity, is fitted with brace pennants and beads for blocks, and everything is set up tight, nothing being crude or

Mr. E. Tebb's bottle model

" heavy." The forward house evidently had two small boats on it at one time, as in the extreme end of the bottle are two which have evidently fallen off.

It is not a model of any special ship, though the maker evidently had the first *France* in mind when he made it ; the second vessel of this name was also a five-masted barque, but had not been launched when the bottle came into my possession ; in fact, when I bought it in Bordeaux, I could see this ship on the stocks on the other side of the river.

The bottle is just an ordinary wine-bottle.

The " Bankfields " Model

The other model I have, says Mr. Poyser, is not so picturesque, but is,

Fig. 1. The hull in the bottle neck   Fig. 2. Mast hinges made from screws

I think, really a fine piece of work. It is of a different character, as it shows a three-masted barque at anchor. This one is also interesting, as it is a model of a particular ship, the *Bankfields* ex-*James Beazley*, built at Sunderland in 1876 and, in order to get the proportions right, it is in an oval bottle.

The hull is 6″ long, but she has the old-fashioned flying jib-boom and bowsprit, which adds another 2½″ or thereabouts, and this is fitted with a dolphin striker and is properly rigged. The masts, though actually in one piece, are beautifully carved to represent the lower, topmasts and topgallantmasts, and are fitted with tops and cross trees, the corresponding rigging being complete, with the exception that it has not been rattled down. On the forecastle head is a capstan and the catheads, abaft the foremast is a house with two boats on the fore end and galley funnel on the after end, whilst all the doors and ports are carefully recessed. Next comes the main hatch, the mainmast, and then the after skids with lifeboats after, hatch poop with skylight, wheelbox, wheel and binnacle.

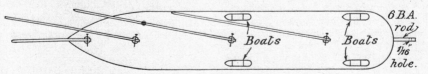

Fig. 3. Diagram showing arrangement of masts on deck.

The rigging of this model is exceptionally good, and the brace blocks are really fine examples of how small a block can be made. Like the other, everything here is set up taut, and the masts and yards are beautifully proportioned. The only fault I can see is that the neck of the bottle has been cut a bit short, which is, I think, a pity, and also the glass is not of good quality.

How to Make a Bottle Model

We are indebted to Mr. Ernest Tebb, another bottle-model enthusiast, for the following notes on a model of a sailing barque, in the South-East trades, of the period about 1850. He writes:—

" I selected a Haig and Haig whisky bottle to hold the model. A start was made on the hull, which was cut from a piece of mahogany 1″ square and 4″ long, care being taken while making this to see that the hull did not take more than half of the bottle-neck. At the same time enough space was left at either side, the thickness of a pinhead (see Fig. 1), as pins, cut short, were used as deadeyes for shrouds and back-stays.

" The four hinges to swing the masts on were made from No. 4BA screws, cuts in the top sawn to $\frac{3}{16}$″ depth, and a $\frac{1}{64}$″ hole bored in each for pegs. (See Fig. 2.) These were then screwed on to the deck. The masts were made from a length of $\frac{1}{8}$″ dia. wood and shaped. A $\frac{1}{64}$″ hole was bored at the bottom of each. The mast was filed at each side, then fitted into the hinges, and pegs were put in, made from pins. Hinges were screwed on the deck slightly askew, so that when the masts were let down they lay side by side by doing this. (See Fig. 3.) I thus gained a little more room for rigging.

" The deck rails were made from pins cut short and connected together with 15-amp. fuse wire. The sails were made from cigarette papers, as also were the flags on top of masts. The method of fixing is shown in Fig. 4 ; No. 36 cotton was used in the rigging.

" I then bored a $\frac{1}{64}$″ hole at one end in a $\frac{3}{4}$″ length of 6BA rod and screwed the other end in the stern of the hull. I fixed an extra-strong length of cotton from mast to mast, then down through the hole in the rod at the stern, leaving about 1′ spare to pull the masts up with after the ship went through the neck.

" The bottom corner of the spanker sail was fixed to the strong cotton just before it went through the hole in the rod. The masts and rigging were now pushed down on to the

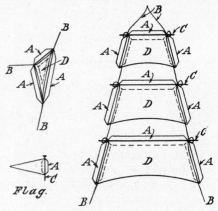

A - Gummed flaps. B - Cotton.
C - Pins.   D - Sails.

Fig. 4. Method of fixing the sails

deck ; by doing this I found room for four lifeboats, two at the stern and two in the middle of the deck.

" The lighthouse was made from the tapered part of a paint-brush handle, top part of a wireless terminal, small clock pinion wheel, and a wooden screw. The sea was made from putty-coloured with Reckitt's blue and green paint mixed. I first put the putty in the bottle a little at a time, care being taken so that sides of the bottle were not smeared. To get the rough-sea effect, I chopped the putty with a length of stiff wire. Being now ready for the lighthouse, I tied it lengthwise to a stick with cotton that broke easily, and pushed it through the neck to the far end of the bottle. Then I took another stick to push the light-house upright, making the cotton break, and bedding the lighthouse into the putty.

" I next took the ship and made sure that nothing would foul as I pulled the masts up once the ship was inside the bottle. Then I held a stick against the stern and pulled the spare cotton till the masts were upright. I dipped a stick in glue to fill the hole in the 6BA rod where the cotton came through, left it to dry, and then cut spare cotton away with a penknife."

Freak Channel Packets of the late 'Seventies

By E. P. HARNACK

IN order to eliminate as far as possible some of the terrors of sea-sickness, several freak vessels of unusual and novel features in design were introduced in the late 'seventies for the Dover-Calais service. Firstly, there was the *Bessemer*, built by Earle's of Hull, in 1874, to the designs of Sir E. J. Reid, Chief Constructor of the Navy. She had a length of 350', a gross tonnage of 1,974, and her engines of 4,600 h.p. were designed to drive her at a speed of 15 knots. The *Bessemer* had a swinging saloon suspended on gimbals, and two pairs of paddle wheels. The saloon measured 70' in length by 35' in width, and weighed 140 tons. It was worked by hydraulic power, intended to keep it in a horizontal position when a rolling motion was set up by the vessel in a seaway. The pitching motion was somewhat mitigated by giving her a low freeboard at the bows, which tended to make her cut through the waves instead of rising over them. In practice, however, these devices were a complete failure, and on her trial run to Calais, she rolled in an alarming manner, whilst those unfortunate enough to be in the saloon, were subjected to a particularly violent and uncomfortable motion. She was, in consequence, withdrawn after a very short career and broken up in 1879.

The *Castalia*, constructed with demi-hulls securely welded together, with two sets of paddle wheels working between the hulls, also made her appearance in 1874. She was built by the Thames Ironworks Co., Black-wall, for the English Channel Steamship Company, formed in 1872 for the purpose of running her. Her dimensions were 290' in length by 60' extreme breadth, and she had a gross tonnage of 1,533. It is recorded that there were but few people who travelled in her who suffered any discomfort, but she was lamentably deficient in speed, and it is doubtful whether she ever attained 10 knots, her designed speed, and because of this she was withdrawn from service in 1876. For many years she was used as a smallpox hospital and stationed off Gravesend, and was finally broken up in Holland, in 1907.

Lastly, as a result of the experience gained in the *Castalia*, the *Calais-Douvres* was constructed in 1877 with two complete hulls welded together. Her builders were A. Leslie and Co., Hebburn-on-Tyne. She had a gross tonnage of 1,925, a length of 302', and a total beam of 61'. On trials she attained a speed of 14 knots, after which she was purchased by the London Chatham and Dover Railway for the sum of £93,000. The *Calais-Douvres* proved herself an excellent sea-boat and was very popular with cross-Channel passengers, but on account of her unwieldy shape and bad steering qualities, she was a difficult ship to handle. Also, owing to her heavy coal consumption—as much as 35 tons being normally consumed for the double trip—she was a costly vessel to operate. She remained in service until 1887, and in 1896 became a coal hulk at Tilbury. She was broken up in 1899.

Notable Ships Past and Present

No. III.—THE HAMBURG-AMERICAN " COLUMBIA "

THE Hamburg - American Liner *Columbia* is one of the old ships of the Atlantic Ferry that is particularly interesting to the student and model maker for a variety of reasons. For one thing she was a remarkably good-looking ship, for another she was one of the last of the many German express liners built in England before the determination of Count Bismarck to encourage the German shipyards had its full effect, and finally she had an extremely mixed and interesting career for an Atlantic liner.

Until she was built at Laird's yard at Birkenhead in 1889, the Hamburg-American Line had generally been contented with the cargo and emigrant business and had left the cream of the express passenger trade to the North German Lloyd, but now they determined to compete for that business as well, and built a number of ships in British and German yards, ships that were slightly faster than their Bremen rivals and had the advantage of twin screws.

The *Columbia* was a particularly good-looking vessel with three funnels and three pole masts, not looking anything like her gross tonnage of 7,363, which is the greatest compliment that can be paid to a naval architect. She was propelled by two 3-cylinder triple-expansion engines supplied by nine double-ended boilers, and in order to get her designed horse-power of 12,500 for a speed of 19 knots, it was necessary to take a very large proportion of her length for her engines and boilers, which seriously cut down her earning capacity, as there was little room for cargo, although she had a very fair passenger accommodation in all three classes.

She was the biggest ship that the Birkenhead shipbuilders had ever attempted up to that day, with the result that they thought it safer not to risk a slipway and built her in dry dock instead, floating her out when she was ready. As soon as she went on service she became popular and, on her maiden voyage, gained the Eastward Blue Riband on the Channel route by a time of 6 days 4 hours to Queenstown. After a few months' service she was fitted with new propellers and then won the Channel record in both directions, although she was later beaten by some of her consorts.

The North German Lloyd did not enter into the record again until 1897 with the famous *Kaiser Wilhelm der Grosse*, and, in the following year, the *Columbia* and her consort, the *Normannia*, were sold to the Spanish Navy to act as auxiliary cruisers during the Spanish-American War. She was re-named *Rapido* and was provided with a powerful battery of four 6.3, four 4.7 and six smaller guns, but unfortunately she was not ready for sea in time to go to the Westward with *Cervera*. Towards the end of the war she was attached to the Spanish Reserve Squadron, which left Cadiz in an attempt to win back the Philippine Islands, but it only got as far as Suez when the war was obviously hopeless and the squadron returned to Spain. Having no further use for the *Columbia* as a man-of-war, the Navy sold her back to the Hamburg-American Line, who incidentally did very well out of the deal, and she returned to their commercial service under her old name.

The Hapag had another opportunity of selling her during the Russo-Japanese War in 1904, when the Russian Government was lamentably short of cruisers and purchased several German liners, doing it through the Russian Volunteer Fleet in order to evade unpleasant consequences under the neutrality law. She fetched

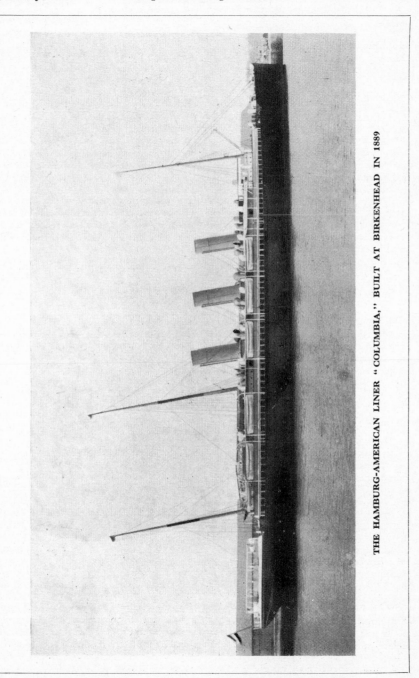

THE HAMBURG-AMERICAN LINER "COLUMBIA," BUILT AT BIRKENHEAD IN 1889

£200,000 which, considering her age and size, was a remarkably good price and, after a short interval, hoisted the pennant as a Russian man-of-war under the name of *Terek*. Like-many of the other auxiliary cruisers under that flag, she began by making herself very unpopular by stopping neutral merchantmen on the very vaguest suspicion of having anything to do with the war, capturing the steamer *Margit Grodal* off Cape St. Vincent, but having to release her almost immediately.

She went out to the East with Rojhdestvensky's ill-fated Baltic Fleet, and when they approached the Japanese coast she and her consort, the *Kuban*, were sent to make a demonstration on the East Coast of Japan in order to make Togo think that the Russian Fleet would be going that way round. Unfortunately her people were not very keen on the job and, instead of making themselves plainly visible, they took every care to keep out of the sight of the Japanese, who accordingly waited for the Russian ships in the Tsushima Straits and annihilated them.

She contrived to miss the battle and seek safety in a neutral port, but after that the Russian Navy had no use for her, and the Russian Volunteer Fleet still less, with the result that she was kept practically idle until the summer of 1907, when she was sold to Messrs. Wards, the well-known shipbreakers, for £21,000, and broken up at Preston, on the Ribble.

Model Making Hints

In the December issue I see a reader has difficulty in making moulds for casting, from plaster of paris, owing to the edges breaking away. I should suggest that he try mixing a little asbestos fibre with the plaster ; this helps to bind it together, and also makes it more heat-resisting. I have not tried it for small and repeated castings myself, but it is an old dodge in the dental workroom, and may help.

Another point is on coiling down the faces of halliards, etc. I have found that by moistening the free ends with a little seccotine, either " neat " or in solution, they can be made to lie practically as they are wanted right away, and it is quite invisible. Another use for this most helpful dope is in putting on whippings, etc., for instance, in fitting blocks on pendants, etc. It is very annoying to find that the cotton will not lie closely, and very difficult when working with " flabby " cord to make a nice job of them. I have found that a dab of seccotine rubbed in with the fingers makes the cotton " stay put," and the end of it tucked through the cord and cut off flush makes a very neat job. Again, when weaving the lanyards for deadeyes, I found my patience and temper sorely tried until I hit on the idea of cutting them to length and doping the ends with seccotine. This is allowed to set and then the ends cut obliquely with a very sharp blade, when they will be found to weave with comparative ease.

I am at present engaged in rigging a full-rigged ship which I picked up in a very dilapidated state as to rigging, in a second-hand shop. I hope to send photographs when I have her completed.

I have made one of the lifeboats, clinker built in the approved style, from strips of paper. I made a plaster model first, covered that with paper in one piece, cut to shape, and then laid in the " planks," sticking them down one by one. Stem, sternpost and keel were of card, also rubbing strake and thwarts, ribs and bottom boards paper and gunwale built up of paper. The whole has had three coats of white and looks very well. I should not recommend it, however, to anyone who dislikes finnicky work.

—OWEN R. WICKSTEED.

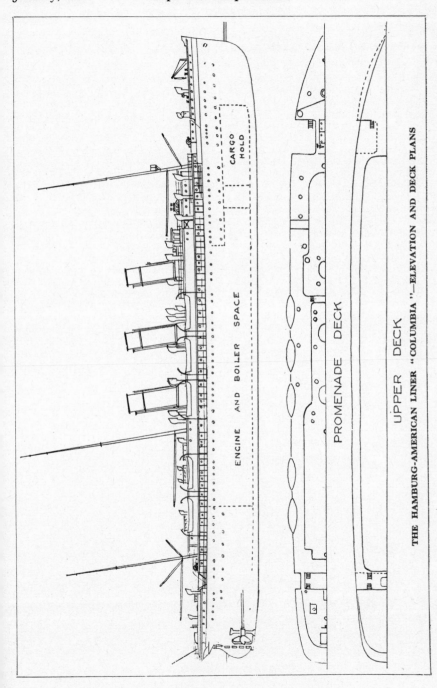

CARGO HOLD

ENGINE AND BOILER SPACE

PROMENADE DECK

UPPER DECK

THE HAMBURG-AMERICAN LINER "COLUMBIA"—ELEVATION AND DECK PLANS

The Oldest Vessels Afloat

THE article published in our last issue has brought us the following interesting replies from readers :—

" The first iron light vessel to be constructed in this country was built by Laird Bros., of Birkenhead, to the order of the Liverpool Dock Trust in 1842, and was named the *Prince*. Her dimensions are 99′ B.P. × 21′ × 11′ ; she is built of Lowmoor iron, and cost £4,810 for the hull only ; her total cost, including all equipment, was £6,110. The *Prince* was used as a Light Vessel until 1896, when she was converted into a Wreck Marking Vessel ; she was sold by the Mersey Docks and Harbour Board in 1926 to Messrs. William Cooper and Sons, Ltd., of Widnes, by whom she is still employed as a sand barge in the Mersey."—J. C. McIVER, A.M.I.MECH.E.

" In Denmark there are some very old wooden vessels afloat, or rather were, because it is 10 years since I left the sea and have never been there since. Still, a newspaper of 1925 says : *Galius Ida* from Thuro, built of oak in 1786, is still afloat in North Atlantic and Mediterranean trade."—CAPT. DIRK VERWEY (Rotterdam).

The following cutting from the *Lennox Herald* establishes the claim of an older steamer than your contributor mentions.—J. C. BURNIE. The cutting reads : " In 1846 my firm built a paddle steamer called the *Premier*. She was built for the Dumbarton Steamboat Company, and records of my firm show that her dimensions were 104′ × 17′ 1″ × 7′, and that her gross tonnage was 127. In the course of 85 years she has probably changed her owners several times, and it is certain that little of the original vessel now remains.

The " Collier "—Built in 1849

Nevertheless, her identity persists. She is now owned by Messrs. Cosens and Co., Ltd., of Weymouth, and I have before me a letter written by them on November 24th, in which they state that she is still going strong, will be running with passengers during the coming season, and that they have no intention of passing her into the hands of the shipbreakers. Until last year it was doubtful whether the *Premier* or the *Glencoe* was the older ship; both were built in 1846, but the *Glencoe* has now passed out of service. The *Premier*, of course, appears in Lloyd's Register, and I think it can truthfully be said that she is the oldest steamboat plying in the world.—MAURICE. E. DENNY.

Several other correspondents quote the claims of the *Premier*, which we illustrate on page 130.

"The *Collier* was an iron three-masted screw steamer of 113 tons net, built in 1849 by J. Reid and Co., Port Glasgow, and lengthened in 1857. I enclose a photograph, which may be of interest."—C. HAWKINS GARRINGTON.

"The *Good Intent*, 38 tons, built at Plymouth in 1790, rigged as a barge in 1870, owned by A. Hubbard of Devon, she was smack-rigged by 1907, when she was converted to ketch rig. In 1907, she was trading continuously between Bridgewater and Cardiff with coal and was still in excellent condition. Her captain was 46 years old and had sailed in her all his life, succeeding his father.

"In 1918, when 128 years old, the *Good Intent* was owned by Mrs. Smart of Bridgewater, and sloop-rigged; she was sold to David Davies of Cardiff for three times her original

The "Good Intent"—built in 1790

cost still in splendid condition. In 1919 she was sold to E. Smith of Cardiff, who sold her to A. Smith of Bristol in 1921 and, in 1926, she was still listed as sloop-rigged."—THOS R. BEAUFORT.

Drawing by]   **The Outgoing Coaster**   [*W. M. Birchall*

The Colouring of Old-Time Ships

WHAT THE WOODEN WALLS REALLY LOOKED LIKE

By A. G. V,

ONE of the first difficulties the model-maker encounters when he sets out to gather material for an old-time ship model is the problem of colour. It is this difficulty which has led many beautiful models of 18th Century ships to appear in the sober black-and-white of the 1840's, or Elizabethan ships to be decorated with carved work or wreathed ports.

The writer has had occasion to go into this question many times, and it occurred to him that a tabulated list of the changes in fashion of warship-painting during the three-and-a-half centuries which principally interest the ship-modeller, together with approximate dates and notes, would be useful to those whose libraries do not include the varied books which have to be consulted to cover the subject adequately.

He therefore compiled the table printed herewith. It must, of course, be understood that the dates given are approximate, since there never was a universal scheme of painting, individual captains having great latitude in details even as late as the middle of the 19th Century.

Tudor ships were painted in bright geometrical patterns above the gun-wale, the colours frequently having a heraldic significance. Green and white, the royal colours, were popular, also red, blue, and black-and-white. Shields, or pavises, were sometimes carried on the fore and after castles. The model of an Elizabethan galleon in the Science Museum shows this method of painting very well indeed.

Carved work instead of painted patterns came in about 1610, the first ship so decorated being the *Prince Royal*. This kind of gilded " gingerbread-work " remained the accepted form of ship-decoration for two hundred years, though curtailed or even suppressed from time to time. Under the Commonwealth the carved work was removed or painted black, but the Restoration brought the gilding back, together with the golden wreaths round the upper-deck gunports which are such a striking characteristic of late 17th Century ships. In 1703 another order abolishing carved work was promulgated, but this was soon a dead letter. By 1712, wreath ports and carved work were as much in evidence as ever.

All through the 16th and 17th Centuries, the hull of the ship, from the lower wales to the gunwale (just above the sills of the upper-deck ports) was not painted at all, but served with a varnish of oil and turpentine. About 1690-1695, it became customary to paint the sides of the ships of the Royal Navy with yellow paint, but some captains never did this, and in any case only one coat of paint was allowed each year. The appearance of one ship, therefore, would differ considerably from that of another, if one had just had her annual coat of paint, whereas the other had eked her's out with many servings of oil and turpentine.

Ships remained very much the same in appearance right up to the end of the 18th Century, except that blue seems to have replaced black on the upper works, only to be replaced by black again about 1775. Wreath-ports died out in the late 1740's.

In the 18th Century, the masts of a warship were treated much the same as the hull-side and appeared as varnished oak. The yards, booms, topgallant-masts, etc., were usually treated with a mixture of oil, turpentine, and lamp-black, which was also used for the wales on the ship's side.

During the French Wars there was a diversity of individual colour-characteristics in ships, although the narrow black lines along the wales,

COLOURING OF WARSHIPS, 1500-1860.

Period.	Hull.	Upper-works.	Interior.	Bottom.
1500-1610	Varnished oak; black wales; port lids as hull.	Geometrical patterns of bright colours.	Red or varnished oak.	White.
1610-1703	Varnished oak; black wales; port lids as hull.	Black or blue; gilded carved work.	Red with gilded carved work.	White.
1703-1745	Yellow or varnished oak; port-lids as hull; black wales.	Black or blue; gilded carved work.	Red.	White.
1745-1775	Yellow or varnished oak; port-lids as hull; black wales.	Blue; gilded carved work.	Red.	White.
1775-1798	Yellow with black wales; sometimes only lower wale black.	Black; gilded or yellow carved work.	Red.	Copper; or white.
1798-1813 (" Nelson Fashion ")	Black with yellow band along each line of ports; port-lids black.	Black; yellow lines on mouldings.	Stone-colour; cabins pale green.	Copper.
1813-1820	Black with yellow band edged with white on each line of ports; lids black.	Black; no lining or carved work.	Stone-colour.	Copper.
1820-1840	Black: white band on each line of ports: thin white line on water-line; black port-lids.	Black; no lining.	Green.	Copper.
1840-1860	Black; white band on each line of ports; red, green or white line on waterline; black port-lids.	Black; no lining.	White; funnel (if any) black.	Copper; or red.

TABLE SHOWING THE COLOURING OF OLD TIME SHIPS

and yellow sides with black upper-works lined in gold was the commonest style. The carved work of the head and quarter-galleries, as well as the stern carved-work, was always picked out in blue and gold, and even in ships painted " Nelson-fashion," the beakhead bulkhead was frequently painted blue and gold.

Some ships in the late 1790's were painted black with red streaks along the line of the gunports, but this style never became general, and was never employed for any ship larger than a frigate. " Nelson-fashion " is first found among the ships which fought at the battle of the Nile, and was always adopted in the fleets there-after commanded by Lord Nelson. This style disregarded the wales, which had hitherto determined the horizontal divisions of ship-painting, and was governed by the lines of the gun-ports, which, of course, ran almost level from stem to stern and cut into the wales where necessary. Nelson's ships were also usually painted stone-colour inside, instead of red, which had hitherto been general, for a practical, if horrible, reason.

During the French Wars, British ships had always had their lower masts whitened before a general action, in order that they might be distin-guished from their opponents, which usually had black masts, though other-wise very similar in colouring to the British vessels.

Some French ships in the Revo-lutionary War were painted blood-red, as the Spanish four-decker, *Santissima Trinidad*, is said to have been at Trafalgar.

After Trafalgar, " Nelson-fashion " became the accepted style of naval painting, although about 1813 a modi-fication was introduced, thin white lines appearing on each side of the yellow streaks. By 1820, white lines had replaced yellow, and the familiar black-and-white appearance, which lasted as long as wooden warships, was reached.

Here are a few points to remember in painting old-time ship-models :—

Remember that when opened, a gun-port lid shows the colour of the *interior*, red or stone-colour.

The black of the lower wale was usually continued down to the water-line where the wale rose aft.

Where the gunports cut into the lower wales, the colour-line cuts across the port lid, too.

When the side is yellow or varnished, the ironwork is black.

Copper-bottoms were first intro-duced into the Navy in 1761, but did not become general until 1785.

Home Made Castings

The following may be of interest to your correspondent :—

Firstly, as regards a suitable white-metal alloy, I think an ordinary solder containing 50% tin and 50% lead, or a harder solder containing 66.6% tin and 33.3% lead, would be very suitable. An equally good mix-ture would be 80% lead, 15% anti-mony and 5% tin. A " type metal," containing 70% lead, 18% antimony, 10% tin and 2% copper, could also be used.

If he were to purchase the tin, lead, etc., separately, he could, by the aid of a set of scales, make his own mixtures. These metals can be pur-chased from a metal merchant. If this method is adopted, melt the tin first, then add the lead, then antimony, and lastly, copper ; use copper-foil or drillings.

As regards his moulds, I think that if he were to smear them with a little thin oil they would stand up better. However, if he intends making a big number of castings, he would be better getting iron moulds. If so, heat the moulds slightly before casting.

A hint in closing : If re-melting old white-metal, drop in a small piece of tallow ; this brings all scum to the top.—DANIEL MORRISON.

The Ship Modeller's Scrap Book
A DICTIONARY OF SHIP DETAILS IN ALL PERIODS.
(Continued from page 122)

Cable

BEFORE the days of chain for anchor work, the thick hemp cable was one of the curses of the sailing ship, for not only had it to be very carefully looked after, but the immense space that it occupied did much to limit the voyages of the ships

Hemp Cable as bent to Bower Anchor

by cutting down the space available for stores, etc. When the anchor cable was too thick to go round the capstan conveniently a MESSENGER was rigged, an endless rope to which the cable was made fast with short strops named NIPS, the custom of calling a smart boy a nipper being due to the fact that it was always the smartest boys in the ship who were given the job of making fast these nips forward and casting them off again as the cable went down into its tier, which was well aft. The cable was secured to the anchor in the manner shown, the ring of the anchor being served with tarred canvas and old rope securely seized (the PUDDENING), in order to prevent chafe.

Cannon

In the early days practically every sizeable merchant ship was armed with guns for her own protection against enemies and pirates. The earliest type was breech-loading, the powder and shot being put into a chamber, of which there were two or three to every gun, which was lashed into its place at the breech of the gun with thongs. A long gun of this type, salved from the *Mary Rose*, which foundered in 1545, is to be seen at the United Service Museum at Whitehall. As the charge and, therefore, the pressure, got greater for increased ranges and heavier shot, it became necessary to turn to the muzzle-loader, in which the whole gun was in one piece, and therefore better capable of withstanding the shock.

The breech-loading system continued to be used with swivels, light guns which fitted on to the ship's rail, but all the heavier guns were mounted on truck carriages, as shown in the illustration. The thickness of the gun itself varied according to the pressure that the particular part had to withstand ; that is to say, they were much thicker at the after end and usually had a

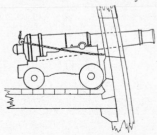

32 Pounder Long-Gun

thicker piece at the muzzle also. The carriage, as fitted in men-of-war and some merchantmen, is shown, two large flat pieces of wood called cheeks, straight at the forward end and stepped down at the after end to permit the working and elevation of the gun, strongly held together by cross pieces. Towards either end there were two strong axle trees, taking the four solid wheels that were called trucks. The transom, or main cross piece, was placed directly over the forward axle tree, exactly half-way down the cheeks. It was usual to make the height of this transom twice the bore of the gun and its width equal to the bore.

A breeching rope went round the after part of the gun and was secured to the side of the ship, checking the recoil, and there was quite an elaborate arrangement of tackles and ropes to prevent the gun taking charge and to permit it to be handled.

The gun shown is the 32-pounder, which was the standard gun of the Navy for many years, 9′ 6″ long with a bore of 6.4″.

In merchant ships the carriage was frequently very much less elaborate and ran on slides instead of having trucks, while as a general rule, except for East Indiamen and other ships taking out Letters of Marque, their armament was confined to 4-pounders (5′ 6″ long with a bore of 3.2″), or 3-pounders, 4′ 6″ long with a bore of just under 3″. The main purpose of this limitation was to prevent them turning pirate.

Cap

The ring at the masthead, and its fittings, used for fidding the topmast, or at the topmast head for fidding the topgallantmast. Originally made of wood, with an iron hoop or band about one-third of the depth of the cap to prevent it drawing, and an iron plate on the upper face. The cap had two holes, one round in the forward end through which the topmast passed, and the other square which fitted over the square end of the masthead and so prevented the cap sliding round. The topmast passed

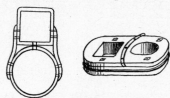

Lower Mast Caps—Iron and Wood

through the round hole at the forward end of the cap to rest on the TRESTLE TREES, which permitted it to be lowered if necessary. In the latter days of sail all caps were made of iron, as being lighter, stronger and neater. A precisely similar cap was fitted at the end of the bowsprit in order to take the jibboom.

(To be continued)

The "Star of Peace"

THE following information is given in reply to a correspondent: It is incorrect to say that the sailing vessel *Star of Peace* carried the first batch of convicts to Australia, for that was in the 18th Century, and was always done by men-of-war or naval auxiliaries. The *Star of Peace* was very much later, a clipper ship built for Thompson's Aberdeen-White Star Line by W. Hood of Aberdeen, in 1855, and designed by Walter Hood. She was a ship of 1,113 tons and shared with the *Omar Pacha* the distinction of being the biggest ship in the Aberdeen fleet for many years. She was a lofty, fine-lined ship, and for some years hoisted rafee moonsails on each mast.

Captain H. Sproat brought her out and had her in the early days of her career, her first four passages to Sydney being 77, 77, 79 and 79 days, surely a record of regular sailing.

In 1866 she is logged as having large repairs effected, and by that time her business was principally in wool, her last wool sailing being in 1874, when she ran from Melbourne to London in 108 days. She was then sold to W. Jamieson, of London, and was the pride of his fleet, although she was cut down to barque rig for economy. In 1880 she was sold to T. Grice, of Bootle, refitted and registered at Melbourne. In 1885 she was bought by Burns, Philp and Co., of Sydney, and was ultimately converted to a hulk at Thursday Island, being broken up just before the turn of the century.

Books to Read

Sea Lore. By STANLEY ROGERS. London : George C. Harrap and Co., Ltd. Price 7s. 6d. Postage 6d.

In this entertaining volume Mr. Stanley Rogers has given us a survey of sea-lore which will be read with pleasure by the landsman who wishes to know about sea life and sea folk. Instruction and romance are woven together in happy fashion, and many a ship modeller will find in these pages something of interest about the original ship he is reproducing in miniature, or about the people who sailed her. Not only are ships and their principal technical details explained, but there are chapters on such interesting subjects as the early navigators, sea language, whaling, and lost ships and lost treasure. The famous wool and tea clippers are dealt with at some length, and the story of the great race of 1866, when the *Taeping* docked 20 minutes ahead of her rival, the *Ariel*, in a 99 days' scramble home from Foochow, is retold in thrilling style.

Mr. Rogers is both writer and artist too, and he has added greatly to the interest of the book by his pen-and-ink sketches of ships and people and sea-scenes. A charming frontispiece in colour entitled " The Sea-Wolves," illustrates some of the old-time pirates about to attack an Indiaman at sea. Altogether, " Sea Lore " is very pleasant reading, not too technical in character, but always adding something to our stock of knowledge of the ways of the sea and of sailor-men.

Sailing Barges. By FRANK G. G. CARR. London : Hodder and Stoughton. Price 18s. net. Postage 8d.

Mr. Frank G. G. Carr's book, " Sailing Barges," will prove a feast of interest to all shiplovers, whether their hearts be in sail or steam. Although a number of books have been published covering a variety of sailing craft, no attempt has, until now, been made to compile a history of this ancient and highly important form of water transport. Written in an amusing and instructive style, it gives a very complete history of the barge and its origin, as well as the people who man them. Many interesting incidents, historical anecdotes, and present-day customs which originated centuries ago are included, which show the amount of research and care which has been undertaken in compiling this book. In the chapter " Early Days on the Thames," the author describes a voyage down river from Putney about the year 1700, in such a manner as to convey the impression that he was actually on board at the time. The old London Bridge, built on very different lines to the present structure, caused the river to rush through the centre arches at a great speed, at the same time dropping in level as much as 5'. For a barge to be steered through an arch with the swirling waters around, required very great skill and nerve. It is recorded that a life was lost nearly every day in this adventure. The vessel round which this chapter is written successfully " shoots the bridge," for which the reader should be very grateful, as had she struck one of the supports and gone down, one feels that Mr. Carr might not have been spared to give us this very excellent work ! In lighter vein is his actual voyage to Antwerp in 1928 as mate of the barge *Davenport*. Again we get a very clear idea of what the bargemen have to face with regard to the weather, tides, etc., and the skill and seamanship which is required to handle these craft in narrow and shallow waters. The story of the lives of bargemen, including their war records of heroism and resource, brings out the humour, romance, and at times tragedy which surpasses any fiction which has been written about them. Now that this country no longer owns any pukka sailing ships, there is a small compensation to be gained from the fact that the sailing barge is the only type of craft left that still remains without any form of motive power, and while they last, they give us a race of seamen in every sense of the word. A feature which will be of interest to many in these days of high taxation and reduced incomes, is the chapter on "The Barge as a Yacht," with its ingenious hints on converting cargo holds into housing accommodation. To those whose hobby is model-making, the dimensions of hulls, measurements of masts and spars and notes on rigging, of a number of barges, enhanced by Mr. R. C. Bingham's sketches, will be found indispensable, a valuable addition to which is a number of photographs of models and drawings of this craft from the extensive collection in the Science Museum. A number of appendices of barge-owners, barges which have sailed from this country to South America, illustrations of the principal house-flags, all carefully indexed, class this amongst the most interesting and valuable literature for the home library.— "CHIPS."

The Story of the Liner. By G. Gibbard Jackson. London: The Sheldon Press. Price 6s. Postage 4d.

In a work of just over 200 pages and 58 illustrations, the author has furnished us with a most fascinating story of the birth and growth of the liner. The liner was not born a liner ; she only became so called when trade had developed and brought into existence pioneer companies whose selected trade routes were termed "lines." From that time onward the ceaseless process of building and developing, scrapping and re-designing went on, interest superseding interest, success following failure ; periods of staid experience again followed by bursts of astonishing development. The story of the liner is, then, the history of these periods, and the way in which it is told is characteristic of Mr.

Jackson's exceptional ability to assemble and present the most pertinent facts in the form of an easily read and readily remembered tale, which in this instance is sub-divided into 18 chapters : The days of sail ; the first ocean steamships ; the triumph of steam ; the first Cunarders ; America's bid for supremacy ; the last of the paddlers ; from paddle to screw ; the early screw ships ; the last of the single screws ; the twin-screw liner ; Britain loses and regains the speed record ; the development of the mammoth liner ; Continental and other liners ; the liner in the first Great War ; post-War recovery and recent developments. An appendix gives in tabular form a list of particulars of notable Atlantic liners from 1837 to date, and another table records some notable runs in the Blue Ribbon contest on the Atlantic over the same period, whilst a third page presents in scale diagram form the comparative sizes of famous ocean liners up to the present year.

Brown's Nautical Almanac, 1932. Glasgow : Brown, Son, and Ferguson, Ltd. Price 3s. Postage 6d.

This well-known volume, now in its 55th year, fully maintains its reputation as a storehouse of information on tides, lights, beacons, buoys, nautical astronomy, port charges, and the hundred-and-one things to which the shipmaster needs to make constant reference. There are nearly 600 pages of useful facts, tables, and data.

Reading Cases for " S. and S.M."

Many readers are no doubt feeling the want of some simple way of preserving their copies of SHIPS AND SHIP MODELS in clean and good condition, and easy of access. We have had some reading cases specially made for this purpose. They are nicely bound in blue cloth, with gilt-lettered title, and are provided with strings, so that each case will hold a year's supply of copies. The price is 2s. 3d. each post free.

The Dead-Eye Difficulty

MANY would-be makers of historical and other ship models hesitate when they realise that perhaps hundreds of small fittings, such as deadeyes, blocks, etc., will have to be made by hand, reasonably to scale, and all alike.

Now, ship-modelling is a job for the patient man, but even very patient people may tire of making dead-

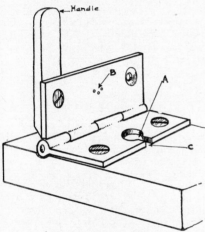

A Jig for Drilling Dead-eyes.

eyes $\frac{3}{16}''$ in diameter or smaller, in quantities, and it is to assist those possessed of only the normal supply of patience that the writer describes his time and eye saving deadeye drilling jig.

The prospective mass-producer should acquire a stout butt hinge, preferably a solid, cast affair, with leaves just under the thickness of the deadeye to be made—drill a hole as at A in sketch, of diameter to suit the deadeye body, and cut a slot as shown at C, about a third of the diameter of the hole in width.

The hinge is now closed, and hole A scribed off on the upper leaf, to serve as a guide when marking out the three holes B, which should be drilled with a drill of the same size as the intended lanyard holes in the deadeye.

Finally screw the lower leaf to a scrap of board, and fix a small handle to the upper leaf as shown.

The procedure now is—turn up the deadeyes from ebonite or other suitable rod, then when a supply is ready, pop one into hole A, close down upper leaf, keeping pressure applied to the handle (as the deadeye is a little thicker than the hinge leaf, this will prevent rotation), then drill through the three jig holes, lift up the top leaf, flick out the deadeye by using the slot C; with the point of the drill (if a hand-drill is used), and there you will have an evenly-drilled deadeye without spoiling your temper or your eyesight.

For those having a treadle drilling machine, the process is easy—the best hand-drill to use is one of the archimedian spring-return type, requiring only one hand.

Of course, the jig may be used for more than one size of deadeye, and no doubt users will be able to add refinements, such as an automatic ejector, etc.

The lanyard holes should of course be countersunk slightly, this is best accomplished by hand, a flat drill in a watchmaker's screwdriver handle is eminently suitable.   A.E.

Miniature Ship Models

AT the recent Engineering and Shipping Exhibition at Olympia, a particularly interesting model was shown by the Thames Model Shipyard, Leighcliff Road, Leigh-on-Sea, Essex. This represented a portion of Tilbury Dock, including the P. and O. berth, old and new dry docks, tidal basin, and jetty. A large number of vessels were shown in the dock, the whole being modelled to the scale of 1″ to 100′. This firm make a special feature of supplying miniature models of any mechanically-propelled vessel to order.

The Ship's Mail

Readers are invited to make use of this column for the discussion of matters of mutual interest and the exchange of ideas and information.

Some Mersey-side Paddle Steamers

DEAR SIR,—I am enclosing three photographs of my own taking of that now rare sea animal, the paddle-steamer. I thought perhaps that they would form a continuation of the famous Mersey-side ships contributed by Mr. Stuart, as these three ships, along with the *Mona's Queen*, were the last four paddle-ships sailing from the Mersey.

La Marguerite, a magnificent example of the now extinct large paddler. Built for New Palace Steamers, London, and used on their service —Tilbury-Margate-Boulogne. Purchased by the Liverpool and North Wales S.S. Co. in 1904, and employed on their Liverpool-Menai Bridge service. Transport from 1915 until released by Admiralty in 1919, during which time she carried 360,000 troops. Built by Fairfield 1894. Last voyage, September 28th, 1925. Broken up at Briton Ferry. Length, 330′; breadth, over paddles, 73′; gross tonnage, 1,554; 19 knots.

St. Elvies, Liverpool and North Wales S.S. Co. Built by Fairfield in 1896. Length, 240′; gross tonnage, 567; 18 knots. Utilised as a mine-sweeper and fleet-tender during the War. In her latter capacity she carried H.M. the King on several occasions. Last trip, September 14th, 1930. Broken up at Birkenhead.

Snowdon, last paddle-steamer sailing out of the Mersey. Built by Laird in 1892. Gross tonnage, 338; length, 175′; 14 knots. Sold for breaking up at Port Glasgow, October, 1931.

Yours truly,

Gorton.   F. C. THORNLEY.

A Frigate of 1750.

DEAR SIR,—Allow me to congratulate you most heartily on the new Magazine, which is just the thing for which we " lone hands " have been sighing.

Already some very fine models have been illustrated, and I was especially interested in Mr. R. W. Prance's frigate of 1750 in the October issue. I remember seeing this model at the

The Paddle Steamer "La Marguerite."

The Paddle Steamer St. "Elvies."

Model Engineer Exhibition of 1930 and admired it greatly, in spite of one rather glaring omission in the rigging, the absence of catharpins and futtocks (sometimes called futtock staves).

It would be very interesting to me, and I am sure to many other students of 18th Century warships, to know the source of Mr. Prance's design, particularly as to the following points :—

(1) *The Poop or Roundhouse.*—I was always under the impression that, up to 1753, or thereabouts, English frigates had only short quarterdecks, with narrow side gangways supported on iron knees, running forward as far as the mainmast, the actual quarterdeck stopping just forward of the

mizzen-mast, and without a poop. Mr. Prance's stern windows seem to me to be a deck too high.

(2) *The Bowsprit.*—Surely a dolphin-striker is out of place for this period, and in any case too far out.

I do not wish to seem too critical, but my impression of Mr. Prance's ship is that of a " fourth rate " from the mainmast aft, grafted onto the hull of a frigate.

It is difficult to see clearly in the reproduced photograph, but there appear to be sternsail booms on the mizzen, which of course would be quite out of character.

I imagine that the reference to " 32-pounder guns " is a slip of the

The Paddle Steamer "Snowdon."

pen, for to put such heavy metal in a frigate of this tonnage would be equivalent to mounting 12″ guns in a destroyer !

Yours faithfully,
Bristol.　　　A. G. Vercoe.

Dear Sir,—In reply to Mr. Vercoe, I am, like him, also a " lone hand," and cannot claim to be an authority on period ship models, so perhaps he will permit me a little indulgence in the matter. The design for my model was originally suggested by a photo appearing in the *Model Engineer*, November 17th, 1921, described thus : " A large model to a scale of 1/24th of H.M.S. *Juno*, one of the first typical frigates carrying her main armament of 32-pounder guns all on one deck. She was built on the Thames in 1757 ; tonnage, 667 ; length, 127.82′ ; beam, 34.25′."

The model was reported to be at the South Kensington Museum. Having little time to spare, I was not able to visit the Museum for reference until the drawings were well in hand. Unfortunately, she was not there, so I decided to continue the model as a representative type, using the *Model Engineer* photo as a check. If, in return, Mr. Vercoe can give me any further particulars of this ship I shall be pleased. I have been unable to trace her so far. To continue, *re* catharpins, futtocks, etc. : These were deliberate omissions. As stated in the article, I found it difficult to put in everything there should be ; please remember the model is only 7¾″ from stem to sternpost. There are a number of details missing, for instance, the foot ropes are not quartered. With regard to poop the position of stern gallery is in exactly the same position as that shown in photo of the Frigate *Juno*, and the position of the dolphin striker is also taken from photo, so I think these must be accurate—for this model, at any rate—I copied the details from the photo very closely. There are sternsail booms on the crojick, and mizzen topsail-yards of

my model ; these have been passed by a good authority, so I think they may be taken as O.K., but in justice to Mr. Vercoe, they were not generally used on mizzen. Last of all, the picture of H.M.S. *Juno* shows her carrying, as main-deck armament, 24 32-pounders. Unfortunately, I haven't a picture of the original model of H.M.S. *Juno* to show Mr. Vercoe. If he could see one, he would soon notice a difference from the more or less standard type of frigate of 1750, or thereabouts. I hope he will accept these replies in all good fellowship, but I think he will admit that my model may stand as a fair example of an early type frigate.

Yours truly,
Deptford Park.　　　R. W. Prance.

Figureheads

Dear Sir,—I was pleased to read that Mr. Wanless had thought of the fine figureheads in Devonport Dockyard. Our National Dockyards hold many relics of interest to the model maker. At Chatham Yard there is a museum containing some well preserved and fully-rigged models of the old warships and many figureheads that have been " returned to store " after the ships have been broken up. But to see figureheads in all their ancient glory one should visit the Chatham Naval Barracks. Near the main entrance stands Queen Adelaide in the flowing robes of her time. The Black Prince guards the Officers' Quarters, whilst Nelson, Anson and Dunche take their station in line on tan Terrace. In the grounds are a few more, placed in positions that well become them. All these figureheads are kept in a wonderful state of preservation, and what is more interesting, are painted in the correct uniform and dress of their time. Finally, one must not forget the wonderful model of H.M.S. *Kent*, which is some 40′ long, and built qy Naval craftsmen, to be seen sailing round the basin during Navy Week.

Yours sincerely,
Malta.　　　C. Worthington.

A " Church Ship " Model.

DEAR SIR,—As you are good enough to invite photographs of ship models of readers' construction, I enclose one, the original of which I have recently built.

A " Church Ship " Model.

She is supposed rather to represent a " church ship " or votive offering, than a scale model, though she is fairly accurate in proportion and detail.

Yours faithfully.

E. E. EGLINTON-BAILEY, Capt.
Putney, S.W.

Model Square Riggers

DEAR SIR,—I was interested in Capt. Hussey's model square rigger and his novel winch for trimming sails. I, like Capt. Hussey, think that square riggers are far more interesting to make and sail and, though I don't approve of his winch on sailing models, it is an advancement in the craft.

I have been working on square sails for some time, and my idea was to make them with as little gear as possible, so that the masts can be unshipped, to take to and from the place of sailing. My square-rigger has no braces. I have fastened the upper

topsail yard so that it will only swing about two or three points forward. All the other yards are free, with hooks into the clews of the foresail. When under weigh, I hook the tack into an eyebolt in the cathead and the sheet in an eyebolt on the rail, fore side of the main mast. On going about, I just change over. The head sails have booms with sheet the required length, and need no attention. My model is 3' 6" long, stem to stern, 6" beam and 9" deep from top rail to keel. The keel is of lead, 8 lbs. weight, made out of water pipe beaten into shape and screwed into the hull. She is easy to handle and is a very fast sailer.

Yours truly,

Burnley.   W. LEWIS.

The Working Model " Cutty Sark "

DEAR SIR,—I write to offer one or two rigging suggestions which · may be of some use to Capt. Hussey in whose article, in your November issue, I am much interested.

I have a 40" L.W.L. model of this famous ship, which first took the water some two and a half years ago. I therefore have the advantage of having had longer time in which to experiment. On the other hand, my model took me three winters to make and, as Capt. Hussey must obviously be very much more expert, since he made his in one, I do not want to appear to be trying to " teach my grandmother, to, etc."

I tried the differential winch, and abandoned it for the reasons which your contributor gives, and others. I then tried one or two other devices, whose description would take too much space for your correspondence columns.

Then I discovered that, on my ship at any rate, it is not necessary to control all the braces. The leech of each square sail sufficiently controls its own yard and, further, just allows the weather yard arm to be checked in enough to give the sails on that particular mast the correct " corkscrew " or slight twist. I expect I need not remind you that correct trim for square sails demands that each yard shall be a little sharper up than the next above it.

This being so, the only braces which have to be dealt with are the fore, main and mizzen. In addition, there are the corresponding tacks and sheets. The problem thus becomes greatly simplified.

I use the " endless " trick almost entirely. If it is neatly done, it can only be detected if its presence is known and it is looked for. My fore brace, for instance, sets up (correctly) to the yard-arm pennant block, runs through the bumkin block, through the yard-arm pennant block, down to the leading block on the main rail, and then along to its belaying pin. Arrived there, it finds a short dummy length already belayed on the pin. So it dives through a hole in the rail, between the pin and the bulwark, crosses the deck, goes up through a corresponding hole in the main rail on the other side of the ship and is rove through the correct blocks just as described for the other side.

The beauty of this arrangement for the lower braces is that it is correct. Capt. Woodget, *Cutty Sark's* crack driver and most successful skipper, ran the little ship a great deal with her lee rail under. Though a strict disciplinarian he was never unmindful of the comfort of his men. He did not wish them to be ploughing about in four feet of water in the lee scuppers unnecessarily. So, I am informed, he took his lee braces across the deck and belayed them on the weather side, out of the water. Thus, what I thought was a land-lubberly " fake," adopted to get me out of a difficulty, turned out to be, in a sense, a standard practice.

The upper braces are, of course, also rove on the endless system and the yards need only a touch or two to help them round when " going about."

I expect Capt. Hussey knows all about the dodge of making tack and sheet one rope. And then there is the trick of reeving a rope through a block so that the block *looks* absolutely " Bristol fashion," but actually works as a bowser. This trick was a godsend to me as it entirely does away with " ends " which are the bugbear of the full-rigged working model.

I find the fore and aft sails, i.e., headsails, staysails, etc., are much more trouble when going about as most of them have to be passed over the stay below to set them on the other side.

The subject is far too large, I should say, for full discussion in your correspondence columns. I expect I have offered more talk already than you will find room for, so I will not enter into the question of scale models not sailing properly. Nor the subject of detachable false keels which is the principle I adopted for my *Cutty*, though she will sail absolutely " scale " with inside ballast, and has done so. I know another working *Cutty*, only 20″ long, which never does anything else and has no false keel at all.

The editorial blue-pencil must be nearly worn out by now, so I had better " pipe down."

Yours truly,

G. DENZIL HOLLIS.

Newcastle-on-Tyne.

An 18th Century Sloop

DEAR SIR,—The model about which Mr. R. Leng inquires in your December number is of considerable interest. First of all, it is obviously a dockyard model and dates from about the middle of the 18th century, when quite small vessels still had raised forecastles and quarter-decks, like their larger sisters. The model appears to represent one of the many 14-gun sloops built between 1740 and 1750. The ports all round the bulwarks, to support the 14 swivel guns with which these vessels were armed, in addition to their carriage guns, are a noticeable feature of the model.

These sloops were of about 270 tons burden. Their normal rig was two-masted, with square-sails on both masts, but they were fitted with a square main course, while the gaff mainsail was hoisted on a trysail mast, on a rope-horse, after the fashion of snows. One or two were rigged as brigantines or as ketches, but the town " brig," and that standard rig was not introduced into the Navy until 1771, and by that time such small vessels were flush-decked. The position of the mainmast shows pretty definitely that the model was snow-rigged.

I should perhaps explain that I am using the term sloop in its general naval sense of sloop-of-war—then the class below sixth-rater—and with no reference to the one-masted sloop rig.

It is worth noting that the three-masted ship-rigged sloop-of-war did not appear in England until 1760. Previous to that all these vessels were, as I have said, two-masters.

Yours very truly,

Science Museum.   G. S. LAIRD CLOWES.

An 18th Century Sloop

DEAR SIR,—In reply to the letter of Mr. R. Leng of Penarth, with reference to his model of an early war vessel, the following information may be of help to him in identifying the model and restoring the stern.

From a study of the photograph, she is undoubtedly an old Navy Board contemporary model and is probably a two-masted sloop of about the middle of the 18th Century. The hole in the deck, just forward of the hatch at the break of the poop and surrounded with a doubling, is for the main capstan. The absence of channels probably indicates the model has never been rigged, although these may have disappeared in the course of time. The beakhead seems to be of unusual character and the head rails are missing.

The above particulars are given on the authority of Mr. R. C. Anderson, F.S.A., a member of the Council and a founder of the Society for Nautical Research, and Editor of the *Mariners Mirror*, whom I have consulted.

The enclosed outline sketch, not to scale, may be of some assistance to your correspondent, and is based on a contemporary drawing of the stern of a very similar vessel in the possession of Mr. Anderson.

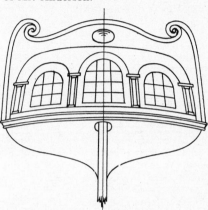

Stern of 18th Century Sloop.

If Mr. Leng would care to supply some dimensions and more detailed photographs, or better still, a dimensioned profile, it might be possible to give him some further information, with the help of the *Mariners Mirror.*

Yours faithfully,

LAURENCE A. PRITCHARD,

Member of the Society for Nautical Research.

Southampton.

The Elizabethan Galleon

DEAR SIR,—With reference to Capt. E. E. Eglinton-Bailey's letter on the Elizabethan Galleon, the following is taken from " Cruden's History of Gravesend," 1843 :—

" 1606. In this year, scenes of unusual magnificence were witnessed at Gravesend, upon the visit of the King of Denmark, to King James and his Queen, who was sister to his Danish Majesty. . . . Two months before, orders were given to Phineas Pott, Master Builder at the Dock Yard at Chatham, to put all the ships of war at that station in complete order, ready for sea service, to be inspected by the King. . . . On

Sunday, August 10th, after attending Divine Service at Rochester Cathedral, they went in barges to view the Royal Fleet lying near Upnor Castle, and went on board the *Elizabeth Jonas*, which had been prepared for their reception. The ship *Bear* (on board of which the Danish Lords and principal persons of the royal suite were entertained) was anchored abreast of the *Elizabeth Jonas*, there being a bridge or platform of near 200' in length, railed in, for communication from one to the other, and between them a hulk, fitted up as a kitchen for the occasion.

" His Majesty entertained the King of Denmark on board the *Elizabeth Jonas*. The great chamber (cabin) being part of the upper deck abaft the mainmast, contained a long table for the Lord Chamberlain and the other Lords of the English Court ; there being on the same deck before the mainmast, another table for the ladies. Between these were stairs leading to a tent lined with silk and cloth of gold, at the upper end, " under a rich cloth of estate," the two Kings, Queen and Prince dined."

Cruden gives as his authorities for the above description, Stow's Annals, *sub anno* 1606 ; copy of a letter from the King of Denmark, Sloane MSS. 149, art. 25, Brit. Mus. ; Letter from John Pory to Sir Robt. Cotton, Cottonian MSS ., Julius ciii, Vol. 34 ; The King of Denmark's Welcome, etc., 8vo, London, 1606 ; and Sir John Harrington's letter to Mr. Secretary Barlow, *Nugae Antiquae*, Park's Ed., 1804, Vol. i, p. 348.

I was greatly interested in the beautiful model of this vessel in the Science Museum. I immediately obtained a copy of the plans from the bookstall. Details of the rigging were not available, however. Perhaps Mr. Laird-Clowes will be so good as to publish these in pamphlet form, so that they may be accessible to the amateur ship modellist. The results of the laborious researches which have gone to make such a model as this should certainly be made as widely known as possible.

Yours faithfully,

Northfleet.   JESSE CLEMENTS.

The Ship Lovers' Association

PARTICULARS of membership were given in full in the September issue of SHIPS AND SHIP MODELS. The Hon. Sec., *pro tem.*, is Mr. Frank C. Bowen, of Customs House Building, Gravesend, Kent.

A considerable number of members have not yet let the Secretary know the sections into which they want to be logged.

Members' Queries and Answers

Could any member give Mr. Robert S. Munn, Harbor Grace, Newfoundland, any information concerning the following sailing vessels on the Newfoundland trade in or about the years mentioned : *Clutha* (1848), *Arabella Tarbet* (1851), *Rose* (1850) and *Miriam Ridley* (1860).

C.J.C. (Bray).—The *Lady Kildare*, of the British and Irish Co., was transferred to the Belfast S.S. Co. a few months ago and is now the *Ulster Castle*. The *Lismore* was sunk off Waterford in July, 1924, within a few weeks of being completed by the Ardrossan Shipbuilding Co.

F.C.H. (Cheam).—Watkins' tugs *Vincia*, *Badia* and *Doria*, form the " Teddy Bear " class—can any London river enthusiast say why ?—and were built at Dartmouth in 1909. All three served the Government in the War, *Doria* under her own name in the Downs Boarding Flotilla, *Vincia* as H.M.S. *Chub* on the same service, and *Badia* as H.M.S. *Chester III* in the Downs and under her Watkins' name at Calais.

Only answers of more general interest are given here ; these and all others of lesser interest are answered by post.

SHIPS AND SHIP MODELS

A Magazine for all Lovers of Ships and the Sea

Editorial and Publishing Offices:

Single Copies, post free, **7½d.**
Annual Subscription **7s. 6d.**

66 FARRINGDON STREET
L O N D O N :: E. C. 4

Vol. I. No. 6.   **FEBRUARY, 1932.**   **Price 6d.**

The Ship's Log

Our Plate

WE make a new departure this month in the presentation of a supplement picture. The drawing is an excellent example of Mr. R. H. Penton's pen-and-ink work, and we believe the subject will appeal particularly to those readers who are interested in the types of sailing vessels to be seen around our coasts. The big sailing ships have disappeared entirely as far as British ownership is concerned, and the coasters are gradually being either displaced by motor craft, or are having their rig cut down, and an auxiliary motor added. Mr. Penton's delightful drawing of the *Kathleen and May* will enable a souvenir of this typical three-masted schooner to be preserved by collectors. We hope to be able to give other plates with future issues, and we shall be glad to have any suggestions from readers as to subjects they would like to see treated, whether sailing ships or steamers, and whether old or new.

The " Good Intent "

We desire to express our acknowledgements to Mr. W. A. Sharman, of Bristol, the owner of the copyright of the interesting photograph of this old craft which we published in our last issue, for his courteous permission to use the picture. Mr. H. L. Summers, of Broadstairs, tells us that in " The Kentish Companion," published in 1804, the *Good Intent* is referred to as " Sailing from the Port of Sandwich, Thomas Jones (Master), chiefly employed in the coal and coasting trade."

*   *   *

The Oldest Vessels Afloat

Mr. G. E. Farr kindly sends us the following further notes on this subject :—" I was very interested to read, in last month's SHIPS AND SHIP MODELS, of the *Premier* of Weymouth, and in view of her history, I shall certainly have to waive my claim for the *John*. A friend of mine, whom I had not met for several years, spoke to me a few days ago and suggested

that the *Premier* has another big point
in its favour, besides years. He was
of the opinion that, whereas the
Premier has kept to her original motive
power, the *John* has been converted
from a paddle-steamer to screw.
However, I have made further inquiries and am led to believe that
though she may have been originally
designed for paddles, she was altered
to screw before even leaving the
stocks. Certainly she was described
in the Press of March, 1855, as a
' screw-propellor,'—as if she was something freakish. The occasion of this
report was when she carried away an
iron bridge spanning the New Cut
at Bristol. The bridge had been
built in 1805 and, after collapsing
without warning in 1808 and killing
or injuring 32 people, was rebuilt
with a single span of 160' the following
year. The *John* had discharged coke
higher up the river and was steaming
back fairly quickly on the ebb tide
when the impact took place. She is
said to have rebounded 10', and then,
somehow miraculously clearing the
wreckage which must have been about
her bows, drifted uncontrolled down
stream, to be stopped from ramming
the next bridge only by grounding
on a convenient ledge.

" I have searched Bristol Docks for
the *Good Intent*, but, though unsuccess-
ful, am certain she is lying somewhere,
though perhaps abandoned. It is a
curious coincidence that her owners
are A. J. Smith and Sons—they also
own the *John*. With reference to the
Collier, the exact date of her wreck
is January 28th, 1914 ; on that
occasion her crew of seven was rescued
by the Ilfracombe life-boat. A large
photograph, by Grattan Phillipse, of
the *Collier* lying a-wash on the fore-
shore, is hanging in the Pavilion there.
It has come to my notice that the
oldest life-boat existing is the *Zetland*
of Redcar ; she is the only surviving
boat of Greathead's build. Built in
1800, she retired from active service
about 1840, but was actually used again
in 1880, when she was instrumental
in saving the crew of the brig *Luna*."

Information Wanted

Several readers are in want of
information relating to certain ships.
Here are their requests :—P.W.E.
(Toronto) would like drawings, particularly deck-plan showing position
of boats, of the *Torrens* ; E.W.H.W.
(Hendon) would like any information
available about the history of the
Ashmore, 1,153 tons, built by J. Reid,
of Port Glasgow, particularly the name
of her original owners, or the line of
ships she was built for ; E.V.P.
(Glasgow) would like deck measurements or deck-plan of the four-
masted ship *Lancing* ; G.T.R. (Leices-
ter) would like full information in
regard to the use and arrangement of
" slab-lines," or reference to book
where information can be found ; R.G.
(Woking) wants authentic plans for
a working model brig ; an American
reader wants information about the
brig *Cabot* after she was sold to the
British Admiralty in 1783. We shall
be glad if readers can help any of the
foregoing correspondents with the
information desired. We shall be
pleased to forward such information,
or to put correspondents in direct
touch. * * *

Colours of Egyptian Ships

A Birmingham reader is anxious to
obtain some information about the
colouring used on Egyptian ships in
ancient days. He writes :—

" I have recently constructed a
model of an Egyptian ship of about
1600 B.C. from a drawing taken
from a temple relief, and I shall be
much obliged if you can tell me if it
is possible to obtain any information
as to the colours which were used on
ships of this period. The drawing gives
minute detail of the *pattern* on the
lotus-shaped stern, etc., but no colours
are shown. Can any of your readers
help ? " * * *

Model Steamers and Power Boats

Several readers have asked for more
articles on this section of ship modelling. We shall welcome any notes,
photographs, or drawings on completed models, or on methods of
building and propulsion.

A Sailing Ship Hunt in the Baltic

By F. T. WAYNE

THE Baltic is an attractive place for anyone, but to the sailing-ship enthusiast it is probably more full of interest than any other part of the world. It was, therefore, not un-natural that I should take the opportunity of paying it a visit when I was ordered by my doctor to take a 10 days' holiday.

I left Hull on a Wednesday on the Finland Line steamer *Ilmatar*, which I found most comfortable. We arrived at Copenhagen on Friday, and I had a good opportunity of seeing the Danish coasting schooners. Most of these have now taken to auxiliaries, but many of them retain their full sail-plan and make good use of their sails. Leaving Copenhagen, I was very fortunate in getting a photograph of the brigantine *Maria*, a beautiful little vessel, probably very old, with a fine figurehead. She went about just as we passed her, about a quarter of a mile away. Before we had passed

Bornholm we had seen at least a dozen schooners, a wooden barque of about 700 tons with painted ports, a barquentine, and another brigantine, but most of these were too far off to photograph.

At Helsingfors there were no large sailing ships, but numerous local schooners and cutters. These were beautiful little vessels of about 50-60′ overall and very beamy. They are very loftily rigged, usually with standing gaffs and brailing sails, the peak of which is hauled out along the gaff on a runner. They have a draft loaded of about 5′ forward and 6′ aft. They have fine lines and are very fast indeed ; in fact, I was told that they can beat a 12-metre yacht under most conditions. Many of them had brought fish, fruit, and potatoes to the market-place and men were selling them off the sterns of their ships. There were also a number of cutters belonging to Sibbo which were loaded with sand. In spite of their huge

The " Carmen " of Mariehamn. 540 tons. Built 1922

A View of Mariehamn showing " Oaklands " in centre

sail-plan these cutters are handled by two men.

At Hango and Abo I saw a number of these cutters and schooners, some of the latter being considerably larger than those at Helsingfors. Many of the larger schooners have their fore topsails set on booms swung above the triatic stay in the manner of the " ranterpikes." They all have booms for their fore-staysails, so that the jib sheets alone require attention when going about. Two schooners at Abo were fitted with wireless.

From Abo I went on a small steamer through the islands to Mariehamn. The 100-mile trip took 17 hours and we called at 16 small islands *en route*. I have never seen any place more fascinating. We threaded our way through narrow channels between wooded islands and into small bays where there would be four or five

houses and an occasional schooner.

At Mariehamn I found no less than 20 sailing ships. There were the big barques *Herzogin Cecilie*, *Archibald Russell* and *Viking* in the outer harbour, while in the inner harbour I found the iron barques *Loch Linnhe*, *Oaklands*, *Lingard*, *Plus*, *Alastor*, the wooden barque *Carmen* (built in 1922), two large four-masted schooners—*Gunn* and *Valborg*, the barquentines *Estonia* and *Dione*, the topsail-schooner *Lideborg*, two three-mast schooners *Hildur* (built 1899) and *Ostrobotnia* (521 tons, built in 1921), and also several small coasters —a total tonnage of about 20,000 in a port with a population of about 2,000. Quite apart from the shipping, Mariehamn is a most attractive place. The harbour is surrounded by woods of fir, pines, and silver birches. In most places the water is deep close

Danish Coasters at Copenhagen

Danish Schooner " Aura "

" Dione "

"Lingard "   Bow View.

" Lingard "—Stern View.

inshore, and many of the ships are tied up to trees on shore. The weather was quite the hottest I have ever known, with a temperature of over 100°F. in the shade, quite warm enough to dispel any ideas that Finland is always a cold place.

I spent one day in Mariehamn before going on to Stockholm, where I found about 25 small schooners and cutters of the usual standing-gaff type—mostly loaded with timber, though one was loading beer for the theoretically Prohibition country of Finland! From Stockholm I went on to Oslo, where there is an excellent museum containing some very good models, but there was not a single sailing vessel in the harbour except yachts. At Bergen I found equally little, but the scenery on the railway from Oslo to Bergen fully made up for the disappointment of finding nothing but a very dirty harbour at Bergen.

To anyone who wishes to see some sailing ships before they die out, which perhaps they may never do in the Baltic, I can strongly recommend a trip to Finland. Living there is extremely cheap, and the people are most charming and hospitable. Added to this, it is a very beautiful country, quite apart from sailing ships, and it is completely neglected by tourists. I went there without knowing a word of Finnish or Swedish, but did not have much difficulty, although a certain amount of Swedish is desirable for comfort, but the Finns are very good linguists, and many of them speak good English.

Ship Models in New Zealand

MR. R. H. FITZ-HERBERT, of Havelock North, Hawke's Bay, N.Z., writes:—"Could you tell me anything of " the wreck of the *Minotaur*," shown in Turner's painting? I cannot find any warship of that name wrecked.

I have three models that I made in an hour or two, to a scale of 100' to the inch. They represent the new Cunarder, the M.V. *Rangitiki* (both with hollow funnels wrapped with coloured paper, and masts of wire-nails with heads filed off), and my neighbour's wooden four-roomed cottage, this model being a particle that is carried in a gramophone-needle box.

I first extract the *Rangitiki* from my pocket, and they think her a cute little thing, until I place the cottage on her forecastle; and, when her great size has been realised, I put the Cunarder model by the *Rangitiki* (16,700 tons in the original), and the result is quite impressive! The two little ship models are very rough and bare, but as all there is of them is strictly to scale, they are very dignified and convincing, for the amount of labour put into them.

If I were rich, I would present a ship-model museum to the district. The main room would be of the same length and width as some " square ended " Indiaman, and equal in height to her depth of hold. In the centre of the room would be a model of the Indiaman, and one of the museum building, and every ship and building model in the room would be to the same scale.

Models of a large steamer and a 1,200-ton ship would be shown at their maximum angles of roll in a " roaring forty " sea. There would also be a model of a 1,200-ton ship in a typhoon's " calm centre," all waves strictly to scale, of course. There would be models of Southampton Docks and Circular Quay, Sydney, at three selected dates, with the finest ships trading there at each date. There would be a working (electric?) model of a single-screw cargo steamer, moving under her own power in a long tank, encouraged by a coin in the slot, and running aground on a sandy beach at each end, to be " warped off " by hand.

House Flags of Shipping Companies
By JOHN S. STYRING

ALL the big steamship companies and shipping lines fly what is termed a " House " or " Company's " Flag. These flags are designed and adopted by the owners as distinguishing marks, and are usually flown at the " main " on entering or leaving port. The owners of smaller boats also have their own house flags. Many of the designs are extremely simple and yet effective, being recognisable at a glance—but the older the firm the wider its choice. In these days it is no easy matter to design a new flag, with the result that a large number merely bear the initials of the owners. In the days of the clippers, the house flags were really racing flags—similar to those flown by yachts at all seaside resorts—but now they are merely the means of ready identification. A shipowner may fly any flag he chooses as his own house flag, provided it does not clash with any of the National or Admiralty flags.

Some Early Flags

One of the oldest flags is that of the Aberdeen Line—red over blue with white star in the centre—remembered particularly by the fine performances of the old *Thermopylae*—and now never absent from the Port of London.

The White Star Line's flag—red swallow-tailed pennant with white five-pointed star—is another old " sailing ship " flag now used for steamers. It was originally the flag of a famous firm of sailing-ship owners, Pilkington and Wilson of Liverpool, and was bought together with the name of the " White Star Line " by Mr. T. H. Ismay for the inauguration of a new steamship line with which he was closely associated—viz., the Oceanic Steam Navigation Co., Ltd.

The flag of the Cunard Line is perhaps the best known of the flags of the present day—yellow lion rampant on red ground—although prior to the year 1880 their flag consisted of two pennants, a blue one with white diagonal cross over a thin red whip-pennant.

The P. and O. Line (the Peninsular and Oriental Steam Navigation Co.) is reputed to have adopted its flag —divided diagonally into four triangles upper white, lower yellow, blue at the hoist and red at the fly—from the Portuguese and Spanish ensigns, the Peninsular countries to which the P. and O. ships first ran in 1837. From the Portuguese we get the blue and white, and the red and yellow is furnished by the flag of Spain.

The Shaw Savill and Albion Line —an amalgamation of Shaw Savill and Co. and the Albion Line—flies the flag of the old Shaw Savill Co.—a white ensign having in the upper canton four white stars on blue field, divided into four by a red cross. This flag was to all intents and purposes the national flag of New Zealand from 1834 to 1840, until the treaty of Waitangi marked the annexation of New Zealand to Great Britain, and the four stars were afterwards incorporated into the New Zealand ensign. The Shaw Savill Co., as the first regular shipping line to New Zealand, adopted the original New Zealand flag as their house flag, and thus saved from oblivion an interesting emblem.

Union Castle and Allan Flags

The well-known Union Castle boats have a blue flag with a red diagonal cross on a white one. The company was formed by the amalgamation in 1900 of the Castle Mail Packets Co., Ltd., and the Union Steamship Co., Ltd., the new flag being a combination of the flags of these two companies. The Allan Line—which originated as the Montreal Ocean Steamship Co.— flew a red, white and blue code " T " flag with a red pennant over it, thus having really a " house signal " instead of a " house flag." In 1916 the Canadian Pacific Railway Co. took over the Allan Line and absorbed it into its huge organisation.

Origin of Blue Funnel Line

Alfred Holt's Blue Funnel Line fly a blue flag with white diamond and black letters " A.H.," and it is said that their familiar blue funnels with black tops originated in the following manner. They commenced their shipping career by the purchase of a " second hand " steamer, the *Dumbarton Youth*, in which was found a quantity of blue paint, some Bibles and muskets. The crew, on taking over the ship and cleaning down, are reputed to have smartened up the funnel by using the blue paint—a " marking " which is still used to this day. The various companies under the Ellerman combination usually fly their own house flag with a blue pennant and white " J.R.E." of the Ellerman Line above it, although the Ellerman and Bucknall Steamship Co. fly a new flag—blue with three white diamonds and red letters " E. and B."—in addition to the Ellerman pennant.

The G.S.N. Flag

A well-known flag on the Thames is that of the General Steam Navigation Co., both on their black-funnelled cargo boats and also on the " Eagle " steamers. They are said to have the distinction of being the oldest steam-shipping corporation in the world, and from small beginnings as carriers on the old smack route between London and Leith, they now have regular sailings to all the chief ports on the European coast. Their flag is white with red globe in centre, flanked by red letters " G.S.N.C." with the date " 1824 "—the year of the company's incorporation. One of the newest flags on the Atlantic route is that of the United States Lines, Inc. Under the old jurisdiction of the United States Shipping Board, their vessels flew a blue swallow tail with white circle and red letters " U.S.L.," whereas under the ownership of P. W. Chapman, the flag was altered to white flag with blue triangle enclosing the letter " Y " in the centre, and a red five-pointed star in the upper corner near the hoist. The flag has

since undergone another transformation and is now white with red triangle with the " Y " encircled by a blue band, having in white letters " United States Lines." The same flag is adopted for the American Merchant Lines with the exception of the white letters—" American Merchant Lines " replacing, of course, the wording " United States Lines."

Railway and Other Special Flags

The Railway Companies also have their " house " flags on the vessels which operate the numerous cross-Channel services ; collieries, iron, steel and chemical companies, telegraph and cable-laying companies all own vessels and fly their own special flags, whilst we must not forget the up-to-date fruit-carrying ships of Elders and Fyffes, United Fruit Co., and the new Jamaica Direct Fruit Line.

Tank steamers which carry both oil and molasses in bulk have quite a host of flags—the flag of the Bulk Oil Steamship Co. of London is an interesting one, being white with a dark blue band across the centre. These are the colours of the ribbon of the Military Cross and the distinction was won by one of the company's directors during the late war and adopted both as their " house " flag and also as a band on the black funnels of their vessels.

The Tilbury Contracting and Dredging Co., Ltd., whose vessels are responsible for the clearing of the channel in the River Thames, also have a flag with a history. The founder of the company was an enthusiastic cricketer and an ardent supporter of the well-known cricket club " I. Zingari," and introduced the colours of that team—black, red and yellow—into his flag.

Zoological Flags

Numerous shipping companies have adopted various designs embodying animals, birds and miscellaneous objects in their flags. Lions, horses, stags, elephants and kangaroos figure very conspicuously, whilst eagles, herons and swans are fairly representative among the birds. Fish appropriately enough, are shown on the flags of several steam trawler owners, and flowers, trees, ships, anchors, swastikas, etc., are found in some hundreds of flags.

" Lloyds "

No article on flags would be complete without those of Lloyd's being mentioned—the great association of marine underwriters. Their ensign, which is flown at all Lloyd's signal stations, is blue with their badge in the fly, while their burgee is white with broad blue cross over narrow red cross and their badge in the top left-hand corner.

A Model Dutch Admiralty Yacht

WE know from our correspondence that a number of our readers are engaged in building the model of a Dutch Admiralty Yacht described in our pages by Mr. Jeffrey Leighton. Here is a photograph of the first model we have seen built from Mr. Leighton's drawings. It is built almost entirely of ivory and celluloid, and is the work of Mr. A. Pepé. The wales and mouldings are picked out in black, and the general effect is very pleasing, the character of the yacht being very well interpreted. No doubt the builders of these models will vary in the degree of ornamental detail they introduce into their work, and in the materials and style of finish adopted, but in attempting a decorative model, Mr. Pepé has been very successful. The model may be seen, for a short time, at our offices.

Model Dutch Admiralty Yacht, by Mr. A. Pepé

The Story of "Mona's Queen II"

MR. C. OLDHAM writes :—" As a lover of ships of many types, and one who heralded with delight the advent of the new monthly, I was very pleased to see in a recent copy a picture and reference to one of my own personal favourites, the *Mona's Queen II*. As the picture was considered worthy of publication, I have taken the liberty of assuming that some additional information will interest you.

The *Mona's Queen II* was a splendid and most interesting old vessel from many aspects, and when I stood at the Douglas Head jetty, over two years ago, and regarded my old friend for what I knew would be the last time, I felt a genuine sense of parting which comes back to me as I write. In spite of her external simplicity of arrangement, with the flush deck extending all fore and aft, with the boats all abaft 'midship, she had a beauty of her own, which was enhanced by the two large and very neat funnels well spaced in relation to paddle boxes, wind heads and masts.

The engines were the last of the oscillating type to be fitted to a Manx Packet, but the ship was not the last paddler to be commissioned. However, she was actually the last to survive, as no others have been used since the Great War, except perhaps as a temporary measure in 1919. There were two high-pressure cylinders, 50" diameter, and two low-pressure, 88" diameter, with a common stroke of 72". The two high-pressure were horizontal, and the two low-pressure were vertical, driving upwards on to the same two cranks as the high pressure. The indicated horse-power was 5,000, steam at 85 lb. sq. in. being supplied by four double-ended steel boilers. It was a weird and wonderful sight to see these huge engines tumbling about the trunnions as they drove the 25' diameter wheels at 30-odd revolutions per minute. Each wheel had 10 feathering floats, which measured 12' long and 4' wide and 1" thick, weighing with the brackets approximately 1 ton each.

Some idea of the esteem with which the *Mona's Queen II* was regarded, may be judged from the fact that of the Manx paddlers which survived the War, she was the only one to return to the holiday service, although three of the vessels were built a little later and were fitted with non-oscillating engines of the two-cylinder compound drag-link type.

The old ship was very sweet-running, very little thumping being evident as her great wheels hit the water at 17 knots, and she could have given a point here to certain well-known vessels which do good business on the Thames during the summer.

In February, 1917, the *Mona's Queen* achieved an unique fame whilst engaged in carrying troops between Southampton and Havre. A molesting submarine was sighted only 500' away, but Captain Willian Cain went right ahead without slackening speed or altering the course. A torpedo was discharged, but this passed under the vessel's shallow bottom, and a few moments later the submarine was struck a shattering blow by the mighty port-wheel. The enemy immediately foundered and, after landing the troops, the old ship returned to Southampton under her own steam, refusing the services of a tug, which was eventually left out of sight."

R.M.P.W. also writes : " Add to your note on *Mona's Queen II*, the Isle of Man paddle steamer whose picture you printed recently, that she served as a cross-Channel troop-ship in the War. She zig-zagged the writer over one night in July, 1915, with nearly 1,700 troops, and a very close fit it was, most of them messing and sleeping where they were halted on marching in, much too close to enable the elaborate orders for defence against submarine attack to be practicable. But later, *Mona's Queen II* took this matter into her own hands, and rammed and sank an attacking submarine with her sponson ! "

The Donegal Curragh

By MANNIN CRANE

ONE of the most remarkable types of craft in existence and in use to-day is the Donegal Curragh. It is a curious mixture of Ancient Briton wickerwork construction and Viking design. The Curragh possesses no keel, and its skin consists of two or three thicknesses of linen sheets. On many occasions nothing stronger than a bed sheet is used. Seamen who use the Northern approach to the British Isles round Ireland, and who pass between Tory Island and the Irish mainland may have sighted this craft at a distance, for, unlike the Welsh Curragh, they are used on the open sea as extensively as in the smooth waters of the Irish bays and loughs of the locality.

The principal dimensions are about 18' long, with a beam of 3', and a depth amidship of about 2' 6". In general shape and appearance they are not unlike the Norwegian pram.

The Curragh possesses a square stern, sloping forward and downward. the midship section is almost semi-circular, and the bow is spoon shape. The only wood used in the construction is that of the gunwale itself, which is usually 2×3 scantling, with lighter pieces of scantling to form the bow gunwales. Through this gunwale are bored holes, varying in size with the hot poker used, or the brace-bit available, but usually about $\frac{3}{4}$" to 1" diameter. After the gunwale has been assembled, it is turned upside down resting on blocks, and through the holes, usually 8" apart, hazel twigs are inserted, so that at this stage of the construction the appearance is the gunwale of a ship with twigs standing upright 8" apart. These twigs are bent over, and inter-twined with the corresponding twigs on the other side, thus forming about a score of ribs in the rough shape of a boat. Fore-and-afters are now tied by any old bits of string which are available, generally there are a dozen to a dozen and a half fore-and-afters made of twigs, which may be in several pieces, all of which are, however, securely lashed in place. The for'ard ends of the fore-and-afters come to a point in the bow, and are usually held in place by a horseshoe right under the end of the bow gunwales. In order to preserve thwartship strength, a cross beam is nailed about a third the distance from the bow, and resting across the gun-wales, with a smaller piece about 1' from the bow. This is the only transverse strength, apart from the stern piece, in the whole construction of the Curragh. Over this wickerwork frame are stretched linen sheets, which are made fast by nailing battens along the outside of the gunwale over the upper edge of the sheets. A coat of tar is applied, and a further skin is added in the same manner. Some of the Donegal fishermen prefer to have a sheet of brown paper between the two skins, but this is not general by any means.

This completes the construction of the Curragh, and a note or two about

    A Donegal Curragh—Broadside View

the materials used may not be out of place. The hazel twigs are usually collected in the Autumn, and given a treatment of drying, which varies in different localities, lasting about six weeks. In some Curraghs examined by the writer, old shoe-laces, stay-laces, pieces of string of a dozen varieties, and spunyarn were used for lashing the twigs together. The gunwale timbering very often comes from the roof of some dilapidated house, or maybe it is a few occasional pieces of driftwood, which have been washed ashore. There is little or no attempt at dressing this timber, because carpentering tools in the locality are, as a rule, scarcely in evidence. Should a break occur in the vicinity of a shake or a knot during the course of construction, the damaged part is securely banded by hoop iron and a few nails.

The equipment of the boat consists of two thwarts and four paddles. The thwarts are simply pieces of board obtained in the same manner as most of the other materials, that is, selected driftwood or other oddments. The thwarts are not secured in any way, but simply rest on short sticks, tied on either side of the Curragh about 6″ below the gunwale. These are placed conveniently for the two oarsmen.

The paddle calls for some comment because of its unique shape and construction. The loom of the oar is roughly shaped, and to a seaman hardly big enough for a full-sized hand. Securely attached to this is a large piece of wood, the same thickness as the paddle, namely, about 2″. This balancing weight, as it might be called, is about 9″ × 15″, and through this piece of wood is a 1″ diameter hole, permitting the paddle to fit over a single thole pin in the gunwale. This paddle, of course, cannot be feathered. In order to prevent wear and tear on the gunwale and this block of wood, metal sheets are sometimes tacked on to each of these as a bearing surface. The paddles may be from 8′ to 14′ in length, they are square in section, and apart from this balancing block of

wood, are in one piece. The blade does not broaden out, but maintaining its 2″ width, thins towards the blade. The reason of this will be obvious to seamen when it is realised that the paddle cannot be feathered, and therefore the narrow blade offers less resistance to a wave-top should the Curragh paddlers be unlucky enough to be caught in heavy weather. As in the North-east Coast Coble the " stroke oar " is for'ard and not aft. The after paddler keeps time with the for'ard paddler, and applies corrective measures when necessary for steering purposes.

Some other particulars relating to the Curragh are as follows—the weight of the Curragh itself is about 120 lb., thus it can easily be carried by the crew of two. They are hauled ashore after use, and turned bottom up on the beach. They will carry as many as eight persons in fine weather. They are used principally for lobster fishing, which is regarded by the natives as the heaviest work to which the Curragh can be applied. They are also used in some districts for loading the local coasting steamers with granite setts, the load of a Curraugh for this purpose being more than half a ton of setts. They will face bad weather, and in expert local hands are remarkably good sea craft. Containing two paddlers alone they can achieve a speed of five knots quite easily, and can tackle a distance of eight or ten miles in the open sea with ease. They do not fear heavy seas as much as they fear a high wind, for they are extremely buoyant. In bad weather three people as a crew can pursue their normal work.

As an indication of the quantity to population, a village of 100 people will have 20 Curraghs between them. The average life of a Curragh is about eight to ten years, but should they be used exclusively for lobster fishing, it is doubtful if they would last for five years. The draught of a Curragh, containing its crew of two men, is about 6″, and when fully laden about 15″.

By courtesy]   **A Donegal Curragh. End view looking forward, showing paddles**   [*Liverpool Museum*

During the recent Shipping Week Exhibition in Liverpool one of these actual Curraghs was on view, and was one of the most remarkable exhibits in the exhibition, exciting tremendous interest not only among seamen but among the general public as well. This Curragh was later presented to the Liverpool Museum, where it is now on view.

The Donegal Curragh should not be confused with the Galway Bay Curragh, which is somewhat different in construction. The Galway Bay Curragh is used for travelling greater distances, but this is not without danger, for several years ago a score of these Galway Bay Curraghs were lost together with their crews in a sudden storm, but that is a happening that sometimes comes to much bigger ships than these unique craft, which although frail are probably one of the finest types of seaworthy vessels in existence to-day.

———

Mr. Robert Gilmore, of Warsaw, New York State, U.S.A., would like to get into touch with readers interested in the collection or disposal of souvenir pieces of famous ships, and other nautical relics.

Ship Models at the Royal United Service Museum

I.—SAILING SHIPS

By CAPTAIN E. ALTHAM, R.N.

TO the student and lover of ship models, no collection will appeal more than that in the Royal United Service Museum. Not only is it representative of naval development from the 17th Century up to the present day, but it is so compact, so well set out and so readily accessible, that the value of the actual models themselves is greatly enhanced.

Let us look first at the sailing-ship models which cover nearly half the floor space of the grand old Banqueting Hall—a truly royal setting for any exhibits. We notice first of all a Dutch ship-of-war of the period 1660 to 1720; although not strictly to scale, the model is a masterpiece of beautiful carving and accurate repre-

sentation of the rigging of that time. Next to this is a 32-gun frigate of the type known as 5th rates in the Navy of 1720, and which bore such names as Lyme, Winchelsea, Rye and Mermaid. This model was built and rigged by Mr. Frank Nye. Then we see a British 64-gun ship of about the same period, a very beautiful model, which was originally in Windsor Castle and later transferred to the R.U.S. Museum by order of His Majesty King Edward VII. A 24-gun frigate, one of the 6th rates of 1745, also deserves notice. Two fine French models, the *Heros* of 74 guns, and the huge *Imperiale* of 130 guns, are of interest as showing typical ships-of-the-line of our chief enemy in the latter part of the 18th

" L'Imperiale "—130 Guns

Dutch Ship of the period 1660—1720

and early-19th Centuries. A famous British 74-gun ship-of-the-line of the Trafalgar period is to be seen in H.M.S. *Mars*; this model was built previous to the construction of the actual ship and was given to a Mr. W. J. Huggins by King William IV when that artist was commanded to paint some pictures of the Battle of Trafalgar; it was presented to the Museum by his grandson.

A fine large model is that of a 5th rate, H.M.S. *Phoebe* of 926 tons, also of the Trafalgar period. This ship had a great fighting record which, as in all cases, is clearly set out on the description card.

Half-way along the line we find

the celebrated model of Trafalgar, showing the position of every ship in the rival fleets at 20 minutes past noon, just as the *Victory* was cutting

" Wappen von Hamburg "—1720

the line. On the far side is a huge-scale model of another 74-gun line-of-battleship, H.M.S. *Cornwallis*, which was built in Bombay Dockyard along-side the ship herself, and is therefore

invaluable as a record of details of rigging and construction. Next we come to a particularly attractive model of H.M. Brig *Raleigh*, complete in every detail ; ahead of her is the huge *Royal Albert* of 131 guns, a remarkably handsome ship which marked the culminating stage of the sailing line-of-battleship. Actually, this ship was subsequently cut in two, lengthened and provided with engines and a screw, but the model shows her in all her glory before she was desecrated by the introduction of steam. Finally, at the far end of the line, is a most striking model of a Hamburg ship of 1719-20 ; the original was, in all probability, the *Wappen von Hamburg*, and the model was obtained from the Arsenal of that city when the contents were sold up in 1804. Recent investigations, which were kindly undertaken on behalf of the Museum by that well-known expert, Mr. R. C. Anderson, have brought to light many details in connection with this ship, and it is clear that in some respects the rigging is not correct for the period. It is intended, in due course, to make the necessary alterations to secure absolute accuracy.

Before leaving this part of the collection to view the more modern ships in the Crypt beneath, we should not miss many beautiful bone and ivory models which include Nelson's *Foudroyant*, Collingwood's *Royal Sovereign*, the *Queen* of 1769, and the *Prince of Wales* of 1794.

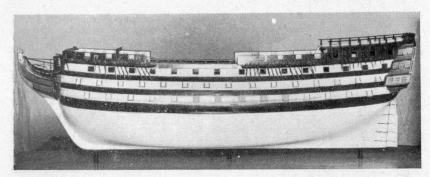

Hull Model of design for reconstructed " Victory "

H.M.S. "Foudroyant"—80 Guns. Nelson's Flagship, 1790

A 24 Gun Frigate of the period 1745

Collecting Photographs, Cuttings and Notes

HOW TO OBTAIN, KEEP AND INDEX THEM

By C. HAWKINS GARRINGTON

I AM expecting my photographs of merchant ships to exceed one thousand this year, while my newspaper cuttings, references to books and notes are too numerous to count. I do not suggest there is anything remarkable in such a collection, as there must be other amateurs who have preserved photographs, books, shipping publications and cuttings over a considerable period ; but how many keep their treasures readily accessible ? Let me assume that I am addressing those who desire to keep a record of ships which they are interested in but have not done so hitherto.

The Outfit

The outfit necessary consists of : (i) a looseleaf binder to take sheets 10″ × 8″, which is suitable for pictures up to half-plate size, obtainable from Messrs. Moore's Modern Methods, Ltd., 12, St. Bride Street, London, E.C., at the special price of 10s., who also supply leaves of stiff paper with slits for mounting, at 12s. 6d. a hundred ; (ii) a book for cuttings about 14″ × 10″, which can be purchased for 7s. 6d. to accommodate about a thousand cuttings, although I have used an old diary successfully ; (iii) an exercise book for notes ; (iv) a card-index box measuring 18″ in length, 8½″ wide and 6½″ deep, to take 500 fairly stiff cards 6″ × 8″, and (v) a camera.

The Camera

An autographic V.P.K. has several advantages : it is comparatively inexpensive both to buy and operate ; can be carried in the pocket ; a spoilt or unsatisfactory negative involves little loss, while good negatives can be enlarged to a suitable size for a few pence. I have enlargements up to 16″ × 10″ which show the minutest detail perfectly. The autographic arrangement enables you to number each exposure, and this number should be entered in a note-book at once with the date, name of ship, port of registry, place, colour details, such as those of the hull masts, upper works and funnel markings. All these details are written subsequently upon the back of the finished photograph together with the name of the company to which the ship belongs, house-flag, signal flags and dimensions ; this will establish definitely the identity of the ship.

Sources of Information

Probably some ships will be of interest about which you know little or nothing, so carry a copy of *Brown's Flags and Funnels*, and if the funnel marking is recorded you will find also the house-flag and name of owners, but similar details of coasters, tugs, trawlers and sailing vessels will have to be obtained by inquiry on the spot. Dimensions and signal flags are found from *Lloyd's Register*, which can be consulted without cost at the British Museum Reading Room, if you apply in writing to the Director, specifying your profession or business and the particular purpose for which admission is sought, but if this is not practicable, the information is available to members of The Ship Lovers' Association, particulars of which are given in this Magazine. The Nautical Photo Agency, 6, Russell Grove, Mill Hill, N.W.7, can supply almost any photograph you are likely to want, at 3d. a copy, post-card size, and a stock may be inspected at the offices of SHIPS AND SHIP MODELS. This Agency specialises in pictures of old ships.

Mounting Photographs

Photographs should be mounted on loose-leaves, an arrangement which enables each company's ships to be kept together and in order of date. The corners are inserted in diagonal slits about 1″ long so that the details upon the backs can be referred to and particular photographs removed for reproduction or other purposes. The binder should be numbered with the letter P as suffix. Mount each photograph, which must be identified by a mark corresponding to its book and the number of the leaf, near the top, and its negative vertically on the left-hand side underneath and as close to the photograph as possible. Half-inch slits are large enough for V.P.K. negatives. Leaves are numbered in the usual way and, when an addition has to be made between, say, leaves 1 and 2, it will become 1A, and so on.

Mounting Cuttings

Cuttings should be pasted into a book having a number with the latter C as suffix, and must bear a date and note indicating where obtained. No index is necessary, as reference to cuttings will be made either in the photographs' book or upon index cards; pages are numbered in the usual way.

Recording News

Newspapers often provide interesting items which should be marked and notes made at the tops of front pages. For instance, recently there was an account of a collision between the *American Trader* and the tug *Royalist*. The *American Trader* was stated to be the first merchant vessel on which an airship had landed; to have made a record Atlantic crossing for a single-screw ship (which was wrong), and to have been battered during a gale. That day's item added a new card to the index *Royalist* and several entries as follows :—

On the existing card *American Trader* is entered 2C39, meaning refer to No. 2 Cuttings' Book, page 39 ; on the card " Pioneers " is recorded *American Trader* first airship landing ;

The Brig "Raleigh"   Period 1806—Royal United Service Museum

" Records," *American Trader* record Atlantic crossing ; " Storms," *American Trader*—battering ; " Collisions," *American Trader* and *Royalist* ; 1931 *American Trader*—collision. In each case 2C39 is referred to for details ; entries are also made upon the cards of the years in which the airship landing, record, crossing and battering occurred.

Indexing Books

This example will make the system of indexing clear, but there remains to be explained the method of dealing with books and periodicals. Mark at the side anything you wish to record and note the page number at the end of a book and, in some convenient place, in a periodical. Then, if reference is made to a ship of which you have a photograph, put the name of the book or periodical and page number in the P book, as well as upon the appropriate cards. If a book is from a library, or referred to in a reference-room, add a note as to where it can be seen if there is too much to copy into your note-book, which you should

number and mark N. Also use the N book to record anything you hear or see, and duly authenticate it. Read and buy as many books as possible, and you will not miss much contemporary news if you subscribe to SHIPS AND SHIP MODELS, *The Nautical Magazine*, *The Shipbuilder*, *The Blue Peter*, and look carefully through a daily paper.

Do not let work accumulate, it will overwhelm you if you do ; wives or sisters can be very useful with cuttings.

I have endeavoured to give the result of long experience in the hope that it may help those who are collectors already, and encourage others to make a start, rather than lay down any hard and fast rules or to suggest that my system cannot be improved upon.

There are events deserving careful record and I am hopeful that these hints will be an inducement to others to take up this fascinating and useful hobby. In doing so, they will derive pleasure for themselves and do a service to ship lovers generally.

The Barque "Sorknes."

THE following particulars are given in reply to a correspondent :—

The *Sorknes* was originally J. D. Clink's *Zinita*. He named all his ships after racing yachts, and when the *Zinita* was built in 1893, the 20-rater of that name had just proved herself the yacht of the year, with 18 prizes out of 24 starts. She was built by Connell and Co., of Glasgow, a steel barque of 1,633 tons gross, and although she was named after a racing yacht, she was no faster than the other ships of the fleet, which is not saying very much. Although she was really one of Clink's fleet, she was nominally owned by the Zinita Ship Co., a single ship concern, whose management was transferred about 1906 to J. D. Hart. In 1907 she had to put into Bahia with trouble among her crew, and then took 155 days to sail from Bahia to

Astoria. Shortly afterwards, Lang and Fulton, of Greenock, took over the management and, in 1909, 40 guineas per cent. was paid for her on the re-insurance market, when she took 276 days from the Tyne to Seattle. A large part of this time was spent trying to round the Horn, but she failed to do so and eventually went via Australia. At the end of that voyage she was sold for £2,300 to J. Bruce, of Tonsberg, who re-named her *Sorknes*. She made a fortune during the War, but in October, 1920, was towed into Barry Roads totally dismasted, by the steamer *Rio Preto*. She was then on a passage from West Hartlepool to Sydney, Cape Breton, but the estimate for repairing her was so great that they decided to sell her, and she was bought by the Channel Coaling Co. to act as a hulk at Dartmouth.

A Working Model Paddle Steamer

By R. O. LOVELL

Model Paddle Steamer, by R. O. Lovell

THE design was taken from *Wonderful Models*, by "Nautillus," but several modifications were carried out during the construction.

The Hull

The hull, which is 48″ overall with a beam of 6″, is made from spruce, on the laminated system. The windows of the saloons below the deck were not cut out in the hull as "Nautillus" mentions in his descriptive article, as I could foresee damage being done to the mullions (or vertical bars), before the completion of the hull. The method I adopted was, to cut solid pieces out of the hull the total length of the window openings shown on the scale drawing. These openings were framed with stripwood about ¼″ thick, glued and pinned, leaving sufficient space at the back for the glass to be put in. The mullions separating each division were cut from stripwood and fitted into the main frames by slotting and glueing into position.

The sponsons were cut from pieces of pine, about $\frac{5}{16}$″ thick, and fitted on to the sides of the hull by glueing, and afterwards secured by brass screws from the inside of the hull.

The portholes are the ordinary black boot-eyes, turned down in the lathe to about ¼″ diameter, and filled with plastic wood and painted blue.

Deck and Funnel

The deck is made of zinc, and is in three sections for the convenience of firing the boiler, etc., etc. Openings were made for the fitting of funnel, ventilators, etc., and for the bridge house and deck saloon structures. On the bridge house is the steering wheel, binnacle and two telegraphs.

The funnel was made from thin-gauge copper sheet, seamed and silver-soldered, and fitted with two thin copper bands to make a finish for the black-painted top band. The base of the funnel was turned up from an old brass ferrule.

The four ventilators were made of copper deposition on lead moulds, similar to that described in *Practical Electro-plating* (No. 9, Marshall's Practical Manuals). The ventilators are not dummies—being hollow, they serve the purposes of allowing fresh air to enter the hull.

The Paddle Wheels

The paddle boxes are made from thin gauge zinc, soldered together, and fitted to the sides of the hull by means of $\frac{3}{8}''$ brass screws. The paddle wheels are of the feathering type, made from sheet brass, on the lines described by Mr. V. W. Delves-Broughton, in the *Model Engineer and Electrician*, under date of January 12th, 1922. These are decidedly an improvement upon the radial floats, and certainly looks more realistic when the machinery is set in motion. The photograph does not show the paddle wheels clearly, owing to the wheels being painted red, and the bottom of the hull black.

The Machinery

The propelling machinery comprises the following : A copper water-tube boiler having six tubes (all silver-soldered), with all the necessary fittings, enclosed in a brass sheet casing, with the funnel uptake directly connected. The firing of the boiler is by means of a methylated-spirit burner of the pan type. The engine is of the slide-valve type, $\frac{5}{8}''$ bore and stroke, on the lines set out in the M.E. Handbook Series—No. 13—*Machinery for Model Steamers*. Except for the cylinder casting and

gear wheels, the whole of the engine was built up from scrap materials.

Deck Fittings

The fittings, such as bollards, fairleads, capstan, ladders, mast-head lamp, port and starboard lights, steering wheel, binnacle, telegraphs, etc., etc., were made from scrap pieces of brass. The davits carrying the four life-boats, and the two flag masts, fore and aft, were made from $\frac{3}{32}''$ brass rod, tapered by filing.

The stanchions are made from large pins, the heads of which were ground down to form a round knob. The railings are of thin copper wire, soldered on to each stanchion.

The paintwork above the W.L. was given three coats of flat white paint, each being rubbed down, and finished white enamel. The deck was given two coats of ivory-colour paint, rubbed down, and lined in the usual way.

I hope to build another model paddle steamer shortly, but this time I shall make the whole of the machinery first, and, if necessary, modify the hull lines to suit such machinery.

Photo by]   [*R. C. Coulson*

The " Cutty Sark " and training ship " Foudroyant " at anchor in Falmouth Harbour

Books to Read

Steel's Elements and Practice of Mastmaking, Sailmaking, and Rigging. London : W. and G. Foyle, Ltd. Price £3 3s.

For many years past one of the greatest troubles of the model maker and the enthusiast on old ships has been the fact that two of the books which he wants most, " Falconer's Dictionary " and " Steel's Elements of Mastmaking, Sailmaking and Rigging," were beyond his reach, for both had got exceedingly scarce and fetched big prices. Messrs. W. and G. Foyle, Ltd., known to any number of sailormen and enthusiasts for their huge second-hand book business, have come to the rescue with the very able and, happily, enthusiastic editorship of Captain Claud S. Gill.

A slightly abridged edition of Falconer was published some months ago at a reasonable price, and has undoubtedly given a great impetus to the study of the sea in comfortable circumstances, and now the invaluable Steel, coveted by every student, is to a large extent re-issued in the original 1794 edition at three guineas nett.

As in the case of Falconer, it has been necessary to cut down the original edition somewhat, omitting such sections as ship handling and naval tactics, but the principal features of the book in the matter of rigging and canvas, are all retained, beautifully printed in a single large volume with well over 50 large plates containing hundreds of illustrations.

Of all the classics on shipbuilding and ship-rigging Steel has been subjected to the least criticism, which is only natural considering that David Steel was in the closest association with the Admiralty when he wrote the first book in 1794. When it was decided to reconstruct H.M.S. *Victory* as Nelson knew her, Steel was one of the principal authorities on which the Admiralty relied. Like most technical books of that day, it was apt to wander from subject to subject in rather a

bewildering manner, and one of the principal tasks of the editor, apart from deleting the non-essentials, has been to re-arrange the material in the handiest possible form, particularly with regard to the position of the plates. In the results of his labour in this direction, the editor is most heartily to be congratulated.

Perhaps two of the most useful features included in the book are at the end, the tables of the quantities and dimensions of the standing and running rigging of merchant shipping, a feature that is very difficult to obtain, and an index which is a model of what such things should be. Everybody connected with this production has earned the very hearty thanks of all who take a keen interest in the old ships and to whom Steel has hitherto been inaccessible.—FRANK C. BOWEN.

Private Men of War. By C. WYE KENDALL. London : Philip Allan. Price 15s.

" When is a pirate not a pirate ? " Nelson and his captains would have said " When he is a privateersman ! " With these words Mr. Wye Kendall opens the absorbing story of " Private Men of War."

Many of the most daring deeds of our Maritime history have often been attributed to privateers, buccaneers or pirates with little discrimination between them. The author, after careful research and much labour, has given to the public a true history of these " professions " of the sea, and has set on record a profoundly interesting story of which little of actual fact has been written.

In tracing the earliest commissions granted to a private Man-of-War in 1243, to " grieve the enemy by sea or by land whensoever they were able," the first privateersman was created, although the name itself was not introduced until the 17th Century.

These commissions, followed some 50 years later by Letters of ·Marque or Reprisal, were the outcome of the lawlessness of the sea which then existed. Our trading vessels, being at the mercy of hostile nations and roving hoards of pirates and buccaneers, were now permitted to arm themselves in self-defence. This, however, in some instances, led to abuse by unscrupulous merchants.

History might have been very different after 1588, but for the large number of privately-owned war vessels which were ready to join forces with Elizabeth's small Navy, and defeat the Armada.

Again, in the 17th Century, the privateer was of the utmost value in combating the fierce attacks of the Algerine pirates, who in their daring, carried out raids as far as the Bristol Channel. The privateersmen reached their zenith at the end of the 18th and the beginning of the 19th centuries, and the concluding chapters relate in a most entertaining way the amazing exploits of these men during the Wars with France and Spain and the American Civil War. With the inclusion of an authoritative bibliography, a general index and a list of over 350 vessels, this work will form a valuable addition to the records of Britain's Maritime History. —" CHIPS."

Blue Water Ventures. By Commander S. W. RYDER, R.N.R. (Retired). London : Hodder and Stoughton. Price 18s. net. Postage 8d.

Recently, there have been published several admirable books of reminiscences by retired master mariners, which have given the reader an interesting insight into life at sea in our great passenger liners. " Blue Water Ventures " is, however, of more than usual interest by reason of the author's varied and adventurous career in so many different types of craft throughout the seven seas. The early chapters, describing his apprenticeship in the old Salcombe Fruit Traders, with references to a number of them, such as the *Creole, Queen of the West, Salcombe Castle* and *Lord Devon,* to

name only a few, will awaken memories of the Clipper ship era in those who were alive in the 'eighties. These chapters will also be appreciated by those who still believe in the necessity of training in sail for the future officer and seaman in the Merchant Service.

In Captain Ryder's words, " . . . this was the kind of life which made a man of him and fitted him for the long struggle of existence. Besides the dexterity of a monkey, it demanded the application of mind and muscle, but (contrary to a boy's routine ashore) it strengthened the will to live and conquer difficulties. As a stout training to be self-reliant and act correctly in times of emergency, this rough seafaring was beyond all estimation." These Fruiters, consisting of barques, barquentines, brigs, brigantines and schooners, of from 500 to 100 tons, were fast sailers and handy vessels. They made quick passages from the West Coast to the Azores, the Mediterranean, and the West Indies. This seems to suggest the possibility of manning a fleet of vessels of a similar type, which could carry a fair amount of cargo, at the same time taking a number of apprentices. His adventures in tramp steamers, and in the *Chigwell,* the first steamer to be converted into an oil-tanker, are vividly portrayed, and emphasise the enormous improvements which have been made in the building of these craft, particularly the latter type, during the last 40 years. The voyage in the *Venture,* a vessel 248 ft. long, which he had to navigate from England to the Baltic and through the narrow and winding rivers and canals across Russia to Baku, a distance of some 5,000 miles, is of absorbing interest. Those who remember the Russo-Japanese War will delight in the story of how Captain Ryder took the *Caroline,* a torpedo-boat disguised as a steam yacht, from London, through the Kiel Canal to Libau. The incident led to serious diplomatic complications, and attention was called to it in all the principal newspapers. The author gives to the public for the first time the full details of this amazing exploit.

In the concluding chapters we see this versatile master mariner in his war-time adventures in various types of warships in all corners of the globe, which will be relished by all who enjoy tales of undaunted heroism and hairbreadth escapes. In a short foreword, Rear-Admiral Gordon Campbell, V.C., M.P., writes : " . . . There is always something to be learned from experiences of those who have found that there is no thrill in life to equal that which comes through duty well done, whether at sea or on shore." And he predicts that this tale of adventure will travel as far and wide among readers as the author has journeyed over the seas and the distant countries of the earth.—" Chips."

The Ship Modeller's Scrap Book
A DICTIONARY OF SHIP DETAILS IN ALL PERIODS.

(*Continued from page* 150)

Capstan

An appliance, *working horizontally*, for hauling great weights, principally cables, etc. ; a round barrel shaped so that a rope will grip it and fixed to the deck by a spindle round which it revolves. The upper ring is slotted with a number of holes to take the capstan bars, against which the men press to turn it, these invariably being made to unship for convenience and generally being stowed against the ship's bulwarks, handy to the geared to the windlass in the forecastle below for cable work.

A ship of the line generally had a fore and main capstan, while many had double capstans with a second crew on the deck below.

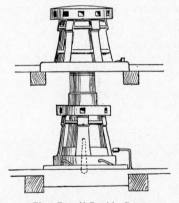

" First Rate " Double Capstan

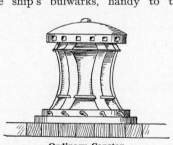

Ordinary Capstan

capstan. In its broad outlines, the capstan was changed remarkably little at different dates, even with the introduction of steam, but it has been considerably adapted to odd jobs, and some of the later ships carried a number of minor capstans, whereas in the old days only the big ones were considered.

In many of the latter sailing ships the capstan on the forecastle head was

Some of the capstan shanties were among the best of them all, having good, cheery airs and being sung much more quickly than the usual shanty, as the men went round with the capstan bars against their chests. In the Navy, where shantying was not allowed, the ship's fiddler, generally known as the Monkey's Orphan, took his seat on top of the capstan to get her round with a run.

Carronade

A short comparatively light gun of large calibre, introduced by the Carron Company in 1778, when the enormous demand for guns had caused a serious shortage. It was somewhat on the lines of the old *Cohorn*, much shorter,

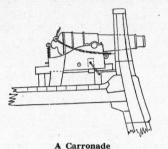

A Carronade

lighter and less elaborate than the ordinary naval gun, but within its short range it was very effective with a very heavy shot, advantage being taken of the shortness of the weapon to reduce the "windage," which was usually allowed in those days. Its special carriage, as shown in the illustration, in which the recoil was taken up by the griping of the carriage on the slide, permitted it to be worked in far less space than the ordinary truck carriage gun (*see* Cannon), and

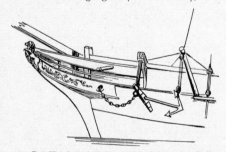

Cat Head and Falls. Fish Davit and Falls

it was therefore very popular with armed merchantmen, as well as with men-of-war as a secondary armament. The carronades were not counted in the number of guns with which the ship was rated until a comparatively late date. Its range was very short

and it had little penetrating power, while if the breeching rope gave way it invariably smashed itself and its carriage completely, but its introduction permitted frigates which had been limited to an 18-pounder gun until then to carry carronades which threw a 68-lb shot.

Cat Heads

Two strong beams projecting one on either bow of a sailing ship, turned slightly upwards and forwards, for the purpose of hoisting the anchor to swing it inboard or of suspending it clear of the ship's side ready to let go. In the outer end of each beam two or three sheaves were placed

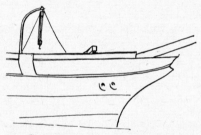

Iron Sailing Ship Cat Head and Fish Davit

through which the CAT FALL was rove to the CAT BLOCK secured to the anchor. The anchor was thus hoisted to the cat head, when a FISH DAVIT was rigged and falls used to lift the flukes of the anchor and get it inboard. In most modern ships a gooseneck davit, after the fashion of those used for boat work, took the place of the spar fish davit rigged whenever it was wanted, and many modern ships dispensed with it altogether and used a tackle with three-fold purchase from the fore topmast head.

The ends of the cat heads of many ships were finely decorated, generally continuing the scheme of the figurehead.   (*To be continued*)

Capt. E. Armitage McCann writes : " In reply to the query by Philip Maddocks, I have after much experiment found that the best material for making the sea on scenic models is Plastic Wood.

The Ship's Mail

Readers are invited to make use of this column for the discussion of matters of mutual interest and the exchange of ideas and information.

Carved Work on Elizabethan Ships

DEAR SIR,—In an article by "A.G.V.," entitled "The Colouring of Old-Time Ships," in the current issue of SHIPS AND SHIP MODELS, the author implies that the Elizabethans never made use of carved work for the embellishment of their ships.

Speaking of the "high-charged" Elizabethan man-of-war, in his introductory remarks to Hakluyt's "Principal Voyages of the English Nation," Mr. John Masefield says : "All had a quantity of carved and gilded work at bow and stern, and most bore a figurehead painted in fitting colours" (p. 17).

Does it not seem reasonable to suppose that Mr. Masefield would take great pains to verify his facts before including them in the introduction to such a great work as this ? I, as a "lone worker," am nonplussed ! for there seems to be so much evidence that is conflicting.

I wonder if "A.G.V." or other readers would be kind enough to say as to whether there is conclusive evidence to show that carved work on an Elizabethan model would be an anachronism, or not !

Yours faithfully,
R. W. TATE.
Instow, near Bideford.

Ships in London River

DEAR SIR,—I have read with great interest the article "Sailing Ships in the London River," by Mr. G. C. Johnson. Although it does not make any great difference as to the value of the essay, I would like to mention that I think Mr. Johnson is mistaken when he states that the s.s. *Preussen* was barque rigged.

I remember having seen this ship in the harbour of Hamburg several times, and it certainly was a full-rigged ship then. I have also before me, right now, a couple of photographs of the *Preussen*, showing five masts with six yards on every one of them, thus 30 yards in all.

Yours faithfully,
KUND SHLAMEF.
Odense, Denmark.

The Oldest Vessels Afloat

DEAR SIR,—I am very interested in the article on "The Oldest Vessels Afloat" in your January issue. I see one of your correspondents states that he is in doubt as to whether the *Premier* or the *Glencoe* were the older ship. Should not the official numbers of these vessels settle the question. They are : *Glencoe*, 6,359 ; *Premier*, 6,387.

I do not make models, but I take a great interest in shipping and shipping matters generally, and was delighted with SHIPS AND SHIP MODELS from the first, but I think No. 5 is the best issue yet.

Yours sincerely,
Bray.   CHARLES J. COGHLAN.

The Model of H.M.S. "Juno"

DEAR SIR,—With reference to the letters of Mr. A. G. Vercoe and Mr. R. W. Prance, I fear that the question of the model called H.M.S. *Juno* of 1750, can only serve as an example of the progress made during the past 30 years or more in the study of the history of Naval Architecture.

The model of the *Juno* was received at the Science Museum in 1898, 13 years before the foundation of the Society for Nautical Research, and at a time when very few ship models had been examined, checked and identified with sufficient accuracy as to form standards by which other models could be measured.

More than ten years ago, the model of the *Juno* was withdrawn from the Science Museum Collections and went, I believe, to America. Consequently,

beyond destroying the negative, there
has been neither opportunity nor
occasion to discuss the model in any
Museum publication later than the
catalogue of 1911.

In point of fact, the model, although
a beautiful piece of craftsmanship,
is not contemporary, and rests on no
historic basis whatsoever.

As Mr. Vercoe points out, the poop
or roundhouse is entirely wrong, and
the stern windows, together with
nearly the whole of the stern, is a
deck too high. His other criticisms
are equally true, but in view of the
model's unfortunate history, I do not
think these points are worth going
into in detail.

May I conclude by expressing my
personal regret to Mr. Prance that he
has been so unluckily led astray.
Knowledge does grow with time, however, and the best information available at the moment is always at the
service of interested applicants.

Yours very truly,
G. S. LAIRD CLOWES.
The Science Museum.

DEAR SIR,—The model of H.M.S.
Juno was in the Science Museum, but
is now removed. In the 1911 edition
of the Catalogue the description is as
follows :—

Rigged model of H.M.S. *Juno*
(scale 1 : 24.) Lent by S. T. G.
Evans, Esq., 1898. This vessel was
built on the Thames in 1757 by Mr.
Alexander to the design of Sir T.
Slade, who then held the post of
Constructor to the Navy. She was
one of the first typical frigates carrying
her armament on one deck and being
built for the Service as a swift independent cruiser. Her armament was
thirty-two 9-pounders, and her complement 220 men.

Tonnage, 667 tons ; length 127.83';
breadth, 34.25' ; depth of hold, 11.83'.

She is illustrated in the Supplement
to this Catalogue and a comparison
leaves nothing to be desired. A
lantern-slide of her is still included in
the list of slides obtainable in the
Museum.

The mistake in her armament is
apparent. Mention is made that an
armament of 32-pounder guns on this
tonnage is equivalent to mounting
12″ guns in a destroyer ; H.M.S.
Adriadne, in 1816, with a tonnage of
only 511 tons, carried an armament of
twenty 32-pounder, six 18-pounder and
two 9-pounder guns on the main
deck, and twenty 32-pounder carronades on the flush upper deck.

Yours faithfully,
L. WITHRINGTON,
London.   Commander, R.N.V.R

Information Wanted

DEAR SIR,—I have discovered, in
a neighbour's loft, a hull of a ship,
a rough sketch of which I enclose.
By the way it is made I should
think it has been a model, but cannot
trace either in books or at the South

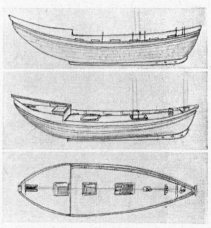

What Craft is this?

Kensington Museum the period or
nationality. I am anxious to rig it
but would like to find out some details.
I can only imagine it to be a type of
fishing-boat, perhaps Greek or Dutch.

The model is 34½″ long, and its
greatest beam is 10″. The opening at
stern, in deck plan, shows where the
rudder has been. Is the fitting right
in the bow for another mast ?

Streatham.   S. C. PRIOR.

Who's House Flag?

DEAR SIR,—I wonder if any of your readers could assist me to trace the company or owner of the enclosed house-flag? I have a model schooner which I am fitting-out, and the flag, crossed with the Red Ensign, appears on the life-belts.

The model was built by an old Blue Nose (shipwright?), who worked for my grandfather in South Africa

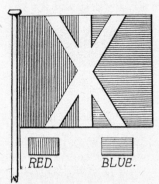

RED.   BLUE.

Who's House Flag is this?

about 1897. Our family were always under the impression that the model was of the *John Knox* until I unearthed the boats and lifebelts with the name *Southern Cross* clearly painted on.

Perhaps some one could also give me the correct colours for the top-sides, etc.?

Later on, when everything is in order, perhaps your readers would like an article and illustrations on my model. She is complete to as far as it is possible to make a $\frac{1}{2}''$ scale working model. The wheel, rudder, compass, skylight, companion-way, hatches and capstans all function. The boats are fitted with oars and rowlocks, etc., which is, I think, exceptional.

Yours sincerely,
Goudhurst.   G. W. MUNRO.

British Coasting Vessels

DEAR SIR,—May I say that I am greatly interested in making models of British coasting vessels, and there is no means of obtaining information

about them in this country. I would be very much obliged if you would publish more articles like the one in the December issue on the three-masted topsail schooner. One on the ketch of the type of the *Ceres* of Bude, also shown in the December issue, would be especially appreciated.

The Oakland Estuary, a few miles from here, contains a large proportion of all the sailing vessels still afloat. There are 13 large iron and steel sailing vessels with their yards still crossed—six of which have figure-heads—as well as many schooners, barquentines and hulks, laid up there. I would like to exchange photographs of them if any of your readers are interested.

Yours sincerely,
JOHN LYMAN.
2928, Hillegass Avenue,
Berkeley, California.

Working Model Clipper Ships

DEAR SIR,—If you can find space in the Ship's Mail, I should like to thank both Mr. Lewis and Mr. Denzil Hollis for their interest in my model, and particularly for their helpful rigging suggestions.

I should like also to disclaim at once Mr. Denzil Hollis's kindly suggestion that I am more expert than he, since I took less time to make my model. Time is not a good criterion in model work, and the rigging details he gives of his ship are sufficient proof that his is the better job. I can well understand that it was the work of three winters.

I, too, have now found that the leech of each sail sufficiently controls its own yard, and have already adopted the "endless" trick, except for the braces from the fore, main, and mizzen courses, which still lead aft to the winch.

I am sorry Mr. Denzil Hollis did not enter more into the question of true-to-scale clipper models—clippers were extreme shallow-draught ships in relation to length and top hamper —and their ability to stand up to full sail without false keels. It was the subject of correspondence between Mr. E. W. Hobbs, A.I.N.A., and myself, when I commenced my model, and he showed me good mathematical evidence why a false keel was necessary, unless provision was made for taking in sail in anything more than a gentle zephyr.

Scale goes to pieces when weights are brought into the picture—one cannot scale down specific gravities—the *Cutty Sark* was over 900 tons net register, and my model is 1/90th scale. The deduction is obvious and I won't labour it.

Quite a small departure from scale in beam, and rather more in depth, would, I know, have given the necessary power to carry sail without a false keel, but theory, anyway, seems against inside ballast only in true-to-scale clipper hulls. I must confess I haven't tried it, for Mr. Hobbs' figures were convincing and the performance of the model in water seems to confirm theory.

Is the subject of sufficient general interest for an article on it in SHIPS AND SHIP MODELS? I suppose, at all events, it is too lengthy a matter to discuss in the Ship's Mail columns.

It may interest owners of *Cutty Sark* models to know her " number " in the International Flag Code ; according to Lloyds Register it was J, K, W, S in that order from the top of the hoist.

Yours faithfully,

Harpenden.   G. S. HUSSEY, Capt.

Northern Notes
By " JASON "

1932 HAS opened well for model ship makers in the North. Already, the Merseyside Club have moved into their new Club Room and Club No. 2 has been opened in Manchester. Preparations are well under way for opening No. 3, in Glasgow, and No. 4 in Hull, while in Bristol and Newcastle arrangements are now being planned. I shall be glad to hear from those who are interested in the districts named. Letters should be addressed : " Jason," c/o Editor, SHIPS AND SHIP MODELS.

I am endeavouring to persuade Commander Craine, the Founder of the Merseyside Club, to contribute a short article as a guide to those who contemplate forming small clubs in their own districts.

Bury, Lancashire

A very successful Shipping Exhibition was organised here last December (3rd-8th). A large number of model ships were on view, but the principal attraction was a " Three Shilling Model Competition," run on the lines of the competition which was so successful in the Liverpool Shipping Week Exhibition last August. Several scores of entries made the judges' work exceedingly difficult, and the 1st prize in the Senior Section was won by Mr. Hartley, of Waterloo, near Liverpool, with his exquisite 20″ model of the four-masted barque *Wanderer*. The Junior Section gave excellent promise for model makers of the future. The formation of a club in Manchester will doubtless prove a boon to many enthusiasts in the Bury district, whence so many of the prize-winners came.

Manchester

The Model Ship Makers' Club No. 2 (Lancashire and Cheshire) was successfully launched on January 13th, 1932, in the Seamen's Mission, Trafford Road, Salford. Nearly a score of members have already given their support. The meeting was convened by Lieut.-Comdr. J. H. Craine, of Liverpool, who attended in person. Dr. W. J. S. Naunton was elected Chairman, and the new Club chose the Rev. R. C. Stuart-Cundy as Vice-Chairman. It was decided to follow along the lines of the Merseyside Club Rules. Many members are model ship makers of some experience. The following are representative of vessels " on the stocks " : A ship of the

Middle Ages, revenue cutter (1800), *Cutty Sark*, *Thermopylae*, a tanker sailing yacht (model), and others. Mr. Authers was appointed Hon. Treasurer, while the Secretary is Mr. Hemmingway, who should be addressed (*pro. tem.*) : c/o Seamen's Mission, Trafford Road, Salford. Meeting Nights, Tuesdays, 8 p.m., at same address.

Merseyside Model Ship Makers' Club

A record attendance greeted Captain F. E. Storey, R.D., R.N.E.—a maker of model ships and whose work is known internationally — when he opened the new Club Room of the M.M.S.M.C. on December 14th, 1931. " It was very important," he said, in declaring the Club Room open, " that models should be accurate. There were many serious errors to be found even in models belonging to important and National collections. Anything, therefore, I can do to help this Club will be a pleasure to me and a duty to the future."

Dr. D. A. Allan, the Director of the Liverpool Museums, supported Captain Storey.

He greeted warmly the advent of the new Club, and he reminded them that there were gaps to be filled in the collection of ship models in the Shipping Gallery of the City Museums. After the formal proceedings, the visitors inspected work in progress on more than a score of models. The room is really a fitted workshop, well lit by a dozen lights, with a draughtsman's table, benches, lathes and an ample supply of tools, wood, metal and fabric. For this, tribute was paid to the " Gentlemen Adventurers," a band of patrons whose generosity made much of it possible, particularly Mr. Robert Gladstone, who has presented a silver cup for annual competition. Hon. Sec. : L. F. Holly, 9, Jasmine Street, Anfield, Liverpool.

Exhibitions of Model Ships

Two Exhibitions, interesting to Northern readers, are announced ; the first, under the auspices of the Merseyside Club, will take place in Liverpool in the late Spring, probably in mid-April. The other will take place in the Autumn, in Manchester. These two exhibitions will strike a new note. A considerable section will be that which shows models in course of construction. Both will also have a section devoted to a " Three Shilling Model Competition."As these competitions will be open to the whole country, a special article will appear next month, giving particulars and hints for this kind of model. As there are many valuable prizes, don't miss the opportunity of competing.

Glasgow and the Clyde

Several readers have already written to me regarding the formation of a Model Ship Makers' Club on Clydeside. There must be many more in the cradle-valley of steamships who are interested in meeting each other to their mutual benefit in particular, and the advancement of model ship making in general. Will those who would support a Clydeside Club write to me before February 10th, so that arrangements may be made for an early meeting.

The Humber District

That ardent ship-lover and indefatigable worker in nautical research, Mr. T. Sheppard, the Director of the Hull Municipal Museums, is keenly alive to the value of a well-organised Model Ship Makers' Club in the Humber district. It is not without interest to record that several entries for the Liverpool Shipping Week Exhibition Competition came from Hull. The Hull Museums are particularly rich in models and other nautical exhibits, one of which, the figurehead of the pioneer transatlantic steamer, *Sirius*, was loaned to Liverpool last summer. So far, I have had two requests from the Humber for a club to be formed. Don't leave it to the other fellow. Perhaps he is leaving it to you ?

The Cockermouth Coracle

An interesting query is before me. " Wirral " asks how many types of coracle are still to be found in Great

Britain. He has challenged my figures and localities. My evidence relates to two, and two others are by hearsay. (1) The *Llangollen Coracle*, on the upper reaches of the Dee, used by salmon fishers. This is, roughly, square in shape. (2) The *Ironbridge Coracle*, on the Severn, in Shropshire, oval in shape and also used for fishing (by nets, in pairs). (3) The *Cockermouth Coracle*, of which I have no definite evidence, but I believe that, at certain times of the year, young men in the vicinity of Cocker-mouth (Cumberland) "shoot" the broken upper waters of a stream in contest with each other. (4) Coracles in various localities of the Scottish lowlands. I shall be glad to have confirmation of Nos. (3) and (4) from readers in the respective localities. Any photographs sent to me will be returned safely.

Model Yacht Clubs

Will Secretaries of Northern Model Yacht Clubs please communicate with me. It may be to the advantage of their Club.

The Ship Lovers' Association

PARTICULARS of Membership were given in full in the September issue of SHIPS AND SHIP MODELS. The Hon. Secretary, *pro. tem.*, is Frank C. Bowen, of Customs House Building, Gravesend, Kent.

A considerable number of members have not yet let the Secretary know the sections into which they want to be logged.

The meetings of London members, to which those from the country and abroad are always cordially welcome, are held at the Admiral's Cabin Restaurant, 167, Strand, on the first and third Tuesdays of each month ; the first an informal gathering, and the third a dinner followed by papers and discussion.

Thanks to the good offices of a Glasgow member, we now have available lines and sail plans of a number of sailing coasters, etc. Will anybody interested communicate with Mr. F. Wayne, 8, Lancaster Gate Terrace, W.2, who has taken charge of Section XIII (Models).

Members' Queries and Answers

(*Only answers of more general interest are given here ; these and all others of lesser interest are answered by post.*)

Several members have expressed interest as to the origin or meaning of the term " onker," always applied on the London River to a sailing ship on the Baltic small-timber trade. Can any member at home or abroad help in this ; the term has certainly been in use for many years, but no explanation ever seems to have been published.

F.S.B. (Bournemouth).—The Antrim Ore Company's steamer *Glenravel* of 1906 was captured by a German submarine on August 8th, 1915, about 25 miles north of Kinnaird Head and sunk by explosive charges.

E.A.W. (Rangoon).—The *Hansy* was originally *Aberfoyle*, a steel ship of 1,661 tons, built in 1885 for J. A. Sillars of Glasgow. She had an unusual experience in 1895 when an Italian steamer picked her up in Gautheaume Bay in charge of the steward. Her master had died from carbolic poisoning and the mate had disappeared overboard ; no second mate had been shipped. Later, she was sold twice in Glasgow and, in 1910, became the Norwegian *Hansy*, being wrecked off the Lizard in 1911.

P.A. (Gravesend).—The very clever parody on Masefield's " Sea Fever " appeared in the *Manchester Guardian* some three years ago, and began :—
" I must go down to the sea again, to
　the lonely sea and the sky,
And all that I ask is a ship done up
　to look like the land that's dry.
With a palm lounge and a ballroom
　floor, and the loose legs shaking,
And a bedroom suite with a bath
　complete, and a bed for the
　morrow's waking."

SHIPS AND SHIP MODELS

A Magazine for all Lovers of Ships and the Sea

Single Copies, post free, 7½d.
Annual Subscription 7s. 6d.

Editorial and Publishing Offices:

66 FARRINGDON STREET
L O N D O N :: E. C. 4

Vol. I. No. 7.   MARCH, 1932.   Price 6d.

The Ship's Log

Our Policy and Progress

NOW that SHIPS AND SHIP MODELS has got so far on its voyage, it is perhaps an appropriate moment to take stock of what our little paper is doing. It is most pleasing to be able to record the expressions of approval which have reached us from readers and subscribers in all parts of the world. It is obvious, from the number of these appreciative letters we have received, that such a publication was much needed, and we are grateful for, and encouraged by, the many kind things which have been said. We do not pretend to have satisfied everybody : it is very rare that any paper succeeds in doing that, but we have a very large majority in our favour. Such friendly criticism as we have received mainly arises from the diversified interests of our readers. It is perhaps natural that the reader who is mainly interested in real ships should begrudge the space given to models, and similarly that the lover of sail should declaim against the space given to steam. Equally the preference may be the other way. This is inevitable with a paper which en-deavours to take a broad view of maritime interests, but we think our readers, whatever their particular liking may be, will find that in the long run they will be fairly treated. In one issue, one particular field of interest may predominate, but over a period of months we think they will find that their pet subject has had a reasonable share of space. We visualise SHIPS AND SHIP MODELS as being a friendly link between ship lovers and ship modellers of all degrees of knowledge and con-structive ability. We do not put our claim for recognition any higher than that. While we have the greatest admiration for classic examples of ship-modelling, and for accuracy of information, we are not high-brow ; we have a tender feeling for the novice, and a desire to give him help and encouragement through articles of a possibly elementary character. If we can improve his knowledge and give him a higher standard of craftsman-ship through the classic and more advanced examples of modelling we publish from time to time, we shall be doing a good work, but we feel at least that the beginner must be catered for in some degree. Judging from our correspondence, we feel that we are taking the right line, and we hope that the good opinions we have already earned may be retained in our future progress.

* * *

The Problem of Queries

We may confess to being a little perturbed by the deluge of queries which has fallen upon us during the past few months. Some of these we have been able to answer right away, others have been dealt with by some of our expert friends, and for this assistance we tender grateful thanks. Some few have been beyond an answer. It is at any rate a compliment that readers who are in search of some historical information, or the plans or history of some particular ship, should turn to us for assistance when they have exhausted every other source of reference. Where we are unable to give the information ourselves, we propose to publish such inquiries, for we think it possible that among our many readers of competent knowledge or fruitful study there may be some who can help. To put it another way, we think our readers should regard our little paper more as a means of intercommunication than as an infallible source of reference. We have already experienced many instances where one reader has very kindly helped another in this way, and we hope that this mutual service may continue to extend. There is one other point ; we are sometimes asked to furnish drawings for a particular ship or model a reader wishes to build. We are not now referring to the blueprints which we supply, but to requests that we should make a drawing to suit a reader's special requirements, in return for a stamped addressed envelope. A little thought will show that such a request is unreasonable. Even if the reference data were available, the expense of preparing special drawings would be quite beyond any gratuitous service which might fairly be expected from us.

Information Wanted

Here are a few recent queries on which readers would like information. We shall be happy to forward any replies which other readers may be good enough to send : (1) Photograph wanted of the s.s. *Milton Star*, a one-time Blue Star boat. Her first name was *Brodhurst*, and she is now *Dniepr*. (2) Dimensions and details of the s.s. *Dundee*, of Dundee. (3) Dimensions and points of interest of B.I. troopship *Neuralia*. (4) Hull plans of the English 100-gun ship *Royal George* of 1715, or of similar ship of same period. (5) What form of block was in use in Portuguese ships of the period 1515 to 1545 ; at what date were sheaved blocks introduced into English shipbuilding ?

* * *

Bristol Shiplovers

The Bristol Shiplovers' Society is now well under weigh with a roll of over one hundred members, and a serious effort is being made to tap the immense store of maritime history that lies buried in and around the West Country ports. When it be noted that among its members the Society counts survivors of the great Peru seaboard earthquake of '76, the old Barbadoes sugar trade, the Gulf of Guinea barter trade, the " Down Easters," the Chilian whale fishery, and the burning of the *Goliath*, to mention a few at random, it will be obvious that there is quite sufficient of the ." hemp and marline spike " tradition to ensure the proper atmosphere for a good yarn. One member still boasts proudly of a ship which he admits, under pressure, normally required pumping 40 minutes to the hour, and responsibilities range from the present command of an Orient liner to the one-time command of the smallest steamer to trade regularly across the Western Ocean. The names of Basil Lubbock, the ship's historian, and Commander Worsley, the Antarctic explorer, among the vice-presidents, add an additional lustre to a good start.

Marine Etchings and Paintings

From a coloured etching]   *[By Oswald F. Pennington*

The Canadian Emigrant Ship " Lake Erie "

WE have recently had the pleasure of looking through a collection of marine etchings and water-colour paintings by Mr. Oswald F. Pennington. Mr. Pennington is obviously a ship-lover as well as an artist, for not only are the drawings excellent in their nautical technique, but the character of the original ship in each case is admirably depicted. The etchings are offered to collectors in two styles, plain and hand-coloured, at very moderate prices. Which is the preferable of the two styles will be a matter for individual choice. They are both effective, but to our mind the addition of a little well-chosen colour puts an additional touch of realism into the picture, which is well worth the additional cost. The subjects of the etchings are the *Cutty Sark, Dreadnought, Garthpool, Lake Erie, Strathearn,* and *White Star.* The

size of the drawing is 6″ × 4″, and they are tastefully mounted for framing to a size of 15″ × 11″. We reproduce the etching of the Canadian Emigrant Ship *Lake Erie,* which shows how effective is Mr. Pennington's draughtsmanship. This picture is reproduced from one of the coloured etchings.

The water-colour paintings depict the *Lightning,* the *Hesperus,* and the *Thermopylae.* These also are notable for the accuracy of their technical detail and good drawing. It is good that the memory of these famous ships should be preserved in picture as well as in story, and Mr. Pennington will undoubtedly please many collectors with his effective contributions to marine history. Inquiries for any of his work should be addressed to B. Pennington, 8, West Graham St., Glasgow, C.4, and mention of this article should be made when writing.

Notable Ships Past and Present

No. IV.—THE P. AND O. TURBO-ELECTRIC LINER " STRATHNAVER "

ALTHOUGH she is not the pioneer turbo-electric liner, the P. & O. *Strathnaver*, and her sister, the *Strathaird*, have particular importance as they take the electric drive which was tried in the *Viceroy of India* very much further than it has been taken in any other merchant ship, they show the readiness of the P. & O. Company to fulfil any new conditions that may Le made on the Australian trade, and in many ways they mark a new era in P. & O. practice. Being a pioneer, the *Strathnaver*, named after the Scottish estate with which Lord Inchcape couples his title, naturally attracted the greatest interest.

As she is very considerably the biggest ship in the P. & O. service, her dimensions are of interest. Between perpendiculars she is 630′ long, 664′ overall, with a beam of 80′ and a load draught of 29′ 2″, which seems very small when one considers her towering topsides and promenade decks. The depth from the keel to E deck is 46′ 6″, to D deck 54′ 9″, to C deck 63′, to B deck 71′ 3″, and, finally, to A deck 81′ 9″. Her gross tonnage is 22,547, her load displacement nearly 28,000, while her deadweight capacity is 9,975, as she is primarily a passenger ship carrying 498 in the first class and 670 tourist-third, her total crew being 487 of all ranks and ratings.

The cruiser stern is already familiar in P. & O. ships, but she has been given rather an extreme raking bow becoming more and more round above the waterline. This roundness permits the fitting of a searchlight room under the forecastle head for navigating the Suez Canal, the watertight door of which is beautifully decorated and is as near to the old-fashioned figurehead as the construction of such a modern ship will permit. Unusually large life-boats, under gravity davits, are another external feature of the ship, which looks more like a crack Canadian Pacific Liner

than a P. & O., with her white hull and three yellow funnels of which only the centre one is active. The old-timers, however, will remember that when the company brought out the famous *Caledonia*, in 1894, and won the Indian record, they painted her in the same way and did not put her into the normal colour scheme of the P. & O. until she was no longer novel.

Fine ship as the *Strathnaver* is from external appearance and the passengers' point of view, it is her engines which are of the greatest interest, and a glance at the plan will show how very compact they are for 28,000 h.p. and how little they interfere with the earning capacity of the ship. They have an added economy in that they permit the company to fulfil the dual speed requirements of the mail contract while keeping the machinery at full efficiency for the whole time. The *Strathnaver*, like the *Viceroy of India*, has two entirely separate turbo-alternator sets, each with its own condensing plant and auxiliaries, generating the power for two double-unit synchronous motors placed on the shafts. The principal advantage of this system is that the turbo-generators can always run at their most efficient speed, and if full power is not required, one can be closed down and the current generated by the other divided between the two motors with excellent results. The turbines, rated for 10,700 kilowatts, run at 3,000 revolutions per minute, while the motors run at 125, from which the full efficiency can be obtained from the screws.

On trial, the *Strathnaver* worked up to 23.003 knots, so that she can easily maintain the 22 knots which is her legend full speed. This permits her to have sufficient reserve of speed in hand to make up for any time lost through bad weather or delays on the voyage, and if the Australian Government demands a higher speed for its

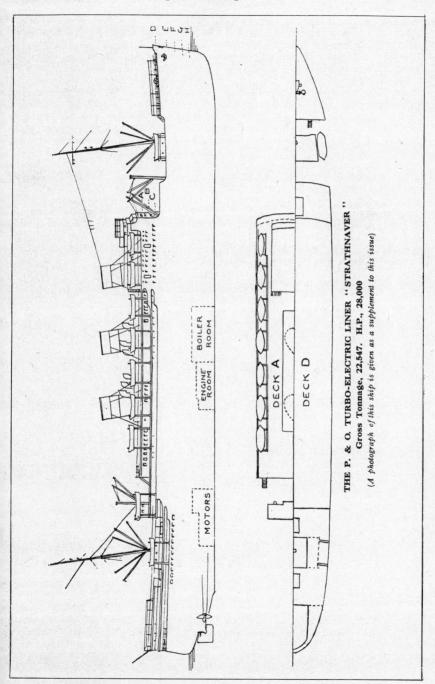

THE P. & O. TURBO-ELECTRIC LINER "STRATHNAVER"

Gross Tonnage, 22,547. H.P., 28,000

(A photograph of this ship is given as a supplement to this issue)

mail contract, as it is always threatening to do, the company is in the position to say that it has the material all ready to fulfil the conditions as soon as the Post Office is willing to pay for the higher speed.

Normally, however, the *Strathnaver* will never run at more than 20 knots, for the time being at least, and at that speed she consumes 136 tons of oil fuel per day. At 18 knots she consumes 100, and at 15½ knots a shade more than 70, and as these figures are for all purposes, it will be seen that she is a remarkably economical ship for her size and class.

Undoubtedly a good deal of this economy must be placed to the credit of the Yarrow boilers, which are of novel design. The small boiler room for such a large power is significant,

for it only contains four main boilers of the very latest double-flow side-firing type, each having three water drums, a steam drum and a super-heater drum. They work at a pressure of 400 lb. to the sq. in., blowing off at 425, while the steam is superheated to 725 degrees Fahrenheit. In addition, there are two smaller auxiliary boilers for auxiliary purposes in port, but they can be linked up to the main set should they require assistance at sea.

Altogether, the *Strathnaver* is a very remarkable vessel, and although she probably has a good many of the troubles of the pioneer which can be rectified with experience, she is a very noteworthy vessel and would make 1931 a special year without any other ships being built.

The " Royal William "

THE PIONEER OF ATLANTIC GREYHOUNDS

By A. M. REID

IN these days of *Majestics* and *Britannics*, it is difficult to realise that one hundred years ago, the Atlantic had never been crossed by steamships. And a wiseacre in authority at that period had pronounced the verdict that it was " as feasible to voyage to the moon ! "

The honour of sending the first steamer, the *Royal William*, across " the herring pond " in 1833, goes to Canada. She had a unique and romantic career. Built in Quebec, engined in Montreal, and owned by Canadians, from " truck to keelson " she was entirely a Canadian product. A brass tablet in the House of Commons at Ottawa commemorates this historic event.

It has been generally accepted by many that the American ship *Savannah* was the pioneer Atlantic steamer in 1819. But her engines were only auxiliary to the sails, and on the round voyage

she only steamed 80 hours out of the 70 days' sailing time. Her engines, being for use in calm weather, it cannot be claimed that she actually steamed across. The fact that her engines were discarded on her return and she reverted to sail, proves that the day of the marine engine for ocean voyages had not yet dawned. Hence the scope for the wiseacres.

The *Royal William* was originally built to trade between Quebec and Halifax, and her builders had no idea that the child of their brains would ever cross the ocean. At that period, the Government wished to facilitate communications between Canada proper and the Maritime provinces, which hitherto had been carried on by schooners and by laborious land journeys. An Act was passed granting £3,000 to the first person or company who would regularly run a steam vessel over 500 tons between these ports.

Thus the Quebec and Halifax Company was formed, one of the shareholders being Samuel Cunard of Halifax, who two years later founded the Cunard Line. The steamer was built in Campbell's shipyard at Wolfe Cove, Quebec, and launched in April, 1831. She was christened the *Royal William*, after William IV, the then reigning monarch, by the Governor's wife, Lady Alymer.

The dimensions may be of interest. Her length of deck was 176′, beam 44′, and depth of hold 17′ 9″. She was rigged as a three-masted topsail schooner. Her tonnage was 1,370, as compared to 60,000 of the new White Star Line. Her cost was £16,000 complete. She was supplied with 400 h.p. paddle engines by Bennet and Henderson's foundry, Montreal.

She sailed on her maiden voyage in August, 1831, with 20 cabin and 70 steerage passengers for Halifax, taking 6½ days to make the trip. In the following year cholera broke out in Quebec, and on her first voyage that year, the chief engineer died and several of the crew were infected. Panic seized the authorities at the various ports she endeavoured to call at, and she was either delayed in quarantine or prevented from entering the harbours. The result was that she could only make the one trip that year before being laid up for the winter, with a resultant loss to the company.

This led to a judgment being entered against the company, and the *Royal William* was sold by the mortgagees for £5,000. The new company sent her to Boston, being the first British steamer to enter that port. It was then decided to send her to England to be sold.

Without any ostentation or ceremony, she quietly left Pictou, Nova Scotia, on August 18th 1833, with seven passengers on board, for Gravesend. The cost of the passage was £20, exclusive of wines. The names of those passengers deserve a place in history. Her engines had never done

three weeks' continuous steaming before. The voyage took 19 days, but for several days she had only the port engine running, due to the starboard engine breaking down. Then, later, she was hove-to with leaky boilers.

Her arrival at Gravesend proved the possibility of steam navigation for ocean travel. She was sold to Joseph Serris, shipowner, for £10,000, and chartered by the Portuguese Government as a transport in the service of Dom Pedro. In 1834, the Spanish Government bought her and had her converted into a warship under the name of *Isabel Segunda*, being the first steam warship they possessed.

Fighting was taking place at that time between the Carlists and the Government. The *Isabel Segunda* first came into action at San Sebastian on August 5th, 1836, by bombarding the Carlists' positions ashore. She has been claimed as the first war steamer to go into action, but that point is doubtful. The Greeks had a steamer in their service during their War of Independence, five years previously, and would likely have used her in action.

In 1837 the *Isabel Segunda* returned to London with discharged soldiers, but was detained there until the claims of the crew, for back-pay, had been settled by the Spanish Government. She was next sent to Bordeaux to be repaired, but her wooden hull was so badly decayed that her engines were taken out. A new hull was built for the engines and, under the name of *Saint Isabel*, she continued in the service of Spain for over 20 years. In 1860 she was wrecked off the coast of Algiers.

So ended the last of the *Royal William*—her hull crumbling at Bordeaux and her engines rusting beneath the Mediterranean. But she had conquered the Atlantic, and the day of the steamship had come, for while she was ending her days as a Spanish warship, the Atlantic liners were coming into being. The seemingly impossible had been achieved.

The " Isle of Sark "

THE NEW TURBINE STEAMER FOR THE SOUTHERN RAILWAY COMPANY'S CHANNEL ISLES SERVICE

THE new Channel steamer, *Isle of Sark*, launched on January 21st from the Leven Shipyard of Messrs. William Denny and Bros., has a special interest in that it is the first ship to be built in Britain to the " Maierform." At the launch, Mr. Maurice Denny said, in explanation of this novel feature :—

" A good many years ago, an Austrian gentleman by the name of Maier came to the conclusion that it was possible to improve the form of ships by a change especially of the lines of the bow. His conception remained dormant for many years, but had recently aroused keen interest, and there were afloat that day many ships built to ' Maierform,' all constructed on the Continent except one, the *Isle of Sark*. Speaking personally, he did not think that Maierform would be found to be of universal application, but it was unquestionable that by its adoption the resistance of a ship may sometimes be reduced in calm weather, and there was a large volume of evidence to show that in rough weather Maierform might be definitely superior to normal forms, enabling a higher speed to be maintained in a seaway, and contributing materially to the comfort of the passengers. The Southern Railway Company deserved much credit for its keen interest in all that pertained to the improvement of ships, and for its courage in being the first shipowner in Britain to try a system novel to shipowners in this country."

The *Isle of Sark* is 306′ long by 42′ broad by 16′ to the main deck, with a gross tonnage of about 2,143, and is intended for passenger service on the Southampton-Channel Islands route. She is expected to attain a speed of $19\frac{1}{2}$ knots on trial. A novel feature in the vessel's lines forward is that they have been designed to the " Maierform " type, and in conse-

quence it is expected that she will be an exceptionally good sea boat.

The propelling machinery consists of two sets of Parsons' geared turbines driving two shafts through single-reduction gearing. The steam to the turbines is supplied by two Yarrow-type water-tube boilers, burning oil fuel, while a separate oil-fired Scotch boiler supplies steam to the auxiliaries.

The hull is sub-divided by 12 transverse watertight bulkheads extending to the main deck. Sliding watertight doors, capable of being quickly closed from the bridge by means of hydraulic control, have been fitted in the bulkheads between the machinery compartments. A double bottom extends for a considerable part of the vessel's length. There are eight lifeboats ; those on passenger promenades being stowed on over-frame davits, so as to increase the deck space available for passengers.

The vessel is fitted with electric light, a Marconi wireless installation, including a direction finder and an auto alarm, and with many other electrical appliances, such as a boat winch, refrigerating machine, clear-view screens on the bridge, electric cooking appliances, electric clocks, an electric submarine sounding fathometer, an electric log, and a panatrope with loud-speakers. Power for these is generated by two steam-driven dynamos. In addition there are two oil-driven emergency dynamos. The steering gear is of Brown Brothers' hydraulic type, having telemotor control.

The vessel will carry about 1,500 first and second class passengers.

Special attention has been paid to the heating and ventilation, the thermo-tank system being installed throughout the whole of the passenger accommodation, while separate hot and cold fresh-air supply systems are fitted to the first-class cabins.

THE SOUTHERN RAILWAY CO'S. NEW TURBINE STEAMER "ISLE OF SARK."
Gross Tonnage, 2,143.   Speed, 19¾ knots.

Hints on the Restoration of Ship Models

By W. LEIGHTON

RESTORATION, the very word makes the collector and dealer look askance.

They seem to have an idea that the ancient beauty will be obliterated and stiff rigging, shiny paint, and mathematical precision substituted. As a matter of fact, it is, in the hands of a craftsman, perfectly simple to restore, without removing the handmarks of age, and to reveal under the coating of grime many beauties hitherto hidden. One must know exactly where and when to stop.

spritsail yard or gaffs on the bowsprit will help to fix the period and the data will help when re-rigging is started. The futtock shrouds may be fixed to a necklace on the mast, or attached to the main rigging, as in the earlier vessels. Apparently, the first ship to have her shrouds brought into the mast was the *Apollo*, East Indiaman, in 1811. Spritsail yards were displaced by outriggers or gaffs in 1830, although it was contended they could be used in an emergency as topgallant yards.

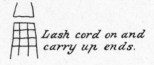
Lash cord on and carry up ends.

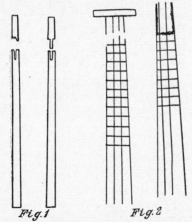

Fig.1

Repairing a Mast

Fig.2

Restoring broken rigging

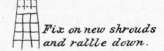
Fix on new shrouds and rattle down.

If the model is a fairly large one and has hatchways, etc., in the decks, it will probably be found that a number of loose pieces, together with boats, blocks, etc., have either found their way down or been placed there by some careful owner. A length of flex, with a pea-lamp at one end and a pocket-battery at the other, will be found very useful; also a long wire with a hook for purposes of extraction. Should these fail to bring up the tiny fittings, try a small ball of Plasticine on the end of a stick.

Before anything drastic is done, the model should be sketched from several positions, and many detailed sketches, coloured if possible, executed. These will be valuable assets later on. Photography is of course quicker, but the mere fact of drawing details helps to memorise them. A few days are very well spent on these interesting operations before anything is touched.

Removable fittings may next be cleaned and put in a box with divisions. They should be studied carefully and notes made as to possible date. For instance, cannons or carronades (1797),

Next may be considered damaged parts that absolutely must be removed and replaced. It depends on the instructions received from the owner how these are dealt with, also time allowed, and price may be taken into consideration. If rigging can be saved by careful manipulation, by all means save it, but if, as in many old models it is rotten, see that it is duplicated in the most careful manner both in thickness of cordage and space between ratlines, etc.

When the model has been stripped as far as possible, grime can be removed with soapy water and a toothbrush, or liquid veneer and a camel-hair brush, taking care to cleanse the brush every few strokes. In this state all repairs can be done to masts, etc., the great object being to save as much as possible of the original fabric. Many models have holes sometimes fitted with sheaves

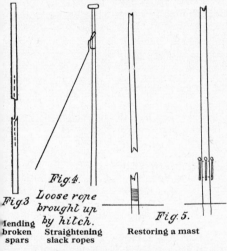

Fig.3
Iending broken spars

Fig.4.
Loose rope brought up by hitch.
Straightening slack ropes

Fig. 5.
Restoring a mast

for the lifts of topsail and other yards, and it will be found that breakages frequently occur at these points.

The smashed mast can be cleared of *debris* and, if the other fragment is there, it may be possible ot glue it firmly in position ; if not, repair as in Fig. 1, making certain it is correct length.

Rigging that has parted close under the tops may be mended as in Fig. 2. If broken backstays, etc., must be saved, soak broken ends in water, unravel them and let in a similar piece of cordage, also unravelled at the ends and soaked in thin hot glue. Make the join by intertwining strands and rolling between the fingers.

French polish that has got slightly thick is useful for coating these repairs and for preventing knots and lashings coming unput. If too thick, thin down with methylated spirits, but allow it to be fairly tenacious. Broken spars, even when surrounded by rigring, can be treated as in Fig. 3 with a fine needle carefully let in each half and glued.

Cracks or holes in deck are filled up with plastic wood (don't forget there is a slight shrinkage) if small, or cut square and a piece of wood let in. In cases of badly damaged decks of small models, it has been found possible to cut stiff Bristol board to exact size of half deck, tone down with water colours, then give a brush coat of white polish. Even if this does not match exactly at first, it can be painted on until uniformity is obtained.

If, on a fairly large model, guns, etc., are missing, use one of the remaining ones to make a plastic mould and cast them in lead. A match-box will be found handy for this. Avoid renovating paintwork on the hull of an old model if possible. Clean it with soap and hot water,; when dry, give a brush coat of polish. Edges of waterlines can be picked out by glueing a thread attached to a pin at bow and stern along them, twisting pin to get all taut. Very slack ropes can be straightened, as shown in Fig. 4.

A case in which the mast (with rigging nearly intact) could be restored is as follows :

If there is enough stump to fit a thin metal collar (as deep as possible), to place same on stump after anointing with glue, place the mast in position and gently raise collar. A band of glued paper may be used if desired. If stump is broken off flush with deck, it must be carefully withdrawn and a slightly longer piece substituted, so as to take the collar.

A pinrail may be formed in order to disguise the join, as in Fig. 5.

The Ramsgate Steamer "Eagle"
By L. P. PERKINS

From a drawing]   [By Loftus P. Perkins

The Ramsgate Steamer " Eagle "—built 1853

THE writer vividly remembers this favourite old paddle-steamer *Eagle*, having often seen her during the summer months, 1880-1887, crowded with happy holiday-makers bound for Margate and Ramsgate. She used to leave Fresh Wharf, London Bridge, every day except Friday, returning in the evening, and called at intermediate piers on her way down the Thames. The *Eagle* was a fast and comfortable vessel, and presented a fine appearance with her shiny black hull and white paddle boxes, volumes of smoke pouring from her old-fashioned bell-topped funnel.

The following data may be of interest :—

Built of iron at Northfleet in 1853. Purchased by the General Steam Navigation Company in 1856.

Length between perpendiculars	.. .. ..	200'.
Length overall	.. ..	209'.
Beam, extreme	.. ..	24'
,, ,, over paddle boxes		42'.
Depth in hold	.. ..	12' 3".
Draft	.. .. ..	7'.

Burthen, in tons, Nos. 450 ; gross tonnage, 325 ; 2 side-lever engines ; cylinders, 49¼" dia. ; stroke, 48" ; revolutions per minute, 48 ; nom. h.p., 130 ; steam pressure, 25 lb. per sq. in. ; four furnaces ; paddle wheels, 16' dia ; 12 feathering floats ; speed, 14¼ knots ; licensed for 466 passengers, to Dover.

A Model Ocean Liner
By L. A. PRITCHARD

THE accompanying photograph is of a model single-screw liner in my possession. There are several points of considerable interest about her. She appears to be built to the scale of ¼" to the foot and is apparently a model of a passenger and cargo

steamer of about 1875. I bought her from an antique dealer in Winchester for quite a moderate sum a few years ago. She is in perfect condition, having evidently been in a glass case since she was built ; in fact, when I bought her the case was screwed

A Model Single-screw Liner owned by Mr. L. A. Pritchard

permanently to the baseboard; this, however, I have since altered, making the case to lift off. The workmanship is of a very high-class order, but she is undoubtedly the work of an amateur builder. Every fitting is shown, with the exception of any rigging details.

The most conspicuous item of the model is the very perfect representation of the strakes of the shell plating which, judging by their widths, are meant to represent those of an iron hull. This is the only model I have ever seen with the strakes of plating actually shown in and out.

Several sailing-ship features will be noticed, such as the narrow rudder, the cat and fish davits on the foc'sle and the double hawsepipes, also the isolated half deck house.

There is no name on the stern or bows, but the name " T. Budden " is painted very small and roughly on the edge of the baseboard. On the bow there is a figurehead device representing a reclining man wearing a curious cap and grasping a spear. The design is repeated on the other side of the stem. The model bears a close resemblance to the old Union Liner *German*, the first of that name,. but the colours are not those of the Union Line, the funnels of whose ships were painted yellow, whereas the model's funnel is black. The hull is painted black with a salmon-pink bottom, white bridge-deck sides, bright varnished deck houses and black funnel.

I wonder if any reader can identify the model or give me any information about her, for which I should be very grateful.

The dimensions are as follows :—

Length overall, 46″; length b.p., 44.25″; breadth, 5.25″; depth to upper deck, 4.5″. On a scale of ⅛″ to 1′ these would represent a ship of 368′ length overall, 354′ between perpendiculars, beam 42′ and depth to upper deck 36′, draught 24′.

Probably she would have been either brig-rigged, or square-rigged on foremast and fore and aft on main.

What is a Model?

By THE EDITOR

SOME comments we have received on models described in our pages seem to indicate that there is a variety of opinion as to when a miniature ship or boat may properly be described as a " model." Exactly the same position arose years ago in the model engineering world, when models of engines and locomotives of all kinds were referred to just as models, without any qualifying word to indicate whether they were real scale copies of a definite prototype, or whether they were modified copies or merely free-lance designs. We therefore introduced a graded system of nomenclature, so that one might know on what basis to judge a model's actual merits. The classification which has been adopted for many years at our Exhibitions is as follows : " True Scale Model," " Representative Scale Model," " Representative Working Model," " Free-lance Show Model," " Free-lance Working Model," and " Demonstration Model." In our entry forms we amplify these descriptive terms, so that a competitor may declare exactly on which basis he wishes his model to be judged. It seems to us that in ship modelling some similar kind of classification is required. We have been told, for example, that it is inpossible to describe a model of the *Golden Hind* as a scale model, since no authentic data of that ship are available. That may be so, and the term " true scale model " might not be applicable. But, on the other hand, sufficient is known about the *Golden Hind* to enable a model to be constructed, having correct general outline and proportions, and having accurate period rigging and fittings, which might quite fairly be termed a " representative scale model " of that vessel. Similarly, with clipper ship models, directly a model builder decides to model a particular clipper ship, he must be careful to reproduce

the characteristic features of the prototype, and to work to scale, but it is not necessary for him to include every minute detail of the original to enable him to describe his production as a " representative " scale model. The work must really be judged not by the standard the critic sets in his own mind, but by what the maker claims to have produced. Some of our readers have criticised the model *Golden Vanity*, described in a recent issue, but that model was not put forward as pretending to be a scale model of any known brig. It was a concession to the romantic imaginings of a youthful mind, inspired by reading " Treasure Island." It succeeded in giving great pleasure to the youngster for whom it was built, and judged from that standpoint was a praiseworthy effort. The purist in ship-modelling is very hard to please. He can even find fault with museum pieces which have passed an exacting scrutiny. Perhaps it is as well that it should be so ; unless a high standard is set there is nothing for the beginner to work up to. Yet all criticism should be mindful not of merely the best possible standard, but of the standard the builder himself set out to achieve when he first took up his tools. If we decided to publish only descriptions of models of the very highest order of merit, such articles would of necessity be few and far between. We think it better to take a broader survey of the activities of model shipbuilders, and while giving due credit to some of the more modest productions, endeavour to raise the general standard of the model-making art by publishing as many examples of classic craftsmanship and exactitude as may be possible. These will serve to inform and to inspire the lone worker who may not have access to the originals, and who needs guidance and encouragement in his work.

The "Bolerion"

A WORKING SCALE MODEL MONITOR, NINE INCHES LONG

By R. V. WALLING, A.I.N.A.

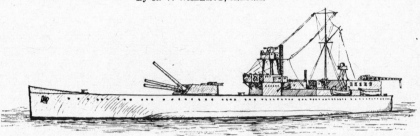

The "Bolerion"—A miniature working model Monitor

I MAKE no claim that the *Bolerion* is the smallest working model built to scale, but she is getting on that way. And her story is an amusing one.

The *Bolerion* is a monitor, of "free-lance" design, to a scale of 48' to 1". Following are the dimensions of her mythical prototype :—

Length (water-line), 420'.
Beam (over bulges), 100'.
Displacement (legend), 10,350 tons.
Guns, three 17" (triple turret) and six 4" anti-aircraft.
Machinery, three sets of Diesels, developing 8,250 s.h.p.
Speed, 15 knots.

The hull of the model consists of one of the "toc-toc" toy speed boats, using solidified methylated spirit as fuel. The "bulges" were hammered out of an old tobacco-tin, and soldered on. The big turret, made of wood, was mounted just forward of amidships, and the remainder of the superstructure was built on to a new afterdeck, which can be lifted at will for "stoking up" and re-fuelling.

The tiny model goes very well in the domestic bath-tub. At first, an adequate supply of air for the "engines" was a drawback, but this was remedied by cutting away the upper deck and providing large engine-room hatches, also a couple of special ventilators.

All the guns, the "Archies" as well as the big fellows, will elevate and depress, and the triple mountings can be trained. The mast-head range-finder and the sea-plane crane are also moveable.

The fittings were made from Bristol board, odd scraps of wood, match-sticks, pins, hooks and eyes and fine-gauge copper wire. The hull lines were altered somewhat by means of plastic wood, and the addition of the bulges necessitated ballasting with a couple of melted-down linotype "slugs." The sheer of the forecastle was also achieved with plastic wood.

Perhaps I should add that the tall chimney shown in the picture is not a "cod" affair. It actually serves to create just the draught required to keep the methylated cubes alight.

The *Bolerion* is painted white, with vermilion boot-topping, cream upperworks and black chimney—not her war colours, of course.

Apart from catching fire on her trial trip, she has had an uneventful career, but she provided me with several hours' interesting relaxation.

This account is offered as an example of practical experimenting on a small scale, with very simple materials and constructive equipment.

An Early 17th Century Model English Warship

By H. P. JACKSON

Model 17th Century English Warship

THE hull of this model is 18″ long by 5¾″ beam, and is of canary pine, built on the bread-and-butter method. It was intended to be an actual sailing model, but as the work progressed, more detail was put in than was at first intended, so that now it is rather too good to put on a sailing lake.

The lines were obtained from a book which came from the U.S.A., and are quite satisfactory, but the details, etc., are far from correct, so that I had some considerable trouble in finding authentic sources of information. Many visits to the South Kensington Museum, and books from the local library, however, enabled me to make a reasonable representation of the period 1600-1604. " Sailing Ships and their Story," by E. Keble Chatterton, and " From Carrack to Clipper," by Frank E. Bowen, were particularly useful.

The sprit topsail and square mizzen-topsail were included, as most authorities are agreed that these items both made their appearance at about the end of the 16th Century or the beginning of the 17th Century.

The scale is one-sixth inch to the foot, and when fitting up poop ladders, ratlines, etc., this was borne in mind so as to make it possible to enable a scale seaman easily to negotiate these items.

There are about 1,600 clove-hitch knots in the ratlines. The guns are of wood painted black. The gun carriages were made from a length of wood moulding, slices ½″ long being cut off, and required very little work to finish. The moulds for casting the guns were made of plastic wood. This mould was made from an aluminium gun pattern, of right shape. Core holes were included, and the holes in gun " casting " for barrel, trunnion, and rear end formed by pushing wires through. The holes for wheel spindles were drilled by the aid of a jig.

The sails were made to my pattern, but the rope edging I sewed on myself, a tiresome job. Anchors from ½″ brass wire, silver-soldered up. The coat-of-arms on stern was fretted out in separate parts, glued on the stern-board and finished off with small chisels and files.

The figure-head, a tiger's head, was cut off a small composition animal obtained from a fancy goods shop. These are very good representations, but are rather too tame-looking, the mouth being closed. To obtain the necessary ferocity, the tiger's mouth was cut and glued open, a few fangs being then inserted.

The upper works above deck were made of 1/16″ plywood and fixed with waterproof glue, and also secured with

Deck View Forward

Model 17th Century English Warship—Stern View

very fine brass pins. All parts, which are fixed on a wood model, should be pinned, or sooner or later they will fall off. The deadeyes and about half the number of blocks were bought from the late Stevens' Model Dockyard, also the cordage for rigging.

The flags are of silk soaked in ricewater, and when dry it was an easy matter to produce the design with ordinary water colours.

The hull was painted with three coats of flat colours, finished with one coat of very thin (crystal) varnish.

This gives a better finish than enamel, in my opinion.

The masts and spars were made from dowel sticks, having one coat of shellac, and are finished with the thin varnish.

In conclusion, I would impress beginners in the art of old-time shipmodelling to spare no pains in getting as much information as possible before making a start, as otherwise they run a risk of mixing two or three periods in the one model, which I have endeavoured to avoid.

Teaching the Young Idea

WHEN training either real sailor men, or ship-modelling enthusiasts, it is a good thing to "catch 'em young." That is the idea of Mr. G. Colman Green, who for the past few years has been organising and stimulating a model yachting movement among the boys attending the schools of the London County Council. He has formed a Boys' Model Yacht Club, the members of which meet and sail their boats about

once a fortnight through the summer months. Here is an attractive picture of some of the boys and their boats on the water at Wanstead Flats. During the summer some hundreds of boys come along to take part in these miniature regattas. The present pond at Wanstead is not ideal for the purpose, and Mr. Colman Green hopes that the day will come when a really good sailing water will be provided by the L.C.C.

"Teaching the Young Idea"

Modelling the "Golden Hind"

Some helpful notes by Mr. Stanley Rogers

THE set of blue-prints from drawings of the *Golden Hind,* prepared by Mr. Stanley Rogers, which we have been offering to our readers, have proved so popular, that they have inevitably produced inquiries for further information about this interesting ship.

The point has been raised that the drawings cannot claim to depict a " scale model " of a ship about which absolutely authentic data are not available. Another point has been made that the drawings show a model with the hull built up from the solid, whereas the original ship must have had a planked hull.

Both these minor criticisms can be answered by the statement that the drawings are offered as a guide to those who want to build a representative model of a ship of that period of which the *Golden Hind* was a well-known example. They are intended for the beginner and for the moderately advanced ship-modeller, rather than for the expert, who in any case would not be content to build from a popular-priced set of drawings, but would rely on his own research and knowledge of period ship construction for his guidance.

Mr. Rogers' drawings have, on the other hand, aroused a great deal of very favourable comment. An admirable ship-modelling craftsman himself, he has visualised the needs of the great majority of historic ship-modellers very well. He shows them in his drawings, how a very representative model can be built, with a minimum of tedious effort. In simplifying some of the details of construction, he enables the beginner to achieve success, where an attempt at more elaborate methods of building might lead to failure. Moreover, the character and period accuracy of the model are so well preserved, that whether the drawings are followed by a novice or

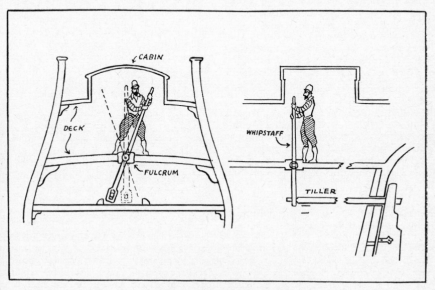

Method of Steering the " Golden Hind "

an expert, a worth-while and pleasing result is bound to be achieved. This is the first time that such reliable and carefully-planned drawings of a period ship have been offered at such a popular price. and we are pleased to say that the favourable opinions expressed by purchasers have fully justified the experiment. We reproduce a portion of one of the sheets of drawings so that readers may get an idea of the helpful style of treatment adopted. There are three sheets of drawings, each 14″ × 20″, in the set, which is supplied post free for 5s. 6d.

Mr. Stanley Rogers has kindly written the following additional notes in reply to some of the queries which have been raised :—

" When the Editor asked me to make some working drawings of the *Golden Hind* for amateur ship-modellers, I had in mind the model-maker who lays out his deck-plan and profile, or sheer plan, on the top and side of a piece of white pine, and proceeds to carve out the block with the aid of his eye and one or two perspectives of the bows and stern. With this idea of keeping the drawings as simple as possible, the vertical intervals on the sheer plan were purposely left out, and the lines on the body plan put in more to suggest the curves than to indicate them by a method which is a closed book to the uninitiated.

" However, this way of working did not appeal to the more scientific-minded of the *Golden Hind* enthusiasts, and an effort has been made to put in the vertical intervals from the lines on the body plan. Where they come a little above the line of the sheer plan, the surplus can be cut off without disturbing the lines at all.

" There has been a number of inquiries concerning minor points on the *Golden Hind* model—how the rudder is governed, and so on—and the rest of this article is concerned with answering these queries. There are no drawings, or authentic pictures of the *Golden Hind* known to exist, and any picture, or model of her, is

necessarily conjectural. The little drawing of an Elizabethan ship on the Hondius map of Drake's voyage round the world, printed 15 years after the event, may or may not be a true representation of the little craft. The evidence is against its being the actual vessel. So the designer can only aim at getting her proportions and armament, and, for the rest, making her a typical ship of the period. Some model builders have been mystified by the absence of any visible steering arrangement on board this type of vessel. The answer is, that the steering was done below the poop by an ingenious lever called the ' whipstaff.' The accompanying sketch explains how it worked. The helmsman steered either by looking forward through the doorway, or forward window, of the small raised cabin, or by orders passed down to him by someone on the deck above.

" Another question is the manner of running the guns in and out. This was done with the familiar gun-tackle comprising two single blocks on either side of the carriage, one fixed, the other movable ; the standing end of the fall being bent to the movable block. There was probably also a breeching to take the recoil, a method in vogue until well into the last century. Guns were made of iron or bronze, or brass, and, for a brief period, a form of breech-loader was common, though this fell into desuetude. A rusty old Elizabethan breech-loader can be seen in the United Service Museum, London. The Elizabethan seamen had a surprisingly large range of guns considering that ordnance was still in a comparatively primitive state. The principal sizes were the Cannon-royal, 60 to 64 pounder ; Demi-cannon, 30 to 32 pounder ; Cannon-periere, 24 pounder ; Culverin, 17 to 18 pounder ; Demi-culverin, 9 pounder ; Saker, 5 pounder ; Minion, 4 pounder, and so on in diminishing calibres, the smallest being the falcon and the falconet, the latter throwing a ball of little over one pound—to be exact one and a-quarter pounds.

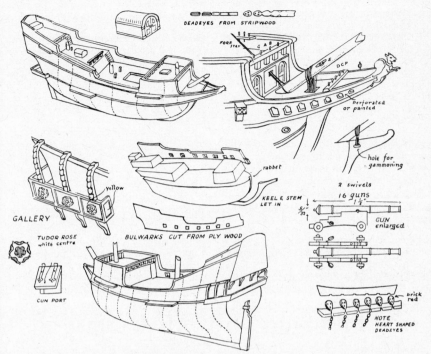

Reduced portion of one of the three sheets of drawings of the " Golden Hind " by Mr. Stanley Rogers, supplied as blue-prints

" In answer to another query, the gun-port lids were raised and lowered by a short lanyard bent to a ring-bolt on the outboard side, and passed through a hole in the bulwarks.

" The fighting tops were frequently built of light lattice-work, though for a model a neater (and quite correct) job can be made by turning them out of pieces of hardwood. There was not much carving on an Elizabethan ship, but she was as gaily painted as a circus wagon. Elaborate carving and gilding came in with the Stuart reign. Anyone building the *Golden Hind*, and living within the greater London area should study the remarkably fine Elizabethan ship model now on view in the Science Museum, South Kensington. Here will be found very definite answer to the questions that exercise the minds of model ship builders. "

Two further queries concerning details of the *Golden Hind* have been brought to my notice, and I will deal with them in order. (1) The absence of a " sternsprit " or bumpkin. All Elizabethan ships did not carry a bumpkin to take the sheet of the lateen sail, and there is no conclusive evidence that the vessel in question carried one. As already explained, in the absence of authoritative drawings of this ship, we designed a typical Elizabethan vessel of the *Golden Hind's* tonnage, with what precious few other details we could gather. The best authorities do not believe that the drawing of the barque-rigged vessel at the foot of the Judocus Hondius map is a trustworthy picture of the *Golden Hind*, for the artists and cartographers of the day were notoriously lax in such matters. I mention it lest some enthusiast holds up this picture to me, as much as to say, " But what about this ? " As for the " sternsprit " that may be put on at discretion, and made to run in and out. The Hondius drawing contains one—a terrific spar that, in my opinion, spoils the look of the ship.

The second query concerns the number and position of the guns. Here, again, we are up against conjecture. I have given the model ten under hatches, six in the open waist, and two swivels. Now, a correspondent sends the following information which other model-makers may like to take advantage of—it is from Zarzate, one of Drake's prisoners, and reads, in part, as follows :—

" The *Pelican* has seven cast-iron pieces a-side under hatches, and two in the nose ; two at the stern, and four above hatches. . . ."

That is 22 guns ! Yet, in the same article, it says that she carried 18 guns ! What is one to make of that ? The only explanation one can offer is that Drake added more guns taken from his prizes, and that he returned with a heavier armament than he set out with. In laying out the plans for the model of this vessel, and having no definite plans to go by, I endeavoured to bear in mind simplicity in building.

These blue-prints have brought considerable praise and some criticism, which only shows how impossible it is to produce plans of a vessel, whose lines and detail are not known, without meeting with some difference of opinion. After all, we are all amateurs when it comes to Tudor shipwrightry and naval architecture. One thing is pretty certain, the *Golden Hind* came back with more guns than she had departed with. Our model is, of course, intended to represent her as she was fitted out in England.

The Ship with Most Masts
By GRAY E. FARR

THE other day I asked a seafaring man what was the greatest number of masts that a vessel had ever had. As I almost expected, he said the famous seven-masted schooner *T. W. Lawson* of Philadelphia, was the winner on that score. Readers will remember that that vessel was, unfortunately, wrecked on Annet Island in the Scillies in December, 1907, whilst on a voyage home with oil in bulk. Her tonnage was nearly five thousand, and it is said that her spread of canvas totalled more than three thousand square feet.

However, the actual winner is a steamship—the *Beukelsdijk* ex *Grangesberg*, which until recently, was a well-known sight on the Maas. She has 14 masts, which, however, are described in Lloyds as being " seven twin masts," since the pairs are side by side.

This peculiar vessel, which was " turret " built, was employed in conveying iron ore between the Baltic and Rotterdam, and to see her loading or discharging with all 14 derricks swaying, was indeed an interesting sight.

She was built at Sunderland in 1903 for Mullers, but was subsequently sold to the Holland-America Line and has since dropped out of the register. Her dimensions were 440′ × 62′, and her tonnage 6,800 gross. I suggest that she would make a fine subject for a model.

A Ship with Fourteen Masts

Books to Read

Ships We See. By FRANK C. BOWEN. London : Sampson Low, Marston and Co., Ltd. Price 6s. Postage 6d.

In turning over the pages of Mr. Frank C. Bowen's latest book, the first impression we get is the thoroughness of the survey he presents of shipping of all kinds. Not only does he deal at length with liners, big sailing ships, cargo steamers, and the larger vessels of the Navy, but we find interesting chapters on ice-breakers, tugs and salvage boats, lifeboats, barges, in-shore fishing craft, racing yachts, motor boats, and lightships. There is even a particularly informative chapter on " Naval Dust," the expressive term invented by a French writer to indicate the smaller and auxiliary vessels which have no fighting value, but which are necessary to the completion of a fleet. Mr. Bowen is always readable, and while the book abounds with facts and figures, it is full of illuminating commentary on the purposes of various types of ships, and on the lives and duties of those who man them. It is, for instance, instructive to read of the conditions of service on tankers, and of the reasons why some men stay in this particular trade, while others are obliged to quit. Similarly, we are initiated into the mysteries of salvage, and into the various problems which confront the master of the river or ocean-going tug. In writing of big sailing ships, Mr. Bowen says that it is only human nature that a thing should never be valued as much as when it is disappearing. " In the old days," he says, " nothing was too bad to be said of them, particularly the real hard cases, and there were plenty of them at sea. But now that they have gone, only their good points are remembered, and the old sailing ship enjoys a popularity that it never had before." The book is illustrated by nearly one hundred photographs, mostly by the Nautical Photo Agency, and Mr. Pelham Jones is responsible for a finely-drawn coloured jacket showing a liner and a sailing ship passing each other at sea. Although written for the general reader, rather than for the nautical expert, every ship-lover will find something to interest him in Mr. Bowen's latest contribution to the story of the sea.

Told at the Explorers' Club. New York : Albert and Charles Boni. Price 3 dols. 50 cts.

In this fascinating volume 33 members of The Explorers' Club of New York have set forth the stories of their adventures, or at least some of the more startling and remarkable adventures which have befallen them in the course of their travels. They naturally vary very much in their character and their setting, but there are several which will make a strong appeal to sailor men. " Bringing the Crippled *Roosevelt* Home," by Robert A. Bartlett, for example, is as stirring an account of an adventurous voyage as one could wish to read. The *Roosevelt*, Peary's Arctic exploration ship, was badly damaged in the ice at Cape Sheridan ; Captain Bartlett's story deals with the navigation of the ship along the Labrador coast, back to New York. Captain Bartlett had a unique record in arctic exploration ; 14 of his cruises ended in shipwreck, and no less than seven of his ships sank under him. " The Cruise of the *Lone Star*, by Warwick S. Carpenter, tells of the adventurous voyage of a canoe in Western Ontario, while in " Walrus Hunting with the Eskimos," Robert Fothingham describes an episode on a cruise of the U.S. coast-guard Cutter *Northland*. Another sea story, related by Earl B. Wilson, describes a voyage of the converted schooner *Dora* on the Alaskan Coast. In this story it is mentioned that on one occasion the *Dora* encountered storm and ice, and in a disabled

condition was carried almost to Japan.
There a storm from Siberia swept her
back again to the U.S. Coast, and she
finally limped into Seattle, after having
long been given up as lost. As an
entertaining book of real life adventure by men who have " been there,"
this volume may be cordially com-
mended. The profits of the book are
to be devoted to the library of exploration maintained by the Explorers'
Club.

Clear Lower Deck. By SIDNEY
KNOCK. London : Philip Allan.
Price 10s. 6d.

Books dealing with the life of lower-
deck ratings of the Royal Navy are
scarce. Of those published since the
War none gives a more comprehensive
picture than this one.

Now that the Disarmament Confer-
ence is sitting, the author's remark in
the preface, " It is not always realised
that the ' Silent Service ' is, in fact,
the most powerful pacifist agent,"
should be borne in mind when reading
the orations of the internationalists
and little navyites. It cannot be
denied that the visits of sailors to
foreign ports play a very important
part in promoting friendly relations.
Moreover, the occasions when British
warships have been the first to render
assistance in times of disaster ashore
and afloat are numberless.

Progress towards International
friendship is not always helped by our
American cousins, whose popularity
lags behind that of the British bluejacket. Mr. Knock considers this to
be due primarily to " latent bombast
in reference to the dollars," a failing
which is not always confined to
nautical circles.

Every phase of the " matelot's "
life ashore and afloat, off and on duty,
is covered, including his hobbies and
occupations in the watch below.

In the concluding chapters on
" Missionaries and Moralists " and
" Religion," it would appear that the
Author's experience of naval chaplains
has been singularly unfortunate. Nor
has he any kind words to say about

Miss Weston, who, despite his criticisms, did devote her whole life to her
ideals.

To some of those with whom she
came in frequent contact she no
doubt appeared a bit of a nuisance.
But, considering she has been dead
for a number of years, it would have
been better taste to have ignored her
failings. However mistaken some of
her views may have been her selfless-
ness and devotion were unquestionable.

The vocabulary of sea terms and
phrases used on the lower deck will
be found as amusing as it is interesting. To the landsman, the multi-
tudinous nick-names which constitute
" nautical parlance " will seem like a
foreign tongue.

On the whole, it is a well-written
book and one which should make a
wide appeal to all interested in the
human side of the Royal Navy.—
" CHIPS."

Easting Down. A Romance of the
Sea. By Commander GREGORY
STAPLETON, R.N. London : Gray-
son and Grayson. Price 7s. 6d.

There is an undeniable fascination
in reading a novel of the sea based on
practical experience, especially so when
the characters are obviously taken
from life.

The opening chapters of " Easting
Down " are devoted to the incidents
of a passage to China in the barque
Serampore, in the days when the
sailing vessel was still in her prime.

A vivid contrast is presented between the terrible weather encountered
by the *Serampore* off the Cape of Good
Hope, and the ghastly monotony of
being becalmed in the doldrums.
Days drag into weeks, until the
crew become listless and ill-tempered
as their thirst increases under the
sweltering tropical sun. Suddenly, it
is discovered that the fresh-water tank
has been leaking and is empty. But
Royeston, the resourceful skipper, is
equal to the emergency. He im-
provises a condenser from an empty
barrel and a few oddments. After
hours of heart-breaking labour, a few

drops of fresh water appear, slowly increasing until a bucketful is obtained !

While the impressions of a newcomer to the Far East are well portrayed, the chapters devoted to life in the Customs Service at Tientsin and Shanghai, full though they are of local colour, lack the vigour which characterises the sea episodes.

But, in his description of the race home to England of the tea-clippers with the new season's crop, Commander Stapleton has excelled.

The following incident occurred when the *Serampore* overtook yet another of her rivals :—

" The *Skyflyer* came towards them at terrific speed, her sharp bow cutting through the seas and throwing up fountains of water on either side. The distance between the two ships shortened rapidly, contracting with every second that passed.

" ' By God, Sir, she'll be into us ! Hard up, Sir—hard up ! He won't give way ! ' The Mate was feeling the nervous strain. . . .

" Nearer and nearer came the *Skyflyer* under her great spread of canvas. Was she never going to give way ? Would her Skipper hesitate until too late ? . . .

" And then, at last ! The anxious watchers on board the *Minim* saw that the head of the other ship was paying off . . . but could she clear ? Was there room ? Was there space for her to turn ? Her long tapering flying jibboom swung through the air, well nigh sweeping over the quarter of the *Minim* and, as she drove under their stern, her side, high out of the water, grazed their lee yardarms."

One would have been glad to have had more of this. But it is possible that to some, the losing fight waged by Abel Marche, the principal character, against the temptations of the East, may make a greater appeal. Disregarding all advice, he ignores the mother of his half-caste children, whose revenge is a terrible one. It is typical of the ineffective personality of Marche that, despite his knowledge of the Chinese language and long residence in the East, he should have so signally failed to understand the Oriental mind.—" CHIPS."

The Ship Lovers' Association

PARTICULARS of membership, etc., were given in full in the September issue of SHIPS AND SHIP MODELS. The Hon. Secretary, *pro. tem.*, is Frank C. Bowen, of Customs House Building, Gravesend, Kent, and the Hon. Treasurer is Basil Lavis, of Egmont, The Ridgeway, Westcliff-on-Sea, to whom subscription (5s. per annum, or 2s. 6d. in the case of cadet members still at school) should be sent.

Members from London and the Home Counties hold meetings twice a month in the Admiral's Cabin Restaurant, 167, Strand, W.C.2, on the first and third Tuesdays of each month, and members from the country or abroad are cordially welcome. On the first Tuesday of the month, it is an informal gathering for the exchange of views and information in the various sections ; on the third, it is an informal dinner, followed by a paper or papers and discussion.

A suggestion has been made that many members might like to make up a party on one of the reasonably-priced yachting cruises that some of the lines have arranged round the British Isles, at Easter or during the summer.

The Shiplovers' Association of Tasmania is making excellent progress, quite as good as its sister association in Victoria.

Members' Queries and Answers

All queries have been answered by post, there having been none during the past month of sufficient general interest to be reprinted here.

The question concerning the origin of the term " onker " for a sailing ship on the small timber trade between the Baltic and Thames or Medway, is still unanswered. Can any Scandinavian friend oblige ?

The Ship Modeller's Scrap Book

(Continued from page 186)

Channels

Wooden platforms placed outside the ship in way of the masts to spread and support the lower rigging. Held down by the CHAINS secured to strong CHAIN PLATES. Sailing ships built in the United States and British North

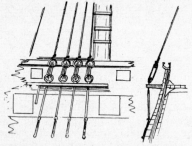

Channels and Plates on a Line of Battleship

America nearly all had upper and lower channels, as shown in the picture. When a ship was heeling to the wind the channels often dragged in the water and impeded her course; this was so general in the tender clippers that often the channels were

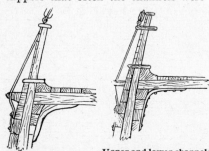

Channel on a wooden clipper.   **Upper and lower channels on a wooden ship. (Generally U.S.A. or B.N.A. built)**

made merely a flat bar. In the old men-of-war the channels had to be wide enough to take the rigging well clear of the nettings, which were placed on top of the rails for the purpose of stowing the men's hammocks in the daytime; they formed the most convenient jumping-off places for boarding parties when the ships were fighting alongside one another.

Chart House

This feature was very slow in coming into general use in sailing merchantmen, in spite of its obvious advantages, and, to the last, many fine ships were built without it. When it was fitted, it generally contained an entrance to the quarters under the poop as well, and was a god-send in bad weather both for examining the chart and

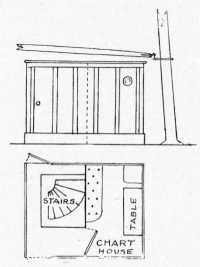

Chart House on poop of Sailing Ship with entrance to Saloon

getting below when the waist was a-wash, although it seldom afforded much protection for the helmsman. In the early steamers, also, it was usually omitted, but it gradually came into favour as a very small and unpretentious addition to their primitive bridges. It gradually became more and more elaborate and complete and, in modern big ships, it is very fine indeed, although sometimes it is completely buried in the towering bridge structure. Nearly every steam or motor vessel is now given a charthouse, although it is sometimes so small that an officer or pilot of any size has to choose whether he will get his head wet or his legs, and generally changes his mind so many times that he gets wet through.

Chess Trees

Originally *Chest Trees*, and also written *Chestrees* in the old authorities.

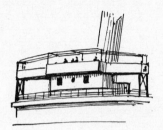

Navigation Bridge and Chart House, 1892 and 1932

Pieces of stout oak bolted to the outside of the topsides abaft the fore chains, with a sheave in the upper end to take the main tack and so keep the clews of the course down and the sail flat.

Cleats

Pieces of wood or iron used for stops and to make ropes fast, their age and shape varying according to their duty, but remaining the same

Belaying Cleat   Shroud Cleat

in general principles for many years. The *Arm Cleats*, sometimes *Sling Cleats*, were made fast to either side of the slings of the lower yard and had one arm only, lying over the straps of the jeer blocks, to prevent chafe. *Belaying Cleats* had two arms and were fastened wherever convenient, to fulfil the same general function as the

Belaying Pin, q.v., *Range Cleats* were similar but larger. *Shroud Cleats* were shaped like *Belaying Cleats*, but the back was hollowed out to fit on to the shroud, and they were grooved to permit them to be securely seized. *Comb Cleats* were semi-circular and were used to keep a rope in place, and there were many other varieties in the old sailing ships. *Cleats* are still fitted in every type of ship or boat as the handiest means of belaying.

(*To be continued*)

Good Work needs Good Light

AN important condition of good model-making is good lighting. It is hopeless to try and do miniature work in a bad light. In the dining or living room, an ordinary table lamp, or electric reading lamp, is an excellent thing to work by. If possible, the lamp should be shaded to direct the light on to the work, and keep the glare from the worker's eyes. This suggests another useful item of equipment—a magnifying glass. A good hand reading glass will be found most helpful for examining the progress of minute work. It may even be fitted to a small stand, so as to be held in focus between the work and the eye, when occasion requires. A small electric torch is yet another useful accessory for examining interior work, or for looking into confined spaces as the work proceeds.

The Ship's Mail

Readers are invited to make use of this column for the discussion of matters of mutual interest and the exchange of ideas and information.

Paddle Steamer "La Marguerite"

DEAR SIR,—In your January issue it is stated by Mr. F. C. Thornley, in his interesting letter, that this boat was built for the New Palace Steamers, Ltd. This is often stated but is a mistake. The vessel was constructed, as were the *Koh-i-Noor* and *Royal Sovereign*, for the Victoria Steamboat Association, Ltd. They all had, when built, the red funnels of this concern, with black tops and two white bands, as can be seen from pictures in the Press of the time (in *Engineering*, for example). The V.S.A. failed soon after the *La Marguerite* came out, and the boats afterwards were run by the New Palace Co., which was really the Fairfield Co.'s creation, it would seem. The model of the *Royal Sovereign* in the G.S.N. Co.'s works at Deptford still bears the name V.S.A. on the description plate, but on the *Koh-i-Noor*, at South Kensington, this has been painted over.

Yours very truly,

Forest Hill, S.E.   T. S. LASCELLES.

The Oldest Vessels Afloat

DEAR SIR,—Probably Mr. G. E. Farr's friend is confusing the *John* and the *Iron Duke*, which was built as a paddle tug in 1857 by T. Wingate and Co., Glasgow, and like the *John*, is registered in Bristol and owned by A. J. Smith and Sons. The *Iron Duke* is now a screw steamer of 24 registered h.p., her dimensions being : 108.3′ × 19.2′ × 9.0′, and net tonnage of 62. She trades regularly between South Wales and Bristol, and was reputed to be the fastest collier of her type.

The very remarkable accident referred to by Mr. Farr, in which the *John* was involved, occurred on March 20th, 1855. Through, it was said, unskilful management, she struck the ribs of one of the bridges spanning the New Cut at Bristol with great violence. The effect was instantaneous, the structure collapsing like a child's house of cards ; not a vestige was left standing, and the carts and passengers crossing at the time were flung into the river. Two persons lost their lives, one being a wagoner, whose cart was found next day below Rownham, two miles down the river. The new bridge cost £5,700.

Yours faithfully,

C. HAWKINS GARRINGTON.

House Flags

DEAR SIR,—Can any reader say how or why the double house-flag originated ?

I mean the flag with a pennant below it ; or two pennants, one close under the other.

I fancy this is a Scottish fashion.

Yours truly,

London, E.C.1.   W. J. T.

A Fine "Cutty Sark" Model

DEAR SIR,—I hope that the enclosed photograph of a very fine, if not the finest, scale model of the most famous ship in the history of marine industry, the *Cutty Sark*, will prove of sufficient interest to publish.

The model was made and presented to me by a real old sea-dog, whose ancestors fought under Nelson. He has sailed on many famous vessels, including the *County of Peebles*, and the great *Largiemore*, and has spent 80% of a long life at sea. The model was made in spare time, and thus took some 15 months to complete. The hundreds of blocks were hand-made by the Captain, who has shown amazing ingenuity in producing the various objects aboard from the most unpromising material. The scale is one-tenth inch to the foot, which proportion has been adhered to in every possible instance.

It will be noticed from the photograph that every single working and standing rope, halliard, ratline, guy and stay has been fitted ; downhauls, lifts, lazy tack, bowline bridles, and braces, all are there, so that, for the *first* time, one can actually visualise this most beautiful and famous clipper, the *only* one now left to Britain, the very last.

The *Cutty Sark* is seen bowling along before a favouring quartering breeze, with stunsails set, and in the actual trim best suited to the following wind, the staysails receiving just sufficient wind to fill them out, though really of doubtful utility as propelling units.

This model has been seen by thousands of sea-faring men of all stations, having been exhibited in the main thoroughfares in Glasgow, London, Liverpool and Dumbarton, the town where she was built, in 1869.

Captain Laird has other models to his credit, one in the Kelvin Art Galleries here, and he is now at work on another *Cutty Sark*, which is to exceed in perfection even the one I have the delight of ownership. Every ratline is correctly knotted to the shrouds, and complete, the ship leans very slightly to leeward as she pushes her nose into the yielding sea, which is realistically reproduced from putty !

I have some 140 photographs of the model, but not one does full justice to the vessel, because, no matter what background there is, some of the ropes, which are of different colours, fail to come out clearly, and sharp focussing of all parts are not to be got if the model is not broadside to the camera, which position is not the most spectacular.

Wishing your publication every success, and assuring you of its great interest to the " Captain " and me.

Yours truly,

Glasgow.   E. W. E. BAILEY.

A Model of the " Cutty Sark " built by Captain Laird

Names of French Ships of the Line

DEAR SIR,—May I draw the attention of Captain E. Altham R.N., to a slight mistake contained in his very interesting study on ships' models at the Royal United Service Museum. The fine model of a French three-decker illustrated on page 174 of the February issue, should be named *L'Imperial.* Ships of the line always bore masculine names, while feminine ones were given to frigates and corvettes.

Captain E. Altham is not at all responsible for this, as the name *L'Imperiale* is given in the official catalogue of the Museum, page 252, heading No. 6126. If readers of SHIPS AND SHIP MODELS are interested in the history of that particular ship, I might be able to satisfy their curiosity.

M. ADAM,
Capitaine de Corvette, French Navy.

Colouring of Egyptian Ships

DEAR SIR,—In reply to your Birmingham correspondent's question about the colouring of Egyptian ships, I have found the following in the chapter on " Egyptian Architecture " in Sir Banister Fletcher's " History of Architecture."

Dealing with ornament, he says : " The Egyptians . . . carried out their schemes of decoration in blue, red and yellow " ; and again, " the painter carried out his work in the strong hues of the primary colours."

This, of course, refers to the ornamentation of buildings, but as all Egyptian ornament was a matter of convention, it follows that the pattern given on the drawing of the ship, " in minute detail," would be somewhat akin to a pattern used in a building at the same period.

I suggest, therefore, that your reader should colour the pattern in blue, red, and yellow, either as his fancy dictates, or after studying the examples of Egyptian ornament to be found in nearly all our larger museums.

I remember having seen Egyptian ship models in the British Museum, but cannot call to mind any details other than that the hull is usually painted ochre all over except for a band of black round the bulwarks and further relief in coloured patterns. Alternatively, the hull is left simply the natural colour of the wood and decorated in colour as in the case of the ship, with an ochre-coloured hull.

Yours faithfully,

Bath.   ALAN CROZIER COLE.

Elizabethan Ships

DEAR SIR,—Mr. R. W. Tate takes me to task for the generalisation that Elizabethan ships should not be decorated with carved work, and quotes Mr. John Masefield's introduction to Hakluyt's Voyages. I have no knowledge of the evidence which Mr. Masefield had before him when he wrote the words which Mr. Tate quotes, but my own impression is, that a great deal of research has recently been made into the exact build and appearance of Elizabethan ships-royal, the results of which may not have been available when Mr. Masefield wrote his introduction to Hakluyt.

My own remarks were based on those of Mr. Laird Clowes, in his book on " Sailing Ships," published by the Science Museum. He states (page 70) :—

" Carving and gilding, as the main scheme of decoration, was entirely foreign to the ships of Elizabeth, but was introduced quite early in the reign of James I."

Elsewhere on the same page, Mr. Laird Clowes says :—

" Carving was restricted to an elaborate figurehead—lions and dragons were about equally common —with the addition of the Royal Arms on the stern, certainly painted in colours, and *possibly* (my Italics) carved too."

Yours faithfully,

A. G. V.

Steamers of 1878.

DEAR SIR,—The interesting article on *Mona's Queen II* leads me to ask if you can give us pictures and particulars of certain of the steam-vessels that were often to be seen in the London River at about the date named above.

For instance, there were two small screw-steamers that ran between London Bridge (S.E. end) and Dunkirk, one the *Sir Robert Peel*, and the other the *Lord John Russell*. One of them was said to have made a passage to Cape Town. One of these boats, I think, tried " patent fuel " for her boiler. I know that one of them had oscillating engines placed fore and aft, not much larger than those in the " penny boats," and with the crank-shaft on top carrying a large wheel with wooden cogs that was athwartship, and geared into a smaller gear-wheel below, to speed up the propeller, instead of speeding it down as is the modern fashion.

Opposite, at Fresh Wharf, one saw the P.S. *Hoboken* and P.S. *Eclair* and, at one time, the Perkins-engined S.S. *Express* and the old P.S. *Arran*, with a single-cylinder diagonal D.A. engine. The *Eclair* was said to be an ex-blockade-runner. But whence came the *Hoboken* and her Dutch or American name ?

From Old Swan I often saw the ill-fated *Princess Alice* start.

Lower down, there was a steamer (the *Elizabeth* ?—but I am not sure of the name) that ran regularly between London and St. Petersburg ; she had formerly been a Russian Imperial yacht and she kept many of the painted panels and so forth from her former state.

Off the Surrey Commercial Docks one often saw the *John Bowes*, the first iron steamer, so it was said ; at any rate, she was a very old craft and kept going till long after 1878, and so I believe did Cory's collier *Black Boy*, a converted water-vessel which was a relic of the Crimean War.

Lower down again, in the Blackwall Point dry-dock, one occasionally saw Watts Milburn's *Hankow*, an exceptionally large ship for her day and service ; I can see her great square yards yet, against the sky, in my mind's eye.

The old Liverpool Register, red leather, was familiar to me in those days. I wonder where I could see one now ?

Come into the light, some of the veterans of Rotherhithe, The Stowage and Blackwall and Greenwich, and spin us a yarn. Don't leave it all to the " sticks-and-string " fraternity.

Yours truly,

London, E.C.1.   W. J. T.

New Model Motor Yacht " Azalea "—by Messrs. Bassett-Lowke Ltd.

New Model Motor Boats

WE illustrate herewith two attractive new model motor vessels just introduced by Messrs. Bassett-Lowke, Ltd., of Northampton. These are the model motor-yacht *Azalea* and the speed-launch *No.* 88. The motor motive power may be either clockwork, or a permanent magnet motor working off two pocket batteries. The speed launch is one of the "Swifta" Series, either electric or clockwork propelled. The hull is

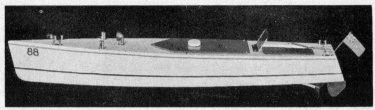

New Model Speed Launch "No. 88"—by Messrs Bassett-Lowke Ltd.

yacht is 30″ in length with a beam of 4¼″. She has up-to-date lines, the decks are lined in white birch, the funnel is buff, and the fittings silver-plated. There are two open life-boats carried on Welwyn-type davits. The finished in white, with assorted-coloured boot-topping, the deck is mahogany, lined in planking, and the fittings comprise bollards, ventilator, port and starboard lights, windscreen, and red ensign. A smart little craft.

Northern Notes
By "JASON"

A Manchester Exhibition

THE outstanding event of the month was the Models and Marvels Exhibition, held in the City Hall, Manchester, from February 16th to 27th. This Exhibition was promoted by the *Manchester Evening Chronicle* and included many things besides ship models. Nevertheless, it formed a test for the newly-formed Model Ship Makers' Clubs, Nos. 1 and 2. Within a week the Merseyside and Manchester Clubs had made arrangements for more than 40 models to represent them in one section, which in itself formed almost a complete story of ships.

A Glasgow Club

The response to my request last month has been very good, and a meeting will be held in the middle of March, in Glasgow, to inaugurate No. 3 Model Ship Makers' Club. It is, judging by letters received, assured of a good start.

And Hull

The above remarks also apply to Hull and the Humber. Please address letters to T. Sheppard, Esq., The Director, Municipal Museums, Hull.

A meeting is to be held in the near future.

Coracles

My note about coracles last month brought an interesting reply from Rock Ferry, Cheshire, regarding the Teifi river coracle, South-West Wales. This coracle is different to the others mentioned and appears to be an older design. I still await particulars of the Cockermouth (Cumberland) and Scotch coracles.

"H.M.S. Victory" Drawings.

Mr. Basil Lavis has now completed his series of Scale Drawings of *H.M.S Victory*, and these are available for purchase as blue-prints. Full particulars are announced elsewhere in this issue, and a sample set of the blue-prints may be inspected at our office.

SHIPS AND SHIP MODELS

A Magazine for all Lovers of Ships and the Sea

Editorial and Publishing Offices:

Single Copies, post free, **7½d.**
Annual Subscription **7s. 6d.**

66 FARRINGDON STREET
LONDON :: E.C.4

Vol. I. No. 8. APRIL, 1932. Price 6d.

The Ship's Log

Certificates of Accuracy

THE problem of deciding the accuracy or the authenticity of a ship model is one which is bound frequently to arise. The Merseyside Model Ship Makers' Club are giving some serious thought to this matter, with a view to instituting a system of giving a badge or a certificate to a model which has passed the close scrutiny of an expert committee. For museum or record purposes the accuracy of a model is a very important matter, and it also affects the value of a model when buying and selling have to be done. It is, therefore, a very helpful thing for a model maker or model owner to be able to get his work certified by some competent authority, and the various ship-modelling clubs in the country might well consider the desirability of following the Merseyside example. The fact that a particular model has gained a prize in an exhibition does not necessarily stamp it as being accurate. It may be that the award has been made primarily on the question of craftsmanship, and therefore the budding enthusiast should not assume that the model which has excited his admiration in the exhibition is necessarily one which he would do well to copy. In all kinds of model making, a careful study of the prototype, or of authentic records, is most important. It is as easy to build correctly as incorrectly, and any time devoted to a preliminary study of correct detail is well spent.

*   *   *

Model Prices

What is the highest price ever paid for a model? A price of 3,500 guineas for a 17th Century model seems fairly authentic, and we have heard stories of a more recent model changing hands for £5,000. These, of course, are very exceptional figures, but even now-a-days prices in the neighbourhood of £1,000 are sometimes asked and obtained. From this high figure, prices may range down to £100, or even less for a period model, but naturally the market is a very limited one, and the price is dictated more by what the purchaser is willing to pay, than the intrinsic value of the model itself. A commissioned scale model of a ship for a museum or private collection, or for exhibition purposes, may cost several hundred pounds, the price depending on the scale of model and the amount of detail required. This type of model can be valued mainly on the number of hours of work involved in its construction ; with the period model, however, both sentiment and rarity enter into the question of price, and it is these factors which largely determine the figure the purchaser is willing to pay.

* * *

The Race Round the Horn

The annual race of the windjammers homeward bound with wheat from Australia is now in progress. Will the *Herzogin Cecile* repeat her victory of last year ? There are eight ships in the race, the others being *Ponape, Lawhill, Pommern, Viking, Killoran, Abraham Rydberg* and *Winterhude*. Although the voyage is regarded as a race, there is actually a period of two months between the departure of the *Winterhude* from Port Pirie on December 23rd, and of the *Pommern* from Port Germein on February 29th. The real racing will probably be between the ships with the February sailings, though every sailorman knows that good luck and good seamanship can make a big bite into the calendar. We shall all watch for the arrivals with the greatest interest.

* * *

Prizes for Ship Models

Many of our new readers may not know that at the annual exhibition organised by us in connection with our other journal, *The Model Engineer*, there are prizes offered for ship models of all kinds. In addition to the Championship Cup which is offered for the best piece of work of any kind entered for competition, there is also a special cup for sailing ship models of any prototype prior to 1900, and there are numerous medals and diplomas for the best work by other competitors. We propose, this year, to develop the ship modelling side of both the Competition and the Loan Sections, and we hope that many

readers of SHIPS AND SHIP MODELS will be represented by examples of their work. The exhibition will be held at the Royal Horticultural Hall, Westminster, from September 1st to the 10th next. Particulars and entry forms for the competitions will be ready towards the end of this month, and will be obtainable, post free, on application to the Editor.

* * *

Blue-Prints of Sailing Ships

In response to various requests for reliable blue-print drawings of sailing ships, we have made some important additions to our list. These include three sets of prints for a wooden three-mast barque, a wooden three-mast barquentine, and a steel four-mast barque respectively. We can also offer a set of drawings for the famous *Cutty Sark*. These drawings have been prepared by Mr. Harold A. Underhill, from shipbuilders' scale plans, and will, we think, be much appreciated, both by ship-modellers and by students of sailing ship detail. Particulars and prices are announced elsewhere in this issue.

* * *

The " Thomas Gray " Prizes

The Council of the Royal Society of Arts are offering two prizes of £100 each under the Thomas Gray Memorial Trust. One of these is for a valuable improvement in the Science or Practice of Navigation, proposed or invented in the years 1931 and 1932. The other is for an essay on the rescue, by another vessel, of passengers and crew of a sinking vessel. Full particulars of these prizes may be obtained from the Secretary, Royal Society of Arts, John Street, Adelphi, London, W.C.2.

* * *

Training in Sail

In a recent discussion on the advantages or otherwise of training in Sail, for officers of the Mercantile Marine, one of the speakers enquired if the advocates of sail training would also argue that a taxi driver should have a preliminary training in a hansom cab!

Coasting Schooners

By JOHN ANDERSON

ALTHOUGH the last British deep-water windjammer has gone to her doom, the Red Duster still flies from the mastheads of a fair-sized fleet of sailing and auxiliary coasters, a motley collection of barquentines, schooners, ketches and Thames barges. In this brief article I propose to discuss the coasting schooners of to-day, of which I have had some little experience, having seen service on two auxiliary craft.

Although many schooners are having auxiliary power fitted these days, many of the purely sailing type, depending only on the free winds for their motive power, still lurk about the china clay ports and the West coast; schooners are seldom seen on the East coast. Most of the wooden sailers are very old, several having been launched before 1870, and they are still sailing round our coasts.

I think the palm in this respect should be awarded to the little topsail schooner *Queen of the West*, built in 1849, and a well-known " fruiter " in her youth ; she still trades between the Mersey and Ireland. Another well-known little windjammer with us still is the three-master *Brooklands*, built in 1859, and formerly the famous Azores fruit-trader *Susan Vittery*. A vessel recently wrecked was the little schooner *Via*, built at Brixham in 1864, and engaged in bygone days in the Newfoundland fish trade, where ships were wooden and men were iron. The schooner *Englishman* also dates back to 1864, and survived a duel with a U-boat during the War, but she nearly closed her career in a heavy

The Three Mast Schooner " Irish Minstrel " of Chester,

gale some months ago. Ships may come and ships may go, but these old-timers seem to last for ever.!

Besides the wooden craft. a few iron or steel sailing vessels still ply round the coast, but most of them have adopted auxiliary power and few depend on canvas alone. One of them, the steel three-mast topsail schooner *Shoal Fisher* of Barrow, recently made a long and very unlucky trip from Firth of Forth to Cornwall.

Britain has now a fair-sized fleet of auxiliary schooners, as most of the old wooden craft have had power installed and many steel vessels have been purchased from abroad. How these wooden schooners withstand the vibration of a Diesel engine is beyond my comprehension, but it is a tribute to their builders. When sailing coasters are converted to auxiliaries, their sail plan is severely cut down, barquentines are converted to schooners, topsail yards are sent down, and sometimes topmasts are discarded altogether.

I recently spent a month aboard the three-master *Mary Jones* of Bideford, built in 1863, and supposed to be one of the oldest auxiliary schooners still afloat. She is a vessel with very fine lines indeed, and a big sail plan, but she is now in a sad condition through neglect. However, London readers may see her soon, as she is being reconditioned for service on the East coast. Other ancient power schooners are *Pacific*, built in 1864, and *Uncle Ned*, formerly a barquentine dating back to 1867. Our largest wooden auxiliary sailing vessel, indeed our largest sailer of any kind, is the barquentine *Rigdin*, 397 tons gross. Changed days from the time when the mighty *Liverpool* was our largest windjammer.

The greatest drawback of these wooden ships, sail or motor, is their excessive draught, so most of our steel auxiliaries are of the Dutch lightdraught type, such as *Crown of Denmark*, *Loch Ryan*, *Emmanuel* and *Cymric*," to mention a few of them. This class of coasting schooner is

TOPSAIL SCHOONER KATE of PEEL I.O.M
AT HOLY HEAD

On board the Topsail Schooner " Kate " of Peel, I.O.M.　　　[*Drawing by A. Bradbury.*

The Topsail Schooner "Doris," built at Salcombe, 1880.

The Topsail Schooner "My Lady" of Plymouth

usually a profitable investment, being economical to run and being suitable for practically any trade or cargo. It is to be hoped that as the old wooden ships die out, they will be replaced by steel auxiliary schooners of modern design and perhaps in this way our depressed coasting trade may overcome foreign competition and thus regain its former prosperity.

So it will be seen, from the above, that sail still lingers in the British merchant marine, even if usually accompanied by a noisy, evil-smelling Diesel engine. I hope that, through this article, some of my readers may take a new interest in these little coasting schooners, the last survivors of the days of sail, as far as this country is concerned.

The Story of the "Torrens"

By LAWRENCE G. ROBINSON *(our South Australian Correspondent)*.

FOLLOWING the publication of a cable in the *Adelaide Advertiser*, stating that the Chairman of Sir James Laing and Sons had loaned to the Sunderland Museum a model of the famous composite clipper *Torrens*. I made a search into the archives to dig up a few facts relating to the old well-known clipper. The *Torrens* was one of the most popular composite passenger clippers in her day which made Port Adelaide the terminal port. And, particularly interesting is the fact that Joseph Conrad, the well-known author, served as a mate from 1891-3 on this ship. Conrad made two important literary associations on board this clipper with W. J. Jaques and Galsworthy, who were travellers on different occasions. Conrad, at the time, was deeply interested in literature, and this was one of the last ships he sailed in before retiring from the sea to follow literature as a profession. Conrad was always scribbling, and his memories of the *Torrens* appear to be very happy ones. Describing the ship, he said "she was a ship of brilliant quality." Apart from her celebrated good looks, she was a comfortable ship and one of the fastest and for many years the favourite passenger ship to Adelaide—the famous *Torrens*.

The *Torrens* was built to the order of Captain H. R. Angel, for the Australian trade, in 1875. Her keel, stem, and sternpost were of finest American elm ; beams, knees, stringers

and keelson of wrought iron ; shell planking and decks of East India teak, copper fastened and braced with wrought-iron diagonals ; and she was sheathed with metal from keel to waterline. Her cost, complete—ready for sea, was £27,257. For 15 years Captain Angel sailed her for the Elder Line, from London to Adelaide, with wonderful success.

A beautifully-modelled ship and a splendid sea-boat, she was very heavily sparred, and crossed a main skysail yard. She was also one of the last ships to hold on to topmast stunsails ; indeed, for many years she was the only ship in the Australian trade with stunsail booms aloft.

Wonderful Ghosting Powers

Regarding her capabilities as a seaboat, it is recorded that in easting weather she would drive along as dry as a bone, making 300 miles per day without wetting her decks. But it was in light winds that she showed up best, her ghosting powers being quite extraordinary. The flap of her sail seemed to send her along at two to three knots, and in light airs she was accustomed to pass other clippers as if they were standing still.

Commander Harry Shrubsole, R.N.R., in a letter to the *Nautical Magazine*, gives an interesting reminiscence of her speed. "Some items of one of her passages are worth noting," he writes. "Crossed the Equator in 15 days from Plymouth ; arrived off Semaphore, Port Adelaide, 61 days

Photo by]   **The " Torrens "**   [*Nautical Photo Agency*

from Plymouth. The last two days were employed in beating up the Gulf from the western end of Kangaroo Island—I forget the name of the point we made—so 59 days could easily be counted as the passage.

" We sighted the *Jennie Harkness*, obviously American, and our Foo-Foo band played " Yankee Doodle." She had Jimmy Greens and water sails, flying jib, topsails, and what-not aloft, but we slid by her as if she was —well—sailing slowly, as she undoubtedly was, compared to our speed."

Change of Command Brought Trouble

Captain Angel commanded her for 15 voyages, and under him the ship became known as a " lucky ship." Her biggest run was 336 miles in 24 hours, and her fastest speed through the water, by the log, was 14 knots. Her average for 15 outward passages was 74 days.

An instance of the extraordinary luck of the ship is evidenced by the following story : The ship ran short of lamp-oil before entering the English Channel. It was essential for a ship to have lights when beating up the Channel. Before soundings were reached a barrel was passed floating on the water. Captain Angel at once hove to and lowered a boat ; the barrel was found to contain oil.

In 1890 Captain Angel retired from the sea, and immediately the *Torrens'* luck deserted her. Captain Cope's first voyage was full of incident. The ship lost her foremast and main topmast in 6 deg. N., 27 deg. W., and put into Pernambuco to refit. Before she was refitted she caught fire. She was eventually remasted and arrived at Adelaide 172 days out.

In 1896, when Captain F. Angel, the son of the first captain, took over the command of the *Torrens*, the Goddess of Fortune again objected to the change, for, on his third voyage, young Angel ran foul of an iceberg in the Southern Ocean ; and, with her bow stove in, and partially dismantled, the *Torrens* managed to struggle into Adelaide 100 days out. Her last passage, under the British flag, also was a disastrous one. She left Adelaide on April 23rd, 1903, and before she was clear of Kangaroo Island, a storm burst on her and she had difficulty in clawing off the land. Another heavy gale caught her, in the Cape latitudes, and forced her back to. Mauritius. At last she got to Table Bay, and, as no cargo was offering, went on to St. Helena, where she took on a load of explosives for the British Government. But even when the Thames tug had got her hawser, the dangers of the passage were not over ; for, while the *Torrens* was in tow, a vessel tried to pass ahead of her and the tug, and was cut down and sunk by the sharp forefront of the famous clipper. When the collision was seen to be inevitable, there was almost a panic on the *Torrens* on account of the cargo of explosives. However, the explosion never came, and Captain Angel was not held blameworthy. But old Captain Angel had had enough of it— her cost of repairs since he had given up the command had come to more than her original cost, and he sold her to the Italians. Again the change of captain brought ill-luck, for the Italians soon ran her ashore. When she arrived at Genoa to be broken up, everyone was so struck with her beauty that the owners went to the expense of repairing her—only to bump her on the rocks. This time she was towed back to Genoa for good and all—to be broken up in 1910.

Recent Italian Shipping Mergers

By JOHN S. STYRING

A MONG the recent amalgamations of the Italian shipping companies, one of the most important is that of the new Soc. di Nav. Italia, which is a merger of the Navigazione Generale Italiana, Lloyd Sabaudo and

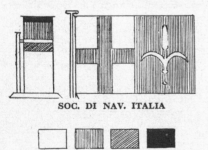

SOC. DI NAV. ITALIA

White   Red   Green   Black

Cosulich Lines. As from January 1st this year, the house flags of the old companies were discontinued and the new flag and funnel adopted. The new house flag combines the emblems of the leading Italian ports of Genoa and Trieste—the cross of St. George, with the white lily of Trieste on a red field. The new funnel markings show the national colours of red, white and green in varying widths, with narrow black band above and the lower half of the funnel white.

The M.V. *Augustus*, formerly of the Navigazione Generale Italiana, was transferred to the new Italia company on January 9th, at New York, with some ceremony, and she sailed on January 11th for the West Indies on her voyage under the new flag and with the new markings on her funnel.

The Lloyd Orientale, which is a merger of the Lloyd Triestino, Societa Italiana di Servizi Marittima and the Marittima Italiana, similarly came into force on January 1st this year, and has adopted a plain black funnel ; the new house flag is identical with that of the Italia company, with the exception that the white lily is in the " hoist " and the St. George's Cross in the " fly."

Another amalgamation of the Soc. Italiana di Nav. Florio, with the Cia. Italiana Transatlantica (Citra), to form the " Tirrenia " company, takes place on April 16th, whilst a still further merger is announced of the San Marco, Costiera and Nautica companies under the title of Cia. Adriatica. The new house flags and funnel markings of these companies will be given in a subsequent issue.

Model Block Making
By A. E.

SOME notes on the writer's methods of turning out quantities of model blocks in small sizes may be of interest to his fellow workers.

For historical and representative models, dummy blocks are usually fitted—the material favoured by the writer is ebonite, as being of even texture, and easily worked—but the methods described apply equally to the use of any other material. If wood is used, select only timber of a hard, close-grained nature, such as box, holly, sycamore, etc.

good enough for quite a number of blocks.

The operation of the jig is simple ; the strip is passed in and a hole is drilled near one end through the nearer jig-hole, then the strip is pushed in until the drilled hole coincides with the other jig-hole—it is then located with a wire pin, as shown in sketch—and the second hole is drilled ; and so on until the whole of the strip is drilled.

The next step is to groove the strip at the sides, as at 2, and is accom-

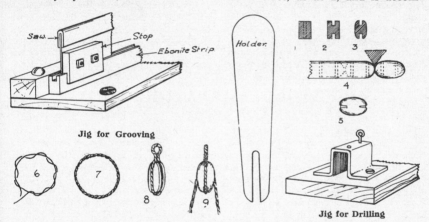

Jig for Grooving

Jig for Drilling

The first step is to cut up the material into strips, rectangular in section, and uniform in size, as at 1 in sketch, and any handy length, say 6".

Next proceed to drill them—those whose hobby of ship-modelling is of a permanent nature will find it will pay them to rig up the simple jig shown ; this consists of a small piece of steel plate bent to fit easily the strip of material, and screwed down to a block or to the bench. This has, on the upper face, two holes drilled to the required pitch of the drilling, and if the tool is destined for continued use these holes could be bushed with steel to give longer service, but for the average man, plain holes will be

plished with a small hacksaw, to which is fitted, at the front end, a metal guard and stop combined, which can be fixed with a couple of screws—the saw-blade is usually quite soft enough for drilling. The grooving is carried out with the strip of material placed against a strip of wood screwed down to a board or to the bench. The whole arrangement is shown in the accompanying sketch.

The grooving completed, it is now best to shape the strip, as shown at 3, with file and glasspaper, after which the shaping up of the individual blocks, as shown at 4, is carried out with a triangular file—each block touched up after parting off with a file made of a slip of wood with fine glasspaper glued on.

Now the strop grooves, shown at 5, may be made with our triangular file —and, as the blocks are difficult to hold at this stage, the writer advises the manufacture of the holding tool shown. This is of flat steel or other metal, about the same thickness as the grooves in the sides of the block, and having a slot, very slightly tapered, into which the block is pushed and held while working on it.

Our dummy block is now finished except for the strop—this the writer makes of very fine brass wire, wound into a grommet strop, as shown, starting at 6 and finishing at 7. Experiment will be necessary to determine the size of the strop—the making of these stops is a nice little job for the fireside. About three complete turns of the wire make a neat-looking strop—the ends should be cut off close and worked into the lay.

The strop is now applied to the block, first bent round by hand and then shaped with a fine-nosed pair of pliers (keeping a bradawl or piece of wire in the eye, as shown at 8), and finally seized, either with the same fine wire or with seccotined cotton as at 9, which shows the finished block with its falls.

The above remarks apply equally to working model blocks as to dummies —the only other steps necessary are the cleaning out of the sheave-space with a fretsaw and fine files, first, however, drilling the hole for the sheave-spindle, which will be retained, on assembly, by the strop.

These methods result in a component which looks remarkably neat if care is taken to get the proportions about right, especially the maker is advised to get the finest possible wire for the strop and to keep the eye as small as possible.

A Model 100-Gun Ship
By B. C. G. Eason

THE hull lines and deck plans were obtained from Messrs. Beale, in Shaftesbury Avenue. Information in connection with the rigging, spars, and the small details were obtained from the Science, Greenwich, and the United Service Museums. Information was also obtained from Mr. F. C. Bowen's book "From Carrack to Clipper"; "Ships and Ways of Other Days," by E. Keble Chatterton; "The Old Wooden Walls," by Falconer and Gill, and the "Encyclopaedia Britannica."

The hull was built on the laminated system of ⅛″ lime boards, which were temporarily fastened together and shaped on the outside with the usual moulds and then separated and hollowed out as far as the lower gun deck. The gun ports were cut out before the final cleaning-up inside, in order not to break away the edges inside. The gun carriages were then fitted before fixing the decks, but the guns themselves were fitted through the ports later.

The forecastle and poop decks were built up on beams and knees, and the various bulkheads fitted with windows and doors, complete with hinges. There is a staircase from the entry port to the main deck and two more from the main deck to the poop decks. The forecastle has two ladders made of boxwood, with threads tenoned into the stringers. The cabins are finished inside, and bear inspection when viewed from any of the stern windows. The hatch covers were halved-jointed and made from $1/32″ \times 1/32″$ boxwood. The figurehead was carved from lime wood and fitted over the stem, but the "tails" were put on separately.

The masts and spars were made from pine sticks, stained and french-polished, and rubbed down to remove the polish which was too bright. The tops were built up on trestle trees and cross-trees, with hounds fitted to the masts to support them.

All the small pillars for the belfry, entry port, and the important doors in the bulkheads were turned for the purpose from bone knitting-needles. The gun carriages were made from

A Model 100-Gun Ship—by B. C. G. Eason

ebonite and the guns themselves from brass which, which were drilled and fitted with trunnions. The photograph gives the impression that the topmasts and the topgallant masts are too heavy, but although they are on the heavy side, they do not spoil the model.

Most of the blocks were bought, but the deadeyes and special blocks were made from bone or boxwood. The parrals were made of very small pieces of pine, shaped correctly, with round beads between each piece, which, when fitted to the masts and yards, looks very well.

At the Admiral's Cabin

By "MAIN ROYAL"

THE lights of London are famous in song and story, and now-a-days they are both numerous and brilliant. But of all the illuminations of London town, there are two lights which stand out beyond any others as a lure to the shiplover ; they are the port and starboard lights of the Admiral's Cabin, to be seen as you pass along the south side of the Strand, a little east of Somerset House. To be precise, at No. 167 in that busy thoroughfare, you will find the lights, and a flight of steps and a side-rope, real ship fashion, leading down to the Cabin itself.

For the ordinary mortal, the Cabin is a very cosy and comfortable little restaurant, where one may start the day with breakfast at 9 a.m. if need be, or where one may drop in for morning coffee, lunch, or afternoon tea, with the assurance of excellent food and good service. For the shiplover it is all that and something more : it is a museum of most interesting models and nautical pictures and relics, and it is a rendezvous of kindred spirits who will talk ships and models till closing time at 7.30

p.m. if you will let them. It was founded in 1922 by Mr. and Mrs. R. G. Rodney, a name which at once suggests the glory of the Navy. Mr. Rodney, in fact, is a descendant of the famous Admiral of that name, and hanging on the wall of one of the rooms is the original telescope of his ancestor. Mrs. Rodney, the charming hostess of the Cabin, can look back through the centuries for her family history to those Norman pirates, the Du Châtels, who, hundreds of years ago, used to raid our southern coasts. Mrs. Rodney makes the catering comfort of her visitors her personal care ; the business side of the establishment is supervised by Mr. R. Stuart Bruce, whose unfailing courtesy and profound knowledge of ships and the sea have made him a much-loved figure in London's maritime circles.

I dropped into the Admiral's Cabin a few days ago, to have a quiet look at some of the models, and, if I could, to get Mr. Bruce to relate their history.

" Tell me, Mr. Bruce," I said, " which do you consider your most interesting model ? " " Well," he

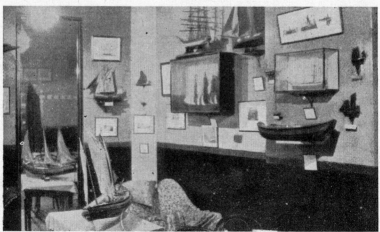

A Group of Ship Models at the Admiral's Cabin

The "Zulu" (left) and the "Fifie" (right)

replied, " I think it is this *Zulu* boat. My further question of " Why *Zulu*, and where does it come from ? " elicited the following little story : " The *Zulu* is a mixture of the lines of the *Scaffa* and the *Fifie*, the former type being a descendant of the Norse herring boats and having a cut-away stem and stern, while the latter has the straight up-and-down stem and stern of the boats hailing from Fife. A certain owner and his wife had decided to build a new boat, but could not agree whether to build a *Scaffa* or a *Fifie*. The husband wanted the one, and the wife wanted the other. Finally, a happy compromise was decided upon. The new boat had the straight bows of the *Fifie*, and the cutaway stern of the *Scaffa*. It proved a great success, having the good qualities of the *Scaffa*, but sailing better into the wind and being quicker in stays, owing to its *Fifie* bows. The Zulu War was in progress at that time, and the new boat being something very weird to the local eye, the Scottish fisherman called it a *Zulu*. The name stuck, and as a type the *Zulu* boat has quite displaced the *Scaffa*." These models are unique ; even the Science Museum does not possess an example of either kind.

Mr. Bruce is a Shetlander, and loves the islands and their people. He has for many years been preparing a book

A Topsail Schooner, a Brigantine, and a Brixham Trawler

on the wrecks of the Shetland shores, and for my edification produced a chart on which he has marked the location of the principal recorded wrecks. " They became so numerous, in the course of my research," said he, " that I finally had no more room on the chart to put my later records." He has a remarkable collection of models of small craft, and I am privileged to reproduce a photograph showing his fleet of models at anchor on a loch in the Island of Whalsay, about twelve miles from Lerwick. I find I have to examine this picture very closely to realise that the miniature vessels are not full-sized craft.

Looking round the Cabin I noticed many pictures and models of interest. In one corner there were models of a topsail schooner, a brigantine, and a Brixham trawler. These and some of the other models are the work of Mr. F. T. Wayne, a regular visitor to the Cabin, who is building a fleet of coasting vessels all to the same scale, so that interesting comparisons may be made. Another example of Mr. Wayne's work on view was a partly built hull, showing the constructional methods he adopts. I am indebted to Mr. Wayne, by the way, for the

pictures of the Cabin models which illustrate this article. Full rigged ships, models of quaint native craft from overseas, and curios in the form of bottle models and match-box models, add much to the variety of this fascinating collection. Perhaps the most remarkable of the curiosities were a model ship in the case of an ordinary watch, and another ship inside the bulb of an incandescent electric lamp. I ought also to mention a model of a Shetland " four-areen," a foar-oared boat, from which all whale-boats are descended, and a model of the first lifeboat put into service at Lowestoft a hundred years ago.

I have said enough to indicate the unusually interesting character of the nautical collection which makes the Admiral's Cabin such a distinctive meeting place for ship-lovers. Here you may also see some of the writers and artists whose names are familiar to our readers, besides many distinguished members of the Senior Service. Mr. T. R. Beaufort dropped in while I was there, and showed me some photographs of his beautiful work in restoration and rigging of period models. The Shiplovers' Association

Mr. R. Stuart Bruce's model fleet at anchor at Whalsay Loch.

hold their regular evening dinner and meetings there, and I hear that the new Naval Photographic Club is to follow their excellent example.

There is no formality or ostentation about the Admiral's Cabin ; there is no need for the visitor to feel that he is a stranger in the land. If good food and good service at very modest prices appeal to him, he will be content ; if, moreover, a kindly welcome and a fascinating array of ships and boats and pictures add to the delights of his visit, as assuredly they will do, he will mentally express his gratitude to me for giving him his compass course to this cosy little harbour.

The U.S. Frigate "Constitution"
(Our Supplement Plate)

THE frigate *Constitution* is almost as celebrated in naval history as our own glorious *Victory*. Launched at Boston in 1797, she is reported to have " won more battles, captured more prizes, sailed more miles, trained more Navy officers and men, received less injury, and sustained fewer losses than any other ship in the world." Her main dimensions were : length over-all, 204' ; length on load water line, 175' ; beam, 43.6" ; draught forward, 21', aft 23' ; tonnage, 1,335, and displacement, 2,200 tons. Her original armament consisted of twenty-eight long 24-pounders, on the gun deck, and ten long 12-pounders on the quarter-deck. At later dates, the number and disposition of her guns were considerably altered. Her active service career lasted from 1803 to 1855, but from then until 1882 she was used as a training ship. During this period she was rebuilt at the Navy Yard at Philadelphia, and in 1907 her final restoration to her present condition was put in hand.

Captain E. Armitage McCann has devoted Volume III of his library on Ship Model Making to the building of a scale model of this famous ship. Full plans and complete instructions on all details are given in the 200 pages which this book contains.

Copies are obtainable from our publishing department, price 12s. 6d., or 13s. post free.

The beautiful photograph of the *Constitution*, which forms the subject of our supplement plate this month, is the work of Mr. W. B. Jackson, marine photographer, of Marblehead, Mass., U.S.A. We are indebted to Mr. Jackson for his courteous permission to publish this picture, and we may add that he is prepared to supply copies of this photograph to any reader who may wish to purchase a souvenir of this fine vessel. He can do these in the 8" × 10" size at 2 dollars each, plus postage.

WM BIRCHALL 1932.

Sketch by]   " Unloading "   [*W. M. Birchall*

Ship Models at the Royal United Service Museum.

II.—STEAMSHIPS

By CAPTAIN E. ALTHAM, C.B., R.N.

IN a previous article, a description was given of some of the most notable sailing ship models in the Banqueting Hall of the old Whitehall Palace, now the Royal United Service Museum.

In the Crypt, below, is another series of models, which depict the gradual introduction of steam into the Navy, and its final complete substitution for sails. The earliest steam men-of-war were small paddle ships, such as the *Rhadamanthus*, of which there is an excellent model. She was a vessel of 813 tons and mounted four small guns; she had engines of 220 h.p., and carried a complement of 60 officers and men. Just a hundred years ago she formed part of the squadron under Vice-Admiral Sir Pulteney Malcolm, which was employed in blockading the Dutch ports. Next in the line we find a model of the *Trident*, which is of interest as being the first steamship used by a British Sovereign. Her Majesty Queen Victoria took passage on board on her return from a visit to Scotland. A smaller model is that of the *Dwarf*, completed in 1840; the first screw ship to be acquired by the Admiralty. A particularly fine and valuable model is that of a corvette of 1860, a class of ship which was fairly numerous in the Navy during the latter part of the 19th Century. It shows a full-rigged ship with the short, stumpy funnel and single-screw propeller, typical of the early steam man-of-war. Last in this line is a hull model of the ill-fated *Captain*, a low free-board turret ship built in 1869. She was the forerunner of a class which marked drastic changes in naval construction, but she lacked free-board and was overmasted. On the night of September 8th, 1870, while cruising with the

The Paddle Ship "Rhadamanthus."

Hull Model of the " Captain."

Channel Fleet, she was struck by a fierce squall, heeled over, filled and went to the bottom ; only 18 out of her crew of 500 being saved.

Two very fine models of the Great War period are those of the battle-cruiser *Queen Mary*, and the German armoured-cruiser *Scharnhorst*. The former, it will be recalled, was sunk at Jutland, and the latter, having carried Von Spee's flag to victory at the battle of Coronel, was sunk in the battle of the Falkland Islands. The Great War is also commemorated by a most interesting collection of miniature models depicting every ship in the Grand Fleet as it was organised immediately before the Battle of Jutland. There are also miniature models representing typical ships of the Allied and enemy fleets.

The models which have hitherto been described are of varying degrees of beauty and accuracy, but the expert will appreciate most of all the latest additions to the Museum's collection : a series of water-line models of the principal types of ships in the Navy of to-day. These have been specially built for the Royal United Service Museum by Mr. Norman Ough, and are probably the most accurate and detailed ship models in existence.

A Corvette of 1860.

The "W" Class Destroyer, H.M.S. "Warwick."

They are $\frac{1}{16}''$ scale, and have been reproduced, by courtesy of the Admiralty, from the original ships' drawings. So exact are they in every particular, including the colouring and 10,000-ton cruiser *London*, the destroyer *Warwick*, the new large submarine *Osiris*, and a sloop-minesweeper. To these will shortly be added a model of the aircraft-carrier *Glorious*, which

The 10,000 ton Cruiser, H.M.S. "London."

metal work, that a photograph of one of these models against a suitable background is indistinguishable from the ship herself. The series includes the battleship *Queen Elizabeth*, the will be even nearer perfection than those already completed.

These are but a section of the more important ship models in the Museum; but there are innumerable others:

H.M. Battleship "Queen Elizabeth."

H.M. Submarine " Osiris."

Chinese junks, a Maltese galley, a Venetian felucca, Burmese canoes, a pirate schooner, horse, troop and ice boats, a sheer hulk, and many other queer craft to interest and intrigue the visitor.

A Fine Model of a Thrilling Sea Battle

A New Panorama Completed in the Royal United Services Museum.

By A. GUY VERCOE.

MORE than fifty models of 16th Century warships are included in the great panorama of the Armada fight which has recently been opened at the Museum of the Royal United Services Institution, Whitehall, London.

The panorama was constructed under the expert supervision of Capt. E. Altham, R.N., the Secretary of the Institution, and the ships are arranged in the order shown in several ancient documents and illustrations in the possession of the Institution, notably a fine volume of engravings of the tapestries which used to adorn the old House of Lords, destroyed by fire more than a hundred years ago.

The actual models were constructed in 1924 for an Armada show which it was proposed to give in the British Government Pavilion at the British Empire Exhibition, but owing to the popularity of the attack on Zeebrugge model, the Armada show was never given. Since then the models have figured at a number of exhibitions in different parts of the world, and have been lent for their present purpose by the Department of Overseas Trade.

While of the pictorial, rather than the exact scale model order, the ships are extraordinarily faithful to their prototypes, and the contrast between the English and Spanish types of ship design is well exemplified. The types included cover all types of 16th Century warships and transports from galleons and oared galleasses to the small pinnaces and other half-decked craft. The English fireships have been very cunningly contrived, and their flames made to flicker and leap by an electrical device which is entirely automatic as long as the lamp in the ship is alight.

The scene was painted by a clever young woman artist, Miss Cynthia Mourilyan, who has also carried out a number of other panoramas in the Museum. The magnitude of the work, which was carried out in distemper colours and occupied five weeks, will be realised when it is mentioned that the panorama is 40' long, with a sea 4' 6" wide, and a sky about 5' high.

The episode chosen for illustration is the attack on the Spanish Fleet off Gravelines by the English fireships. The scene is in semi-darkness, lit by the red and yellow gleams of the flaming hulks, with blood-red lights playing on the sails of the ships and on the clouds above. Seen in perspective from the point of view of the English Fleet, the sight is extremely lifelike and impressive.

The Armada, it will be remembered, was sighted off the mouth of the Channel on the afternoon of Friday, July 19th, 1588, and on the Sunday began the running fight which lasted all the way up the Channel, and in which the Armada was so harried and hunted that it was quite unable to effect a landing in the Isle of Wight, as had been intended. On the Thursday a stiff gale from the south-west hastened the Spanish ships in what had already almost developed into a flight from the tenacious English.

On the Saturday evening the Spaniards anchored in Calais roads, there to wait until it was possible to embark the army of the Duke of Parma and proceed with the invasion of England. But the English would give the Spaniards no peace. They anchored so close that the nearest ships of the rival fleets were within a quarter of a mile of one another.

On the Sunday the English commanders held a council of war aboard the flagship *Ark Royal*, and planned an attack by fireships. A number of merchantmen were filled with explosives and combustibles, and at midnight they were released to drift down among the Spanish ships. Driving before the wind, each ship blazing furiously, the fireships advanced upon the Spaniards, the crews abandoning them as the heat became too fierce to remain.

This is the stage of the action depicted by the panorama. The clumsy Spanish carracks, having cut their cables and hoisted their sails, are shown trying to tack clear of the floating furnaces which are already in among them. The fleet is in confusion as each ship makes frantic efforts to get clear of the danger.

In-shore of all is the great galleass *San Lorenzo*, with her banks of huge seeps pulling towards the shore, where she ultimately grounded and became a total loss. Among the other Spanish ships shown are the flagship of the Admiral, the *Duke of Medina Sidonia*, the *San Martin*, the great *Rata Coronada*, the *Gran Griffon*, and all classes of ships down to tiny craft of 20 tons or so.

To seaward, in ordered lines, lie the ships of the English fleet, silhouetted against the dark sky by the glow of the blazing fire-ships. Here are shown such famous vessels as the *Ark Royal*, flagship of Lord Howard of Effingham, Drake's *Revenge*, Hawkin's *Victory*, Frobisher's *Triumph*, the *Elizabeth Bonaventure*, and the *Margaret and John*, one of the 30 ships fitted out, manned and armed by the City of London.

The panorama is a spectacle which should not be missed by any student of naval history or ship construction, for it shows the northern and southern types of warship at the end of the 16th Century in perfect contrast, and gives a magnificent impression of the terror and confusion caused in those days by the use of fireships.

Sketch by]   **" Heavy Weather."**   *[S. E. Beck.*

The Ship's Mail

Readers are invited to make use of this column for the discussion of matters of mutual interest and the exchange of ideas and information.

Bending a Cable to an Anchor

DEAR SIR,—In the Ship Modellers' Scrap Book column of January appeared a sketch illustrating the method of bending on a rope cable to an anchor. I venture to point out that I think there must be a mistake.

According to the drawing there

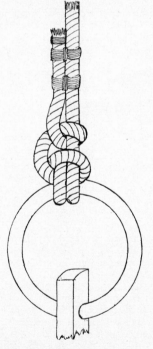

Bending a Cable to an Anchor.

appears to be no sign of a bend or hitch, just simply three seizings. Now this method would not hold, where any chafing was likely to occur, such as on a sandy or rocky bottom.

The enclosed drawing will show you the bend used by seamen before the days of Nelson. It was easily

cast adrift when the cable was stowed, and could be depended on when riding at anchor.

The method of securing the cable to the anchor is as follows : Take two round turns with the end of the cable through the ring of the anchor, and one half hitch around the standing parts, and under all parts of the turns ; then one half hitch around the standing part above all, and stop the end to the standing part, as shown in the sketch.

Yours truly,

Woolston.   C. W. BASS.

The Derivation of " Onker "

DEAR SIR,—In answer to the question from whence came the name of " onker " for a sailing ship on the small timber trade between the Baltic and Thames, I offer the opinion that this name is derived from the word " hooker," by pronouncing this " ooker," later " onker." Harkers, or similar-shaped vessels, were used in former centuries as freighters in large numbers.

Another possibility seems that the word is derived from " hawker," a vessel which sold out its cargo in small lots to all-comers, as did the onion-schooners from Brittany in former years in British ports, especially in the Welsh coal ports. The derivation would thus be : hawker-awker-onker. The word " drogher," used also for Baltic timber-traders' may have its origin therein, that these vessels were obliged to pass the Drogden bank in Ore-sund. To those of your readers who think these explanations far-sought, I may add a few examples of how your Queen's English gets altered abroad to suit the local tongue.

In my last ship (Dutch) I had a boatsman, a Dutchman, who served a long tine in Rhine craft. This worthy proposed to me, one day, to paint the anchor-line black. As I did not comprehend his proposal, he pointed the object, which he had in his mind, out to me. This proved to be the angle-iron connecting the hatch-coaming to the iron deck. Derivation : angle-iron (?) ankerlyn, whilst the correct technical name for this work in Dutch is hockyzer. Other examples of " English as she is spoken " by Dutch sailors are : kommers for coamings, stoert for steward, pusser for purser, wins for winch, hiewen for to heave, etc., etc.

In explaining nautical slang, it is often very difficult to find out which way to look first, as our profession is a very international one.

Yours faithfully,
Rotterdam.   D. VERWEY.

Steamers of 1878

DEAR SIR,—I think that W.J.T. is confusing the *Carbon* with the *Black Boy*. The *Carbon* was the ship reputed to have been built to carry water to the Crimea ; she was long afterwards sold to Cork owners, and had rounded gunnel plates, so prevalent in early steamers. I remember being sculled off in the *Carbon's* boat to see a capsized barque, *Childers*, on the Tyne about 1897.

I had dealings with the *Black Boy* about 1899. She had a clipper stem, engines aft, and was about 670 tons deadweight.

One peculiarity of many of these vessels was that the steam winches were quite evidently an afterthought, as the donkey boiler was a separate fixture on a sheet-iron bed, held down to the deck by wire lashings and eye-bolts. The only steam winch carried was just aft of the foremast. The windlass was " dumb," and was power-operated by a " gipsy " wheel on winch and windlass, with an endless ordinary link chain as belt, the slack being taken up by a snatch block hoving up alongside foremast, the outfit being the last word in noise and clatter.

I once had dealings with a very archaic little German steamer running pit props from the Baltic. On being asked what horse-power she was, the

skipper replied : " Two hunerd und dirty, but dey vas very little horses." Evidently they were the candle-horse-power type.

Yours truly,
South Shields.   TYNESIDE.

Steamers of 1878

DEAR SIR,—The letter of your correspondent W.J.T. interests me very much indeed, and I trust that you will see your way to publish from time to time particulars and, if possible, pictures of these old steamers.

With reference to the *Sir Robert Peel*, my records of old vessels contain a wood-cut showing a screw steamboat of that name, dated 1852, and stated to be " the first mail steamer into the Bay of Natal," no doubt the vessel

Sketch of the "Sir Robert Peel"

referred to by W.J.T. The *Hoboken*, a paddle-boat with one large funnel, forward of the paddle boxes, was owned by the General Steam Navigation Co., and I have a small sketch of her bound for Yarmouth from London Bridge.

The *Eclair* I seem to remember about 1879, in Ramsgate Harbour, with passengers on board for a trip to France.

The s.s. *Express* was engined by my father on his well-known system of high pressure, and was fitted with quadruple compound engine with triangular connecting-rod driving on to *one* crank. Boiler pressure, 600 lb. per sq. in.

In the year 1887 she ran from Blackwall Pier to Southend and Sheerness, in opposition to the paddle-boats *Arran* amd *Bonnie Doon*. According to my records, the *Arran* (ex *Dunoon Castle*, 1867) was very fast and " was the last of the Clyde steamboats to be fitted with a *steeple engine*."

My records also contain a photograph of the *Glen Rosa*, a fast paddle-boat belonging to the London Steamboat Co., and a great favourite with holiday-makers, circa 1878.

Yours truly,

Cricklewood.　　LOFTUS P. PERKINS.

Steamers of 1878

DEAR SIR,—With reference to W.J.T.'s interesting letter in the March issue of SHIPS AND SHIP MODELS, I, in common with others, would like to hear of any Thames steamers. The *Hoboken*—of which I have a very excellent photograph—I knew well ; she ran to Margate and Ramsgate, captained by that popular Charles Sargent. The *Hoboken* ran in conjunction with the *Eagle*, and the clipper-bowed, two-funnelled *Hilda*, all belonging to the G.S.N. Co. They ran the service until cut out by the new *Halcyon*, *Mavis*, etc.

A very famous Thames steamer was the *Baron Osy*—Capt. Verbist—which ran bi-weekly from London to Antwerp.

Those who knew the Thames, no doubt can call to mind the cattle-boat *Racoon* that used to lie off Deptford Foreign Cattle Market.

It may interest W.J.T., and others, that these steamers are mentioned in my "History of the Cross-Channel Paddle Boat," now in course of preparation.

Yours truly,

FRANK BURTT,

Lewes.　　M.I.Loco.E.

Irish Cross-Channel Boats

DEAR SIR,—As a reader of your very interesting paper, I enclose a photograph which, if you care to make use of same, may be of interest to some of your other readers.

There must be very many who, like myself, greatly regret the passing of the " City of Dublin Steam Packet Company," with its long and honourable association with the Irish cross-channel service. The photo shows R.M.S. *Leinster* leaving Holyhead. I took her just about a month before the outbreak of the Great War, that

R.M.S. "Leinster"—City of Dublin Steam Packet Co.

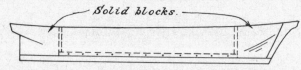

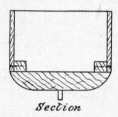
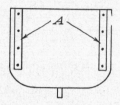

Section

A simple method of making a model steamer hull

fatal time which was to claim so many fine ships, including the *Leinster* herself, which, it will be remembered by many, was sunk on October 10th, 1918, with great loss of life.

The four splendid vessels, *Ulster, Leinster, Munster* and *Connaught*, with their beautiful lines and black raking funnels, were the product of Laird's, of Birkenhead, and came on the Holyhead station in 1897. They had a length of 370′, with a beam of 41.5′, and draught of 15.6′, with a tonnage of 2,630. With a speed of 24 knots, they were at the time the fastest cross-channel steamers afloat.

The war claimed the *Connaught* and *Leinster*, but I cannot trace, with certainty, the subsequent career of the two remaining sisters, *Munster* and *Ulster*. A German firm bought them, and they were towed out of Holyhead, destined, apparently, for the breaker's yard. But, last year, I was told that they were still afloat, and that one had recently been seen at Folkestone. Another report says that they are now coal-hulks. Perhaps some of your readers could answer this question ? One would hope that such fine boats have escaped so ignominious an end ; but, if true, I certainly would go to Folkestone, or further, to see my old friend.

Yours faithfully,

Chiswick.   (Rev.) CHARLES O'REILLY.

A Simple Method of Model Hull Construction for Model Steamers

DEAR SIR,—I enclose rough sketches of a cheap, quick method of making a model hull for either sail or steam, but particularly adapted for engines, as it gives so much room in the hull.

On a thick board you fasten upright boards for the sides, and then fasten on securely soft wood blocks. The strips of wood (A) in end view are nailed on the solid ends, to prevent sides being crushed in. Plane down bottom edges to give the bilge and carve stem and stern and the hull is complete. Seams and screw holes can be filled in with plastic wood. This is my idea, and I have never heard of anyone making one like it.

I commend it to the notice of your model steamer readers.

Yours truly,

Southsea.   R. WILSON.

The Cro'jack

DEAR SIR,—Was it the custom, in full-rigged ships, not to have a sail bent on the cro-jack yard ; or, alternatively, was it the custom, even if it were bent, not to set it ?

Your cover-design shows no canvas, bent on the cross-jack. Contrariwise, see *Lake Erie* on page 195 of No. 7.

Yours truly,

London, E.C. 1.   W.J.T.

C. HAWKINS GARRINGTON
1932

The Union Liner "**Trojan**"—Built in 1880

Carved Work on Elizabethan Ships

DEAR SIR,—The Pipe Office Accounts prove that one at least of Elizabeth's great ships was so decorated. This was the *White Bear*, for whose carved wooden figures and painting and colouring £121 13s. 8d. was paid in 1563.

On being rebuilt, her carvings included an image of Jupiter sitting upon an eagle in the clouds, side boards and train board, with compartments and badges and fruitages, 16 brackets supporting these boards, 36 " peces of spoyle or artillerie " round the hull, and on or between the stern uprights " the greate pece of Neptune and the Nymphs about him." The cost for carving alone was £172, and the gilding and painting £205 10s.

At the same time, it must be admitted that this ship was exceptional ; no other of the Queen's ships had anything like as much spent on them for " spit and polish," with the exception of the *Elizabeth Jonas*, and her finery apparently consisted of paint and gold-leaf only.

Faithfully yours,
E. E. EGLINTON-BAILEY,
Putney, S.W.　　　　　Captain.

Identity of Model Liner

DEAR SIR,—The model liner, illustrated on page 205 of the March issue, resembles the old Union liner *Trojan*, built in 1880. Points of similarity are : the dimensions to $\frac{1}{8}''$ scale would be, roughly, length 45.5″, beam 5.3″, depth 3.5″ ; four davits on the forecastle head ; double hawse pipes ; scroll work at bow and stern ; same number and spacing of portholes in the plating protecting bridge-house (there were doors in the larger spaces separating the third and fourth and sixth and seventh) ; accommodation ladder in similar position ; and the ash shoot between ports six and seven. The chief differences are : the *Trojan* carried her main exhaust pipe aft of the funnel ; a donkey boiler uptake was carried into the after side of the funnel ; there were two boats each side aft, with a deck-house between the for'ard pair.

It is interesting to note that a similar Union liner of the period, the *Spartan*, carried her main exhaust pipe for'ard of the funnel, but had four boats each side of the bridge deck and one aft, but no after-deck house. In both these vessels the waterline was pink, and a drawing I have of the Union liner *Mexican*, dated August, 1886, shows a black funnel. The *Trojan* was schooner-rigged in the early 'nineties, and W. Clark Russell, in an account of his voyage to the Cape, dated 1889, referring to the *Spartan*, says: "Had she carried square yards, there were moments when I should have looked to see the yardarms harpooning the swell."

The deck-house, pierced by the main mast, was similar in the *Trojan* to that of the model, but in the *Spartan* the bridge-deck is extended over it and carries the fourth boat; it is supported at the sides on stanchions, forming an alley way. This may have been added, or perhaps was a natural development, as the *Spartan* was built a year later than the *Trojan*.

The *Trojan* was re-engined, had electric lighting installed and refrigerating apparatus placed on board in 1887, and it is possible that the extra deck-house and boats were added at this time.

I cannot make out the details of the device on her bows, but it appears to be similar in shape to that of the model. The reclining man, grasping a spear, may represent a Trojan; the *Spartan's* device is quite different.

Yours truly,
C. HAWKINS GARRINGTON.
Caversham.

Identity of Model Liner

DEAR SIR,—In the March number of SHIPS AND SHIP MODELS you ask for information *re* same. It is a model of the Union Line *Trojan*—not the German—she was a different vessel in build. In the old days the funnels were black. I should say it was about 1887 when they changed to yellow. I recognised the picture by the figure on the bow, as I sailed in her for about 12 months as a junior engineer. She was built by J. and G. Thompson, Clydebank, Scotland. Her official number was 82,404 and registered tonnage 2,283. When she was first out she carried two yards on the

foremast only, but they were afterwards taken down. As regards the name on it, I seem to think that was the carpenter of the ship, as the name seems familiar, and he was always busy at small models. Trusting this may be of help to you. With kind regards.

Yours faithfully,
Southampton.   W. H. TROTMAN.

"L'Imperial"

DEAR SIR,—I am very much obliged to Capitaine de Corvette M. Adam for calling my attention to the mistake in the name of the French ship *L'Imperial*, which will be corrected forthwith.

Possibly the error came about from the English tradition of always alluding to a ship as "she."

Yours very truly,
E. ALTHAM.
Captain R.N., Secretary.
Royal United Service Institution.

A Model 13th Century Ship

DEAR SIR,—I have always been interested in ship models and have already made half-a-dozen. My difficulty in the past has been to obtain details of ships, and I have generally had to build from old prints and photos of models.

This has also been the case with the model, the photograph of which I enclose, I obtained a photo of a model in the Science Museum of a ship of the Cinque Ports of the 13th Century.

I made a scale drawing from the photo (an awkward business), increasing the size from about 4" to 12", and built my ship from this drawing.

She is 12" overall, with a beam of 4", and is carved from the solid and hollowed out to the level of the floor of the hold.

She has a couple of heavy beams running across the hold at the deck level, and is decked fore and aft, and has connecting side decks, all of these being planked. She also has a small deck at the foot of the mast, with a pin rail, and she carries a cargo of barrels, all hand-made.

There are bollards, fore and aft, for the anchor ropes and sheets respectively. The anchors are, of course, of the grapnel type.

Other points of interest are the sprit, with its bowline, the bonnet on the foot of the sail, and the quarter rudder, and the yard, which is made up of two pieces, fished together in the centre, although this is not visible in the picture.

Leigh-on-Sea.   G. H. DAWSON.

The Oldest Vessels Afloat

DEAR SIR,—Whilst waiting for a train at Bournemouth, the other morning, I strolled along to the bookstall and casually looked along the various magazines, when SHIPS AND SHIP MODELS attracted my attention.

On close inspection, I noticed, with great interest, the reference to several old vessels, namely the *Premier*, *John* and *Good Intent*. It may interest you to know I was for many years Marine Superintendent of the *John* and *Good Intent*, owned by Messrs. A. J. Smith and Co., of Bristol, and am now Marine Superintendent for the company which owns the *Premier*.

On looking up the records, I quite agree with your correspondent that the *Premier* is older than the *John*, and the *Premier* is also the oldest vessel afloat, which has a Board of Trade Certificate for carrying passengers. With reference to the remarks of your correspondent *re* the *John*, I think he must be under a misapprehension, as no provision at all has been made in this vessel for paddle engines. A very old vessel, owned by the same company, the *Iron Duke*,

A Model 13th Century Ship—by G. H. Dawson

built in 1857, was originally a paddle vessel, the construction amidships, with raised floors and web frames, are still there ; she was altered many years ago to a screw boat for cargo carrying.

With regard to the *Good Intent*, she was built in 1796. Alf. J. Smith, Ltd., bought her for a coal hulk, her mast and rigging being taken out. Subsequently, she was sold to a firm at Pill and has been broken up.

Another vessel owned by the same company is the *William*, which was built in 1809. This vessel was built of wood, and is of the open-trow type with canvas sides, fitted with main and mizzen, and is complete with a set of sails. She is in very good condition, and is used for carrying coal and burnt ore to the South Wales and Severn ports. By the date, you will observe that this vessel is now 123 years old, and is still going strong.

I am writing you because it may be of interest to your readers, and it is also a coincidence that I am now Marine Superintendent of the *Premier*, and was formerly Superintendent of these old craft, and should any further information be required, I shall be only too pleased to supply same if it is within my power.

Yours faithfully,

J. Moore Ward, M.I.Mech.E.
Weymouth.

15th and 16th Century Blocks

Dear Sir,—I shall be much interested in any replies that may be forthcoming on the subject of blocks used in the 16th Century.

Since writing to you, I have made some further inquiries regarding the point in question. I have verified the reference in Paris' " Souvenirs de Marine," and find that the sketch in my letter was not quite correct, the type of block shown being more of the form indicated in my sketch.

The reference to this block reads as follows :—

" Les poulies au XVI siecle ne sont pas generalement rondes elles sont un peu allongees et au lieu d'une estrope la caisse de la poulie a un oeil ou passe une estrope avec cabillot " (toggle).

I have also obtained a copy of the Navy Records Society's publication of the Naval Accounts of Henry VII, in which there are numerous references to blocks and their fittings, such as the following :—

The " Grace Dieu " (1485).

Poleis with stroppes.

Poles with sheves of brasse and stroppes.

Checke poles with V sheves of brasse.

Left poles with iiij sheves of brasse.

Blokkes for the meson with iij sheves of brasse.

Poles of iij sheves and colkes (pins) of brasse.

Stroppes of russewale.

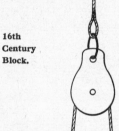

16th Century Block.

Double poles with a stroppe for the bote staye.

Double poles with treen sheves.

The " Mary of the Tower " (1485).

Snache poleis (snatch blocks).

The " Sovereign " (1495).

Shyvers of brass with polies for the same.

Snache poleyes with oon shever of brasse.

Jere poleyes with a shyver of brasse.

The " Mary Fortune " (1497).

Polleys bound with yren for the mayne tyes.

The inventories show plainly that blocks and tackle were well developed at the end of the 15th Century, but of course do not indicate the manner in which the strop was affixed, though sheves were evidently much of the same type as in modern blocks.

I have tried to find some evidence from contemporary art, but unfortunately have not access to much material. The only references bearing on the point which I have been able to find, are as follows :—

Volpe.—"The Embarkation of Henry VIIIth at Dover." In a reproduction on about ¼-scale, the blocks are too small to show any detail. Possibly a close inspection of the original might show some evidence.

Holbein.—The drawing of a small ship reproduced in the Science Museum Guide (Sailing Ships) shows blocks which do not appear to be stropped in the modern way, but the reproduction is not sufficiently clear to make the point certain.

Holbein.—"Death and the Sailor," in the wood-cut. Dance of Death (about 1525) shows clearly a block of type given in sketch.

"Plancius Taking a Sight."—An engraving reproduced a few years ago in the "Studio," under this title, shows a fairly typical 15th Century carrack and appears to be more or less contemporary. The blocks are rather crudely drawn, but show no sign of modern strops.

Pintoricchio.—"The Return of Odysseus." There is a very interesting carrack, with much detail, in the background of this picture, with some blocks shown conspicuously. I do not know the size of this picture, but it is probable that the blocks are represented on a scale large enough to show the strops.

I think it is probable that a more complete inspection of contemporary drawings would yield enough evidence to settle the matter.

With regard to recent models, I see that the "Elizabethan Galleon" in the Science Museum has stropped blocks, for which there is doubtless historical evidence. I have not been able to detect, from photographs, the type of block used on the *Santa Maria* or "Flemish Carrack" models, but it would be interesting to know what form of block is fitted and what evidence it is based upon.

The pulley is a device of considerable antiquity ; its invention is traditionally ascribed to the Greek mathematician, Archytas of Tarentum, about 450 B.C. It is probable that some references might be found in classical or mediaeval writings on general engineering, such as Vitruvius or Da Vinci.

It is obvious that a block, as described above, with two holes on the diameter, would transmit strains along the grain of the wood, and tend to split. It seems probable that the peripheral strop must have been introduced for this reason, as strains increased. Possibly the "polleys bound with yren" of the *Mary Fortune* indicate the beginning of this practice.

I hope you will not think that I have laboured the point too much, but it seems to me to be of some importance to anyone interested in the naval archaeology of the 15th and 16th Centuries.

Yours truly,

Newcastle-on-Tyne.   L. D. MORPHEW.

A Model Fittings List

A NEW list of model yacht and ship fittings has recently been issued by Messrs. E. Gray and Son, Ltd., 18-20, Clerkenwell Road, London, E.C.1. The list covers eight pages, and illustrates and describes a variety of fittings for both sailing and steam ship models. Anchors, binnacles, blocks, bollards, capstans, fairleads, old-type and modern guns, steering wheels, stanchions, telegraphs and ventilators are among the many requisites of the ship-modeller which are included. Propellors and propellor shafts, engine-room skylights, searchlights, funnels, and anti-aircraft guns are among the details which will appeal to the builder of modern prototypes. The model yachtsman will be interested in the automatic steering gears. The list may be had post free on application.

The Ship Modellers' Scrap Book

(*Continued from page* 219)

Clew Lines and Clew Garnets

Sometimes spelt *Clue* in the old days. On square sails, the ropes used for hauling the lower corners or *clews* of the sail up to the yard for furling, etc. *Clew Lines* and *Clew Garnets* fulfilled precisely the same topsails, the clews of the sail being shackled to the lower topsail yard, to which is attached the upper topsail down-haul. In the old days of big jackyard topsails for fore and aft craft, *clew lines* were often fitted across them.

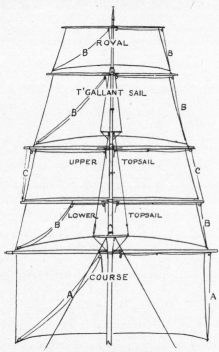

Clew Lines and Clew Garnets

Types of Companions

functions, but the latter term is only applied to those on the courses. Until comparatively recently, they always led up to the slings of the yard, but the more modern practice is to lead them to the yard-arms, even to the royals in some ships. The illustration shows both methods, the old on the port side and the new on the starboard (A *Clew Garnets*, B *Clew Lines*). C is the *upper topsail down-haul*, for clew lines were only fitted to the upper topsail in the earliest days of double

Companion

Properly, the cover over a ladder on shipboard, particularly one giving access below, but very often loosely applied to the ladder itself. Of all types and sizes, from the more or less standardised and inexpensive half-round of the coaster to the elaborate deck fitting of the passenger-carrying sailing ship, generally beautifully decorated and often combined with the functions of skylight and deck seat.

(*To be continued*)

Northern Notes

By "JASON"

Welcome to the New Clubs

AS will be seen below, two new Clubs have been launched, one on the Clyde, No. 3, and one in Hull, No. 4. It is just as well at this stage to re-state the value of these Clubs. Their aim in every case is to provide an organised workroom so that members may work on models in view of each other. When one refers to the Editorial of last month, regarding the purpose of this Magazine, one might also use the same remarks as applying to Club Rooms. Not everyone can be accurate, and not everyone cares to go deeply into the subject, but inevitably each one is almost an expert in some particular small detail of model-making. Therein lies the value of practical workshop-club. And now for Bristol !

Bristol and the West

I shall be glad to hear from some more members who are interested in the formation of a model-makers' club in that district. Already a number of people have written, and it seems that before the month is out, sufficient progress will have been made to warrant the formation of No. 6 Model Ship Makers' Club.

No. 2, Lancashire and Cheshire

The indefatigable Secretary of No. 2 reports a very busy month and, what is more important, the addition of something like a score of new members to the Club's books, mainly due to the exhibition of members' models at the Models and Marvels Exhibition held in the City Hall, Manchester, under the auspices of the *Manchester Evening News*. In club types, Manchester is now fast approaching Liverpool, for they cover almost a dozen different periods and types. Manchester also have made definite progress toward their new Club Room, which is the aim of all the Model Ship-makers' Clubs.

Secretary: W. F. Hemingway, "Withens," Lake Bank, Littleboro', Nr. Manchester.

The Clydeside Club

A meeting was held on March 11th, at 19A, Renfield Street, Glasgow, for the purpose of forming Model Ship-makers' Club No. 3 (Clydeside). Unfortunately, Commander Craine, from Liverpool, was unable to be present, as previously arranged, but I hear that he will visit this new Club possibly before this issue comes into the hands of our readers.

The new Club has promise in plenty of a good future and widely varied interests, including early and modern steamers and sailing ships, and some of the earlier period ships, notably 17th Century vessels. Model ship-makers throughout the country will welcome this extension of activities.

Secretary: Robert Lawton, Esq., 224, Armadale Street, Dennistoun, Glasgow.

Model Ship-makers' Club No. 4 (Hull and the Humber)

The inaugural meeting of this Club was held on March 13th in ideal surroundings, namely, the Pickering Museum of Fisheries and Shipping, under the guidance of Mr. Shepherd, the Director of the Hull Municipal Museum.

At the time of going to press, full details are not yet to hand, but no fears are entertained for this young Club when it is under the guidance of such an indefatigable workman as Mr. Shepherd.

Intending members should write: T. Shepherd, Esq., M.Sc., F.G.S., F.Z.S., etc., The Director, The Municipal Museums, Hull.

The Merseyside Club

The Merseyside members had a very interesting and busy month, the early part of which was devoted to the arrangements for exhibiting members' models in the Models and Marvels

Exhibition, City Hall, Manchester. A very interesting paper was read by Captain Niger W. Kennedy on " The Earliest British Steamboats," and a unique feature of the evening was the speaker's exhibition and demonstration on early steamers of his own construction.

Sub-committees are now being formed to deal with the forthcoming Model Ship Makers Club Exhibition, to be held in May. This pioneering effort will be watched with interest by all those who have a love of model ships.

Secretary : L. F. Holly, Esq., 9, Jasmine Street, Everton, Liverpool.

More About Coracles

At last I have got on the track of the Cockermouth Coracle, although details are not yet to hand. Nevertheless, I should still be grateful for sketches or photographs from any others who can help in this particular type.

Recently, in a newspaper article, reference was made to a Coracle on the River Dart in the " West Countree." Perhaps there are some living in the locality of Dartmouth, or on the upper reaches of the Dart, who could give me some particulars regarding this type of Coracle.

Three Shilling Model Competition

THE enormous success of the Three Shilling Model Competition in the great Shipping Exhibition held in Liverpool last summer was such that it might be, with advantage, copied in many parts of the country. It has a wide appeal to the expert, and to the uninitiated alike. It tempts the very poorest of people to try their hand at model-making ; it gives scope for artistry and ingenuity.

Two important exhibitions which are to be held during the present year, which are of interest to model-makers, will be as follows : The First Annual Exhibition of the Merseyside Model Ship Makers Club, in conjunction with its associated clubs, particularly that of No. 2, Lancashire and Cheshire, held in the middle of May, in Liverpool, and the second will be that of the Missions to Seamen Exhibition, to be held in the autumn, in Manchester. In each of these a feature will be made of the Three Shilling Model Competition. Some brief remarks, therefore, may not be amiss. There is a limitation of size, namely, no model shall exceed 20" overall length. It may be of any type or period. There is a limitation of cost in the materials, namely, three shillings. The total cost of materials, therefore, must not exceed three shillings, but competitors may use scraps from the home, from the work-basket, from firewood, and things which are ordinarily found in any house. These are the brief and simple rules of the Three Shilling Model Competition.

Some hints regarding packing may be of assistance. Make a box, having one side hinged at the bottom, make a base to fit inside the box and which can be inserted when the hinged side is open. This base should run between grooves or strips at either end of the box. Upon this base erect chocks to hold the model, and use lampwick or broad soft tape in order to tie the model down to this base. A model can thus be sent safely when properly marked and labelled. Do not forget, when sending such models in. to have a card on the baseboard, and on the model itself, giving the following particulars :—

Full name and address.

The name, type and period of the ship model.

A list of the materials used, together with their cost.

Generally speaking, the three shilling model entries are judged by a committee, and valuable prizes are as a rule awarded.

Particulars regarding the Three Shilling Model Competition, to be held in connection with the First Annual Exhibition of the Ship Model Makers Club at Liverpool, may be had on application to any of the Secretaries, whose names will be found in Northern Notes in this issue.

SHIPS AND SHIP MODELS

A Magazine for all Lovers of Ships and the Sea

Single Copies, post free, 7½d.
Annual Subscription 7s. 6d.

Editorial and Publishing Offices :

66 FARRINGDON STREET
LONDON :: E.C.4

Vol. I.   No. 9.   MAY, 1932.   Price 6d.

The Ship's Log

New Science Museum Models

SEVERAL notable additions have recently been made to the models on view at the Science Museum, London. One of the most interesting of these is a contemporary model of the *St. Michael*, an 1,100-ton ship built for the Navy by Sir John Tippetts, at Portsmouth in 1669. Two other period models have also been placed on view, a Stuart yacht, lent by Mrs. Drogo Montagu, and a 50-gun ship of 1682, lent by Mr. R. C. Anderson. The model of the *Torrens*, recently made from the original plans, by Sir James Laing and Sons, will interest admirers of this famous ship, while the additions of smaller craft include several models of modern Chinese boats, a model of a Shetland " Ness Yole," and a model of a Zanzibar canoe with outriggers upon either side.

* * *

Ship Models at Liverpool

In accordance with their policy of development of their ship model gallery, the Liverpool Museums Committee have just added to their collection a scale model of the *Comet* of 1812, the first passenger steamer built in Europe. This has been specially built to the order of the Committee. They have also secured a model of the steamer *Poplar Branch*, a turret-deck ship with ten masts, arranged in five pairs.

* * *

And at Belfast

Belfast is another shipping centre, where the preparation of a representative collection of ship models in the Municipal Museum is receiving active attention. Several models have recently been added to those already on view, and a separate shipping collection is in process of being formed. The new exhibits include scale models of the *Greenore* and the *Menevir* of the L.M.S. Railway, a typical coal boat, the *Monarch*, and an old-time timber ship, the *Star of India*. Nautical photographs and plans are also to be included.

Sail Training

That the Belgian Government hold to a belief in the virtues of sail training is evidenced by the handing-over of their new training-ship *Mercator* by the builders, Messrs. Ramage and Ferguson, Ltd., of Leith. The *Mercator* is rigged as a three-masted schooner with square sails on the foremast, and is engined with a Diesel motor of 500 h.p. She will carry about 70 cadets, in addition to the officers and crew. She is 190′ w.l. length, 34′ 10″ beam, and has a displacement of 1,050 tons. Her trial trip under power showed a speed of over 10 knots. She is to be used both for summer cruises in Northern waters, and for longer trips overseas between seasons.

*   *   *

Bristol Shiplovers

It is interesting to hear that the Bristol Shiplovers' Society has gained its first overseas' member through SHIPS AND SHIP MODELS. The new member, Mr. Charles E. Lauriat, of Boston, is one of our subscribers, and had the distinction of being proposed for membership by Mr. Basil Lubbock, and seconded by Mr. Roy Baker, the U.S. Consul in Bristol. Although overseas' readers may not have many opportunities of attending the meetings of shiplovers' societies in the Old Country, we believe that through membership they might establish contact with valued correspondents interested in similar branches of nautical history and research.

*   *   *

An Acknowledgment

Mr. R. P. Hirst, of Wallasey, sends us a friendly note, pointing out that the photograph of the schooner *My Lady*, published in our April issue, is his copyright. We make this acknowledgment with pleasure. It is important that contributors and correspondents sending us photographs for reproduction should be careful on this point. Unless the photograph has actually been taken by the correspondent himself, its source should always be stated. Photographic post-cards, and other purchased prints may not be reproduced without the permission of the owner of the copyright, and we are anxious not to offend unwittingly in this direction.

*   *   *

An Old-time Modeller at Work

A feature of the recent Ideal Home Exhibition at Olympia was the stand of Mr. S. J. Lethbridge, of Plymouth, where a number of ship models were on view. An old-time model-maker, dressed in the sailor fashion of a hundred years ago, was busy making and rigging model ships, and he proved vastly interesting to the public. Mr. Lethbridge, in addition to making attractive furniture from the timber of old ships, also has a model ship-building side to his business. One of his productions is a model in teak, of the *Mayflower*, built to a scale of 1/60th. Several models of West Country fishing craft were also shown on his stand.

*   *   *

To Correspondents

We have to thank a number of correspondents for interesting letters for "The Ship's Mail," which are unfortunately crowded out from this issue. We regard this feature of our magazine as being an important means of interchange of information and opinion between our readers, and welcome all letters intended for those columns. We hope to give increased space to this feature next month.

*   *   *

The " Cutty Sark "

The new blue-prints of the *Cutty Sark*, prepared by Mr. Harold Underhill, have aroused a great deal of interest. Mr. Underhill has taken considerable trouble to check up his figures and details, and there is no doubt that these drawings are the most reliable plans of this famous ship which have yet appeared. Mr. Underhill says that the various authorities he has consulted do not all agree on some of the minor dimensions, but he is satisfied that the figures he gives may be taken as being as nearly authentic as it is possible to get.

Aboard the Barquentine "Waterwitch," of Fowey

By ARTHUR BRADBURY

THE barquentine *Waterwitch* is the last vessel so rigged, sailing under the Red Ensign. She is 206 tons gross, 170 net. Built in 1871 by Meadus, of Poole. Length, 112′; beam 25′ 8″; depth, 12′ 8″.

Up to a few months ago there were two other barquentines trading around the coasts, the *Hilda* and the *Francis and Jane*. The *Hilda* was sunk in collision with the steam trawler *Kudos* off Hartlepool on December 10th, 1930. The *Francis and Jane* is laid up at Fowey.

The *Waterwitch* is commanded by Captain C. H. Deacon, a Cornishman. Famed as a hard driver, he gets to sea at the first opportunity, and stays there, and has made some wonderfully fine passages in his vessel.

The *Waterwitch*, being a fine sailer, with a fresh wind on the quarter, can pass the average steam coaster. A few weeks ago she made a fine run from Plymouth to Goole in 48 hours.

It is said that her oak timbers were made from wood taken from an old wooden battleship, rigged as a barquentine. She carries on the foremast a fore course, lower and upper topsails and topgallant sail, flying jib, inner jib, middle jib and drummer. On the main mast is the fore and aft mainsail, and gaff topsail and three staysails. On the mizzen mast the mizzen and mizzen topsail. Forward is the old-fashioned windlass and the fo'cs'le scuttle, then comes the fore hatch, foremast, and abaft the foremast is the galley, which is divided in half to take the motor winch; abaft this is the main hatch with the longboat on chocks; a smaller boat is carried on the after-hatch; on the low poop-deck is the cabin companionway, skylight and wheelhouse. The fo'cs'le boasts of four swing cots, canvas stretched on iron frames. There is a coal fire, and it is usually snug and comfortable, except when

The Barquentine "Waterwitch"

she is bucking into a big head sea, then things become somewhat moist. The cabin aft also has a coal-burning stove. The mates' cabin is at the foot of the companion-way ; the masters' leads off the cabin. There are also two small bunks—one on either side of the cabin—locker-like affairs, into which one has to climb, and lie diagonally if you are anywhere near 6'. I berthed in one of these, when on the two trips I made in the *Waterwitch*.

On my first trip I joined the vessel at Fowey. Having bought a donkey's breakfast—(sailor's mattress) for 2s. 11d., I went aboard. The crew

Capt. Deacon at the wheel

were busily washing her down. The vessel seemed a mass of clay from truck to deck, the clay dust having blown into the wet rigging. We were bound from Fowey to Newcastle with china clay. The crew consists of the master, the mate (Jim), who signed on as bos'un, " Bert " (an able seaman) and three young men, holding masters' tickets in steam, putting in twelve months in square rig to qualify for the Trinity House Pilot Service. These " embryo " pilots sign on as the mates. This re-shuffling is necessary, on account of the scarcity of square-rigged vessels on which training can be obtained.

The easterly gale blew itself out, and the old man was eager to get under weigh, as a Danish schooner, the *Marie*, had left four hours previously,

bound to the East'ard. We were given a pluck-out by a local tug ; we soon got the canvas on her, and a course was set East by South.

It was wonderful to watch how the old vessel ghosts along under a light breeze. The watches were picked and everyone settled down. Dinner was at 12, tea at 5, breakfast at 8, hot cocoa at eight bells (midnight), when the watch was changed.

The first night out was perfect, very clear and calm, the stars came out and the moon rose. The square sails made a velvety black silhouette against the eastern sky, the gear in the rigging creaked in a thousand different ways, and the sails idly flapped ; a heavy dew fell, and everything aloft and below became wet. Aboard a sailing vessel at night time, things seem different somehow. Ghostly shapes appear in the form of shadows, cast by the sails and rigging that flit across the deck.

Next day was bright and clear, and at 2 p.m. a sail was sighted ahead, which turned out to be the *Marie* ; we were overhauling her fast, and the old man seemed pleased with himself. At about this time we ran through a fleet of Brixham trawlers. We passed the Dane next morning, about 11 a.m., gave her the weather report, and at about 6 a.m. that night she was out of sight astern. Two small finches flew aboard in the first dog watch— one landed on the jib-boom stay.

The weather came on thick with fog, and the fog-horn was kept going. The watch below slept in their clothes. There were steamers all around us, and the fog was so thick that we could hardly see the length of the vessel. One steamer approached us, stopped her engines, gave three blasts, and crossed our bow. The old man gave the order to swing the yards and put the vessel aback, which took some of the weigh off her. The steamer loomed up through the fog and seemed right on the top of us—a German, the *Ugo Ferdinand*—I read the name on her bow ; she started her engines

From the Poop

Getting the canvas on her

Buntlines and Clewlines

From the Jib Boom

and sheared off to starboard. The fog lifted about 4 a.m., and breeze came from the Sou'-West course, set N.N.E.

On Sunday, April 13th, the wind freshened, and all hands were called at 2 am. to take in the foresail; up aloft one's hands became cold, and the wind and hail seemed to cut right through you. The wind was freshening, with a falling glass. The ship was pitching badly; the fore topgallant sail was clewed up and made fast, outer jib and main topmast staysail taken in, and we were somewhere off the Norfolk coast. At 9 a.m. next morning a Grimsby trawler came alongside and offered to tow us into Bridlington, and said a gale was expected from the S.E., which would have put us on a lee shore. We tacked ship again and again, until our arms ached, and beat up to Flamborough Head for shelter, and dropped anchor. All sail was stowed and the vessel rolled badly. A strong gale was blowing, and a

Lloyd's agent advised the crew to leave her. But the old vessel hung on for four days. There was some doubt whether her two anchors would hold. A Yorkshire cobbleman came off with fresh fish and newspapers. Eventually, the wind eased up, the anchors were got up, sails loosened, and we were once more on our way. Newcastle was reached without further incident.

The second trip I made was one from Runcorn to Falmouth, during the early part of 1931. The passage took two weeks, much time being spent windbound in the Mersey River and at Holly Head. But this is another story. When we struck a strong north-westerly gale, the foc'sle was flooded out and pumps had to be kept going half an hour out of every hour, and the galley was washed out. The "old man" was at the wheel for 12 hours without a break—a wonderful seaman, a survival of a nearly extinct class of seamen of the days of wooden ships and iron men.

Drawing by]   **The " Waterwitch " taking a tow**   *[Arthur Bradbury*

The Navy "At Home"

Drawing by]   **" Showing her Teeth "**   [*S. E. Beck.*

THE vast majority of readers will have a considerable interest in the Silent Service, whatever section of ship modelling their hobby may be.

It will not be out of place, therefore, to draw attention to the visits of H.M. ships of the Home Fleet, the new name for the Atlantic Fleet, to various seaside resorts in the British Isles during June and July, which give the public an opportunity of acquiring first-hand knowledge of our modern warships and the men who man them.

It has been the custom for some years now for municipal authorities to invite units of the Fleet to visit their resort during the season. This adds to the holiday programme, and enables the local people to see something of the Navy. Entertainments are arranged ashore for the ships' companies, who in return organise dances and, at times, theatricals on board. These are invariably a great success, as the sailor has no equal when it comes to providing hospitality. It is during these visits that the ships are open to the general public, who are allowed on board free of charge.

Those who have not had an opportunity of visiting a man-of-war, or who may be inclined to think there is nothing much to see in the " unromantic mechanical Navy," will be agreeably surprised. They will probably find that the time usually allowed on board is too short to appreciate all there is in a modern war vessel.

Others who have not seen inside a ship since the war, will be amazed at the changes which have taken place in both ships and men. One of the recent innovations which will be most noticeable is the elaborate system of loud-speakers installed throughout the big ships. The familiar blast of the bo'sn's pipe, followed by the spoken order, is no longer repeated round the mess decks by the call-boys, but is quietly said into the microphone and carried to every compartment in the ship by the raucous voice of the " talkie " machine.

The following is the list of coast resorts to be visited :—

ABERYSTWYTH : June   21st - 24th, H.M.S. *Furious*, Aircraft Carrier.

AVONMOUTH : June 30th-July 6th, part of the 5th Destroyer Flotilla.

BALLACHULISH : June 5th-13th, H.M. Cruiser *York*.

BANGOR (Co. Down) : June 13th-25th, H.M. Battle Cruiser *Hood*.

BARRY : June 22nd-30th, H.M. Cruiser *York*.

BELFAST : June 11th-20th, part of the 5th Destroyer Flotilla.

BOURNEMOUTH : July 15th - 21st, H.M.S. *Warspite*.

BRISTOL : June 11th-21st, H.M. Sloop *Snapdragon* ; June 30th-July 7th, part of the 5th Destroyer Flotilla.

CARDIFF : June 7th-14th, H.M. Cruiser *Dorsetshire*.

CLACTON : July 15th-21st, H.M. Cruiser *York*.

DARTMOUTH : June 22nd-28th, H.M. Sloop *Snapdragon*.

DEAL : July 15th-21st, part of the 6th Destroyer Flotilla.

EASTBOURNE : July 2nd-7th, H.M.S. *Malaya*.

FALMOUTH : June 23rd-July 1st, H.M. Cruiser *Dorsetshire* ; July 1st-8th, H.M. Cruiser *York* ; July 15th-21st, H.M. Aircraft Carrier *Furious*.

GOUROCK : June 11th-20th, part of the 5th Destroyer Flotilla.

GREENOCK : June 11th-20th, H.M. Aircraft Carrier *Furious*.

GUERNSEY : June 27th-July 8th, H.M. Battle Cruiser *Hood*.

HEYSHAM : June 11th-20th, part of the 5th Destroyer Flotilla.

ILFRACOMBE : June 21st-29th, H.M. Cruiser *Exeter*.

JERSEY : July 15th-20th, part of the 6th Destroyer Flotilla.

LARNE : June 11th-20th, H.M. Aircraft Carrier *Courageous*.

LERWICK : June 5th-9th, H.M.S. *Rodney*.

LIVERPOOL : June 10th-20th, H.M. Cruiser *Exeter*.

LLANDUDNO : June 17th-27th, H.M. Cruiser *Norfolk*.

LOCH EWE : June 5th-10th, H.M. Aircraft Carrier *Furious*.

LYME REGIS : July 15th-20th, part of the 6th Destroyer Flotilla.

MANCHESTER : June 21st-29th, the 5th Destroyer Flotilla.

MARGATE : July 15th-21st, H.M.S. *Valiant*.

NEWCASTLE (Co. Down) : June 14th-21st, H.M. Cruiser *York*.

OBAN : June 4th-9th, H.M. Sloop *Snapdragon* ; July 5th-10th, part of the 5th Destroyer Flotilla.

PENZANCE : June 15th-23rd, H.M. Cruiser *Dorsetshire*.

PORTREE : June 5th-10th, H.M. Aircraft Carrier *Courageous*.

PORTRUSH : June 11th-20th, part of the 5th Destroyer Flotilla.

ROTHESAY : June 5th-13th, H.M. Battle Cruiser *Hood*.

ST. IVES : June 29th-July 7th, H.M. Cruiser *Exeter*.

SANDOWN BAY : July 15th-21st, H.M. Battle Cruiser *Hood*.

SCARBOROUGH : June 25th-July 6th, H.M. Battleships *Rodney* and *Valiant*.

SCILLY ISLES : June 28th-July 5th, H.M. Cruiser *Norfolk*.

SEATON : July 15th-21st, H.M. Cruiser *York*.

TENBY : June 24th-30th, H.M. Aircraft Carrier *Furious*.

TOBERMOREY : June 5th-10th, part of the 5th Destroyer Flotilla.

TORBAY : June 20th-30th, H.M. Aircraft Carrier *Courageous* ; July 1st-8th, H.M. Cruiser *Dorsetshire* and Aircraft Carrier *Furious* ; July 15th-21st, H.M.S. *Rodney*, Depot Ship *Lucia*, Sloop *Snapdragon*, Flotilla Leader *Stuart* and 2nd Submarine Flotilla.

ULLAPOOL : June 5th-9th, H.M. Cruiser *Exeter*.

WEYMOUTH : July 8th-12th, H.M. Cruiser *Centaur* and 5th Destroyer Flotilla ; July 8th-15th, H.M.S. *Nelson*, *Rodney*, *Warspite*, *Valiant*, *Malaya*, Battle Cruiser *Hood*, Cruisers *Dorsetshire*, *Exeter*, *Norfolk*, *York*, Aircraft Carrier *Furious*, 6th Destroyer Flotilla, Depot Ship *Lucia*, Sloop *Snapdragon*, Flotilla Leader *Stuart* and 2nd Submarine Flotilla.

YARMOUTH (Isle of Wight) : June 28th-July 8th, H.M. Sloop *Snapdragon*.

Following these visits, Navy Week will be celebrated for the sixth year in succession at the three principal Naval dockyards, affording unsurpassed opportunities for seeing not only all classes of ships from the great *Hood*, *Nelson* and *Rodney* to Destroyers, Submarines, etc., but numerous interesting and spectacular evolutions, including " Firing a Torpedo," '' Diving,'' '' Q Ship Encounter,'' etc. Incidentally, a small charge of admission to the Dockyards is made, the proceeds of which are devoted entirely to Naval Charities.

Each port has its own particular attraction during this week.

Plymouth, with her long associations with Britain's Sea Kings, Drake, Raleigh, Frobisher, &c., will attract many people to the West country.

Chatham is "London's depot," and one of the prized possessions here is the original "Chatham Chest." Established by John Hawkins in 1588 after the defeat of the Armada, it was the foundation of Naval Charities. Also there will be a 42-foot sailing model of the 74-gun ship "*Kent*," launched in 1762. She is manned by a crew of

12 and takes visitors for trips round the dock.

Portsmouth claims to have the most famous ship in the world. H.M.S. *Victory*, now permanently docked in the oldest drydock in existence, is fully restored to appear as she did at Trafalgar. A visit to her affords a unique opportunity of observing the progress in ship-building and manning which has taken place during the past century and a-quarter, and also of appreciating many of the traditions and customs of the Service which have been handed down through the ages.

It is well to remember that the Navy of to-day is not so much a fighting force as an element of defence. Moreover, it is a very powerful pacifist agent. It is still written in the Articles of War that, " It is upon the Navy that under the good Providence of God, the wealth, prosperity and the peace of these Islands and of the Empire do mainly depend."

Merchant Ships and their Names
By W. G. JAMES

COULD you tell by the name of a merchant ship who are her owners ? It is not generally known, but ships are usually named in a manner that is in accordance with a definite idea, and not in a careless, haphazard way. For this reason a sailor usually knows by the name of a ship who her owners are, and can form a general idea as to the trade in which she is engaged.

Different companies have different schemes. Thus the Cunard names end in the suffix " ia "—*Mauretania*, *Aquitania* and *Ausonia*—and the White Star steamers end in " ic "—*Majestic*, *Adriatic*, *Baltic*, etc. Other companies favour names which hold a flavour of the countries to which they trade. The Peninsular and Orient Steam Navigation Co. have Indian and Chinese names, such as *Ranpura*, *Rajputana*, *Nankin* and *Mongolia*, although a departure from this idea is being made in the case of their latest

steamers, which begin with the name of " Strath." Other companies which adopt this idea are the New Zealand Shipping Co. — *Otaki*, *Tekoa* and *Remuera* ; Messrs. Elder, Dempster and Co., who adopt West African names—*Aba*, *Accra* and *Appam*, in addition to the names of prominent people who have been connected with the development of Africa—*William Wilberforce* and *David Livingstone* ; The Atlantic Transport Co., who have the American State names such as *Maine*, *Maryland*, etc.

Three companies adopt the names of counties. The Federal Steam Navigation Co. take the names of *Kent*, *Surrey*, *Norfolk*, etc., whilst the Bibby Line, trading to Burma, name their ships after the English shires— *Cheshire*, *Yorkshire*, *Shropshire*, etc. The Scottish shires—*Banffshire* and *Buteshire* — indicate the vessels of Messrs. Turnbull, Martin and Co., trading to Australia.

One company name their ships after the Scottish Clans ; another commence with the name of Glen— *Glenapp* and *Glenshane*, whilst the ships of the Ellerman Lines are mostly " Cities "—*City of Newcastle, City of Oxford*, etc. Another firm—Messrs. W. R. Smith of Cardiff—also use the name of City—*Atlantic City, York City*, etc. In the same way, Messrs. Haldin's fleet are known as the " Courts "—*Wellington Court, Ovington Court*, etc. Various companies use the named of Halls, Granges, Rivers, Kings and Princes. The Union-Castle steamers, trading to South Africa, are named after castles—*Windsor Castle, Warwick Castle*, etc. The " Empress " steamers are owned by the Canadian Pacific Railway Co., who also use the title of *Duchess* for one class of their liners, and the cargo-boats commence with " Beaver," giving them a typical Canadian air.

The oldest steamship company in the world, The General Steam Navigation Co., Ltd., of London, call their ships after birds—*Gannet, Petrel, Teal*, etc.—and the names of the professions such as *Historian, Actor* and *Dramatist*, are used by Messrs. Harrison

and Co., of Liverpool. Probably the names that sound most beautiful in the ears of the average person are those of Messrs. Alfred Holt and Co. (The Blue Funnel Line) who give their ships the names of the Greek heroes— *Ajax, Titan, Jason*, etc.

The London suburban names, such as *Epsom, Hampstead* and *Putney*, are carried by the fleet of Messrs. Watts, Watts and Co., but this idea is also followed by the South Metropolitan Gas Co., who have ships by the name of *Brixton, Catford* and *Camberwell*.

The Anglo-Saxon Oil Co. have adopted the names of shells in christening their ships—*Clam, Donax, Pearl, Shell*, etc., and the Anglo-Mexican steamers all commence with the Mexican prefix " San." Another firm whose steamers are named in a distinctive manner is the British Tanker Co., all of which are called " British " —*British Sergeant, British Courage*, etc.

The Gas Light and Coke Co. of London, whose steamers bring coal from the Tyne to London, use names indicating light — a novel method that has some bearing upon their occupation—such names as *Homefire, Torchbearer, Gaslight* and *Suntrap*.

How I found the "Amazon"

It was while wandering round the back streets of one of our ports I found her ; she was looking down at me from a shop window, a pretty water-line model of a steamer with two funnels and clipper bow, in all about 18″ long, stained black, the sombreness relieved by the red paddles, and the gracefully fluted light wood paddle-box, she was barque-rigged with bow-sprit and jib-boom, carrying an Amazon as figure-head, her namesake.

Can one imagine the sensation that would be caused to-day if the original could appear moored at Southampton as she actually was on Friday, January 2nd, 1852, before sailing on her maiden voyage. The Royal Mail Steam Packet's new steamer, built by R. H. Green, of Blackwall, of 3,000 tons burthen and 800 h.p., at a cost of

£100,000, bought off the Cunard Company, for whom she was built, while still on the stocks, to replace the R.M.S.P. Co.'s then new steamer *Demerara*, lost by stranding in the Bristol Avon while being towed.

The *Amazon* caused as much admiration on that day when she sailed to the West Indies with mails and 50 passengers on board, also carrying a valuable cargo, as she would excitement to-day, if seen side by side with one of our gigantic ocean liners.

The *Amazon* was destroyed by fire during the early hours of Sunday morning, January 4th, in the Bay of Biscay.

On taking the model out of the case, for easier transport, I found the starboard side quite unfinished, and wondered if this is usual with builders' models.—C. M. YORK.

The "Santa Maria"

WHAT KIND OF VESSEL WAS SHE?

By CAPT. E. ARMITAGE McCANN

NEITHER the writer nor anyone else knows much about the famous vessel in which Christopher Columbus, in 1492, first crossed "The Gloomy Ocean," as the Atlantic was then called.

It is safe to say that more exhaustive study has been given to this *Santa Maria* than to any other vessel that ever sailed, yet it still ranks with the

[*From a contemporary woodcut*
Light Bark or Caravel of the 15th Century, Venice.

Roman galleys as a matter of conjecture and dispute.

What we do know is that Queen Isabella of Spain ordered Columbus to be supplied with three vessels, and that he finally obtained two caravels, the *Pinta* and *Nina*, and another larger, but still small vessel, presumably a carrack, called the *Gallega*, solid, but old from service, which re-named the *Santa Maria*.

There is no certainty as to her measurements or shape, and there is

dispute as to exactly what sail she carried. All anyone can do is to devise a vessel of the period suitably rigged. Many attempts to do this have been made in small and full-sized models. To analyse them all would be a lengthy task, and really the first to which serious attention need be paid is the so-called replica built for the Spanish Government in 1892.

This vessel is important because it was sailed across the Atlantic to America and went to the World's Fair of Chicago, and is still afloat on the Great Lakes spreading false information. Having been given the chachet of the Spanish Government, most people at once accepted it as correct, countless models have been made to the same lines, and these are even to be found in such museums as South Kensington, Milan, Munich, and Washington. The Deutches Museum, in Munich, is still distributing them as the correct thing. I do not know how the South Kensington one is labelled.

Now this 1892 carrack is a fine carrack and very gay, a French writer dubs it a " parroquet." Had Columbus made his voyage in the late- or mid-16th Century, it would have served fairly well; unfortunately for this model he sailed in 1492. The features on her that had not yet been invented, and other mistakes are more numerous than the correct parts. Some of the principal may, however, be enumerated. (Though from here I will speak positively, I am still quite open-minded, but it gets so tiresome repeating " I think " or " I believe.")

The hull, though round, is not round enough; the stern should have a round, not a square tuck; the poop and forecastle should be of lighter construction and different in shape, and the well deck should have cow-bridges.

Model of the " Santa Maria " of Christopher Columbus.   By Capt. E. Armitage McCann

In the rigging there should be no bobstay; the bowsprit should be to one side of the foremast, not central; the foresail should be smaller; the topsail should not sheet-home to the yardarms; the forestay should be single, setting up with hearts to the stem; the lateen mizzen is peaked up too much. There should be a Jacob's ladder abaft the mast in place of ratlines; some of the shrouds (pendants) should come further forward and set up with tackles, probably all the chains were of chain, and then there are details such as no bands on the anchor stocks required.

It is unlikely that a decrepit old vessel such as this, which Columbus could not even get properly caulked, would be painted up and decorated like a Chinese Christening, but she might very probably, as was the custom of the time, have a cross on her mainsail. As Colombus was an Admiral sailing under Royal patronage, she would probably have the flags usually depicted, and might have some of his companions' shields hung on the pavisades.

In 1926 a magazine asked me to write a story on how to make a model of the *Santa Maria*. To this I agreed, but not to make another copy of the 1892 vessel. The model I made was not supposed to embody every last little detail, but I did endeavour to get it correct in essentials. I used the compasses for a straight-edge, as seems to have been the manner of old, and made the model here depicted. I still think this model fairly correct, except that the foremast is a bit long, and there are perhaps too many windows in the stern. I am also in

Sketch of model of Catalonian Caravel of Early 15th Century

doubt as to whether I should not have given her a spritsail. I find that it was not invented when this vessel was probably built, but may have been when she sailed. In *translations* of Columbus's log one finds : " I set all sails to the ship, the mainsail with two bonnets, the foresail, the spritsail, mizzen, maintopsail, and the boats' sail on the poop." An Italian version gives stu'n sails for bonnets, and in the original Spanish I can find no mention of the spritsail. To set a spritsail, the bowsprit would have to be lowered. Take your choice.

With regard to the size of the hull, the 1892 vessel was 74′ 6″, on the water-line by 25′ 7″ beam by 13′ 5″ hold. The 1929 vessel, 78′ 8″ by 25′ by 11′. Mine is a bit larger. All the measurements are conjectural.

In 1927 I received a letter from Sr. Julio F. Guillen, at the Naval Museum of Madrid, saying that he had spent some 30 months investigating the *Santa Maria* and offering to send me his plans—he had mine. During the following years, under his able direction, a new full-sized replica was built by the Spanish Government and was at the Spanish-American Exposition at Seville in 1929-30. This

vessel is to sail to America carrying a stone from Spain to the Columbus Monument in Santo Domingo.

This vessel was built so far as possible with the same wood as was the original (was she built in Spain or Italy ?) and with 15th Century tools, she is to be sailed with navigation aids of the same date. She is very much more like what the *Santa Maria* might have been than the previous attempt. Everything about her has been most carefully worked out and all details are possible and probable.

I would hesitate to pit my version against this, but, of course, am permitted my own personal opinion, especially about some details such as cow-bridges (the half decks over the well deck), some of which opinions have later been borne out by a model since discovered.

I did not receive her lines, after all, because the concession for lines, models, moving pictures and booklets was given to a gentleman in Madrid who kindly offered me the concession for America for the sum of $32,000.00 and some sundry percentages. As I was unable to forward this trifle to Spain, I have only pictures of the ship to guide me as to what she is like. If, however, any reader would like to take up the concession I will gladly furnish the Don's name and address.

In conclusion, I do not wish to discourage those who have made or want to make *Santa Marias* like the 1892 one. It is a good-looking carrack of the 16th Century, but it is not Columbus's *Santa Maria*. I would suggest that those making it, at least, omit the bobstay which can never go with a spritsail.

A Notable Ship Modeller and his Work

AN INTERVIEW WITH MR. NORMAN OUGH

By A. GUY VERCOE

IN a little courtyard not a hundred yards from Piccadilly Circus, I found a shipyard whence scores of great warships have set out on their travels.

Of course it is only a model shipyard, but what models ! Small enough to carry in a suitcase, most of them, yet perfect in scale and finish right to the last rung of the last ladder.

The presiding genius of this dockyard is Mr. Norman Ough, who is best known for his work in connection with the Museum of the Royal United Services Institution in Whitehall, and with the Imperial War Museum.

When I called on Mr. Ough I found him hard at work on a great model of the aircraft-carrier *Glorious*, which is to take its place shortly in the collection of the United Services Institution. Mr. Ough has been at work on this model since last May, and it is truly a masterpiece of the modeller's art.

Mr. Ough's workshop is so small that when he and I and the *Glorious* occupied the floor-space, there seemed no room for a single thing more. But every inch of space is used, and every inch is crammed with tools, half-finished models, books, files of drawings and photos, and stacks of material. In one corner is a small lathe, while the model on which Mr. Ough is engaged occupies a special revolving stand in the centre. Under the window is the bench, littered with pieces of wood and metal which, under the magic touch of the craftsman, resolve themselves into delicate parts of a warship.

" How did I begin ship-modelling ? " said Mr. Ough, in reply to my first question. " In the usual way—as a hobby. I was an art student at Exeter, and one of my sailing ship models, a working model which I have sailed in Dawlish Bay, was put on view in Exeter Museum. Then they asked me to do a series of models showing the development of ships, so I built them 14 models. In fact, one of the models is not finished yet " —and he indicated the hull of an Elizabethan galleon which stood on a shelf. " While I was at the Art School I began my model of the Grand Fleet on a scale of 100′ to the inch, and applied to the chief of the Naval Section of the British Government Pavilion at the 1925 Wembley Exhibition. I showed him my small model of the *Hood*, and he said that I could show the Grand Fleet there if it was finished in time. Well, it was finished in time, and after the Exhibition was over I sold it to the Royal United Services Institution.

" After Wembley, I got the job of reconstructing a number of models for the Imperial War Museum, and afterwards of building several more, including the *Iron Duke*, the *Lion*, and others. I built for this museum a model of the *Vindictive* as she was when she took part in the attack on Zeebrugge Mole in 1918. This meant a great deal of research, for so great

Mr. Norman Ough at work in his model shipyard

had the care been that the preparation of the vessel should not be made known to the enemy, that the shipwrights in Chatham Dockyard were kept in ignorance of the object of their labours, and the drawings destroyed immediately the work was complete.

"In making the model, the plans of the ship were obtained from the Admiralty, and details gradually pieced together from various sources of the alterations made for the raid. Further information was supplied by a shipwright who had assisted in fitting out the *Vindictive*, and who, fortunately, was possessed of a long memory.

"The model was made to a scale of $\frac{1}{16}$" to the foot, and is about 20" long. It is a waterline model, but shows the rig and armament of the ship in full detail. I believe this model is the only accurate record of the ship as she went into action on St. George's Day, 1918.

"After that I was kept busy on a variety of jobs. I built a small model of the *Queen Elizabeth* for Lord Howe, and he presented it to Earl Beatty at a re-union dinner. Afterwards I made Lord Howe another—larger—model of the famous Grand Fleet flagship.

"My present job, the *Glorious*, is by far the most difficult I have yet undertaken. I began her in May, 1930, and she is not quite finished yet. After her I am to make the submarine-tender *Alecto* for the same Museum, and possibly another cruiser.

"Just to show you how it is the labour and not the material which is the main expense in producing ship-models," concluded Mr. Ough, "I may say that the *Queen Elizabeth* I built for Lord Howe, which I sold complete for £200, cost only 2s. 5d. for materials—all the rest was time and labour at only about 2s. an hour!"

Notes on modelling a Dutch Admiralty Yacht of 1706

By L. A. WESTWATER, S.N.R.

THE photographs accompanying these notes are of a model representing the vessel described by Mr. Jeffrey Leighton in his recent articles in this magazine.

Hull of Dutch Yacht Model

The obvious differences in outline and detail are accounted for by the fact that several models of this yacht are in existence. The one in the Sheepvart Museum, in Amsterdam, which I am copying, is, in Mr. Leighton's view, the builder's model.

Mr. Leighton's articles were of the greatest interest and assistance to me. I had just completed the drawings from photographs and other data from Holland, when SHIPS & SHIP MODELS launched its first number.

The hull, which is now complete, is cut from a block of yellow pine, hollowed out to the deck level, which is planked.

The keel and stem are cut out of three-ply wood.

Points which have presented the greatest difficulty, so far, have been mostly in connection with the roundhouse at the stern.

The stern itself was carved out of a piece of cherrywood (blocks can be

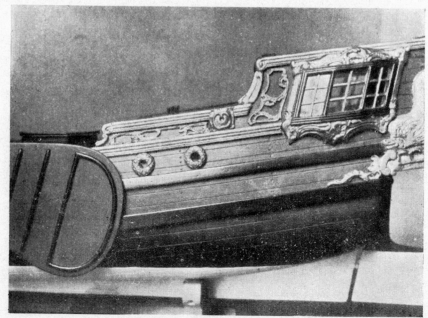

Enlarged view showing the Quarter Badges

The carving on the Stern

obtained from art dealers, who supply them for wood-cuts). I tried oak first of all, but rejected it when completed, as the grain made it impossible to obtain a sufficiently fine finish.

The cherrywood was more difficult to carve, but made a better job in the end.

The quarter badges, or side windows, of the round-house proved almost too much for me.

I experienced such difficulty in their construction that the following account may help others :—

The Quarter Badges

The outline of the carving was traced on to a cherrywood block, thick enough to shape into the bow of the window. The centre was then cut out, leaving nothing but the part to be carved, as in the sketch.

After filing it more or less to the general contour, the detail of the carving was drawn in and completed.

The upper and lower sashes came next ; they were cut to the bow shape and the mouldings worked on to the three-sided surface.

The two side frames, which were the same moulding as the upper sash, and making mitred joints with it, were then fitted and recessed at the back to take the glass.

Lastly, the two centre frames, which were double recessed at the back and counter-checked into the upper sash.

The glazing was done with microscope slides which were very nearly the correct size and, being of good clear glass, proved very suitable and easily cut to shape. Plastic wood was used instead of putty.

The astragals were cut from thin larch strips and glued on to the glass.

As there were ten different mouldings in various parts of the ship, a moulding tool had to be devised.

They catalogue a selection of strip wood down to $\frac{1}{32}''$, which should be of use to all model makers.

I did not use barbola or plastic wood for any of the carving on this model. Its use, to me at least, would have been a confession of failure.

Personally, I would rather have a rough carving in wood on a model in any but the smallest scale than a plastered job.

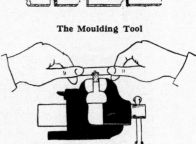

The Moulding Tool

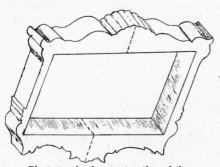

First step in the construction of the Quarter Badges

Moulding Tool in use

This consisted of a strip of steel, $9'' \times \frac{1}{2}'' \times \frac{1}{16}''$, with one edge filed into the negative shapes of the various mouldings. It is used like a spokeshave on the strip of wood held in a vice, as shown in the sketch.

The planking of the model, astragals, and various other small parts, were made from fine strip wood, supplied by Messrs. A. E. Jones, of 97, New Oxford Street, W.C. for aeroplane models.

This is the first carved model I have attempted, and the fourth of any kind, so that I may have made too much of the difficulties, but perhaps this account of the part I found most troublesome may be helpful to someone who is keen enough to attempt the carving.

The original plans were revised and drawn by the authorities in the Royal Scottish Museum, Edinburgh.

Drawing by]   **" The Commercial Thames "**   *[W. M. Birchall*

A Working Model Steam Coaster

By N. W. MARSHALL

THE model is built to a scale of ¼″ to 1′, and is based on a typical steam coaster, of 880 tons, with mid-ship bridge, and engines aft. It is constructed of 24-gauge tinplate arranged in strakes of scale width, the building was carried out on 16 moulds or frames erected on a suitable base board, as described and illustrated on page 31 of the *Model Engineer* Handbook on " Model Steamer Building." On these moulds the strakes were formed to shape (the vessel, of course, being built upside-down) and correctly lapped, i.e., strakes alternately outside and inside, not overlaid as in a clinker-built vessel, and soldered. The stem and stern posts were formed out of a piece of " scale " railway track, when the hull was fully plated it was removed from the moulds. It was intended that ribs should be fitted, but it was found to be so strong and stiff that these were quite unnecessary and were omitted.

The rail was formed by slitting a piece of small-bore brass tube and fitting it over the top of the bulwarks, all angle " iron " struts and stays being fitted to the inside of the bulwarks after the decks were in position, the decks are formed of wood, with the exception of the fo'castle which is of tinplate.

The ship is complete with all fittings, i.e., ventilators, winches, windlass, ladders, etc., and " clinker " built boats. The motive power is provided by a Bassett-Lowke No. 10 " Nautilus " motor, 1¼″ armature 6 volt 2 amp. when under load. The accumulator is a 6 volt 10 amp.-hour (this is its ignition rating, so that its actual capacity for driving a motor would be about 5 amp.-hours). It is now proposed to use two of these accumulators connected in parallel ; there is plenty of room for this in the boat, and it would bring her down nearer to trim without needing so much

A Working Model of a Typical Steam Coaster

ballast, the total weight of the present power unit is 5¾ lb., and she will carry a further 10 lb. of ballast to bring her down to her marks. The motor has plenty of power; in fact, it drives her too fast for scale speed.

The motor is installed below the engine-room casing, the deck of which is made to lift off for inspection or removal of motor, the accumulator being fitted under the after hatch, the additional accumulator could be fitted below the fore hatch, both these hatches being large enough, at scale size, to pass them.

The switch operating the motor is arranged below the after capstan and operated by it, so that when out

of the water she is a perfect scale model without having her deck marred by an ugly switch.

The ship proved to be very stiff and will stand up without either power plant or ballast, and even if thrown over almost on her beam-ends she will return at once to the upright.

The actual length of this model is about 3′ 9″ over-all.

(A scale blue-print drawing of the prototype of this model, showing elevation and deck-plan, can be obtained from our publishing department, 2s. 6d. post free. A separate blue-print of the hull lines is also obtainable, price 2s. 6d. post free.)

Towing Hooks for Tugs

There are almost as many arrangements of towing gear as there are tugs. The simplest is the plain hook, mounted on a semi-circular bar fixed to the top of the fiddley and supported at an angle of about 30 deg. by two forged brackets; the hook running freely on the length of bar between them. Another form has a plain hook swivelling about a vertical bolt in a bracket attached to the after-side of the fiddley, or to a tripod of steel

by a pawl, locked in place by a trigger with a slotted lug on its after-side, which engages with a rib on the pawl. The tripping line may be led to the bridge, but is sometimes only a short length left dangling, as a man is always at hand on deck when craft are in tow. A pull on the line frees the

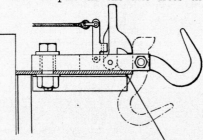

Towing Hook used on Large Tugs

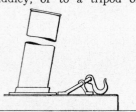

A simple towing hook

bars mounted directly on the deck between the boiler and engine casings. Such simple mountings are found usually in the smaller tugs.

The larger tugs often favour some form of slip-hook, one type of which is shown in the sketch. The body of the hook consists of a slotted forging swivelling about a vertical bolt, the hole for which may have a brass bush. When towing, the hook is held

pawl, which can then be knocked back by a touch, releasing the hook which swing into the vertical position by its own weight. The form of the hook is more open than the usual " crane hook," so that the hawser slips freely off. The whole contrivance traverses upon a semi-circular flat plate (shown in section in the sketch) supported by two brackets of plate and angles against the after-end of the boiler casing, and about 2′ 6″ above the deck.

The " Lancing "

(For photograph see Supplement Plate with this issue)

WE are indebted to Captain Norman P. Forbes for the following interesting details of this famous ship.

The sailing vessel *Lancing* was, in my opinion, the fastest of all sailing vessels—either wood, iron or steel—a vessel of whose exploits we have heard very little, perhaps owing to the fact that she was once a steamer, and what is known as a converted ship.

It is an authentic fact that this vessel could clip off with favourable winds, and plenty of them, such as one might expect to get running the easting down to 18 knots, quite easily, and on one occasion she is known to have kept this speed up for 72 consecutive hours—this was on a run from Buenos Aires to Noumea, New Caledonia, while running her easting down on a parallel of 47 degrees south. The distance from Buenos Aires to Noumea, on a composite great circle track, is more or less 11,000 miles, and she covered this in 42 days, practically a speed of nearly 262 miles a day, so possibly at some time during the passage she was going at speeds over 20 knots. Of this she was quite capable, her only trouble being lack of men to handle sail in blowing weather.

This vessel was built on the Clyde, by the firm of Napier and Sons, in the year 1866 to the order of the Compagnie Generale Transatlantic ; more commonly known as the French line, who ply between Havre and New York. Her original name as a steamer was the *Periere*, and she ran as a mail steamer for 22 years. Her sister ship was a vessel called the *Ville de Paris*, and she was also converted from steam to sail, and was named the *H. Bischoff* and, I think, went to German owners, for about that time the Germans had many steam vessels that were converted.

The *Periere* got ashore off St. Nazaire, France, in the year 1888, and the French Line abandoned her

to the Underwriters ; and Captain George Hatfield undertook the job of refloating her, and persuaded A. E. Kinnear, of London, to form a company to purchase her. After her cargo was salved, her engines were taken out, and they still seemed to be in good condition, for they brought a considerable sum when sold. The hull was floated off the beach, and towed to Blyth, England, where she was converted into a four-masted square-rigged sailing vessel ; this work was done by the Cowpen Dry Docks and Shipbuilding Co., of Blyth.

She sailed under the British Flag for many years, but did not distinguish herself to any extent ; she was sold to Norwegian owners, and changed hands twice under that flag, her last owners being Melsom and Melsom, of Larvik, Norway. She was, I believe, sold to the Italian ship-breakers, and her last resting-place was Genoa ; this was, I think, about 1927. She fetched a good price, owing to the wonderful material of which she was constructed, and her last owners were sorry to part with her, for she had made lots of money for them ; but, owing to the lowness of freights, they let her go. She was running all through the World War.

Her dimensions were as follows : Length, 356′ ; breadth, 43.8′ ; depth, 27.3′ ; she was very long and narrow, and sharp at both ends. When re-rigged, her main and mizzen masts were 200′ from keel to truck, and 175′ from the main deck. Her cross-jack yard was 92′ long, and one of the shortest spars on board was the spike bowsprit she had, which, through being so short, detracted from making her a good ship in stays, for with more head sails I feel sure she would have been an easier ship to handle.

(Captain Forbes would much like to obtain authentic plans of the *Lancing*, and we shall be pleased to put any reader who can assist, into touch with him.—ED., S. AND S.M.)

Books to Read

Fishermen and Fishing Ways. By PETER F. ANSON. London: George G. Harrap and Co., Ltd. Price 7s. 6d. Postage 6d.

The story of deep sea fishing has a twofold interest to most of us. As sea-girt islanders, we have a big fishing industry on our coasts, and it is but right that we should know something of the lives of the people who provide us with a substantial portion of our daily food, and of the conditions under which their arduous work is done. But beyond that we have a definite interest in the types of boats and ships employed and the manner of their equipment and handling. Mr. Peter F. Anson, in his newest book, deals with both these aspects of deep-sea fishing in his usual informative and interesting way. The earlier pages, devoted to folklore and superstitions of fishermen, are very entertaining. However much we may feel inclined to scoff at superstitions, there is no doubt that they are regarded with a very tenacious belief, and it is remarkable that similar superstitions, perhaps of a very trivial nature, should hold sway in widely separated countries. Both in Scotland and in Sweden, for example, they say that if a woman steps over a fishing-line, no fish will be caught with it. How many of us know that if an Iceland fisherman wishes to do harm to a neighbour's boat, he sprinkles it with sulphur, or that the men of the Isle of Man used to carry salt in their pockets to ward off the devils who destroy nets and lines. The Chapter on " Fishermen and the Law " gives us some interesting inside details of the poaching which regularly goes on in prohibited areas, and of the methods adopted by cunning skippers to avoid capture. The methods used in trawling, drift-net fishing, and hand-lining are very fully explained, and, in the pages devoted to the cod fisheries, Mr. Anson details the life of the men who face such terrible hardships on the Newfoundland Banks. It is difficult to believe that men and boys can be found to man the *Voliers* which set sail each year from the French ports for a long spell of weary months in the fog and cold of the grey seas of the Banks. The insanitary and over-crowded accommodation, the monotonous food, and the strenuous work which these men have to face, are vividly described by Mr. Anson, and it is rather a relief to read that modern steam trawlers and improved conditions are beginning to displace the hardships of the old-time sailing ships.

As with Mr. Anson's other books, the illustrations are a delightful feature of this volume. His line drawings of fishing craft are beautifully executed, and will be a source of valuable reference to those in need of authentic detail for modelling or other purposes. A coloured drawing of Macduff Harbour makes a very charming frontispiece.

Sea Dogs of To-day. By A. J. VILLIERS. London: George G. Harrap and Co., Ltd. Price 7s. 6d. net. Postage 6d.

In his latest work the author is to be congratulated in covering such a wide field. It is a revelation of adventure and heroism that is happening every day in all the Seven Seas, but goes unnoticed and unrecorded. He has personally known some of the men of whom he writes and has sailed long voyages with them.

Although well known to a very large following of ship-lovers, a few remarks on Mr. Villiers' career may not be out of place. At an early age he went to sea as a cadet in a square-rigger, but the master died, and the new one was mad, so he cleared out. But only to find another ship. For a year or two he sailed before the mast, until, in a four-masted barque on passage from France to Australia, the vessel was cast ashore.

After this he " left the sea and went into steam," but the salt of the sea having got thoroughly into his veins, he found steamers dull. After one voyage he decided to try whaling. Sailing in a 12,000 ton whaler, he went to the Antarctic under the Norwegian Flag, and after five months, returned to New Zealand.

He then turned his hand to journalism, and for this we have every reason to be grateful, as few writers have the same easy and attractive style of writing combined with the practical experience of sea life with which to record these amazing sea adventures.

However, this was not by any means to be the end of Mr. Villiers sea career, for in 1928 we find him in the *Herzogin Cecilie*, and later in the *Grace Harwar*. It was in the latter vessel that he made his world-renowned film record of the voyage round the Horn.

" Sea Dogs of To-day " is undoubtedly a book that will inspire all who read it. Here we have the story of the " John Stewart Line," the last of the English sailing-ship lines ; " The Garth Line " of Montreal, which owned the last square-rigged vessel to sail under the British Flag ; and Captain T. C. Fearon, " Veteran of 36 Cape Horn roundings."

The life of Captain Gustaf Erikson, " the sea cook who became sea captain," is of particular interest at the present time, for he owns more than a dozen of 19 sailing vessels which are racing to Europe from Australia with cargoes of grain. Then there is the life of Captain Carl Larsen, " the founder and guiding spirit of modern whaling."

So wide is the scope of this book that a chapter on " Women in Windjammers " has been included. Although so many of the " gentle sex " have encroached upon the occupations which were at one time solely those fulfilled by mere man, sea life for women, other than as a stewardess in a passenger liner, is hardly to be recommended. Those who are unwise enough to try it, even though " Amazons," will find there is a great deal more to be endured than Mr. Villiers has described.

The work is profusely illustrated, and contains a number of appendices, lists of sailing ships, and records of voyages, which will be found of the utmost value.—" CHIPS."

The Ways of the Navy. By Rear-Admiral D. ARNOLD-FORSTER, C.M.G. London : Ward, Lock and Co., Ltd. Price 7s. 6d. net. Postage 6d.

With the approach of summer, thoughts will be turning to holidays. During the next few months, units of the Home Fleet will be visiting various holiday resorts for short periods to give members of the public opportunities of seeing something of life afloat in the Royal Navy. Also, " Navy Week " will be celebrated as usual in the three great Naval ports during the period July 30th to August 6th.

Those who wish to get the maximum of interest out of a visit to one of H.M. ships, will be well advised to procure a copy of Rear-Admiral Arnold-Forster's book. Well indexed, and written in most entertaining style, it deals with every phase of naval life, in all kinds of craft, from monster battleships down to sloops, minesweepers and destroyers. The author remarks, " I have written chiefly of the modern Fleet, but since many naval ways are handed down from one generation to another, I have included a little about earlier times, so as to round off the picture."

Many quaint customs and expressions in use in the Service are lucidly explained. It is a pity certain of the lay writers on naval subjects cannot be induced to study this work, which might enable them to avoid some of the egregious mistakes that appear.

In these days of oil-burning vessels, the chapter on " Coal and Oil " is of historical interest as a record of the practically extinct art of the stoker.

For those who remember the days of sail, the concluding chapters will have exceptional interest, especially in view of the desire expressed by the First Lord of the Admiralty to revive sail training in the Royal Navy. Details given of the exercises undertaken by the famous Training Squadron at sail and spar drill during its cruises, clearly illustrate the great benefits to be derived from this form of training. Imagination will be further stirred by the vivid descriptions of stunsail work, including the actual terms and orders used in setting and taking in sail.

There is no lack of humorous anecdotes, of which one may be quoted here :—

" One of the quickest actions in emergency I ever saw was that of a gunner during an Admiral's inspection. General quarters, fire and collision drills had been exercised ; the sheet anchor had been let go and weighed by hand ; and other seamanlike feats carried out in incredibly short times.

" The Admiral, looking on from the bridge, was pleased with the ship, and said so, but decided to spring one more little surprise on them. ' Send a diver down from the port accommodation ladder,' he said, as he collected his staff and began to move aft to leave the ship.

" Almost as the order, ' Out diving gear,' rang out, the gear was being rushed aft to the quarter-deck, and long before the Admiral arrived there, a diver, ready dressed, was standing at the bottom of the port ladder. Four men were heaving round the diving pump, another was holding the front glass of the great copper helmet, and waiting to hear the hiss of air before screwing it on.

" But something was wrong with the pump and no air came. The gunner, who is responsible for all diving gear, was horrified. Suddenly he made a dash for a bucket, and calling out, " Wet the diver ! " threw it to the men at the bottom of the ladder, who quickly dipped it into the sea and soused the diver.

" ' Oh ! I see he has been down already ! ' remarked the Admiral, glancing over the side as he arrived on the quarter-deck. ' Very credit-

able ! ' he added, as he crossed to the starboard ladder, where his steam barge was waiting to take him away." —" CHIPS."

A Century of Atlantic Travel.

By FRANK C. BOWEN. London : Sampson Low, Marston and Co., Ltd. Price 12s. 6d. Postage 6d.

Our first impression on opening the book is one of arrangement, partly at the industry of Mr. Bowen in adding to his already long list of books another volume of over 300 pages, and partly at the encyclopaedic knowledge displayed in this record of Atlantic shipping. At a rough estimate there are references to nearly a thousand individual ships, and Mr. Bowen has something of interest to say about each one of them. Moreover, the book is a narrative, and not a catalogue, and the story of Atlantic travel is unfolded in logical and historical sequence, with the reasons for the changes of types of ships and methods of propulsion most interestingly explained. The early days of sail, the trials of the emigrants, the challenge of steam and the fine passages made by the clippers in competition, the financial problems of the shipping companies, the early days of the Cunard, Inman, White Star, Anchor, and Allan Companies, the progress of the Hamburg-American, North German Lloyd, Red Star, and other Continental lines, the decades of the war, and the coming of the turbine and motor ships, and the giant liners of to-day, are all matters of great appeal to shiplovers, and their story is told with unflagging interest and a wealth of informative detail. Mr. Bowen says, in his " Epilogue," that " it is difficult to believe that the next hundred years of Atlantic travel can possibly contain half the interest and excitement of the century which has just finished." This is an opinion with which we are sure every reader of this fascinating book will agree. Some eighty or more photographs of the most famous ships mentioned add much to the value of the book as a record.

The Ship's Mail

Readers are invited to make use of this column for the discussion of matters of mutual interest and the exchange of ideas and information.

Steamers of 1878.

DEAR SIR,—The writer, although not such a veteran as your correspondent, " W.J.T.," was born, and lived, in Rotherhithe for the first 20 years or more, and happens to remember some of the steamers mentioned in his interesting letter. According to Lloyd's Register, 1925-26, in the Sailing Ship portion, the old *Sir Robert Peel* and *Lord J. Russell* are mentioned as belonging to the Lighterage Company, of Liverpool, being described as " Barges for being towed." I well remember the second *Sir Robert Peel*, which for years traded to Dunkirk, berthing at Fenning's Wharf. Of the old paddlers, in addition to the *Hoboken*, the General

S.N. Company had the *Hilda* ; another regular trader was also the *Baron Osy*, which ran from one of the wharves to Antwerp.

Referring to the *Elizabeth*, this, I think, must be one of the earlier steamers of the Bailey and Leetham fleet, which used to use Church Hole for loading and discharging. Other vessels of this company were *Una*, *Oria*, *Argyle and Lorne*, etc. They were familiarly known as *Tombstone* funnelled boats, owing to the white panels on their funnels. This line was some years ago absorbed by the Wilson line, of Hull.

The *John Bowes* was the first iron collier to be built specially for the coal trade, and my grandfather frequently used to unload her, as at this time he was the contractor to the South Metropolitan Gas Company, the colliers coming into the jetty in the Surrey Commercial Dock, but which has long since been demolished.

Photo by]   **The " John Bowes "**   [*Nautical Photo Agency*

as their jetty in the River has replaced it. This steamer was still running recently, but converted in rig and under the Spanish flag.

The *Black Boy* was also a regular coal carrier from the North, as were also similar steamers, such as *Newburn, Newpelton, Trevethick*, etc., under the same ownership. I think your correspondent is under a misapprehension regarding the first named ; the converted water vessel referred to by him was the *Carbon*. She was, I have always understood, built to convey water to the troops in the Crimea, but the war was over before she was finished, and she was a very old and regular visitor to the Surrey Commercial Dock. When loaded, she looked almost like any other steamer, but when in ballast she very much looked like a later date turret ship.

Yours faithfully,

Addiscombe.   GEO. J. PAYNE.

Ships' Plans Wanted

SIR,—I wonder if any readers could help me in the tracing of the builders' plans of two old steamers in which I am very interested, also one old wool-clipper. Perhaps some of the readers on the Clyde could help.

The steamers were sister ships, *Ghazee* and *Pathan*, built in 1883 by Aitken and Mansel, of Whiteinch, for Messrs. Gellatley, Hankey and Co., of London. The owners have no trace of the plans, neither have the present occupiers of the yard where these steamers were built.

The ship is the *Harbinger*, built in 1876 by Steele, of Greenock, now defunct, for Messrs. Anderson, Anderson, of London.

Both the steamers and the ship have been off Lloyd's Register for many years, but they were beautiful examples of the shipbuilder's work when ships were ships and steamers could honestly be called steam-ships.

Yours truly,

Fife.   KENNETH W. CRABB.

Bending a Cable to an Anchor

SIR,—I was interested in Mr. C. W. Bass's correction to my Ship Modeller's Scrap Book which appeared on page 245 of the April number, but I beg leave to be unrepentant.

If Mr. Bass will turn to Captain George Biddlecombe's famous " Art of Rigging " and look up the plate facing page 52 in 1he 1848 edition, he will find his bend illustrated as being the one used for a kedge anchor, while the method used for a bower anchor was the one I illustrated. For a stream anchor they used a round turn and hitch, with the end stopped.

There is no doubt of the logic of Mr. Bass's letter, but I think that Biddlecombe was in a position to know. He was a captain in the Merchant Service before he went into the Navy, in which service he rose to the rank of master, and he had actual personal experience of the seamanship about which he wrote. The book was issued by Charles Wilson's Navigation Warehouse and Naval Academy, who had a great reputation for technical books on the sea, so that we may take it that it had an added check to accuracy beyond the actual knowledge of its author.

Yours, etc.,

" THE MAN WITH THE SCRAP BOOK."

London.

The " Calais-Douvres "

SIR,—In your January number you published an interesting article entitled " Freak Channel Packets of the Late 'Seventies." Referring therein to the *Calais-Douvres*, it is stated that this vessel was broken up in 1899. I do not think that is correct. About that time a company was formed, called The Liverpool and Douglas Steamers, Ltd., who bought a *Calais-Douvres* amongst other steamers, and ran them in opposition to the old-established I.O.M. Steam Packet Co., Ltd. This competition lasted till about 1902, when the Liverpool company collapsed, and the

Calais-Douvres was bought by the I.O.M. Company. She was re-named *Mona III* and continued in their service till about 1909, when I presume she was broken up. I wonder if any of your readers could tell me what happened to a steamer named *Westonia* which plied on the Bristol Channel about 1908 for, I believe, the Barry Railway Company. She had two funnels forward of the paddle-boxes.

Yours truly,

Glasgow.   " CLYDESIDER."

The " Light Brigade "

DEAR SIR,—Possibly the enclosed photo of a model of the *Light Brigade*, which I have in my possession, may be of interest to your readers.

I think it is a very beautiful model, and I am very fond of it. It was purchased for me a few years ago by a friend in a country village near Bath. She was laid up as a " white elephant " in a Parish Hall, and in a dusty broken case, with her mizzen mast sadly smashed ; she awaited a modest purchaser, and my friend obtained her, case and all, for a very small sum.

You will notice the beauty and proportion of the fine rigging. Mr. Basil Lubbock's book, " The Colonial Clippers," gives a photo of this ship in commission, and from this book I quote the following particulars :—" *Light Brigade*, original name *Ocean Telegraph*. Tonnage, 1,495. Built Medford, U.S.A., 1854. Purchased by the Black Ball Line."

Unfortunately, about an inch or more of the bowsprit is missing and the mizzen mast is in a fragile condition, otherwise she compares very favourably with the photo of herself when in commission.

The Model of the "Light Brigade"

She carries the flag of the Black Ball Line, on her main, the initials L.H.E.B. in diagonal on the fore— and the mizzen her name-flag—yellow on a blue ground, Union Jack on white ground at bows. In addition there are several flags of the international code. All these flags are of silk, and embroidered by hand.

From "hearsay," this model is said to have been made by the skipper of the ship, a Captain Walker. Perhaps some readers can give me further information.

Yours faithfully,
Felixstowe.   E. MASON.

The "Trojan"

DEAR SIR,—I must thank your correspondents, Messrs. Garrington and Trotman, for the interesting information contained in their letters in reply to the query on the model liner in your March issue.

From Mr. Garrington's sketch and the description given in both letters, together with certain other facts sent to me by another correspondent, Mr. R. W. Smith, of Woolston, it seems pretty well certain that my model represents the Union liner *Trojan*.

On comparing the sketch on page 249 with the model, there are the following slight differences : The sketch shows the donkey boiler uptake leading into the afterside of the funnel, in the model there is none. There are no gangway doors in the bridge of the model as shown in sketch. The model has only one quarter boat each side aft, whereas two aside are indicated in the sketch. The model has two large skylights aft in place of the deck-house between the forward pair of quarter boats. In every other respect the drawing and model agree.

It is quite possible the model represents the ship as originally built, and the sketch at a later stage in her career, the differences being accounted for by alterations and additions from time to time.

My correspondent, Mr. Smith, also confirms Mr. Trotman's remark about the name on the stand being possibly that of the carpenter. Several Buddens apparently lived in Woolston or Southampton at one time, and most of them appear to have sailed in the Union Line in various capacities. If the model was the work of the ship's carpenter, he must have been a very clever man, as the workmanship throughout approaches very closely to exhibition finish.

There are two further points of interest I might mention and which I omitted in my article. The forecastle is built round a large "well," the after end forming a transverse gangway, reminding one somewhat of a modern liner's docking bridge. The propeller is fitted with the old-fashioned after-bearing in the rudder-post. I was under the impression this fitting went out of use in the middle of the 'seventies.

Yours faithfully,
LAURENCE A. PRITCHARD.
Southampton.

The Colouring of Egyptian Ships

DEAR SIR,—May I, through the medium of your journal, thank Mr. Alan Crozier Cole for the details of the colouring of Egyptian ships which he supplied in your March issue.

Yours truly,
Birmingham.   H. ZIMMERMAN.

Paddle Steamer "La Marguerite."

DEAR SIR,—The builder's model of the steel P.S. *La Marguerite* (1894) is exhibited in the Shipping Gallery in the City of Liverpool Free Public Museums, and bears the original plate, with the following inscription : " Built and Engined by the Fairfield Shipbuilding and Engineering Company, Limited, for the Palace Steamers, Ltd., London."

Yours faithfully,
D. A. ALLAN,
Free Public Museums,   Director.
City of Liverpool.

The Ship Modellers' Scrap Book

(*Continued from page* 254)

Counter

STRICTLY speaking, the underside of the overhang abaft the stern post, but more loosely applied to the whole of the ship's body abaft the stern post, except in ships with cruiser sterns. It was one of the principal

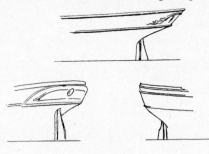

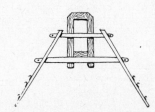

Types of Counter—(*Top*) Tea Clipper "Lahloo," 2 American built, Green's "Swift Sure," and the "W.D. Lawrence." (*Bottom*) Mid-19th Century "Blackwaller."

features in determining the district and date of a sailing ship's build, and was often very beautiful indeed in its lines. On the other hand, it was often capable of spoiling a very fine-looking ship, frequently the case in ships built in America or B.N.A., and this trait of an ugly counter is inherited by many modern steamers built there.

Courses

The lowermost sails on each mast in a square-rigged ship, the word being taken from the same derivative as the word " corpse," (body), that is, they were the body of the sail in the old days of single square sails, and bonnets and topsails were merely

added to them. The fore course was more usually called the foresail, the main course the mainsail, and the mizzen course the cross-jack, invariably

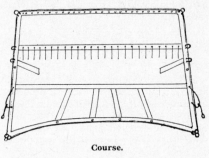

Course.

pronounced cro'j'ck. In many of the earlier full-rigged ships the cross-jack was not bent until the Americans brought it in with their clippers.

Cross-trees

The athwart-ship supports to the tops of the lower masts in square-rigged ships, bolted across the trestle trees. They were also used to spread the topgallant shrouds at the topmast head. In fore and aft masts they are used for spreading the topmast shrouds

Plan of square rigged vessel's topmast cross-trees with outriggers for backstays

which are set up from the channels or from the rail abreast the mast. As a rule, fore-and-aft cross trees were two in number, but in many recent ships there has been only one. Each timber of the cross trees is called a horn.

(*To be continued*)

The Ship Lovers' Association

Members' Queries and Answers

M. PIERRE LE CONTE, of La Villariou, rue des Bastions, Cherbourg, the well-known French marine artist and writer, is very interested in peculiar British man-of-war names. Will any member who has gone into this aspect of the subject communicate with him direct ; there seems to be a very big field of interest.

E.W.H.B. (Hendon).—The emigrant sailing ship *Ashmore* was built for J. Stewart and Co., by Reids in 1877, an iron full-rigged ship of 1,179 tons. She was employed principally on the Australian trade, but in 1881 and 1882 she was chartered to the New Zealand Shipping Co., and had most unfortunate voyages with weather, losing spars on each. In 1903 she was cut down to a barque and, in 1907, was sold to Norway for £3,050. She was wrecked in April, 1918. There is a very interesting chapter on John Stewart's ships in Mr. A. J. Villiers' latest book, "Sea Dogs of To-day," just published.

E.P.H. (London).—Of the packets you mention, the *Great Western* of 1867 was sold to David MacBrayne in 1891 and re-named *Lovedale*. She was scrapped in 1904. The *Cherbourg* of 1873 was not broken up until 1930, and the *Pembroke* of 1880 in 1925. The *South Western*, built in 1874, was torpedoed without warning by a German submarine on March 16th, 1918, off St. Catherine's, 24 lives being lost. The *Guernsey* of the same year was a marine casualty during the war, being wrecked on Cape La Hogue with 7 deaths on April 9th, 1915.

A.A.H. (Meopham).—*Port Logan* was a full-rigged ship built by Russell, of Port Glasgow, for Crawford and Rowat in 1895, 1,984 tons gross. In 1914 she was sold to H. H. Schmidt, of Hamburg, and renamed *Mimi*, contriving to reach Talcahuane just before. war broke out and being bottled up there.

Among the spoils of war she was allocated to France, but they had no use for her, so she was sold back to H. H. Schmidt in 1922. He re-named her *Bertha*. She was posted missing in May, 1925, on a voyage from Jacksonville to Hamburg, a lifebuoy picked up in January being the only clue to her fate.

B.L. (Westcliff).—There were three brig-rigged *Boxers* in the Navy. The first had 12 guns and was built on the Thames in 1797. She took part in the Ostend Expedition in 1798 and, in 1800, was with H.M.S. *Dart* in a particularly gallant cutting-out expedition in Dunkirk Roads. She was sold in 1809 and replaced by another 12-gunner in 1812. She was the one captured by the V.S.S. *Enterprise* (16) in 1813, after a gallant fight, honoured on both sides of the Atlantic. The third was an American prize, captured in the 1812-14 War, and employed in American waters only.

There were many *Darts*, but only one schooner-rigged, the one mentioned above being a 20-gun ship sloop. The schooner was built at Sheerness in 1847, mounting 3 guns only, but having a burthen of 319 tons on dimensions 90′ × 29′ × 11′. She was employed on coastguard service only and later became a station hulk as Watch Vessel No. 26, at Beresford. She was scrapped in 1875.

H.S. (Preston).—James Little and Co., of Barrow, acquired the *Rouen* from the L.B. and S.C. Railway Co. in 1903, and re-named her *Duchess of Buccleugh*. She was finally scrapped in 1909. The *Lady Wolseley*, of the British and Irish S.P. Co., went to the Limerick S.S. Co. in 1915, to be re-named *Kinvarra*. Once sold, her luck changed, for in the following year, after a further transfer to Tyneside owners as the *River Tyne*, she foundered off Oporto with a cargo of minerals for Hull.

Northern Notes

By "JASON"

Manchester

THE Secretary of this progressive Club is anxious to get suggestions for the Summer Programme not only from his own members, but from anyone interested and having a love for ships. Among other ideas is a Club visit to a liner in the Manchester Docks, under the guidance of a navigator club member for deck descriptions, and an engineer club member for the engine room. It is hoped to make arrangements to have tea on board at a small nominal charge and perhaps finish up by a quick tour round the docks in a motorboat belonging to the Manchester Ship Canal or some shipping company.

Another excursion consists of a visit to the flotilla of destroyers due to visit Manchester at the end of June. Here, again, members with naval experience will be able to help the interest of the afternoon by instructional talks.

One more suggestion which is offered is that the Manchester members pay a day's visit to the now greatly enlarged Shipping Gallery of the Liverpool Museum. No doubt arrangements could be made for an official of the Museum staff or one of the Liverpool members to conduct them on, what would probably be, one of the most instructive experiences to be obtained outside of London itself.

No. 2 Club is particularly strong in power boat members and, accordingly, one of the summer meetings will probably be an exhibition of power boat work on one of the public lakes at Manchester.

3/- Model Competition

The Secretaries of the four Model Ship Makers' Clubs have preliminary information of the 3/- Model Competition which will be held in the Autumn of the year. Particulars will gladly be sent to any inquirer who sends a stamped, addressed envelope.

The Merseyside Club

The Pioneer Model Ship Makers' Club have now had an opportunity of of reviewing their progress over a period of six months and, at meetings recently held, the value of the workshop-club room as opposed to the social and library club room, was fully discussed. It was felt that the workshop is not used to the extent it might be, and that the library facilities might be developed. The decision, although not unanimous, was yet strong enough to warrant some change in the future and, accordingly, the Committee have decided to concentrate more on the social side than the workshop side. In the meantime, a questionaire is being sent out in many directions seeking further views. It remains to be seen whether the Manchester, Clydeside and Humber Clubs will still continue to make the workshop-club room their objective, for there is much to be said in favour of it.

Hon. Secretary : L. F. Holly, 9 Jasmine Street, Anfield, Liverpool.

An Annual Meeting

The first annual meeting of No. 2 (Lancashire and Cheshire) will be held on May 3rd, in Lockart's Victoria Cafe, Manchester. There are some important additions to the existing Rules, and all who are interested are cordially welcomed. Part of the programme progress of this Club is a series of lectures and talks on matters of interest to model makers in general.

Secretary : W. F. Hemingway, Esq., Withens, Littleborough.

Tasmania, No. 5

A Model Ship Makers' Club is now in process of formation at Hobart, Tasmania, on the other side of the world. There are many in that district who are keenly interested in ship models, not only of the windjammer types but many others as well. Those who are interested should communicate with Capt. A. C. Alexander, of the Ozone Tea Rooms, Long Beach, Sandy Bay, Hobart. One of the members of this new Club has made a model of a ship which conveyed St. Paul to Rome 2,000 years ago. Other models belong to the periods 1450 and 1700, together with a number of windjammer models.

Merseyside's Spring Exhibition of Model Ships

The Exhibition which it was proposed to hold in May has been postponed until the end of September, as it was not possible to obtain suitable rooms for the requisite period prior to the opening of summer conditions. The 3/- Model Competition has accordingly been postponed to the same date. More particulars will be announced later, but a preliminary notice may be had on application to the Secretaries of the Model Ship Makers' Clubs.

Clydeside Ship Lovers' Club

No. 3 Club is now well under way. Meetings are held at Miss Buick's Restaurant, 19a, Renfield Street, Glasgow, and the first president is Mr. Macmaneny. No. 3 is following along the lines of Nos. 1 and 2, particularly with regard to the call of Gentlemen Adventurers, and Glasgow feels that the Gentlemen Adventurers should exist throughout England in the support of those interested in the making of model ships.

Hon. Secretary : Robert Lawson, Esq., 224, Armadale Street, Dennistown, Glasgow.

The Lucky Humber Club

The members of the Model Ship Makers' Club, No. 4, are indeed fortunate, for they meet in the Pickering Museum, the galleries of which are crowded with interesting models of many periods, together with actual relics of other times. Their usual meeting night is on Sunday, and they are doubly fortunate in being under the direction and leadership of Mr. T. Shepherd, the Director of the Municipal Museums, Hull, to whom intending members should write for further particulars. Already the Club is in a flourishing state ; the interests of the members cover half-a-dozen periods of model making.

And Sunderland

This Club concentrates on sailing models and power boats, with a total membership of over two score. The Secretary writes an interesting report, during the course of which he makes some complaint on behalf of the Club regarding the Model Lake, which badly requires cleaning, but unfortunately, like many other bodies to-day, the Borough Council are obliged to economise, and the £2,000 necessary for cleaning, cementing and building a boat-house is not available. It is felt by those of the locality that the importance of Sunderland as a shipbuilding centre is worthy of better facilities for a progressive Model Ship Club. Address the Secretary, 15, Warwick Street, Sunderland.

An 18th Century Coaster

A VESSEL arrived at Whitehaven lately, from Strangford, which is known to have been coasting, chiefly in this channel, for 130 years. She is called the *Three Sisters*— Donnan, master—but is better known by the name of the Port-a-Ferry Frigate ; she is of the burthen of 36 tons, at present rigged as a brigantine, but there is a report that she formerly appeared as a ship. However this may be, it is certain that she was employed at the siege of Londonderry in 1689, and was successful, on an emergency, in supplying the garrison with provisions. This venerable piece of architecture (which, from the great improvements made in the course of the last century, is now viewed as a curiosity), is allowed, we are informed, the privilege of using any of the public docks at Liverpool, free of all port charges, and this, in consequence of her having been the first vessel that entered the old dock. —Extract from the *Naval Chronicle*, Volume 8, published in 1802.

SHIPS AND SHIP MODELS

A Magazine for all Lovers of Ships and the Sea

Editorial and Publishing Offices:

Single Copies, post free, **7½d.**

Annual Subscription **7s. 6d.**

66 FARRINGDON STREET

LONDON :: E.C.4

Vol. I. No. 10.   JUNE, 1932.   Price 6d.

The Ship's Log

The Grain Carriers

PROBABLY the news of last month which was of most interest to ship-lovers was the arrival in the Thames of the *Abraham Rydberg*, the winner of the great race home of the grain-carrying windjammers from Australia. The *Abraham Rydberg* made the passage from Wallaroo, South Australia, to the Downs in 121 days. She sailed via the Cape of Good Hope, and berthed on arrival in Millwall Dock. She is a four-masted barque, Swedish owned ; commanded by Captain Tamm, she has a crew of 40 cadets, who are getting the full benefit of sail training. The *Winterhude*, another of the grain fleet, has reached Queenstown from Port Pirie after a passage round the Horn, the full voyage lasting 145 days. Some fine pictures of the *Abraham Rydberg* arriving in the Thames, were published in the London papers, and these must have stirred the pulse of many a landlubber, as well as of sailormen, at the beautiful sight such a ship always presents. The well-known barque *Hougomont* is out of

the race, owing to being dismasted off Kangaroo Island. Fortunately, she was safely towed to harbour.

*   *   *

The " Passat "

The largest sailing ship in the world, the *Passat*, berthed in the Tees a few weeks ago, coming from Bilbao for a cargo of nitrates. She is just over 30 years old, and has been latterly used as a training ship for German cadets. During her stay in the Tees, a new owner's flag was hoisted, as she has been purchased by Captain Erikson, the famous Finnish sailor and sailing fleet owner, of Mariehamn.

*   *   *

The Oldest Port ?

Having devoted some space in our columns to discussing the question of the oldest ships afloat, a kindred question might well be put—Which is the oldest port ? Probably the correct answer is Mount Ararat, but we do not invite readers to respond with alternative replies, as we can visualise an avalanche of contestants for the honour. We mention the matter because of a statement that Hull could claim to have been connected with shipping or water transport since the year 2000 B.C. This was made by Mr. Thomas Sheppard, the Director of the Hull Museum, in a very interesting address he recently gave before the Hull Luncheon Club. He related how the finest and largest specimen of a pre-historic naval boat existent in the world was found embedded in the Humber silt. It measured 40′ in length and was 5′ in width, and it had been made out of a single oak tree. From the excavations at the time that the Guildhall was being built, they obtained another dug-out made from a solid trunk of pine which was made about the year 1500. Mr. Sheppard also traced the history of the Port of Hull through the Middle Ages and mentioned that ships and guns from Hull played a considerable part in the defeat of the Spanish Armada.

*   *   *

The City of Liverpool Free Public Museums

The Shipping Gallery in the Liverpool Museums has received an excellent scale model of the barge *Nordic* (1921) scale 1 : 48, specially constructed by order of the Liverpool Grain Storage and Transit Co., Ltd. There has also been acquired one of the two original builder's models of the s.s. *City of Paris* (1866), the other being on view in the Shipping Section of the Science Museum at South Kensington. This is a valuable addition to the Gallery as models of early steamships are difficult to secure.

*   *   *

Prizes for Ship Models

The prize list and entry forms for the forthcoming *Model Engineer* Exhibition in September next are now ready. A special Competition Section has been arranged for ship models of all kinds, and the prizes include a cup for the best sailing ship model, and a cup for the best steamer model. In addition to these premier awards, silver and bronze medals, and diplomas

will be awarded to work considered by the judges to be of sufficient merit. We may perhaps mention that the Competition Section at this popular exhibition is intended to encourage all grades of model-making skill, and the efforts of less advanced workers are just as welcome as the very high class models. Offers of interesting models are also invited for the Loan Section.

*   *   *

New Books

In addition to the books reviewed in this issue, we have received copies of "The Sea in Ships," by Alan J. Villiers, published by George Routledge and Sons, Ltd., price 7s. 6d., and "Model Sailing Craft," by W. J. Daniels and H. B. Tucker, published by Chapman and Hall, price 25s. We hope to publish full reviews of these next month.

*   *   *

Information Wanted

Here are a few extracts from queries recently submitted by our readers. We shall be glad to forward any replies to the correspondents concerned, or if of sufficient general interest to publish them in our " Mail " columns :—

(1) Where to get a hull about 4′ long, suitable for rigging as a sailing model of a brigantine. (2) Information as to rig and deck-plan of *Francis Hoyle*, Bacup. (3) How to make new brass guns look old. (4) Book about old warships' ordnance, dealing with calibres, ranges, rate of fire, weight and nature of shot, and other details of firing practice. (5) Correct method of mounting bowsprit of fairly late type of fore-and-aft schooner. (6) Data concerning small paddle-steamer *Alexandra*, now being converted in London. Did she sink a German submarine during the war while troop carrying ? (7) Data *re Foudroyant* (1790), or reference to good source of information. (8) Data *re* Bristol Channel pilot boats built by Hambly, of Cardiff, 1900-1908, particularly *Baroque*, *Curiad* and *Mischief*.

Bristol's Paddle Fleet

By C. HAWKINS GARRINGTON

IT can be said, without fear of challenge, that the paddle-steamers of P. and A. Campbell's White Funnel Fleet, of Bristol, are the handsomest best-kept and fastest of their type and size afloat.

The flag-ship, *Britannia*, is 36 years old, yet such care and attention has been bestowed upon her by the owners that it was difficult to believe she had long left the builders' yard when she made this season's opening trip from Bristol to Ilfracombe on March 24th. The present fleet is composed of the following up-to-date, thoroughly well-equipped passenger steamers :—

red boot-topping. Paddle-boxes and the plating from the promenade deck to bulwarks are very pale grey ; funnel-casings, ventilators and boats are white, the funnels having black cowl tops and the ventilators french-blue interiors. All carry one pole mast and a short mast at the stern on the promenade deck for the wireless aerial ; funnels and masts are well raked and the steamers present a pleasing and yacht-like appearance.

Glen Gower, *Lady Moyra* and *Devonia* each have two funnels, the other eight, one.

The house-flag is a blue pendant

	Gross tonn.	Built.	Builders.	Length.	Beam.	Depth.
Glen Gower ..	522	1922	Ailsa S.B. Co., Troon	242'	26' 5"	9' 3"
Glen Usk ..	524	1914	Do. do.	224' 3"	28' 1"	8' 9"
Glen Avon ..	509	1912	Do. do.	220'	27' 1"	8' 9"
Waverley ..	398	1907	J. Brown, Clydebank	225' 6"	26' 6"	8' 7"
Lady Moyra ..	519	1905	Do. do.	245'	29'	9' 7"
Devonia ..	520	1905	Do. do.	245'	29'	9' 7"
Brighton Belle ..	320	1900	J. Scott, Kinghorn	200'	24' 1"	8' 2"
Britannia ..	459	1896	S. McKnight, Ayr	230'	26' 6"	9' 6"
Cambria ..	420	1895	H. McIntyre, Alloa	225'	26' 1"	9' 4"
Westward Ho	438	1894	S. McKnight, Ayr	225'	26' 1"	9' 5"
Ravenswood ..	345	1891	Do. do.	215'	24' 1"	8' 5"

Messrs. P. & A. CAMPBELL'S PRESENT BRISTOL FLEET

It is useful to note here how misleading it is to compare ships in terms of tonnage. For instance, the gross tonnage of *Glen Usk* is four more than that of *Devonia*, although the latter steamer is about 20' longer and 1' broader ; the net tonnage of *Glen Usk* exceeds that of *Devonia* by 27.

All the steamers are built of steel and, excepting *Ravenswood*, have the promenade deck carried right up to the stem ; wireless is fitted, except in *Westward Ho* and *Glen Avon*. Hulls are painted black with either one or two buff lines on the bulwarks ; water-lines are pale green above light

with white chevron and ball and is worn below a blue pendant with the ship's name in white ; with the usual Campbell thoroughness, these two flags are worn under the French flag on the South Coast steamers when crossing to France.

Ravenswood carried two funnels with the bridge aft between her paddle-boxes, until 1909, when she was sent to the Clyde where her two haystack boilers were replaced by a single boiler of the marine type and the single-cylinder engine by a two-cylinder compound ; this type of engine is used throughout the fleet.

Photo by]   **The original " Waverley "—built 1885.**   [Pincock Bros.

Ravenswood returned to Bristol with one funnel and her bridge forward.

Westward Ho was the first excursion steamer south of the Clyde to have the plating under the promenade deck carried right up to the stem, and was thus the prototype of the modern Bristol Channel, South Coast and Thames paddlers.

It is also worthy of note that the progenitor of the present Campbell family was the first private individual to introduce the modern type of deck saloon steamer on the Clyde. *Brighton Belle*, as *Lady Evelyn*, was lengthened in 1904 ; she was purchased in July, 1922, from the " Yellow Funnel Fleet," one of P. and A. Campbell's competitors.

Cambria was renamed *Cambridge* for War service ; *Devonia* was purchased in 1911 from Bristol Channel Passenger Boats, Ltd. ; *Lady Moyra* was purchased in 1922 from the " Yellow Funnel Fleet.'

Waverley, purchased in 1911 from the same coampany as *Devonia*, was originally named *Barry* and has borne her present name since 1925. During the War she was known as *Barryfield*. The name *Waverley* was borne by the first steamer of the fleet, which was built in 1885 by McIntyre, Paisley, and was 205′ long, 21′1″ beam, 7′5″ deep, with a gross tonnage of 240. She ran on the Clyde for about two years, when she was purchased by P. and A. Campbell to start marine excursions from Bristol in 1888. She was considerably improved by an extended promenade deck and entirely redecorated for the opening of the

Photo by]   **The " Waverley " as finally altered.**   [Nautical Photo Agency

Photo by]   **The "Glen Usk," built 1914**   *[John_York*

1889 season. *Waverley* was a success from the start, and three years later *Ravenswood* made her first trip from Bristol on July 3rd, 1891. When the writer watched her departure he little thought that, 41 years later, and after more than 3½ years' war service, she would still be sailing looking as spick and span as she did on that day.

Then followed *Westward Ho, Cambria, Britannia, Lady Ismay* (1911),

Glen Avon, Glen Usk and *Glen Gower*, all specially built for the Company, while *Lady Margaret* (1896), *Brighton Queen* (1897), *Glen Rosa* (1897), *Bonnie Doon* (1899), *Scotia* (1899), *Albion* (1900), *Devonia, Waverley, Tintern* (1911), *Lady Moyra* and *Brighton Belle* were purchased from other concerns.

During the season regular daily services are maintained between Bristol and Ilfracombe, Cardiff and Weston,

Photo by]   **The "Glen Gower," the latest Steamer of the fleet**   *[James Randall*

and Swansea and Ilfracombe. Very popular short trips are run from Bristol, Cardiff, Clevedon, etc., out and home on the same tide, and there are frequent trips from Bristol and Ilfracombe to Tenby, Clovelly and Lundy Island. From Ilfracombe, steamers go as far as Newquay. Operating from

being sunk and three returned unfit for reconditioning. The dates of departures and return were as below :—

The amazing development of marine excursions in the Bristol Channel is entirely due to the energies and personalities of Captains Peter and Alec Campbell. Captain Peter Camp-

	Date of Departure.	Date of Return.
Devonia	September, 30th, 1914.	May 2nd, 1919.
Brighton Queen	September 30th, 1914.	Sunk October 6th, 1915.
Cambria	December 2nd, 1914.	May, 4th, 1919.
Westward Ho	December 2nd, 1914.	April 1st, 1919.
Glen Avon	December 2nd, 1914	March 11th, 1919.
Lady Ismay	December 2nd, 1914.	Sunk December 21st, 1915.
Britannia..	February 5th, 1915.	April 8th, 1919.
Glen Usk	February 5th, 1915.	April 11th, 1919.
Ravenswood	July 1st, 1915.	March 5th, 1919.
Albion (broken up) ..	July 1st, 1915.	February 15th, 1919.
Barry	July 24th, 1915.	September 27th, 1919.
Waverley (broken up) ..	May 30th, 1917.	March 17th, 1919.
Glen Rosa (broken up) ..	May 30th, 1917.	March 23rd, 1919.

THE WAR SERVICE OF THE CAMPBELL FLEET

Brighton, *Devonia*, *Waverley* and *Brighton Belle* maintain a service to resorts from Folkestone to Bournemouth and across the Channel to Boulogne and Calais.

The whole fleet of P. and A. Campbell's fleet of 13 steamers was requisitioned for war service, two

bell has the unique distinction of possessing an Engineer's Certificate in addition to his Master's Certificate and Bristol Channel Pilot's licence. Captain Alec Campbell, the founder of the Company, and one of the most genial and kindly of men, died in Scotland in December, 1928.

ROUNDING SOUTH ROCK LIGHTSHIP.

Sketch by]   **Rounding South Rock Lightship**   *[Harold A Underhill*

Some Unusual Funnels
By GRAY E. FARR.

A FEW months ago, in SHIPS AND SHIP MODELS, there appeared a paragraph on the subject of funnels and the chances of their disappearance. I think, however, that I am voicing the opinions of most people when I say that the chances of this are almost negligible, even though the internal-combustion engine may come into exclusive use. It is well known that however many ejecting forces

The double funnel of the "Malaya."

are employed, the exhaust gases of these engines are very prone to "hanging around" the interior of the vessels.

A good example of this (though on a smaller scale) is found in the larger motor lifeboats fitted with cabins. The first Barnett type twin-screw lifeboat built, in 1924, had no funnels, the exhaust pipes being directed through pipes leading out at the sides. It was found that however much the

A fore-mast funnel on an S.O. Co's. Barge.

intervening bulkhead was sealed, the fumes managed to leak into the after-cabin. The result was that on later boats of this type, such as were sent to Plymouth and Aberdeen, twin side-by-side funnels were used to carry the gas well overhead. Now, all the larger motor lifeboats are being fitted with funnels.

(The side-by-side arrangement was very popular in the 19th Century, and it is highly probable that it may come into use again after this fashion.)

The same idea of clearing the atmosphere was behind the adoption of the " double " funnel in the *Queen Elizabeth* class of warship. From the accompanying illustration of the midships section of one of this class, the *Malaya*, it will be seen that the former first funnel has been converted into a diagonal trunk leading into the after funnel and thus effectively keeping the smoke away from the control top, which was formerly liable to become uninhabitable with a following wind.

Another peculiar funnel, or mast-cum-funnel, is to be seen in the other illustration. This is on the Standard Oil Company's oil barge *S.O.Co.No.* 94. This and similar vessels were once a common sight in Avonmouth (Bristol) and other western docks. They were towed across the Atlantic by the stern-engined tanker *Navahoe* of the same line, and as they were of about 4,000 tons and about 360′ in length, I imagine they made quite an exciting tow. The engine, by the way, making the smoke from the fore-mast, was merely a donkey engine for working the pumps.

The " Lancing " ex " Periere "

By CAPITAINE DE CORVETTE M. ADAM.

AMONG the numerous iron side-wheel mail steamers ordered by the French Line to start its services from Havre to New York, two were allocated to the Napier shipyard at Glasgow, their names being *Periere* and *Ville de Paris*. Very quickly, the French Line realised that the days of paddles were gone, and wisely decided to alter these two boats on the stocks, to make them screw steamers. They were given very fine lines, with a clipper bow, and their new dimensions became as follows :—

The " Periere " Mail Steamer in her early days.

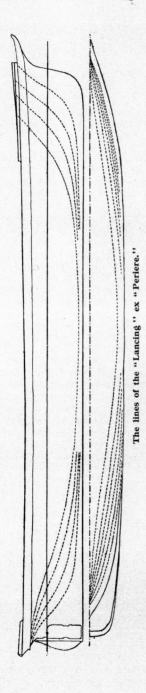

The lines of the "Lancing" ex "Periere."

Length, 113 m. overall; breadth, 13 m. 36; depth 11 m. 80. Displacement, 5,600 tons; gross tonnage, 3,200. Their engine was a two-cylinder, mean pressure engine of 3,200 h.p., also built by Napier.

A similar ship, *Saint Laurent*, built by the Chantiers de l'Atlantique, Penhoet, underwent the same modification, but she got a straight stem, instead of the clipper bow. She never was so successful on service as her two sisters.

Periere was launched in November, 1865, followed in December by *Ville de Paris*. Both were very successful ships from the beginning. *Periere's* speed on trials reached 15 knots 3, a very fine speed for her time, and she crossed the Atlantic on her first passage in 9 days 4 hours, at a mean speed of a little more than 13 knots.

She could accommodate 284 first class passengers, 104 second class and 32 third class.

In the year 1873, she got practically new engines by the addition of a third high pressure cylinder placed in front of the two others; the economy of fuel thus obtained reached 26%. At the same time, her external outlook was changed, as she received two funnels instead of the single one she had before.

According to "Mail and Passenger Steamships of the 19th Century," she caught fire in 1881 at Goletta, at the time the only harbour of Tunis, and had to be sunk by a torpedo to avoid trouble for the other ships in harbour. I have no other information to allow me to know exactly if this is correct, and if, having been salved, she was again in commission when she went ashore in 1888, as suggested by Captain Norman P. Forbes, but, in fact, it is in 1888 that she was converted into a sailing ship. The rest of her history is given in the May issue of SHIPS AND SHIP MODELS. She was finally broken up at Genoa in December, 1924 (and not in 1927).

I include a picture showing her as she was in the early days of her life, together with a plan of her hull lines.

Notable Ships, Past and Present

No. V.—THE WHITE STAR "COPTIC" OF 1881

THE White Star *Coptic*, of 1881, was for many years one of the most famous ships on the New Zealand trade, and even in her old age was able to maintain a great name for herself. She and her sister, the *Arabic*, were, like all ships which have been originally laid down for the White Star Line, built by Harland and Wolff, of Belfast, and they have the distinction of being the first two ships of the company to be built of steel, and were so successful that they were closely followed by the *Ionic* of 1883, which was practically a duplicate. They were originally intended to maintain a secondary transatlantic service, with the result that their lines and passenger arrangements were a reduced copy of contemporary mail practice.

That was before the day of twin screws on the Atlantic, although the Hill Line was just making the experiment, and the *Coptic* was a single-screw steamer with a gross tonnage of 4,367 on dimensions 430.2 × 32 × 17.5 depth of hold. At that time, Harland and Wolff's had not yet completed their marine engineering works and were generally going to the Thames establishments for the machinery of their ships, but as the White Star Line's Liverpool connection was so strong they gave the local firms an opportunity, and the *Coptic* was given four cylinder compound engines by J. Jack and Company, of Liverpool, the cylinder diameters being 32″ and 71″ and the stroke 60, giving the ship a speed of 14 knots. Steam was supplied by three boilers, and she was lighted throughout by electricity, a feature which was not then usual in a ship of her size. In addition to good passenger accommodation she had excellent cargo stowage, like all White Star ships being fitted with good deck machinery for a rapid turn round.

She began her career in rather unfortunate circumstances, for on her maiden voyage to New York, in November, 1881, she had her decks swept fore and aft by a huge sea, two hands being washed overboard and the third officer seriously injured. She did quite well on the Atlantic trade, but the working partnership between the White Star and the Shaw-Savill and Albion concern seemed to offer a better opportunity and, in February, 1884, she was withdrawn from it and sent to Belfast to be thoroughly overhauled and fitted with refrigerated space for 750 tons of cargo, her bunkers also being slightly altered to fit in with the very much

Photo by]   **The White Star "Coptic" of 1881**   *[Nautical Photo Agency*

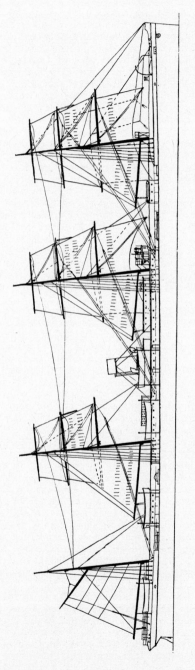

THE "COPTIC" OF 1881—DIMENSIONS OF MASTS AND SPARS

	Fore	Main	Mizen	Jigger
Extreme length from Iron Deck to Truck	109' 6"	110' 4"	102' 6"	90' 3"
Masthead	12'	12'	11'	10' 3"
Lower Yard, Extreme	72'	72'	65'	—
,, Diameter and Arms	16" 3' 0"	16" 3' 0"	14½" 2' 6"	—
Topsail Yard, Extreme	60'	60'	51'	—
,, Diameter and Arms	14½" 2' 6"	14½" 2' 6"	11½" 2' 3"	—
Topgallant Yard, Extreme	44' 6"	44' 6"	39' 0"	—
,, Diameter and Arms	10¼" 1' 9"	10¼" 1' 9"	9" 1' 6"	—
Boom	47'	53'	55'	55'
,, Diameter	12"	13¾"	13¾"	13¾"
Gaff Extreme	—	—	—	37' End 6'
,, Diameter	—	—	—	9¾"

longer voyage to New Zealand that
was contemplated. The work was
pushed forward rapidly and, on May
28th, 1884, she left Plymouth for
Hobart and Otago on her maiden
voyage in her new service.

From the first she was a success on
the New Zealand and Tasmanian
service, particularly when she was
under the command of Captain R. E.
Bence, one of the best-known of the
junior masters in the White Star
Company, who had attained great
fame when chief officer of the *Germanic*
by his gallant rescue of the crew of
the steamer *Hurworth* in mid-Atlantic.
He, unfortunately, died on board
during her twelfth New Zealand
voyage in 1887, and soon afterwards
her luck began to change. One or
two minor mishaps culminated in
October, 1889, by her grounding on
Main Island, soon after leaving Rio
for Plymouth on her homeward voyage,
when carrying a valuable cargo and
35 passengers. She slid off into deep
water, and although there was 24′
of water in her forward compartments,
her stout construction saved her, and she
limped back to Rio for repairs. They
were soon completed and she returned
to the New Zealand run until 1894.

During this period, it may be mentioned, there is a strong tradition in
the Company that it was on
board the *Coptic* that Kipling found
the inspiration for his well-known
" MacAndrews' Hymn."

In 1894, the New Zealand tonnage
having been steadily improved, it
was decided to take the old *Coptic* off
the run, and when she finished her
passage in the Thames she was sent
round to Belfast to have her
passenger accommodation thoroughly
reconstructed and to be given new
engines and boilers. The former consisted of a set of three cylinder triple
expansions with cylinder diameters
28″, 47″ and 78″, the new boilers
supplying the necessary steam pressure
and restoring the ship's speed to its
original 14 knots with a small margin.
These alterations completed, she went
out to Hong Kong early in 1895 and

relieved the famous White Star pioneer
Oceanic, on the service which the
company was running between San
Francisco and the Orient under the
title of the Oriental and Occidental
Line. She ran under this flag until
1906, when the service was dropped
and the *Coptic* and *Ionic* were taken
over by the Pacific Mail Steamship
Company of San Francisco.

American running costs were then
very high and the two ships were
kept under the British flag as owned
by single ship concerns, the *Coptic*
being re-named *Persia* and officially
transferred to the Persia Steamship
Company of London. She was, however, really on the Pacific Mail transpacific service until 1916, when they
were forced out of that business by
the expensive requirements of the
La Follette U.S. Seamen's Act and,
not foreseeing the war boom that
would have made their fortune, no
matter what the crew cost might have
been, they dispersed their fleet.

The *Persia* went to the Toyo Kisen
Kaisha and continued on the transpacific service under the Japanese
flag as the *Persia Maru*. She was
no longer in her first youth, and even
her new engines were beginning to
be very extravagant, but she was a
wonderfully satisfactory investment
for her owners until 1922, by which
time she was outclassed on the direct
transpacific run and was put on to
the East Indian service. In the
summer of 1924 she was laid up at
Yokohama and, in December, 1925,
she was dismantled preparatory to
scrapping, the beautiful fittings which
had been built into her by the White
Star Line attracting considerable attention and being eagerly snapped up by
Japanese buyers, who used the famous
old ship's furniture in hotels, restau-
rants, and the like. She had an
unusually varied career for a first-
class liner, and although, as a rule,
she kept commendably clear of acci-
dents and incidents which would have
made her story more interesting, she
was a wonderful investment for every
company that owned her.

The Downeaster "Olympic"

By JOHN LYMAN

The Downeaster "Olympic"—a "Jackass Barque."

THE four-master *Olympic* was a typical product of an American ship-yard. In hull, she differed little from the other wooden ships built in Maine in the early 'eighties ; the only refinement being that she was designed to sail at sea empty without ballast. She successfully accomplished this feat on several short trips. Her dimensions were 224.4′ × 42.1′ × 21.3′, and she registered 1,402 tons net.

Her rig was the idea of her managing owner, Capt. William H. Besse, of New Bedford, who had owned and sailed the similarly sparred *Hattie C. Besse*. It consisted of square yard on

the fore and main, and gaffs on the other two masts. Upon first coming out, the *Olympic* had double top-gallants and a main skysail yard, but she was soon cut down to single top-gallants and royals. It was under this rig she became best known. Her fore and main masts were 80′ and their topmasts 60′ in length.

She was built to carry spars and ship timber between Puget Sound and the Atlantic, but made only two passages in this trade. Most of her lumber cargoes were taken to ports in the Pacific. She sailed well both with lumber and with nitrate, and her passages were better than average. Her first cargo from Puget Sound went to Boston in 114 days, and her five passages from Atlantic to North Pacific ports averaged 125 days.

On March 17th, 1897, the *Olympic* was sailing up San Francisco Bay, having just arrived from Philadelphia. The stern-wheeler *Sunol* attempted to cross her bows, but misjudging her speed, was run into and carried ahead for several minutes. The passengers and crew of the *Sunol* managed to climb aboard the *Olympic*, but the steamer listed so far over that her safe and boilers fell out and sank. The safe contained a shipment of gold bars from up the Sacramento, but divers eventually recovered it and the boilers.

In July, 1899, a group of San Francisco and Honolulu business men bought the *Olympic* for trade between California and the islands, forming the " Bark *Olympic* Co." They sold her in 1910 to the North Alaska Salmon Co., who used her in connection with their salmon canneries. Thomas

Crowley, of San Francisco, bought her in 1917 for the export lumber trade, and at this time the yards on her mainmast were sent down, making her a four-masted barkentine.

The *Olympic's* last voyage as a sailing vessel was made between September, 1920, and September, 1921, when she went from Eureka, California, to Sydney, then to Callao from Newcastle, N.S.W., and back to San Francisco, where she was laid up. In 1925 the Hermosa Amusement Company bought her and took her to Southern California for use in the production of motion pictures. She is now a fishing barge there.

There has always been an argument as to the exact name for the *Olympic's* rig. Some insist upon the term " jackass bark," while others favour simply " four-masted bark." While I am in no position to settle the discussion, I cannot help liking the name given to it by an old seaman, who upon seeing it for the first time, exclaimed : " It's a schooner chasing a brig ! "

Full-sized Models

By G. W. TRIPP, F.C.G.I., M.I.Mech.E., M.I.C.E.

MANY and varied are the incentives that prompt the construction of a model vessel. Some are built for the sheer joy afforded to the embryo naval constructor, for the delight that comes from fashioning something beautiful from the crudest components, some are destined to be used in tanks for the purpose of determining such things as bow waves, lines of hull, and the like, while the function of others is to advertise the steamship company which owns the large vessel of which the model is a true to scale, if diminutive, representation. Certainly the beautiful miniature steamers which grace the windows of the offices of many steamship lines make an irresistible appeal to the ship-lover and sea-lover to book a passage for a cruise on the vessel which he can readily imagine

full size, and riding majestically on the water.

Models of the sort mentioned can readily be understood, but probably the idea of full-sized models will appear somewhat strange to those who have their own very definite conception of what constitutes a model.

The sort that the writer has in mind is one that is in the nature of an experiment, with the development of a new invention in view, so constructed that basic principles can be determined and the practicability of the design tested under working conditions without incurring too high an initial expenditure.

When Sir Charles Parsons had satisfied the marine mind that his steam turbine had yielded very encouraging results in his experimental launch *Turbinia*, the possibility of its appli-

Photo by]   **"King Edward"—The first Passenger Turbine Steamer.**   [*G. W. Tripp*

cation to Atlantic liners was at once mooted. It was, however, wisely determined, in the first place, to construct a steamer of more modest dimensions—indeed, a full-sized model —one which could carry passengers, maintain regular and efficient services, and so test the principle somewhat exhaustively.

Fortunately, an enthusiastic ally was forthcoming in Captain Williamson, who had been for many years actively associated with passenger services on the Firth of Clyde, and designs were prepared for a steamer which was built by the celebrated firm of William Denny and Brothers, Ltd., and, in 1901, *King Edward*, the first passenger turbine steamer, commenced to sail regularly from Glasgow to Inveraray at the head of Loch Fyne. She was a vessel of 550 tons gross, and 250′ long. She became a favourite from the start, so much so that a sister ship 20′ longer, was built the following year. The success of this class of vessel was assured, the principle was adopted for cross-Channel steamers,

Photo by]   **"King George V"—the first high pressure turbine steamer.**   [*G. W. Tripp*

and later, with eminent success for the largest liners. To the old South Eastern and Chatham Railway belonged the credit of placing on service the first turbine cross-Channel steamer *Queen,* and the first liner was *Virginian* of the Allan Line, which has since been absorbed by the Canadian Paciffc Line.

Before the liners that were destined to win the blue riband of the Atlantic for Britain and hold it for over 20 years, the *Lusitania* and the *Mauritania,* were constructed, it was deemed expedient to make some experiments on large-sized model turbines. It is interesting to record that when these engines had fulfilled their original purpose, they became the driving force of the well-known Clyde steamer *Atalanta,* belonging to the Glasgow and South Western Railway, a vessel that is still sailing on the romantic waters that wash the shores of the Isle of Arran, but now, of course, flying the flag of the L.M. and S.R. Perhaps, therefore, we may justifiably look upon the *Atalanta* as a model steamer.

But of the full-sized model none can be considered of greater interest than the *King George V,* again ostensibly built for excursion services on the Clyde, but her primary function was to determine in a comparatively small, but none the less practical manner, whether the principle of high pressure boilers could be satisfactorily applied to steamships.

Whereas a fair boiler pressure for turbine steamers had been considered to be about 200 lb. per sq. in., the Yarrow boilers installed in the *King George V* were designed for a pressure of 550 lb., a wonderful innovation, although of course more common in land practice. Many other problems attended the experiment, as for example, the high temperature of the steam, 750° F., necessitated special metal for the turbine blades, this being found in Monel metal. Again special attention had to be given to the steam pipes, and they were made of solid-drawn steel tube, tested to three times the working pressure, and care has been

taken to have them efficiently lagged to minimise heat losses. Even a casual glance would convince the passenger that here is no ordinary ship, for the number of indicators that are provided for a variety of different purposes clearly suggest the experimental nature of the craft. In view of the fact that no passenger services are maintained during the winter months by this particular line, the whole of the winter season is available for trial runs when required, and much valuable information has been obtained from this smart little model, whose performances have been watched with the keenest interest by distinguished engineers and naval architects, all unknown to the thousands of holiday-makers who have sounded the praises of the spacious shelter decks with their large glass windows.

Incidentally, the lower Clyde is a noted locality for testing out a steamer, and its fleet of pleasure steamers is an unrivalled one. Even now, the once popular and highly efficient paddle steamer still holds her own, and the new steamer *Jeanie Deans* is perhaps the last word in this class of vessel.

Two Bottle Ships
from Captain A. F. A. Howe's Collection

WE are permitted to reproduce photographs of these two exceptionally good specimens, one a French sailing-ship and the other a British steamer. The former was made in Dunkerque during the Great War, and represents a four-masted barque under sail. The model is 8″ overall, is named the *Ada,* but whether she is a miniature of an actual ship the owner does not know. The set of the sails, with a fair wind, is remarkably realistic, and all the details are good, e.g., the four boats carried on the deckhouses have painted reproductions of their canvas covers. The other vessel, which is 6″ long, is a perfect little model of the *Star of New*

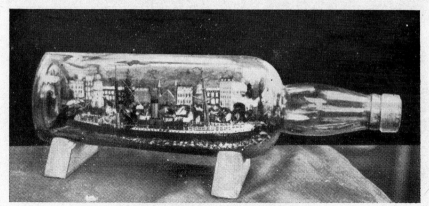

" The Star of New Zealand,"

Zealand, a steel screw steamer, brigantine rigged, built in 1895 by Workman,
Clarke and Co., of Belfast, for J. P.
Corry and Co., (Star Line), of London
and Belfast. Her gross tonnage was
4,840, and her dimensions 393.5′ ×
46.8′ × 28′. In December 1915, she ran
aground close to Molene, near Ushant,
and became a total loss. The owner
of the model takes this opportunity
of thanking Mr. F. C. Bowen the
Honorary Secretary of the Shiplovers'
Association, for kindly furnishing these
particulars of her. She is here shown
entering a Mediterranean port, and
in the background may be seen a
dozen typically French buildings,
together with a lighthouse, wind-
mill, flagstaff and palm trees.
These are not painted on the glass,
but are made separately, appropriately
coloured, and most naturally arranged
on a rocky bluff. The ship has
Corry's house-flag at the main and
Tyser's at the fore (these two firms
amalgamated). The maker of this
beautiful specimen is not known, but
his must have been a labour of love,
and one can conjecture the time he
spent upon it. The photographs of
these very difficult subjects (which are
the owner's copyright) reflect great
credit upon the Keystone View Company, who took them.

A four masted barque under sail.

An Artist in Restoration

THE WORK OF MR. THOMAS R. BEAUFORT, F.R.S.A.

By "MAIN ROYAL"

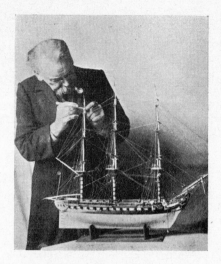

Mr. Beaufort at work

THE restoration of a model or a work of art requires something more than good craftsmanship. The restorer himself must be an artist, keenly sympathetic with his subject, and thoroughly versed in the period and the style of the work he is restoring. Such an artist is Mr. Thomas Richard Beaufort, so well known in the ship-loving world for his perfect restoration of numberless valuable models.

Like many artists, Mr. Beaufort is enthusiastic about his work, but very reticent about himself. It is only because he has a very kindly regard for SHIPS AND SHIP MODELS that I was able to persuade him to tell me a little of his personal history. Over a friendly pipe, he actually told me a great deal, but his cautionary interjection, " You mustn't put that in," occurred so frequently, that I am restricted to some facts which are few but solid. Not that Mr. Beaufort had any alarming confessions to make; when I pleaded the natural interest of my readers, he merely remarked, " But they don't want to know about *me*."

He started life as a pupil to an architect and surveyor, and subsequently filled some important posts as secretary and librarian to several prominent people in the artistic and theatrical world. But, always a student and a craftsman, a time came when he had so many requests for his personal skill as a restorer of works of art that he had to devote his whole time to executing these commissions. His artistic restoration has not been limited to ship models ; he has made picture restoration a special study, and has even exercised his skill on stained glass windows and heraldry. When not busy in his workshop, he sometimes writes. He

A French Prisoner-of-war Model before restoration

French Prisoner-of-war Model as restored by Mr. Beaufort

has written an authoritative volume on " Pictures and How to Clean Them," and has contributed numerous articles of historical value to the *Times*, the *Graphic*, and other important journals. Some-times, as our readers know, he sends a valued item to SHIPS AND SHIP MODELS.

I asked him which, out of his many interests, pleased him most. " Ship models," he replied, as he handed me a bunch of photographs of beautiful period models which had passed through his hands. " Yesterday," he said, " I worked 14 hours on a model. I frequently work 16 hours in a day, and I could not do that if I did not love the work." " And what do you do when you want a change from ship-modelling ? " I asked. " I get out my microscope," said this wonderful man.

Mr. Beaufort works only on sailing ship models, and has a special preference for restoring and re-rigging dockyard and French prisoner-of-war models. There is probably no greater authority on the prisoner-of-war model, and he related several interesting experiences of both " fake " and genuine models which had come to his notice. I asked him at which period in marine history model making was at its zenith. He expressed the opinion that the dock-yard model of about 1745 represented as high a standard of craftsmanship as any. " There is too much paint and varnish on the modern model," he added ; " I like to see the actual workmanship." Even in workman-ship, as in handwriting, there is individual character, and Mr. Beaufort said he was frequently able to identify the source of a particular model by his recognition of the tool-marks or other signs of the individual craftsman.

A beautifully made model of a brass carronade, which Mr. Beaufort handed to me, showed him to be as much at home in metal working as he is in other materials. In his well-equipped workshop, he can, in fact, produce anything in wood, or bone, or ivory, or metal, as occasion requires. Indeed, the complete restoration of a model, with only a derelict hull as a starting point, requires all-round craftsmanship, and in some of the period models the internal mechanism for moving the guns in and out is quite a complicated affair.

Ship-model restoration has occupied most of Mr. Beaufort's time for the past 20 years. He has many friends and many clients, both privately and in business. He is very punctilious about not confusing the two. " It is only by my regard for business etiquette," he said, " that I keep my business friends. I restore many models for customers with whom I do not come into personal contact, and I do not seek to discover them. My only interest is to execute a com-mission to my client's satisfaction, and I may say, to my own satisfaction also, for every piece of work I do is a pleasure to myself and must be done as well as I know how."

Mr. Beaufort is a member of the Shiplovers' Association and of the Society for Nautical Research and a Fellow of the Royal Society of Arts. I am glad to be able to illustrate a little of his work. Our supplement plate this month shows a splendid example of the French prisoner-of-war model, restored by him ; this model is unusually interesting because it is complete with sails, a characteristic generally absent in models of this nature. My other two pictures show another prisoner-of-war model in two stages. The first view shows the hull as handed to Mr. Beaufort ; the second shows the model as he rigged and restored it. Perhaps better than anything I can say, these pictures illustrate the delicacy, the accuracy, and the completeness of Mr. Beaufort's art. The hundreds of models he has restored are now treasured in public and private collections the world over, as masterpieces of historically valuable craftsmanship.

You Can Help Us

BY making SHIPS AND SHIP MODELS known to your ship loving friends.

By sending a photograph and a story about any ship you know.

By sending a photograph and a description of any model ship, steam or sail, which you have built.

By sending short practical hints and tips on ship modelling from your own experience.

By using our correspondence columns for discussing ship and ship-modelling matters of interest.

By ordering SHIPS AND SHIP MODELS to be supplied to you regularly by your newsagent.

15th and 16th Century Blocks

By SAM SVENSSON (Stockholm)

A   B   C   D

WHEN dredging the harbour of Ystad, Sweden, a few years ago, an old block, believed to be from the 15th Century, was found in the mud and slime brought up. This block (see A) was 8″ long and about 3½″ in diameter, and was circular in shape, having possibly been turned on a lathe. Through the collar-shaped top two holes, about ⅞″ in diameter, were drilled obliquely towards each other and, coming out below the collar, they continued as a groove around the shell to take the strop. The sheave was made of oak, 3″ in diameter, and had originally been about 1¼″ thick. The pin was also of wood, rather heavy and conical, 1¼″ and ¾″ each end respectively. The shell and the pin was of a close-grained wood, possibly grained birch.

When excavating for a new bridge over the Ridderholm Canal at Stockholm, in 1930, a small clincher-built warship was found embedded in the muddy ground, which later was proved to have sunk between the years 1450 and 1523. In the ship was found about 20 blocks of different types. Some were of the type described above, and others were as shown in the sketches. B was a larger block, possibly a jearblock, with the top slanting off to one side (or rotted away) and with a groove to take the strop.

C was of a long square pattern, with a hole in the top to take the strop, and another hole in the lower end, possibly to take the standing part of the fall. D was like C, but smaller and narrower, with the hole at the bottom at right angles to the hole at the top, and with the sheave slightly projecting from the sides of the shell. None of these blocks were built blocks; they were all cut from a solid block of wood.

Launch of L.M.S. Railway's New Clyde Steamer

THE Duchess of Hamilton performed the ceremony of launching a new steamer named after her— the T.S. *Duchess of Hamilton*, to be employed by the L.M.S. Railway on Firth of Clyde cruises—which was launched on Thursday, May 5th, from the shipyard of Messrs. Harland and Wolff, Govan.

The general design of the steamer is on similar lines to the *Duchess of Montrose*, launched in 1930, which has proved to be extremely popular with Clyde and Ayrshire Coast excursionists. She will be driven by triple-screw turbines and has a length of 260′.

The *Duchess of Hamilton* will take the place of the paddle-steamer *Juno* which has run on the Clyde services for a number of years.

The Ship's Mail

Readers are invited to make use of this column for the discussion of matters of mutual interest and the exchange of ideas and information.

H.M.S. '' Juno ''

DEAR SIR,—A few months ago some correspondence appeared in your columns concerning a model frigate copied from a model which was formerly in the Science Museum, and which was alleged to represent H.M.S. *Juno*, of 1757. This model, it will be recalled, turned out to be spurious.

A model of a frigate on the launching ways in the Science Museum has now been definitely identified as the *Juno*, and is described in the official catalogue as follows :—

" This model represents one of the 32-gun frigates, first introduced in the year 1757. Previously, the largest vessels to carry their main armament on a single gun-deck had been the sixth rates of 20 and later of 24 guns. These sixth-rates had been built and designed essentially as two-deckers, although none of them ever carried more than six guns on the lower gun-deck, and the model shows the continuation of this usage, inasmuch as, although the oar-ports have been raised to the upper deck, the hawse-holes still open on to the lower deck, where the cables are worked. . . .

" The dimensions of 32-gun frigates differed only slightly from one another, nor was there any marked increase in size during some 30 years, and as a result the exact identification of the vessel represented is difficult. The figurehead of a goddess with peacocks at her feet, however, renders the name *Juno* highly probable, and with this identification the dimensions of the model agree with reasonable accuracy.

" The model, which once belonged to Mr. T. Ditchburn (1801-70), a well-known naval architect, was long known as the *Cleopatra* of 1779, but although the dimensions agree closely with those of that ship, no 32-gun frigate of that date was built with a square beakhead bulkhead, while such identification receives no support from the figurehead."

Yours faithfully,

Bristol.   A. GUY VERCOE.

The Dutch Naval Steamer '' Curacao ''

DEAR SIR,—With reference to the interesting account of the *Royal William* in your March number, can any reader speak authoritatively on the performance of the Dutch naval steamer *Curacao* and its claims to be the first steamship to cross the Atlantic Ocean ? This vessel, which was certainly fitted with engines, as can be seen in a contemporary aquatint, performed the trip from Rotterdam to Dutch Guiana and back in 1827, taking about 29 days each way, which seems to suggest a considerable use of steam. She therefore antedated the *Royal William* by nearly four years.

Do the logs of her various trips to the Dutch West Indies still exist, or failing these, are there any contemporary printed newspaper accounts which might supply information as to the extent to which the *Curacao* made use of steam ?

Yours truly,

L. McCORMICK-GOODHART.

Washington D.C.

Bone Models

DEAR SIR,—It is fairly well known that a large number of bone models of line-of-battleships, frigates, etc., of the Napoleonic period were the work of the French prisoners of war, excepting, of course, where copies of them have been made by modern craftsmen. How comes it, then, that so many of these models are given the names of British ships of the period, when they are obviously French in almost every detail ? They certainly are not correct models of the ships they are named after. For instance, there are bone models of the *Prince of Wales*, the *Royal Sovereign* and the *Foudroyant* (the latter launched at Plymouth in 1798) that neither Calder, Collingwood, or Nelson would recognise as the ships they sailed in.

The explanation is : the models were sold by the French prisoners of war (often for trifling sums of money) to British officers and seamen, who named them after the ships in which they themselves had served, the general outline of the model being near enough.

Those that have their original rigging intact, which in many cases would be over 120 years old, are more or less reliable from a rigging point of view—the work having been performed by French seamen—but so many of them have fallen into decay and have been re-rigged as Victorian sailing ships, or simply dressed with a smother of meaningless gear " to make them look pretty."

The hulls, of course, are not made to scale, and many are profusely decorated with carving on the bone, which is beautiful to look at, but not exactly what would appear on the real ship. For example, elaborately-carved balustrades may often be seen on these models, round the opening at the waist where the boats would be swung in and out from the skid beams (hardly a suitable place for carved balustrades) and, again, carved bone drapery, hanging in festoons between the gangways and the main gun-deck, is very much in evidence on many of them—beautiful work, but not realistic.

The value of genuine French-prisoner bone models (and they are reliable) lies in their antiquity, the beauty of their carving, and the original rigging of those that still possess it ; otherwise they must not be taken too seriously as correct reproduction in miniature of the ships they are intended to represent.

London, W.1.   A. J. BROWN

Steamers of 1878

DEAR SIR,—I wonder if any of your readers remember the old *Mileta*. She was a paddle boat with engines of the oscillating cylinder type, and, as such, I should imagine, one of the last steamers of that kind afloat. She had one funnel, painted white with black top, and one mast forward. So far as I can remember, she had no main mast. The hull was painted black with white squares, which gave her the appearance of an early steam warship. During the first decade of this century she used to ply between Ramsgate and Dover, calling at Deal, weather permitting, to pick up and set down passengers. She used to make the passage once each way daily throughout the summer, and she was owned, I believe, by the then South Eastern and Chatham Railway Company.

No doubt there are some of your readers who will call her to mind, and I should be much obliged if anyone can inform me who her builders were and the year in which she was launched, and also what eventually became of her. Did she survive the ship-breaker's yard to perish in the war ?

     Yours faithfully,
Barnham.   ANDREW HAMMOND.

Steamers of 1878

DEAR SIR,—With reference to the letters of " W.J.T." and " Tyneside," *re* s.s. *Carbon* and *Black Boy*, according to my records of 1885, there was an iron screw steamer named *Carbon*, built in 1855, at Liverpool. Her dimensions were as follows : 194′ 7″ long, 27′ 6″ beam, and 19′ 1″ depth, 714 gross tonnage, and engines of 90 n.h.p. In 1885 she was then owned by G. Headley, Newcastle.

The *Black Boy* was also an iron screw steamer, built at Yarrow in 1854. Her dimensions were : 166′ 2″ × 26′ 7″ × 15′ 7″, gross tonnage 504, and engines of 70 n.h.p. Owned by N. Wood, Durham, in 1885.

S.s. *Sir Robert Peel*, an iron screw steamer, built in 1846 at Blackwall.

Length 131′ 3″, beam 23′ 4″, depth 11′ 9″, 265 gross tonnage, and engines of 40 n.h.p. Owner, E. F. Carey, London.

The *Eclair* was built at Port Glasgow in 1865, being registered at London in 1877, then owned by the River Thames Steam Boat Co. She was 179′ 8″ long, 20′ 2″ beam and 8′ 5″ deep, gross tonnage 237, and engines of 120 n.h.p.

The well-known *Glen Rosa* had a very interesting history, which the following records show. Built in 1877 by Caird and Co., Greenock, for working on the Clyde, her owners being Shearer Bros., of Greenock. In 1882 she came to the Thames and was owned by the Thames and Channel Steamship Co. In 1883 her owners were the London Steamboat Company. In 1885 by the River Thames Steamboat Company. In 1889 by the Victoria Steamboat Association. In 1897 she left the Thames for Bristol, having been purchased by A. Campbell, later the well-known firm of P. and A. Campbell, Ltd. In 1920 she was purchased by Pugsley and Co., and broken up. Her length was 206′ 1″, beam 20′ 1″, depth 7′ 5″. She had a single cylinder engine, the cylinder being 50″ × 72″, n.h.p. 163. New engine in 1887 and a new boiler in 1891.   Yours truly,

Lewes.   F. BURTT.

The '' Calais-Douvres ''

DEAR SIR,—In reply to '' Clydesider,'' the *Calais-Douvres*, referred to in the article '' Freak Channel Packets of the Late 'Seventies,'' was not the vessel of the same name that ended her career as *Mona III* of the Isle-of-Man Steam Packet Company. The latter was built in 1889 by the Fairfield Company, Glasgow, and had a gross tonnage of 1,212. She was acquired from the London Chatham and Dover Railway Company in 1902 by Liverpool and Douglas Steamers, Ltd., and in the following year was purchased by the I.O.M.S.P. Co., Ltd. She continued in service until 1909, when she was broken up.

The *Westonia* ex *Rhos Colwyn* ex *Sussex Belle* ex *Tantallon Castle*, built in 1899 by J. Scott and Co., Kinghorn, was sold to Portuguese owners by the Barry Railway Co., in 1913, and was re-named *Tintern*, and later, *Alentejo*. She disappeared from the 1928-29 Register.

Yours truly,
          E. P. HARNACK.

We thank other correspondents who have kindly replied with similar details.—ED. S. and S. M.

The First Iron Collier

DEAR SIR,—In the May issue of your magazine I saw that the *John Bowes* was again mentioned as the first iron collier. I thought that the enclosed extract from the *Newcatle Evening Chronicle* might be of some interest, as it would appear that there was an earlier iron collier than the *John Bowes*.

This is the first time I have seen the claim of this ship challenged, but there has been no further correspondence on the matter, and I am sending it to you for what it is worth. As the *Q.E.D.* was wrecked soon afterwards, she has no doubt been forgotten. Still, 80 years is a pretty long life for a ship, and a pioneer one at that, probably embodying many new ideas in her building.

Yours truly,
Gateshead.   J. GORDON ROBSON.

Extract from '' Evening Chronicle ''

'' In ' A.S.R.'s ' interesting article in the *Evening Chronicle* of April 19th, with references to ' Palmer's, of Jarrow,' credit is given to that firm for having built the first steam collier in 1852. This is quite a general impression, and has often been repeated, but it is on record that Mr. John Coutts, of Aberdeen, who established the first iron shipbuilding yard on the river at Low Walker in 1840, built a vessel to carry coals from Newcastle to London, propelled by a high pressure engine of 20 h.p. She was the first screw collier ever built, and was fitted with a double bottom for water ballast.

" This vessel was named the *Q.E.D.*, was 150′ long and 27′ 6″ wide, and carried 340 tons on a mean draft of 11′. She was barque rigged, and the mizzen lower mast was of iron and formed the funnel. The propelling machinery was constructed by Messrs. R. and W. Hawthorn, of Forth Banks.

" The vessel was launched on St. Swithen's Day, 1844, and sailed for London in September. She was soon afterwards wrecked at the mouth of the Seine, otherwise she might have played an even more important part in history. She thus preceded by eight years the larger and more famous *John Bowes*, which is generally regarded as the pioneer screw collier."
—ROBERT SLOAN.

(The essay Mr. R. Sloan quotes from, specifically mentioned the *John Bowes* as " the first screw collier to run in the London trade," and not the first built anywhere. The article in the current issue of *The Navy*, actually speaks of the *Bedlington* as " the first iron collier," but no date of this vessel's launching is given. This latter vessel seemingly plied between the Tyne and Blyth.—A.S.R.)

Bending a Cable to an Anchor

DEAR SIR,—May I offer my congratulations on SHIPS AND SHIP MODELS, of which I have been a reader since No. 1. I find it of great interest, and it embraces many subjects of interest to any ship lover. I should like to mention that, in the Ship Modellers' Scrap Book of the October issue, there is a diagram and explanation of a Bentinck boom.

I once sailed in a brigantine so rigged, and have only seen one other vessel fitted with one ; she was a Scandinavian, also a brigantine. I was very interested to see it in print, as I have found very few shipmates since who knew that rig.

What really moved me to write to you is the discussion in the April number " Ship's Mail " regarding

Bending a Cable to an Anchor. The sketch shows a cable bent on by a fisherman's bend, a half-hitch and the ends seized back. This method is generally used when bending a hawser to a kedge anchor for temporary use (often without the half-hitch).

The other method, illustrated in the January Ship Modellers' Scrap Book, is known as a clench (either an inside or an outside clench). It is not quite clear, though the only difference between the two is that the end is seized on top of the round turn in the outside clench, and underneath in the inside.

This was the method used to bend a hemp cable to a bower anchor, as stated in January's issue.

My authority for this is the H.M.S. *Victory* who, now she has been reconditioned, has hemp cables bent with a clench.

Clenches were also used in vessels I have sailed in, as follows : Inside clenches for making halliards fast to jib-headed sails having single halliards such as flying jib, main topmast, stay sail, etc. ; outside clenches for making fast bunt lines and back lines to foot and back of sail respectively.

Trusting this may be of interest, and wishing your Magazine all the success it deserves.

Yours sincerely,
Swanage. E. G. HARDY.

The Oldest Vessels Afloat

DEAR SIR,—A few days ago a Danish three-masted schooner, built of oak, 212 R.T.N., called at this port. As I am a lover of sail and, as the sight of a wooden sailing vessel is not often met with nowadays, I decided to have a look at her.

So, yesterday, I went to the docks and was soon at the quayside where the *Cornwall* was unloading barley. I jumped on board. I was happy to be on the deck of an old wind-jammer once more. Then I went aft and called on the master. His welcome was simple, but sincere, and as soon as I had told him of my admiration for the sailing ship, we were friends at once. In his tiny cabin we spoke of ships, of the big ships that sailed the seven seas, of the ill-fated *Koben-havn*, and of the smaller but equally fascinating coasters, schooners, bar-quentines, etc.

Then the talk drifted to the age of some of the wooden ships still afloat. At the mention of the old vessels still afloat, my mind went back to SHIPS AND SHIP MODELS, and to the articles I read therein about the oldest British vessel, the *Good Intent*. I mentioned her to the captain. " I can beat that," he replied, with a smile. " A few weeks ago I saw the old *De Wende Brodre* of Marstal. She is called the *Ida* at the present day, but was built some 146 years ago in the good year 1786. She's what we Danes call a *Jagtgalease*. Her tonnage is 75 R.T.N. and she is owned by Mr. C. F. O. Larsen, of Thuro. Oh yes, she is still doing good service."

Another old one mentioned by the captain is the *Anna* ex *De fire Brodre*, a yacht built of oak, at the same port of Marstal, in 1794. Actually, she belongs to Mr. J. Fano, of Vejle, Denmark, and her tonnage is 14 R.T.N. or 20 T.D.W.

This seems to confirm Capt. Dirk Verwey's statement in the January number of SHIPS AND SHIP MODELS concerning some very old wooden Danish vessels.

I hope the above information will be of interest to those connected with shipping and especially to your readers.

Yours faithfully,
F. H. VAN DEN BROECK.
Brasschaet, Antwerp.

Technical Terms

DEAR SIR,—May I suggest the following for The Ship's Mail in one of your next issues :—

(1) There appears to be a printing error in the letter from Mr. D. Verwey, in as much as the correct Dutch word for angle iron is hoekijzer and *not* hockyzer, as given. However, this is a general name for all kinds of angle irons, hoek meaning angle and ijzer, iron. The correct English name for the angle bar, to which he refers

(anchor line) would be (hatch-) coam-ing angle bar, and, in German, lukensullwinkel. However, " anker," in German, means likewise " stay " ; for instance, in a boiler or in machin-ery, and it is not impossible that the expression " anchor line " has some-thing to do with this fact. In so far as the examples of Dutch sea slang given are concerned, I am not quite sure whether I must agree with Mr. Verwey or not. It seems rather that what he gives are Dutch words of best quality, English and Dutch being both languages of Germanic origin and often not unsimilar. Moreover, in German too, you say, e.g., " hieven " for " heave," and this is by no means slang, but genuine German.

(2) " W.J.T." is mentioning the de-sign of your cover. Curiously enough, the ship-rigged vessel shown in it not only has no cro'jack, which may be understood, but has no spanker either, a fact much more difficult to be explained.

(3) On page 254 you are speaking about clew lines and clew garnets. I have followed up the question and found that, exceedingly seldom, if at all, they are mentioned in literature. However, it would appear that not only the upper topsails, but likewise the upper topgallant sails, in vessels with double topgallant sails, are having *no* clew lines. You state, further, that " until comparatively recently, they always led up to the slings of the yard." Is it not rather that the clew lines were led to a point about two-fifths of the half-yard length from the mast, as shown in your illustration for the lower topsail? About what year did the change take place ?

(4) House-flags of Shipping Com-panies. Before the war there was an Italian shipping company—I cannot remember its name—called by the sailors in the Mediterranean " the U-Line," because of the resemblance of its house flag with an international U. As a matter of fact, it was an inverted U. Very faithfully yours,

Dr.-Ing. WLADIMIR V. MENDL,
Bucharest. A.M.I.N.A.

The " Glen Morag " Figurehead

DEAR SIR,—Noting several articles concerning figure-heads, I thought you, and possibly yours readers, might be interested in the enclosed photograph of the figure-head of an old British ship—the *Glen Morag*—wrecked about 20 miles north of the entrance to the Columbia River, opposite the town of Ocean Park,

**The "Glen Morag" Figurehead in
Morehead Park**

Washington, March 19th, 1896. She came ashore on the sandy beach on an even keel, and for many months remained upright with most of her sails set. As a boy, I have fished, at high tide, from her bow. When the hulk was broken up, the figure-head was saved, and is now in a park a few miles from the scene of the wreck.

I enjoy your magazine very much and find the articles instructive and interesting.

Yours sincerely,
Portland, Oregon. LOUIS M. DILLON.

Electric Propulsion for Models

DEAR SIR,—I have great faith in electric propulsion for scale models, and I consider that the poor opinion which many people hold about the use of it, is due to the fact that only a very small and scattered band of enthusiasts have devoted any intelligent thought to its development. My own ideas on the subject are as yet in their infancy, but nevertheless, the record speed of my *Viking Maid* stands at 3.3 knots (3.9 m.p.h.), and her longest total running in one day is 1½ hours. My smaller vessel, *Lady Margaret*, is a tiny tramp of only *four* pounds displacement, yet her electric machinery has driven her at 2.2 knots, and she carried off a steering event at Ilford Regatta. She has also circumnavigated the Round Pond, taking only 40% longer time than the 90-lb. boats in the club. The biggest difficulty seems to be to obtain accumulators whose design even approximates to my idea of what boat accumulators should be.

I agree with Mr. T. R. Thomas's statement in " Elements of Model Steamer Design," some issues back, that twin-screws are worse than awful for steering competition work.

My experiences with *Viking Maid* convince me that the worst feature by far is, that as the ship takes on only a small list, say to Starboard, the port screw runs slightly less deep than it's fellow, and round she comes to port or *vice versa*. I am trying partly to obviate these troubles by means of a device automatically to swing the rudder as the ship heels. It is, however, possible by the exercise of a little seamanship to keep the vessel out of collisions, and also to cause her to return from the point from whence she started, steering a zig-zag course according to the wind. This manoeuvre greatly mystifies the crowd and can be likened unto dodging torpedoes.

There are two points on which I would argue with Mr. Thomas. Firstly, my vessel has a great deal of top hamper for her weight, and yet she is perfectly stable and safe, even in a gale of wind. I think that far more depends on the general design and weight distribution than on the actual expanse of wind-catching surfaces. It is also a definite advantage on such a large lake as the Round Pond, to possess a ship which in the event of weed trouble is rapidly blown inshore. Secondly, as I have always made channel-type steamers the first favourites among my many loves, I have yet to learn the name of any such vessel which is credited with a pace of 30 knots. I mean as a genuine maximum, not running shallow, with a half gale and a three-knot tide to help her. I think it must be admitted that Mr. Thomas is at least four knots out here, and four knots at such speeds is *some* difference.

Yours truly
Romford.   C. OLDHAM.

Fairfield Paddle Steamers

DEAR SIR,—With reference to the correspondence regarding the P.S.S. *Koh-i-Noor, Royal Sovereign* and *La Marguerite*, Mr. T. G. Brew, of the North Wales Steamship Co., Ltd., has very kindly supplied me with the following information given by Mr. J. L. Wilson, London Registrar for the Fairfield Shipbuilding and Engineering Co., Ltd.

Yours faithfully,
                        D. A. ALLAN,
City of Liverpool   Director.
Free Public Museums.

Mr. J. L. Wilson's letter is as follows :

P.S. *Koh-i-Noor* was ordered by the Victoria Steamboat Association, Ltd., in the Autumn of 1891, and was placed on their London, Clacton and Harwich service in 1892.

" P.S. *Royal Sovereign* was ordered for the London and East Coast Express Steamship Service, Ltd., in the Autumn of 1892, and was placed on the London, Margate and Ramsgate service in 1893.

" P.S. *La Marguerite* was ordered for the Palace Steamers, Ltd., in 1893, and was placed on the London, Margate and Boulogne service in 1894.

" The above three vessels were all built by the Fairfield Shipbuilding and Engineering Co., Ltd., and were all run, in the first instance, under the same management as the Victoria Steamboat Association, Ltd., but were owned by separate companies.

" In April, 1895, the New Palace Steamers, Ltd., was incorporated, and, under its management, the three vessels above mentioned ran for many years in the Thames pleasure service, the owners being the Fairfield Company."

The P.S. "Westonia"

A CORRESPONDENT inquires, in the May issue, regarding the paddler *Westonia*. Built as *Tantallon Castle* in 1899 by J. Scott and Co., Kinghorn, for Galloway Saloon Steam Packet Company, this steamer had a varied career. After running some time on the Firth of Forth, she came south as *Sussex Belle*, later becoming *Rhos Colwyn*. In 1907 she was purchased by the Barry Railway Company and re-named *Westonia*; in 1910, she was owned by Bristol Channel Passenger Boats, Ltd. ; in December, 1911, she was acquired by P. and A. Campbell, re-named *Tintern*, and sold some years later to buyers in Lisbon. When I saw her in 1900 as *Sussex Belle* on the South Coast, her funnels were, I believe, buff with black tops ; in 1908 she had red funnels with black tops, grey hull and raised fo'castle ; in 1910 her hull was black with a narrow white line above red boot-topping, funnels red but the raised fo'castle had disappeared. Originally built with two funnels and bridge aft, Campbells altered her to one funnel, moved the bridge for'ard, replaced the square windows of the saloon with ports and painted her in their standard colours.

Her dimensions were : Length, 210′ 1 ″, beam 25′ 1″, depth 8′ 4″, quarter deck 18′ and saloon deck 144′ ; tonnage, gross 393, net 97 ; engines, compound 206 N.H.P.—C. HAWKINS GARRINGTON.

The Ship Modellers' Scrap Book

(*Continued from page* 285)

Cunningham's Patents

A patent gear for reefing square sails with the minimum of trouble and labour. Invented by Henry W. B. Cunningham, R.N., and for some years in the middle of the 19th Century adapted by many shipowners anxious

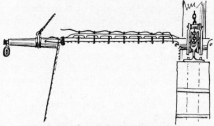

Cunningham's Patent Reefing Gear

to economise in men and a few Queen's ships, but heartily cursed by the man who had to use it. The idea was to make the yard revolve by means of tye chains running down to the deck, hauled from the deck they parbuckled the yard and rolled the sail round it,

Ordinary Boat Davits

thus reefing it. The footropes, etc., were on a small yard, which did not revolve. In the centre of the sail a separate cloth was attached to travellers in order that it might not interfere with the rolling gear.

Davit

A small crane used for various purposes in working a ship, both sail and steam. The best known are the boat davits, which began in a very simple form with wooden beams projecting from the ship's side in whalers and men-of-war at a time when the ordinary means of lowering a boat was by the yardarms. They gradually became more elaborate and efficient, until for many years they were stabilised as curved iron standards (goose-neck) fitted in sockets at the rail of the ship with falls to the boat at the outer end. They were capable of being turned right round in order to swing the boat inboard for safe stowing and outboard for use. Recently, and particularly since the war put a premium on lifeboat work, various patent davits have been introduced into steamers, mostly the big passenger ships, some of which are very elaborate indeed. A quadrant davit is shown.

Deadeye

The disc blocks used for setting up lanyard rigging, invariably used in pairs. The "dead" is because the holes, generally three in number, had no sheaves in them, and were thus called

Modern Quadrant Davit   **Upper and Lower Deadeye**

dead like every other block without a sheave. The similarity of the three holes to a face supplied the rest, the name being sometimes amplified into "monkey face deadeyes." In due course they gave way to the more convenient rigging screws and now are only very occasionally met with in small craft.

(To be continued).

Books to Read

In Great Waters. By CAPTAIN S. G. S. McNEIL, R.N.R. London : Faber and Faber, Ltd. Price 15s. Postage 6d.

It is fast becoming an established custom for merchant service captains to write their reminiscences on retirement. Most sailors, despite their association with the traditional " silence of the sea," can spin a good yarn when their natural reticence has once been penetrated. It is not surprising therefore, that some excellent books have been turned out by them.

From such reminiscences as these, the landsmen can form a clear and impressive idea of the last days of the sailing ship. A very close link is thus established with the days of wooden ships and iron men. Those " bad old days," with their hard discipline, indifferent and scanty food, and unhealthy accommodation, turned out a magnificent breed of seamen, both physically and mentally, which the present system is hard put to it to reproduce. Captain McNeil's remarks on this controversial subject are especially instructive, and his views on the proposed re-establishment of sail training are undeniably sound.

His experiences with passengers and crew make delightful reading and are indeed the best things in the book. During the time he had command of the famous *Mauretania*, a well-known American woman artist was returning to England in the ship. Of her the following amusing incident is related :—

" On my way down to dinner, just three hours after leaving New York, a feminine cyclone in skirts bore down on me, and, arriving alongside, backed her maintopsail right athwart my course and signalled.

" ' Captain, I am a Miss Yoshkowitz, and I do want to paint your picture. I want to paint the Captain of the fastest ship, and I promise that I shall do it in record time.'

" Against my will, I fell. Fortunately, the weather was clear all the passage, but sometimes I felt sorry for the artist, because she was not a good sailor, and sometimes had difficulty in finding the right spot on her canvas owing to the liveliness of the ship. She worked hard and the portrait was finished the day before we arrived in Plymouth. Many people thought it was most lifelike. Confirmation of this may lie in the fact that when the picture was standing unframed in a rather dark corner on a settee in my cabin, the Chief Officer informed me that he had just come from there, having reported to my portrait, thinking he was talking to me."

In the chapters relating to Captain McNeil's war experiences one is sorry to detect an unfortunate note of bitterness. It is fairly common knowledge that in the early days of the war a certain amount of friction existed between the Royal Navy and the Merchant Service. But this was not all the fault of the Senior service as is sometimes too hastily assumed. Allowance must be made for the tendency of certain merchant captains to adopt a tactless and domineering attitude, which contributed in no small degree to make relations unhappy. It is a pity that Captain McNeil should deem it necessary to re-open these old grievances, when every effort has been used by responsible and conscientious officers of both Services to " bury the hatchet."— " CHIPS."

The Kaiser's Coolies. By THEODOR PLIVIER. Translated by WILLIAM F. CLARKE. London : Faber and Faber, Ltd. Price 7s. 6d. net. Postage 6d.

Yet another German War book. This time, however, there is a noted absence of anti-British propaganda. It is pleasing to come across a work which gives the public the impressions of naval activities through the eyes of a German seaman free from exaggerated stories of maltreatment of their prisoners in enemy countries.

" Kaiser's Coolies " deserves a record circulation, because for the first time it exposes the true facts which led to Germany appealing for the armistice. Conditions on the lower deck in the German Navy at the outbreak of the war seem to have been little better than those which were general in the sea service during the 18th Century. Impressed into the service, underfed, and badly clothed, they were officered by veritable nigger-drivers.

In all cases of war, stern discipline and strict censorship are imperative, but these were administered with the most extreme severity. The officers, however, were allowed exceptional freedom. This, combined with an ostentatious display of excess in all things, and an utter disregard of co-operation or good-will with the ratings, was sooner or later bound to end in disaster.—"CHIPS."

The Ship Lovers' Association.

Members' Queries and Answers.

F.S.B. (Bournemouth).—The *Ben Croy* of 1892 was sold to Germany in 1912, renamed *Curt Retzlaff*, and was wrecked in October, 1913, carrying iron ore from Lulea to Stettin. *Armstor* of 1909 was sold to Belgium at the end of 1912 and was posted missing in the following year. *Mistor* of 1906 was sold in 1913 to the Greeks and, as *Ellispontis* was sunk by a German submarine in the North Sea in April, 1915. A similar fate befell the *Hillmere* of 1905, which was sold in 1912 to the Royal Holland Lloyd, renamed *Saaland* and torpedoed by a German submarine in the Channel in January, 1917. *Hillbrook* of 1904 was sold to the Italians in 1912 and, as the *Genova*, was torpedoed by a German submarine in the Mediterranean in July, 1917. *Furtor* of 1904 was sold to Germany in 1913 and re-named *Emil*, but was re-sold back to Britain before the war, renamed *Aquarius*, and sunk in collision in November, 1918.

E.P.H. (London).—The *Rotterdam* was built for Rankine, of Glasgow, in 1896, bought by G. Gibson and Co., of Leith, in 1920, and three years later resold to the Limerick Steamship Co., who renamed her *Cloudananna* two years later, selling her for scrap in 1929. The *Eugenie* of the South Eastern Railway, built in 1862, was soon afterwards sold to P. L. Henderson's and eventually went to the General Steam Navigation Co., who

sold her for scrap in 1890. The *Calvados* of 1878 was originally built for the London Brighton and South Coast Railway, and was sold to London owners in 1911. She was finally lost in the Sea of Marmora in March, 1913. Little's *Duchess of Edinburgh* was originally a South Eastern steamer, built in 1880. She was bought by King, of Garston, for breaking up in 1907.

G.E.P. (Jersey).—The *Honfleur* of 1873 was sold to Greek owners in 1911 and renamed *Chrysalis*. After the Armistice she was bought by the French Government and was later renamed *Fauvette* and *Ahsani*. In 1925 she went under the Turkish flag as *Aibin* and apparently finished her career in 1928.

H.S. (Preston).—The *Tamesis* of 1870, whose numerous previous names include *River Thames*, was sold to Spain in 1925 and renamed *Dimats*. She is still going as the *Antonio Ferrer*, which name she took in 1927.

F.S.B. (Bournemouth).—The Australian coaster *Keilawarra* was rammed by the *Helen Nicoll* on December 8th, 1886, when bound from Sydney to Brisbane. Forty-five lives were lost, including several passengers of the *Helen Nicoll*, who had jumped on board the sinking vessel in the mistaken impression that their own vessel had got the worst of the encounter.

(Only answers of more general interest are printed ; these and others have been sent through the post).

Northern Notes
By "JASON"

A Sixpenny Book

The Handbook and Guide to the Liverpool Shipping Gallery has been published recently, and all those who are interested in ships should obtain one from the Director, Liverpool Museums. It is an astonishing revelation of the immense strides which have been made to make the Liverpool Shipping Gallery worthy of that great seaport. In the first few years of the post-war period there were no ship models worthy enough to be called a collection. To-day that is changed. Among the many scores of models on view there are many which are unique, particularly in modern builder's models. Among others may be mentioned a splendid example of a modern motor tanker, and also one of the famous " Empress " liners. A ten-masted tramp attracts a lot of attention.

Britain's Only Whaleback Steamer

A builder's model of the s.s. *Sagamore* (1893) causes visitors to look twice. At first glance she appears to be a submarine. She has the rounded deck and her hatchways rise up like stunted conning towers. Her decks were awash even in moderate weather, and often vessels rushed to her aid needlessly. Lack of ventilation led to the extinction of her type. She was lost by enemy action in 1917 after 24 years of profitable service. Two 1812 steamers (the first of them) are represented in the *Comet* and the *Elizabeth*. The *Garibaldi* is outstanding. She is a completely rigged snow, and a builder's model, of which there are very few examples in existence. Two valuable contemporary models of 18th Century merchantmen are on view. One is a privateer and the other a whaler.

Merseyside's New Headquarters

The Liverpool Club has now moved to its new headquarters, viz., the Minsterley Cafe, Rumford Street, alongside the Town Hall. As mentioned in this column last month, Merseyside has departed from the workshop clubroom and is concentrating on the social side with a well-equipped library and reference department. The weekly meetings are held on Fridays at 7.30 p.m. The title of the Club has been altered to The Model Ship Club. Secretary : L. F. Holly, 9 Jasmine Street, Liverpool.

The Bosun's Pipe

This is the title of the Manchester Club's new monthly magazine. True, it is only a sheet of foolscap, but the energetic Secretary is using every endeavour to keep Club members " warm " during the summer months. Particulars of various summer outings by the Club members may be obtained on application to the Secretary, W. F. Hemmingway, " Withens," Lake Bank, Littleboro', Manchester.

The Manchester Annual Meeting

Important decisions were made on May 3rd at the first annual meeting of No. 2 Club. They confirmed by actual experience the conclusions of the Liverpool ship modellers that the library should have a prominent place in the Club's activities. They also fell into line with the new name, and the Lancashire and Cheshire Club will now be known as The Model Ship Society No. 2. Commander Craine was given a hearty welcome, and tributes were paid to the officers.

British Coracles

The hopes of tracking down a Devon Coracle have failed. Several Devonshire correspondents have convinced me that there is no such thing as a Devonshire coracle. The blame will have to be placed upon hikers for importing a canvas boat for their convenience in crossing streams. The Cumberland Coracle also has failed to materialise as yet. One well-known writer and lecturer uses a coracle of his own construction. I still believe however, that there is a Cockermouth Coracle. No news has yet been received from Scotland regarding a Highland Coracle. I should be glad to have any news of these.

SHIPS AND SHIP MODELS

A Magazine for all Lovers of Ships and the Sea

Editorial and Publishing Offices :

Single Copies, post free, 7½d.
Annual Subscription 7s. 6d.

66 FARRINGDON STREET
LONDON :: E.C.4

Vol. I. No. 11. JULY, 1932. Price 6d.

The Ship's Log

Our Supplement

THE famous old *Victory* is such an outstanding feature of British naval history that we are sure the plate we give as a supplement this month will be generally appreciated. It has an additional interest to ship modellers as presenting a beautiful example of the high standard of model making craftsmanship which prevailed towards the end of the 18th Century.

* * *

Sail Training

The arrival during the past few weeks of some of the sailing vessels with grain from Australia, and the recent suggestion by the Admiralty that sail training for officers and men of the Royal Navy was being considered, has aroused considerable interest. As a good deal has been written on the subject of sail training for the Merchant Service, we propose to publish, in the next issue, an outline of the system of training which existed in the Navy at the end of the last century. Some of the older readers will remember the picturesque training brigs such as the *Martin*, the *Liberty* and the *Pilot*, to mention only a few, which were to be met with in the Channel, in which midshipmen and boys gained their early knowledge of seamanship. There seems no reason why a similar method could not be adopted to meet the present needs of the Service.

* * *

A Shipowner's Views

Sir Walter Runciman holds very definite views on the value of sail training, and is now actually negotiating, in Denmark, for the purchase, or building, of two three-masted brigantines for this purpose. He says :—
" The sailing vessels we had up to the time of the war were all too large —many of them over 5,000 tons—and I have always maintained that many of these vessels were lost in consequence of the larger part of the crew not being able to handle the sails in heavy weather. They were obviously too large to handle in narrow waters or when on a lee shore. My belief is, that we must come back in some way to the sailing ship system, both on economic and training grounds. We must not go beyond 1,000 tons deadweight. My idea is not to go beyond 550 tons."

Clyde Shiplovers

We are asked to state that all inquiries and correspondence for the Clyde Society of Shiplovers should, in future, be addressed to Mr. R. Macmenemy, 35, Bellwood Street, Glasgow. Membership is not restricted to model makers, but is open to all who are interested in ships and the sea generally. We understand that the Society is making good headway, and that new members will be welcomed.

* * *

What is a " Snow " ?

Some of our readers may be interested in an authentic definition of a "snow." Here it is : " A vessel similar in construction to a brig, but the largest of vessels fitted with two masts. It has a square foresail and mainsail, with a trysail abaft, resembling a mizen of a ship, and hoisted by a gaff upon a small mast, close abaft the main mast, which is called the trysail mast." This is quoted from a very interesting lecture by Mr. Charles Lyon Chandler, given before Princeton University, in February last, and reproduced in full in the Journal of The Franklin Institute, for May, published at Lancaster, Pa., U.S.A. Mr. Chandler's lecture was entitled " Early Shipbuilding on the River Delaware," and it gave a most instructive survey of this section of American shipbuilding of the period 1682-1810.

* * *

An International Marine Encyclopaedia

We hear from Mr. R. de Kerchove, of the Agence Maritime Internationale, 12, Rue Chauveau-Lagarde, Paris, that he is engaged on the preparation of an International Marine Encyclopaedia in four languages—English, French, German, and Spanish. It is intended to give an accurate translation of the terms in the various languages most frequently used by the shipping community; and also, to make clear, by definition, for the benefit of those who are not familiar with some of the highly specialised branches of shipping, the true meaning of each term. The work will be illustrated by line drawings. Mr. de Kerchove says he would like to get into touch with any of our readers who can assist him with information on any doubtful points which arise from time to time in the compilation of the book.

* * *

The First Mersey Steamer

A model recently added to the shipping gallery of the Liverpool Museum represents the *Elizabeth*, the first steamer to enter the River Mersey. She was the second steamer built on the Clyde, and after some service in local waters, voyaged to Liverpool by way of Ramsey. She reached the Mersey on June 28th, 1815, and inaugurated the ferry service between Liverpool and Runcorn, her speed being between 9 and 10 miles an hour. It is rather sad to record that, due to her lack of financial success, she was converted into a horse-operated vessel three years later.

* * *

Ship Models in Tasmania

The Secretary of the Ship Lovers' Society of Tasmania has kindly sent us a cutting from the *Hobart Mercury* describing some of the local shipmodellers and their work. In addition to mention of the late Mr. Thomas Bennison, Captain Joseph Creese, and Captain J. C. Ives, all noted model makers in their day, a good description is given of the *Torridon*, modelled by Mr. Lionel S. Rogers, and his latest piece of work. It is pleasing to find that so much is being done in far-off corners of the world, to preserve the form and the traditions of the famous ships which have played so great a part in the development of our Empire.

* * *

Information Wanted

We wish to thank those readers who kindly furnished information in reply to the queries in our last issue. Here are two more inquiries : (1) Correct colouring and house flags for a model of the clipper ship *Stonehouse* of 1866. (2) Information about the sail called the " Jamie Green," and has it been tried on a sailing model ?

The Ramsgate Sailing Trawlers

By FRANK C. BOWEN

NOTHING on the Kent coast shows up more clearly the great differences wrought during the last few years on the conditions at sea than the state of the Ramsgate fleet of sailing trawlers. When war broke out their numbers were already sadly depleted, but they still made a fine fleet and their brown sails as they left the harbour in scores, made a picture to delight the heart of any artist. Now there are scarcely any of them left on the Kentish coast. Some are working from West Country ports, it is true, but the great majority have gone and will never be replaced, the once prosperous fishing industry of the port being left to a handful of drifters employed more or less successfully as trawlers.

It is a great pity from every point of view, for not only did a very large part of the prosperity of the town and district rest on the trawler fleet, but it

produced a race of sailormen second to none, a race whose members are still appreciated by a hundred shipowners. And to the lover of ships, particularly the old sailing ships, it has meant the death of a particularly interesting type of vessel, small it is true, but pre-eminent in seaworthiness and other qualities.

It must be remembered that Ramsgate was one of the first of the Eastern ports to take to long-distance trawling seriously, and to see the value of the Dogger Bank and the seas round it. But it is only natural that they should borrow to a certain extent from the Western ports where trawling really originated, and successive types have all shown this Western influence.

The Ramsgate smack was therefore strongly akin to that from Brixham, although it varied in minor details. In the early days the fish were brought home in a well-free flooding to the

Photo by]
A Ramsgate Sailing Trawler leaving Port
[Nautical Photo Agency

sea. This system, which is still met with occasionally on the Continent, permitted a proportion of the catch to be brought ashore alive and, still more, to be kept in reasonable condition, but the import of ice from Scandinavia and its consequent cheapening, permitted quantities to be taken to sea and the fish to be brought home roughly preserved in it.

In the early days, also, cutter-rigged smacks were quite usual, but a second mast proved far better for towing the trawl, and by the 'eighties the single-masted vessels were rapidly disappearing. Similarly with the square transom stern which was once quite usual ; latterly, there was not a single one to be found in the fleet. It must be remembered that practically all the smack owners of Ramsgate had been to sea for many years themselves, starting as boys and working up to their command before they began to buy their own smacks. Thus every development of design was carefully thought out in the light of practical experience, and experience in the hardest possible school. That is certainly the reason why the Ramsgate smacks were such magnificent sea boats.

To take them feature by feature, the bow was almost invariably straight with a curved forefoot. In the older boats this curve was comparatively small, but in the last few years before the war there was a tendency to round it far more and to fit a larger rudder. Boats built on these lines proved very much better in a seaway, handled beautifully, and were so handy that they would carry way to sail round and round the " a " while waiting to leave the harbour. Those who remember the sight of a big fleet of smacks leaving Ramsgate Harbour in pre-war days will appreciate the value of this point. There were three well-remembered boats which differed from this practice, the *Vie*, the *Vis* and the *Vic*, whose stems were cut away sharply and which were always known locally as the " snib-bowed boats." The idea was to render the jibs un-

necessary in working, but the boats proved far too light-headed and were not satisfactory for towing the trawl.

In the matter of the stern it was a case for the taste of each individual owner. Some preferred square and some the elliptical stern that was introduced into the port from Lowestoft. There was no difference in strength or seaworthiness, but the square stern was far cheaper to repair if there was an accident. Similarly, the line of the rail depended on the taste of the owner, although they were all given a good sheer forward and spring aft. The Brixham boats all broke to sheer at about the main rigging ; some Ramsgate smacks did, but many did not. When the owner was indifferent on the point, and very few Ramsgate owners were indifferent to the slightest detail that affected their beloved little ships, it depended very much on the district in which they were built. Many of the smacks came from Brixham, others from Galmpton and Rye, while a few hailed from Ramsgate's own shipyard alongside the West Pier.

The change from the single-masted cutter to the two-masted ketch or dandy rig—the word ketch originated in a Hindustani word meaning one and a half—came gradually, for the cutter rig was generally faster and could sail nearer to the wind. But the ketches were undoubtedly the better trawlers, so that before the cutters disappeared altogether they were employed for carrying the catch of many smacks back to the harbour, their smart sailing often permitting a day's market to be saved.

In those days there were plenty of fishermen available, and the supply of the right type of youngster to make smack boys appeared to be steady. Therefore the sail plan was apt to be elaborate. The tall main topmasts of the smacks permitted a big jackyard topsail to be fitted over the mainsail, and a rather smaller one was almost invariably carried on the mizzen. Jib topsails were also carried, but when the shortage of

The Ramsgate Steam Trawler "Wishful"

men began to be felt, the rig was simplified. The jib topsails were abandoned, the main jackyard topsail gave way to a smaller jib-headed topsail of a shorter topmast, while the mizzen topsails went and bigger mizzens were fitted. They thus had a big spread of canvas and, in reasonable weather, could make their markets with the minimum of delay, but they also had to stay out and work in the very worst of weather at all seasons of the year, and therefore particular attention was paid to the reefing. The mainsails and the later big mizzens were fitted with three reefs, using lacing and eyelets instead of points, while the foresail had one reef. A particularly big foresail, called the tow foresail, was carried for trawling and, boomed out, it made a useful spinnaker.

Captain and crew all lived aft in a single cabin, surrounded by five 6′ berths with locker seats under and in front of them. In the older boats the stove and oven were in the cabin, but latterly they were fitted in the engine room, while the later boats were also given the refinement of a table ; formerly all hands eat off the floor.

While the supply lasted, the smacks carried five hands—skipper and mate working on shares and the third hand, " deckie " and cook being apprentices. These apprentices did not share in the catch, but they were given what was known as spending money— in the old days the third hand one shilling a night, the deckie sixpence, and the cook threepence. They also had as a perquisite all small fish, and the less saleable catch which were known as stockerbait and which were sold for the benefit of the juniors of the crew.

It was round about the year 1886 that the steam capstans were introduced, the first coming down from Grimsby and being regarded with a good deal of attention when she reached Ramsgate Harbour. It was realised that they meant a colossal saving in the heavy labour of working the trawl and they soon became popular, firms desiring an improved capstan which became standardised and which, although not as powerful as the first ones, did all the work on half the coal consumption.

Even with this aid, however, the work was terribly hard. Until the middle 'eighties the Ramsgate smacks fished in fleets under proper fleet discipline, and when that was abandoned there was a spell of what was known as partner fishing, when two or three owners would let their smacks fish together and transfer their catch at sea.

When this system was carried out the boats would stay at sea for eight weeks, but when each smack worked on her own and brought her own catch back, seven ways was the usual length of a trip.

In this fleet or partner fishing a premium was put on good boat work, and it is doubtful whether there were any finer small boatmen in Europe than the hands of the sailing trawlers. When they had to transfer the fish in the middle of the North Sea in any weather, everything depended on the way the boat was handled and designed. The smack owners evolved the most suitable and safest type of boat and then felt that they could leave it to their men with confidence.

These notes are necessarily brief, but enough to give some indication of a life and a phase of the fishing industry that has gone for ever. The supply of smack boys began to slack off in the latter part of the 19th Century, and with the general migration towards the towns this slackening became more rapid until the outbreak of war. Yet there are few callings which offered a better chance for the right man to become his own master and to attain material success.

But the life was undoubtedly hard, as it must have been with the work indicated carried on by vessels of very moderate tonnage. This tonnage varied greatly, but latterly 24 tons nett, about 38 tons gross, was the most popular. A nett tonnage of 25 saw the towing charges at Ramsgate doubled, and necessitated captain and mate possessing certificates which comparatively few of them desired to worry about. But they were grand seamen, among the finest in the British Isles.

A Model of Full-rigged Ship "Hilston"

By LAURENCE A. PRITCHARD

THE badly-damaged hull of this model was discovered by the writer some years ago outside a marine store in Southampton.

The model was so damaged, it was at first doubtful if restoration was possible, but the photograph will show what can be done with care and patience.

The hull was obviously a shipbuilder's model, probably made by the builders of the actual ship, Russell and Co. of Port Glasgow, in 1885. It was at one time in a glass case but was not originally rigged.

The restoration has included a new bar keel and stern deadwood, sternpost and rudder, figurehead, new decks throughout, a complete set of fittings, masts, spars, rigging and mahogany stand.

This model is one of the few exceptions where identification was definitely

possible as, fortunately, the ship's name was still quite legible on the topsides at the time I bought her, and by referring to Lloyds' Register, the dimensions were obtained and the scale of $\frac{3}{16}''$ equals $1'$ was determined.

Hilston was an iron full-rigged ship built as before-mentioned, by Russell and Co., in 1885, for Graham and Co., and was of 1,998 tons register, $278.1' \times 40' \times 24.4'$. She was sold to T. Beynon and Co., of Cardiff, who owner her until 1915, when they sold her to J. G. P. Murphy of Mobile (Ala), but she remained under the British Flag and registered in London.

She was sunk by collision off the Chico Bank with the steamer *Fahrwohl* when bound from Buenos Aires to New York in February, 1920.

I am indebted to Mr. Browning Dick, late of Lloyds, for the above particulars.

Mr. L. A. Pritchard's Model of the Full-rigged Ship "Hilston"

Vanished Shipyards

By J. FOSTER PETREE, A.M.I.N.A.

NATIONAL Shipyards Security, Ltd., the company which is dismantling redundant shipyards in the interests of the industry as a whole, has caused some well-known names to disappear from the list of British builders, but nothing they may do is likely to be so drastic as the force of economic circumstances, which has blotted out scores of yards, big and little, during the past century.

Some are by name household words to every student of shipping history, and a great deal of dependable information is available regarding them and the ships they built, although it is sometimes rather widely scattered. Cases in point are Scott Russell and Co. and Samuda and Co., on the Thames ; Evans', Potter's, and Royden's yards on the Mersey—all builders of fine sailing vessels ; Mitchell and Co., and Miller, Ravenhill and Salkeld, on the Tyne ; William Pile and Co., on the Wear ; Napier, Shanks and Bell on the Clyde ; and the warship yard at Buckler's Hard, Hants., where Nelson's *Agamemnon* was constructed.

There were many others, however, of which little is remembered to-day beyond the bare fact of their existence, testified by entries against some of the more ancient vessels in Lloyd's Register Book ; and many more again which are quite unknown to the present generation, and not even to be found in the Register, for the practice of naming the builder of a vessel was not regularised until the early 'seventies, though some names appear from 1859 onwards.

The rapid development of iron shipbuilding killed many of the wooden-ship yards, and it was not every firm which managed to establish itself effectively, of the numbers which tried to " get in on the ground floor " of the new industry.

Often, these little firms were only small family concerns, started inconspicuously by working shipwrights, staffed by a coterie of friends and relatives in many cases ; dependent for their custom upon little more than local repute and local requirements, and ending as quietly as they began when the founder died, or his family drifted into other pursuits, or shipbuilding suffered one of its periodic slumps.

Some, such as Pilcher's yard at Northfleet, near Gravesend, progressed to the building of ships of considerable size ; Pilcher's built for the Royal Navy the *Eagle* 74, which was the R.N.V.R. training ship at Liverpool from 1862 to 1927. Others, like Bowdler, Chaffer and Co., at Seacombe, on the Mersey, builders of the famous yacht *Sunbeam*, are chiefly remembered by some single ship. Most of them did nothing very spectacular, even at second hand, but steadily turned out sturdy little ships in wood and iron, and advertised themselves by their work, quite effectively. In 1856 there were 150 wooden ships under construction on the Wear alone.

No elaborate plant was needed to start a wooden ship yard. Seldom were they even fenced, 50 or 60 years ago—many a riverside right of way was quietly filched from the public when the fencing of shipyards became general. Each shipwright had his own tool-chest, a small building housed the office staff and the master, who usually lived in or very near to his yard, and a firm shelving bank, with the minimum of timbering, supported the half-built ship.

Thus, when a small " family " yard closed down, nothing very monumental remained to interest future historians, and it is only by diligent search in the files of local papers, in libraries, rate-books, legal records, account books or harbour authorities, and amongst the treasured possessions of " oldest inhabitants," that a detailed history can be pieced together.

It is probable that a great deal of research of this kind has already been done merely from personal interest and the pleasure of doing it, by private individuals with an antiquarian bent, but has not been published for lack of a suitable medium, the absence of details felt to be important, or possibly a failure on the part of the collector to realise that what has interested him may also be of absorbing interest to others.

This is a field in which the Model Ship Makers' Clubs and similar organisations can play a valuable part. By pooling their members' own knowledge, exploring local quarries of local information, and particularly by arousing local interest before it is too late, they may be able to add materially to the present imperfect records of British shipbuilding.

Many of the smaller wooden craft were not built from " lines " at all. A half-model was frequently employed as a guide, and numbers of these still exist in private ownership—although the existence of a model alone is no guarantee that the vessel was ever built, as they were sometimes used for estimating and tendering purposes. When a yard finally closed, it is readily understandable that the models had a better chance of survival than the dusty rolls of drawings and the obsolete ledgers from the office.

The bygone firms have been mentioned as typical, at Northfleet and Seacombe respectively. Other names that may serve to whet local antiquarian zeal are :—

Thames.—Chas. Lungley, of Deptford ; W. Joyce and Co., Greenwich ; Bilbie and Co., Rotherhithe ; F. Dadd, Woolwich.

Clyde.—T. Wingate and Co., Whiteinch ; John Reid and Co., Whiteinch ; Lawrence, Hill and Co., Port Glasgow.

Mersey.—Brundit and Co., Runcorn (barge builders) ; T. Vernon and Son, Liverpool (very early builders in iron) ; the Canada Works, Birkenhead.

Tyne.—T. and W. Smith's yard (formerly Row's) at St. Peter's, where many East Indiamen were built ; Airey's and Headlam's yards (18th Century) ; Wright's, Hopper's and Errington's yards (early 19th Century) ; J. H. Coutts, Walker (iron).

Wear.—Hume and Easson, Pallion ; R. H. Potts and Bros., Bishopwearmouth ; J. and J. Robinson, Deptford, Sunderland.

Various.—William Allsup, Preston (precursor of the Caledonian S.B. Co., which closed in 1908) ; Ann Deakin, Winsford (probably only a barge yard but the only instance I know of a yard started by a woman) ; A. Ferguson and Son, Connah's Quay ; J. Kay and Sons, Kinghorn ; H. McIntyre and Co., Alloa ; J. Payne, Bristol ; Thos. Turnbull and Son, Whitby.

Finally, I should personally be very glad of any odd scraps of information regarding the Wearside yards operated at North Hylton and, later, at South Hylton, by my great-grandfather, William Petree (1799-1878), and his brother, John Petree. He was related by marriage to James Laing, who is sometimes credited (whether correctly, I am not certain) with introducing iron shipbuilding on that river.

ALL PLAIN SAIL.
Sketch by]   **" All Plain Sail."**   *[Harold A. Underhill.*

"Built-up" Model Hulls

By FRANCIS T. WAYNE

THERE are many methods of building the hulls of models ranging from the block-and-pen-knife system to the most elaborately built-up ribs and planking. But most builders of scale models require something more accurate than can be produced from a solid block without great skill and pains, but they do not wish to spend either their time or patience on the intricacies of timber ribs. If, however, the frames of a model are built from 3-ply wood cut out in one piece to form both frame and deck-beam, much of this trouble is avoided. I have used this system on three models and find that it is extremely simple to work. On my most recent model,

A Model Brigantine.　By Mr. F. T. Wayne.

which is still only half complete, the entire frame of the model only occupied six hours in the making, and the planks took about 10 minutes each. This actual model—a Finnish coasting cutter—of which rough drawings are reproduced here, may be seen in the Admiral's Cabin in the Strand, probably already familiar to most readers. There, also, are four complete models built on this system, including a very fine barquentine built by Mr. A. R. Stone.

The method of building is as follows : Assuming that the scale is about 60 to 1 and that the model will be between 12″ and 24″ long, the keel should be about ¼″ square. Strips of this size (or larger sizes if required)

A Model Topsail Schooner. By Mr. F. T. Wayne.

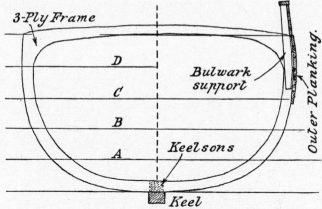

Cutting out the Three-ply frames.

can easily be bought ready cut out. The stern and stern-post are held in position by 3-ply knees, while strips of wood similar to that used for the keel are laid along the keel in the place of the keelson to keep the frames in position. To cut out the frames, take a large sheet of 3-ply and rule lines on it similar to those in the plan so that the distance from the centre line to the inside of the planking can be plotted at the different water-lines (A, B, C, etc., on plan). It is, of course, necessary to have the midship and other sections of the ship drawn out first on a piece of paper on the same scale as that used for the model. The 3-ply frames are easily cut out with a fretsaw and are then pinned and glued into position on the keel. Supports must then be made to keep the frames from moving sideways.

These need only be temporary until the first few planks are in position, and they can be cut out in a very short time, as they will all be the same length, namely, the distance between the frames less the width of one frame.

For planking the model it is best to start with the plank immediately below the deck. To get the sheer the same on both sides, rulers laid across the model and resting on the two planks will soon show any fault when looked at from the bow or stern.

The first few planks may be made the same breadth over their whole length. After the first few, however, we are confronted with the usual trouble of building with planks,—namely, that they have to taper from the point of greatest beam to the two ends of the ship, with a sudden bulge

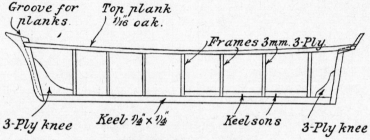

Showing the frames in position.

out again as they go onto the counter. The simplest way of tapering planks is to place a small plane upside down in a vice and then draw the plank across the plane. The finishing touches can be done with sandpaper.

The next trouble that arises is the question of putting on the bulwarks so that the model is quite watertight between the deck and topsides. It is possible to make the bulwark supports in one piece with the ribs, but it is neater and quite as strong to make separate supports, which are glued alongside the ribs and also half-way between the ribs. I find the simplest method is to make a "sham" deck on which the real deck rests and which is slotted to take the bulwark supports. This "sham" deck need only be roughly made and about ½" in width, and in a number of different sections covering about 3 frames each. The deck can then be cut out of one sheet of $\frac{1}{16}$" oak, with lines ruled down it to give it the appearance of planks. It is then laid on the "sham" deck and the spaces between the bulwark supports filled with short planks put in with plenty of glue.

The following points are worthy of the attention of those who are thinking of trying this method for the first time. When planning the ribs, be careful to take into consideration the position of the masts and hatches.

There should be half as many frames as in the actual vessel. Only the finest pins should be used for the planking or the frames may split.

The Finnish Coasting Cutter "Edla"

Steps should be taken to prevent the keel "hogging" on any model with a strong sheer, as the bending of the planks will tend to cause this.

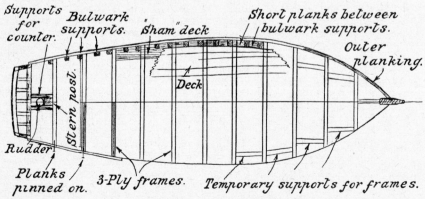

Plan showing method of planking.

How I Make My Ship Bottle Models

By JOHN MITCHELL

SHIPS in bottles have a charm of their own, and apart from their value as a model, there is always the discussion amongst the uninitiated as to how the ship was put into the bottle. Many and varied are the methods I have heard put forward ; for example, the bottom is cut out of the bottle, the ship inserted, and the bottom stuck with a transparent adhesive. Others say the bottle is blown round the ship. Either of these means would be considerably more difficult than the actual method, which, when you know it, is comparatively simple.

First of all, procure a glass bottle, a round 40 oz., one with a short neck is the most suitable. These are usually about 8″ long from base of neck to bottom, and 3½″ in diameter, and I may say I find the procuring of a good bottle the most difficult part of the whole procedure. Perhaps some reader could say where bottles of the type illustrated can be obtained.

A 4″ model can easily be inserted in a 40 oz. bottle, together with a tug, a lighthouse, and some houses or cottages.

The tools and materials required are a fine fretwork drill, a sharp pen-knife, a reel of white silk thread, a tube of seccotine, a piece of bees' wax, a long piece of thin wire which can be easily bent into any shape, a second piece of thin wire with a needle soldered on to the end, a long piece of tin about ½″ wide, which is used for putting the sea into the bottle, and a piece of wire with a small piece of safety-razor blade soldered on to one end. This is used for cutting the threads when the model is complete.

The secret of inserting a ship in a bottle is to make it in such a manner that the masts will fold down level with the deck and the yards cockbill so that they will be in line with the masts.

The model I intend to describe is the full-rigged ship *Star of France*, which I have constructed with the aid of a good broadside photograph. She is 4¼″ long overall.

The first thing to do is to cut out a waterline model from a piece of yellow pine or other suitable wood, making sure it will pass easily through the neck of the bottle with plenty of space between the deck and the side of the neck for the masts and yards to lie on. (See Fig. 1, in which A is

The finished bottle model of the "Star of France"

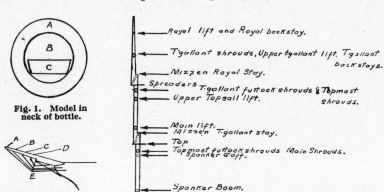

**Fig. 1.   Model in
neck of bottle.**

**Fig. 3.   Bowsprit
Rigging.**

Royal lift and Royal backstay.

T'gallant shrouds. Upper t'gallant lift. T'gallant
backstays.

Mizzen Royal Stay.

Spreaders T'gallant futtock shrouds & Topmast
Upper Topsail lift.   shrouds.

Main lift.
Mizzen T'gallant stay.
Top
Topmast futtock shrouds Main Shrouds.
Spanker Gaff.

Spanker Boom.

Fig. 2.   Showing holes as drilled in masts.

the neck of the bottle, B the space for masts and yards, and C the model.)

Cut three small slots in the deck running fore and aft, one for each mast. These should be very small, just big enough to hold the foot of the mast, which should be cut to the shape of a tiny wedge, in order to fit into the slot prepared for it.

Abaft of the slots for the main and fore masts a small hole should be drilled through the deck to the ship's side to allow the mizzen and mizzen topmast stays, also the main and main topmast stays, to be rove. The ship should now be painted and the deck varnished.

Now cut out the deck houses, boats and capstans from small pieces of yellow pine. The poop fitting from mahogany and the hatches from fine cardboard. These should be painted and stuck in their places. Fine needles cut down and painted black can be stuck into the top of the house for galley and donkey funnels. I have also made two life belts, which are attached to the poop rail. These are cut out of thin white celluloid, but are hardly worth the trouble, as they are so small they are difficult to see against the white rail. The wheel is also cut from celluloid.

The poop and forecastle rails are made from No. 10 crewel needles, as follows : Take three long pieces of silk and thread them through the eyes of the needles. On this model there

are 11 needles on the forecastle and 20 on the poop. Cut the needles with a pair of pliers, leaving about $\frac{3}{16}''$ on the threads. Now drill small holes in the forecastle and poop, and place the needles in them, sticking them down with seccotine. When set, the threads can be pulled taut and the ends stuck.

The masts can now be cut out and should not be more than $1/12''$ thick at the foot ; they can be made with lower masts topmost and t'gallant masts in one piece, and the spreaders and tops can be made out of the celluloid. (The *Star of France* had main and topmasts in one, and no spreaders.)

When making the masts, leave the lower masts about 2'' or 3'' longer than required, as they get a lot of handling when rigging, which tends to spoil the varnish.

They should now be drilled to take the lifts, shrouds, backstays, and stays ; then painted or varnished, as required.

Fig. 2 shows where the holes should be drilled. Main mast (only no holes for spanker boom and gaff). Fore mast, similar, only main royal and main t'gallant stays lead through fore and aft holes. Mizzen, similar only no fore and aft holes for stays.

The spars may now be cut out and painted or varnished like the masts. The bowsprit should have five small holes drilled through it, to take the stays. The one which takes the forestay should be drilled after the bowsprit is stuck on, and will, of course, have to be drilled down through the ship.

The *Star of France* was fitted with a dolphin striker which I made from a No. 10 crewel needle. The head of the needle should be cut off and inserted in the bowsprit before it is fixed to the ship, and the bowsprit rigging done afterwards. (See Fig. 3.) Pass all threads through needle eye first, then peg all threads into the ship's side. Haul A and D taut and stick with a drop of seccotine. Haul B and C taut, hold in position and stick; when dry, make fast loose ends E. No. 10 crewel needle head.

The ship is now ready for rigging, and a start should be made with the mizzen mast. First of all, pass two

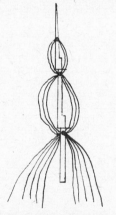

Fig. 4. Mast rigging before hauling tight.

threads through the hole shown in the sketch for t'gallant shrouds; take plenty of thread, then pass them through the hole under the spreaders, two ends from one side and two from the other. This will give you two t'gallant shrouds at each side, also the futtock shrouds; then pass a single thread through the same hole as the four. Quite easily done with the aid of bees' wax or a fine needle. Now pass the three through the hole

under the " top " from each side, which gives three topmast shrouds. Another thread will require to be passed through this hole, which makes four mizzen shrouds. Pull the whole lot taut and put a spot of seccotine in the holes under the spreaders and " top " which will hold the mast rigging in position. Fig. 4 shows the mast rigging before it is hauled taut.

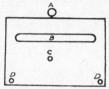

Fig. 5. Stocks for setting up masts.

The back stays may now be set up. The royal and t'gallant back stays may be rigged by passing threads through the holes shown in the sketch, while the remaining back stays will require to be made fast round the mast.

The royal, t'gallant, topmast and mizzen stays should also be rigged; these should be very long, as they are required to haul the mast into position, and should therefore come out of the neck of the bottle.

The spanker boom and gaff are attached by drilling a small hole in the end of each of the spars, and sticking into it with seccotine a piece of thread. The thread is then passed through the holes in the mast, stuck with seccotine, and cut off. Care must be taken not to pull the boom and gaff too near the mast, as they require some play when the mast is folded down. A piece of thread can then be attached to the mast below the spreaders, led from there to the end of the spanker gaff and boom, and when the mast is set up, pegged into the stern. The shrouds on the main and foremasts are rigged in a similar manner. Two t'gallant shrouds, three topmast shrouds, and four or five main shrouds. The back stays are then made fast, also the main royal and main t'gallant stays, etc.

(To be concluded)

A Famous Ship Model

Some Notes on the Original Model from which H.M.S. " Victory " was built in 1765.

By B. LAVIS

THERE is no doubt that the art of the ship modeller is as old as the Pharaohs. Models of early Egyptian vessels have been discovered during excavations in the tombs of the ancient rulers, where they have been placed with jewellery and other treasures belonging to the deceased.

One of the first collections of models appears to have been made by the famous Samuel Pepys.

During his term of office as Secretary to the Admiralty, he wrote with enthusiasm of the models built by the master shipwrights for the Admiralty Board. On one occasion, after seeing a particularly fine piece of work, he wrote : " It pleases me exceedingly . . . I do want one of my own." It was not long, however, before he had acquired an excellent collection, which he desired should be preserved for the benefit of the public.

Unfortunately his wish was not granted, for at his death the collection was allowed to be dispersed to the irreparable loss of the naval historian.

It is only in comparatively recent years that the ship model has begun to come into its own in public regard and interest.

As such models are of considerable value to the historian it is not a little surprising, in view of its standing as a Maritime Nation, that this country should have made so little effort to preserve and identify them.

A little over a quarter of a century ago the Americans began to realise the value of ship models, and not a few excellent and rare specimens crossed the Atlantic at absurdly low prices.

It was then made plain that our maritime history had been sadly neglected, except by a few enthusiasts whose interests was mainly personal.

Partly as a result of this state of affairs, the Society for Nautical Research was brought into being. Not only does it do work of real value, in identifying a number of old models, particulars of which have long since been lost, but its intensive research among records has brought to light much interesting material on the development and growth of the ship. Another valuable outcome of its activities is the founding of the National Maritime Museum, in which a number of interesting historical models will be housed, together with pictures, documents, and other records of maritime progress.

It was in 1654 that the practice of constructing scale models by the master shipwrights for submission to the Navy Board was first established. In 1716 this practice was expanded, the Board issuing instructions for draughts or models to be submitted of every ship ordered.

The method of construction, the carved work and ornamentation of figureheads, galleries, etc., were the principal features of these models.

During recent years very high prices have been obtained for some of these works of art. In 1928, three thousand guineas was paid for one reputed to be the *Royal William* of 1719. A dockyard model of H.M.S. *Burford*, Admiral Vernon's Flagship at the capture of Porto Bello in 1739, was sold for two thousand guineas. But the record deal must surely be the thirty thousand pounds paid by Sir James Caird for the famed Mercury Collection, comprising 176 models. Through his generous action this wonderful collection was saved for the Nation.

The model of H.M.S. *Victory* of 1765, illustrating this article, is a particularly fine piece of work. It is the original model from which this famous ship was built, and is considered to be the most interesting and valuable model in existence.

It was the property of His Majesty the King, who graciously presented it to the Victory Committee, formed in 1922 for the purpose of restoring the vessel to her Trafalgar appearance. This valuable and highly appreciated gift, although representing the *Victory* 50 years before Trafalgar, supplied the research workers with a great deal of information and reliable data concerning the original construction of the hull.

It is here shown in a cradle on a slip ready for launching. Actually she was built in a drydock, the old Single Dock at Chatham, and on completion was floated and towed through the dock gates to the sheer hulk.

During the *Victory's* lifetime she was in dockyard hands a number of times for repairs, the three which altered her appearance most having been effected in 1787-90, 1797-1803, and 1812-16. The most noticeable changes were to her bow and stern,

her bulwarks and channels, and the colouring of her hull.

At the time of her building the usual method of protecting the underwater section was the application of a mixture of white lead and linseed oil. Copper sheathing had been introduced, but still under experiment. It was not until 1780 that it was applied to the *Victory*.

At that time there does not appear to have been any fixed rule for the colouring of ships. At the end of the 18th Century it was the generally accepted practice to paint them with a mixture containing yellow ochre and turpentine, with a band of black along the wales. There were, however, variations from this according to the ideas of individual captains. In some cases the black bands were thicker than in others, and white was added to the yellow ochre mixture, thus varying the shade of yellow.

Just before Trafalgar, Lord Nelson introduced a more uniform pattern, by

Photo by]   **The Original Model of H.M.S. Victory of 1765**   [*Stephen Cribb*

having all vessels under his command painted the same shade of yellow with the black band running between the lines of the gun ports following the level of the decks. The lids of the ports were painted black also, and when closed formed a chequered pattern, which became known as the " Nelson Fashion."

Although white was substituted for yellow about 1816, this pattern was adhered to in sailing war vessels and training ships, until the last of the wooden walls afloat, the *Victory*, was docked for restoration in 1922. She then reverted to the yellow. Many of the clipper ships affected painted ports, so popular was this fashion.

The interiors of warships, as well as the gun carriage, were at one time painted red, the reason sometimes given for this being that the blood of the killed and wounded would show less vividly. But at the end of the 18th Century, this gave place to yellow for all inside works, bulkheads, partitions and gun carriage.

Names of vessels were not displayed anywhere on the hull until 1771, when the Admiralty issued instructions that they were to be painted on the stern.

The original figurehead of the *Victory* was a very ornate affair. It consisted of an elaborate grouping of figures supporting a bust of George III, the carving of which is so beautifully reproduced on the model. The present figurehead, an illustration of which appeared in the November number, has adorned the vessel since the great repair of 1797-1803. It consists of a shield of the Royal Arms surmounted by a crown, and supported on either side by a Cherub.

A brief extract from a document recently reproduced in the *Mariner's Mirror* gives some idea of the elaborate details contained in the figurehead of 1765 :—

" A new large figure for her head cut in the front at the upper part with the bust of His Majesty, the head adorned with laurels and the body and shoulders worked in rich armour, and his George hanging before, under the breast is a rich shield partly supporting the bust and surrounded with the four cherubs' heads and wings representing the four winds smiling, gently blowing our successes over the four quarters of the Globe. On the starboard side of the headpiece the principle figure is a large drapery figure representing Britannia, properly crowned, sitting on a rich triumphal arch and in one hand holding a spear enriched and the Union Flag hanging down from it, and with the other hand supporting the bust of His Majesty with one foot trampling down Envy, Discord and Faction, represented by a Fiend or Hag ; at the same side, above and behind Britannia, is a large flying figure representing Peace crowning the figure Britannia with laurels and holding a branch of palms denoting Peace and the happy consequences resulting from Victory. At the back of the arch is the British Lion trampling on very rich trophies of war, cut clear and open, and the arch on this side supported by two large figures representing Europe and America, properly dressed agreeable to the countries, and at the lower part of this side the headpiece is cut a young Genius holding in one hand a bunch of flowers belonging to a rich Cornucopia or Horn of Plenty filled with fruit or flowers, cut clear, denoting Abundance or Plenty, which are the happy consequences arising from Victory, by bringing about a peace, and the Genius standing on contrast works and holding a branch of palms in the other hand is an emblem of Peace, etc. . . ."

It may be mentioned that the larboard side contains an equal amount of detail !

When the *Victory* was building, it was the custom to construct vessels with what are known as " open sterns." In three-deckers the after part of the quarter-deck and the upper deck projected some two to three feet beyond the level of the stern, and were finished with a brestrail forming galleries, where the captain and officers, whose quarters were situated on either side of these decks, could obtain a breath of fresh air, without having to go up on deck. In two-deckers the quarter deck only was open in this way.

However, during the great repairs at the end of the 18th Century, these galleries were done away with, the sterns of all ships being glazed in flush with the profile of the stern. At the same time great economies were effected in all ornamentation work and the much simpler design now to be seen in the present ship was substituted. At the same time, the frieze along the bulwarks was dispensed with.

Another noticeable alteration is to the channels. Originally, the fore and main channels were below the upper deck gun ports, and the mizen above them. It appears that in this same repair the fore and main channels were raised above the gun ports to the level of the mizen channels.

The question of protection on the quarter deck does not appear to have been regarded as so important a consideration as grace of appearance. Up to the end of the 18th Century this deck was almost entirely unprotected, except for a very low bulwark over which the guns could fire. Above this

was a narrow rail rising aft in a graceful line to the poop, where it joined the taffrail. But about 1800, a stout bulwark some 6′ in height was built, forming a substantial defence for the officers and guns' crews. The artistic sheer of the rail, however, is still retained.

It is interesting to relate that in 1807 dry rot was discovered in the hull. The only remedy known for this was the ancient practice of " snail creeping," and although this method had not been used for nearly a century, the Admiralty issued an order that it was to be carried out.

In the space of this article it is not possible to describe fully the many interesting and instructive alterations which have been made in the *Victory*, but enough has been said to show the vast amount of research work that has been necessary for her restoration.

It is a great piece of good fortune that it should have been possible for comparison of the original model, representing all that was best in the shipbuilding and decoration of the 1760's, to be made with the ship herself as she appeared nearly half a century later, within the gates of the same dockyard.

(The *Victory* model is temporarily housed in the Portsmouth Dockyard Museum.)

W.M.BIRCHALL.
1932

Sketch by]   **In Eastern Waters**   [*W. M. Birchall*

A Small Scale Cunarder

By S. E. BECK

THE water-line model illustrated measures 6⅜″ overall, and represents a Cunard " intermediate " vessel, running on their Canadian service.

These ships are about 14,000 tons gross, twin-screw, propelled by steam turbines, the boilers being oil fired, under forced draught.

I was unable to get hold of any drawings, or even accurate measurements, and consequently, to my lasting regret, the model is not exactly correct in detail or proportion.

A visit to the docks when one of the ships was in port did not help much, either, as I was not then thinking of making a model, and did not take particular notice of this ship.

However, work was begun with the little knowledge acquired, and a large amount of guesswork.

The hull was carved out of an odd piece of soft white wood up to the bridge deck, and cut away fore and aft to the level of the working deck.

On this were fixed wooden deckhouses, and above them the boat deck, made of postcard, also the bridge and wheel-house.

Stanchions along the promenade deck are very thin strips of card, cut with a razor blade. The chief difficulty with these was to cut them *exactly* the same size.

A short length cut from an old quill pen came in handy for the funnel, being a convenient size, hollow, and

oval. It was sandpapered smooth, trimmed up correctly, and narrow strips of paper were stuck on to form the upper rim and bands round.

The steam pipe abaft the funnel was made from a pin with the head filed down so as to leave just a slight bell top.

Syrens were made up of odds and ends of wire, etc., mounted on a small platform of paper.

Pins of various sizes served for the masts, derricks, and sampson posts. The kind that are used for setting butterflies were found to be most satisfactory, as these are thinner than ordinary ones, and do not rust.

The only parts of the model that came near being tedious to make, I think, were the boats—28, almost exactly alike, carved out of wood and just under ⅜″ long.

Now came a problem over which I puzzled over for weeks, and one which seems to have bothered several of my fellow model builders.

Ventilators!

After many weird and wonderful experiments these were successfully constructed by halving mustard seeds, hollowing out the centres, and mounting each half on a shaped wooden upright. The join does not show when painted over. Of course it was necessary to choose well-formed seeds of suitable size.

Winches were next built up with

A Small Scale Model of an intermediate Cnnard Liner.

pieces of card and pin-heads, and after this came all the small stuff, in what order I really don't remember.

Ebonite anchors ; a binnacle on the wheel-house made from a pin ; ensign and house-flag made of thin paper, and painted with water-colours ; davits

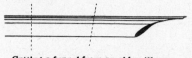

Cutting a funnel from an old quill pen

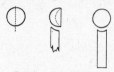

Details of ventilators

of wire ; blocks for boat tackle of wood ; hatches ; deck rails of fine copper wire ; crow's nest, etc.

Deck ladders were made of thin card, light buff colour, the gaps between steps being drawn in black with a fine pen.

One of the for'ard hatch covers is removed, showing a case of cargo being swung out of the hold between two derricks.

All the rigging is fine human hair, except the wireless aerials, which are fine-drawn strands of seccotine.

It is a curious things about these aerials that they sag in wet weather, until almost touching the funnel top, and tighten up again as soon as the atmosphere becomes dry.

The black part of the hull is painted with indian ink, and the rest with water-colour.

I did not feel capable of making a really good imitation sea, so mounted the model on a piece of satin walnut, bevelled and polished, which gives quite a neat setting without any imperfect attempt at realism.

Along one side of the base is fixed a piece of miniature ivory with the names and other particulars of the class of ship.

The model was about two years building, but this does not, of course, give much idea of the actual working time, as it was split up into so many odd scraps of spare time.

I note I should like to make is, that these ships now have the white paint carried a deck lower than when the model was made, which, of course, takes it right along to the stem and a little further aft.

A Model Electric Motor Launch

By C. EDWARDS

THE idea and general design were obtained from *Model Steamers and Motor Boats* under the heading A Clockwork-driven Model of a Motor Launch—*Lady Barbara*, although it differs in many details and mode of construction.

Dimensions

The overall dimensions of the model are as follows : Length, 44" ; breadth, 7½" ; depth amidships, 4½" ; height to top of mast, 21".

The Hull

The hull consists of two side strakes of an ⅛" three-ply wood screwed to three wooden blocks. The bow of the launch is the first block, which is 5½" long and is shaped accordingly, the

three-ply wood strakes being let in flush with the sides for 1½", so that the remaining 4" surface of the block forms the bow. From this point the side strakes gradually widen, leaving a flat bottom to the stern. The stem block is cut with a slight angle, thus giving the necessary slope to the side of the launch. The stern block is cut square. The three blocks are bored with ½" holes for the sake of lightness. All joints were made completely watertight by the use of glue and white lead. The port holes are ¼" in diameter, small washers being turned in the lathe to the required size and glued over the edge of the bare hole. Pieces of celluloid served as glass, being glued

The Model Electric Motor Launch " Lady Barbara "

on the inside with white lead for a watertight joint.

The Deck and Fittings

The decks are of $\frac{1}{16}''$ whitewood lined with ink and varnished and the fittings were made from the following materials. The deck-house and hatches are made from $\frac{1}{8}''$ mahogany, stained and varnished. Matches were very useful for framing windows and doors, while fine, glazed, transparent paper (often found in the wrapping of sweets) was utilised for the glass. The six ventilators are ordinary white clay pipes bought at a tobacconist's, cut short at the bowls and sandpapered. They were painted red inside. The bollards are simply white studs placed in pairs on a small block of $\frac{1}{16}''$ wood and painted black. The six lifebuoys consist of thick rubber wire bound round with white tape, the name being put on with pen and ink. All the stairs leading from the decks are bent out of tin and painted, while the rails leading from the fore to the aft deck are bent from fine wire, covered with tubing, allowing the wire to fit in flush to the deck to the end of the tubing. The ladder leaning against the deck-house to the bridge is entirely made from matches. Long pins

served as stanchions, being bound with white cotton for rails.

The steering wheel, which really operates, is part of a clock-wheel to which has been soldered some small cobbler's nails to form the spokes. The pedestal is made from wood. The launch is steered by means of a small wooden, grooved drum (which has been turned in the lathe) attached to the wheel, and strong cotton winding round this, and a similar, only larger, drum fixed to the rod of the rudder. The rudder is of single sheet tin bent round and soldered to a meccano rod which passes through a watertight gland. The compass and engine-room telegraph are turned from brass. The side-lights, lockers, galley funnel, engine-room skylight and small winch placed forward are made from wood with the help of a penknife. The wireless aerial, of the twin type, is of fine wire, while small beads acted as insulators. The mast is a bamboo cane, the end off a diary pencil forming a suitable top. The beading to which are fixed the stanchions is $\frac{1}{2}''$ dowelling planed down to give a flat surface. It is painted brown and varnished. The mast head light is made from a long tapered bead with a drawing-pin for a top and, touched up, it makes a very good dummy. The anchor, made from tin, is attached by a chain running through the hull. The other end of the chain is threaded up the main hatch, from where it is lengthened or shortened as required.

Life-boat and Fittings

The life-boat is made in two halves from two solid pieces of wood which were scooped out and glued together. The oars and seats are made from thin strips of mahogany. The davits are the ends of motor-cycle spokes which have the requisite knob at the end. Small beads acted as pulley blocks.

The Machinery

The *Lady Barbara* is a twin screw driven by two electric motors, coupled by a belt and running off a 6-volt accumulator. The control switch is placed on the deck. The charging of the accumulator is accomplished without removing it from the hull of the launch, the negative wire being hidden inside a ventilator and the positive under the deck-house stairs. I find this system very useful, because I only require to place the launch on the charging table and connect the wires which are readily accessible, the launch then again being ready for another trip. This model runs for fully three-quarters of an hour at a fair speed on one charge.

Books to Read

The Indian Ocean. By STANLEY ROGERS. London : George G. Harrap and Co., Ltd. Price 7s. 6d. net.

For some time past, Mr. Stanley Rogers has been entertaining an increasing number of readers by his popular books on the Sea and Ships. In the work under review he is to be congratulated on the amount of ground covered within the pages of an average book.

He touches on the early voyages and discoveries of Vasco da Gama, Bartolomew Diaz, and Affonso de Albuquerque ; the history of the East India Company ; pirates and buccaneers ; storms and shipwrecks. A chapter on "War Days" describes the exploits of von Müller in the *Emden*, her destruction, and the escape of a handful of her crew under Lieutenant von Mücke, who had been landed on the Cocos-Keeling Island to destroy the wireless station, in the *Ayesha*, a small and badly leaking sailing craft.

It is to be regretted, however, that so many errors have been allowed to pass unchecked, particularly where statistics have been quoted. In the story of Vasco da Gama's voyage to India, after his merciless revenge on the ruler of Cannanore and the plundering of the native fleet, we read that the implacable sailor departed for Cochin, which, according to a footnote, is in China. The map on page 74 shows Cochin to be about 100 miles to the south of Calicut, whereas Cochin China is over 2,000 miles away. In the *Emden's* exploits, the light cruiser *Newcastle* is stated to be of the same armament, whereas the latter was more heavily armed.

The Sea in Ships. By ALAN J. VILLIERS. London : George Routledge and Sons, Ltd. Price 7s. 6d. net.

A "story in pictures" is Mr. Villiers' latest work.

Deserving of the highest praise, it is undoubtedly the best pictorial record of the last days of the sailing vessel yet published. The 112 pictures taken from all angles, alow and aloft, in fair weather and foul, are surely unique in the annals of ship photography. Of special merit are the ones taken from aloft, looking down on the men working on the upper yards with the boiling sea beneath. To the model-maker they will be invaluable, for they show a vast amount of rigging and other detail remarkably clearly.

In an introduction of less than a dozen pages, the author conveys a realistic impression of life in sail. "'Twas ever thus ; it is a hard road," he writes, "but it is an interesting one. It is a man's life. It has very great compensations. It is one of the few unspoilt walks of life which still remain. There are no artificialities about it. There are no newspapers, no stock exchanges, no politicians. It is extraordinary how one may make a long voyage in a sailing ship, through calm and storm, under blue skies and grey, in rain and in sunshine. There are passing clouds, but on the whole all is well with the world. There are no crises. There are no " grave political events." There are no Stock Exchange slumps, or bank failures ; no rumblings of war.

"And yet, when you come into the first port and the pilot brings aboard a newspaper, you find that half the world is mad and the other half dangerously sick ; that there are grave possibilities of at least two wars ; that the politicians of all countries have made a terrible mess of things, and that there have been at least eighteen murders in the preceding week. One throws the newspaper down in disgust and longs for the freshness of the sea outside and the beauty of the swelling sails."

Much useful and informative information is included, details of running costs, wages and port charges, which will greatly add to the interest in the annual race of the grain-carrying sailing ships.

A large diagram of a barque is provided for the benefit of any who are in doubt of the names of the principal sails and spars. " CHIPS."

The Nelson Collection at Lloyd's.

Edited by WARREN R. DAWSON, Hon. Librarian to Lloyd's. London : Macmillan and Co., Ltd. Price 10s. net.

Comparatively few of the general public realise how large and important is the collection of Nelson relics in the possession of the Corporation of Lloyd's, in Leadenhall Street. It comprises plate, swords, medals and a number of autograph letters of Nelson. In addition, there are numerous other letters and documents,

which, although not directly concerned with Nelson, bear on the history and events of the period.

The nucleus of all this was formed by seven pieces of plate, part of a service presented by Lloyd's to Lord Nelson in honour of his victories of the Nile and Copenhagen, and acquired by the Corporation in 1910. In view of its historical importance the Committee of Lloyd's recently decided to publish an account of the collection for the benefit of the public.

Mr. Dawson, who for many years has devoted much painstaking research to the subject, was requested to undertake this task. He is to be congratulated on having produced a work in every way worthy of the collection it describes.

He has taken the utmost care to transcribe every letter and document exactly as it was written. In the preface he writes : " All eccentricities of spelling, punctuation (or lack of it), abbreviation, and other features of the original documents are here accurately reproduced, so far as the conventions of printed type will allow. I hold the opinion that to edit ancient documents in accordance with modern custom is to rob them of all the little mannerisms (often very distinctive and characteristic) of their writers, and to deprive them of half their charm, and I hold that to print a Nelson letter lays upon the editor the obligation to reproduce it in all respects as Nelson wrote it, and not as a 20th Century writer would have rendered it."

Appended to this unique record of over 500 letters, documents, etc., are biographical notices of 445 of the persons mentioned in them. Enormous labour must have been entailed in accumulating and checking these details, which add considerable to the interest of the book. There is also a list of over 500 vessels, with details of their armament, date of launch, etc., which should prove of great value to the student of naval history.—" CHIPS."

Model Sailing Craft. By W. J. Daniels and H. B. Tucker. London: Chapman and Hall. Price 25s.

The information presented in this book represents the combined experience of two outstanding members of the model sailing yacht fraternity. Mr. Daniels is known to every model yachtsman for his exceptional skill as a designer, as a builder, and as a skipper of model racing yachts, and Mr. Tucker is equally well known as an organiser and keen enthusiast in all that pertains to association and club affairs. The opening pages deal with the various aspects of model yacht racing and with the rules in force. Then follow some excellent chapters on design and practical construction which give the model yachtsman all the information he requires to design and build his own boats. The instructions on hull building, both by the " bread and butter " and the " planked " methods, are particularly complete and well illustrated. Keels, rudders, steering gears, spar making, rigging fittings and sail-making are all dealt with in full detail, and there is a helpful chapter on sailing. Other important sections for the racing men are those explaining the M.Y.A. and International racing rules, and open-water racing rules, the methods of model yacht measurement, rules for model yacht clubs, and regatta arrangements. Some space is also given to fore-and-aft and square-rigged sailing models. The book is profusely illustrated with diagrams and interesting photographs, and there are a number of folding plates giving the lines of selected racing and other sailing models. A preface by Mr. C. N. Forge, the Hon. Secretary of the Model Yachting Association, states the case for the hobby very well. Altogether, this is the most complete and authoritative guide to model yachting in all its aspects which has yet been published. It should be an indispenable reference book in model yachting club circles, while the unattached enthusiast could have no better source of instruction in enabling him to build and sail craft of which he may well be proud on any water and in any company.

The Ship Lovers' Association.

THE usual bi-monthly meetings of the Ship Lovers' Association in London are suspended for the summer months and will be recommenced in the Autumn as in previous years.

Members' Questions and Answers

N.B.—Only those of more general interest are reprinted here.

H.S. (Preston).—The famous *Earl of Erne*, of 1855, was built for the Dundalk (later Dundalk and Newry) Steam Packet Co. She was sold to the Greeks in 1923 and renamed *Sophia Inglessi*, being scrapped three years later.

E.P.H. (London). — The packet *Boulogne*, of 1878, was sold to the British Central African Co. in 1903, and was broken up during the war.

The London Brighton and South Coast Railway's *Honfleur*, of 1865, was sold to E. Bates, of Liverpool, three years later for the West Indian trade and remained on it until the early 'seventies.

F.S.B. (Bournemouth).—The *Aranmore* was stopped and sunk by a German submarine off Eagle Island, Co. Mayo, on March 21st, 1916, and the *Astarte* of 1909 was sunk in collision in January, 1915.

The *Monnow* was an auxiliary four-masted schooner, built in 1918, and owned by T. Berg and Co., of Cardiff. She was burned out off Southend in December, 1920.

Can any member assist Mr. W. F. Barnaby, of Post Office Box 51, Hudson Terminal Annex, New York, in his search for hull and sail plans of the sailing ship *Imberhorn*. It is the former that are wanted particularly for making a model.

The Ship Modellers' Scrap Book

(*Continued from page* 317)

Deadwood

THE timbers filling in between the forward and after ends of the keel and the keelson. In a fine-lined wooden ship they were baulks bolted one above the other, and in iron or steel ships the tapering sections in the same position. In a sailing ship they not only gave added strength but helped her to grip the water; in a modern man-of-war, and in some merchantmen, they are generally cut away altogether in order to increase handiness.

Deckhouse

Any house erection on deck which is not an integral part of the ship's structure like the topgallant fore-

the ship got into soundings and the anchors were got out as a precautionary measure, the discomfort was appalling. Deck - house forecastles could be wet too, and were not infrequently washed out, but, generally speaking, they were much preferable. Many of them divided the crew into the two watches, which was a godsend for getting rest, while others even had the refinement of a little space for drying clothes and keeping oilskins.

In many sailing ships the half-deck in which the apprentices lived was also a deck-house, generally the one next before the poop. There was, however, no rigid rule, and in some ships the half-deck was actually under the poop.

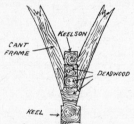

The position of Deadwood

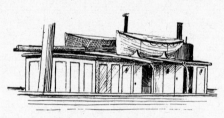

A Sailing Ships' Deckhouse

castle, poop, etc. It may vary from the little caboose galley of a sailing coaster to the whole passenger accommodation of some types of liner.

In sailing ships deck houses were fitted for various purposes from the earliest times. Even in the Roman days there was a sort of deck house aft; in mediaeval times the forward and after castles, by whose construction a merchantman was immediately converted into a man-of-war, were nothing but deck-houses. In the later sailing ships a deck-house forecastle instead of the topgallant or below-deck fore-castle, was quite usual and, generally speaking very much better liked by the men. If the forecastle were in the eyes of the ship, it was always wet, no matter how carefully the hawse pipes were caulked, while when

Many sailing ships also had a deck-house for the accommodation of the petty officers, the donkey boiler and its primitive engine, the carpenter's shop and suchlike. In steamers, innumerable uses are found for deck-houses, according to the type of ship.

It may be mentioned that the "Liverpool House," or midship section of a very modern sailing ship like the *Garthpool*, which stretched right across the ship, was not, strictly speaking, a deck-house, as it was an integral part of the ship's structure.

(*To be continued.*)

Have you got your entry form for the Ship Models Section of the "Model Engineer" Exhibition? Do not leave it till too late.

The Ship's Mail

Readers are invited to make use of this column for the discussion of matters of mutual interest and the exchange of ideas and information.

The "Lancing"

DEAR SIR,—I was most agreeably surprised when, upon opening the May issue of SHIPS AND SHIP MODELS, I found the fine picture of the ship *Lancing*. It brought back pleasant memories not only because I made a voyage in her, but also because it was my first trip as an able seaman.

It is rather sad that such a fine ship should have met the fate it did ; one almost wishes that she would have found a last resting place somewhere in Davy Jones's locker.

I signed the articles at New York City, on November 8th, 1917, and was sent from there to Cape Chat, Canada, where I joined her a few days later. I do not remember the date of departure, but at any rate we made the trip across to Queenstown in eleven days, and the royals were not furled once. From Queenstown the *Lancing* was towed to Adrossan, where her cargo was discharged, and thence to Glasgow, where she took a cargo of briquettes for Brazil. Her master at that time was Captain O. Olufsen, and her port of registry Christiania (Oslo).

Captain Olufson was a man of distinction, an exceptionally fine sailor, and very proud of his command. He loved sail and despised steam. I have heard since that he leaped overboard down in the roaring 'forties, but that is only hearsay, and I cannot vouch for the truth of it.

Iron deck, ballast tanks, and a wheel-house half below the poop deck were some of the things which I found unusual in the *Lancing*. The latter made quite hard steering when in tow.

Other ships I have sailed in were : 4 m. barque *General Gordon*, Haugesund, 1916-17 ; 3 m. ship *Majanka*, Drammen, 1919 ; 3 m. barque *Novo*, Montevidio, 1919 ; 3 m. barque *Fiol*, Haugesund, 1915, shipwrecked Christmas, 1915, on the island of Anholt, in Kattegat.

Besides the above-listed ships there are a few schooners and some steamers.

In conclusion, I thank you for the fine picture, and hope, perhaps, that some day I will find another, to me, well-known ship.

Very truly yours,

Chicago. BEN WILSON.

The "Yawry"

DEAR SIR,—Can any of your readers give me information as to the ultimate fate of the four-masted barque *Yawry*, in which I served as apprentice for, roughly, 12 months from 1917 to 1918 ? The ship's bell had the name "Forteviot" (MacVicker and Marshall), and the ship's name-plate at the break of the poop, "Werner Vinnen Altona." I believe she was originally British owned, sold to the Germans and captured at the outbreak of war in 1914 by H.M.S. *Highflyer*, taken into Freetown Harbour, Sierra Leone, as a prize and renamed H.M.B. *Yawry*. A full crew was sent out from Liverpool in 1917 to put her into shape for going out to sea, but we found that the running rigging had to be renewed, owing to the German crew having poured some kind of acid over most of it. We also found that the upper topgallant yards were in such a bad state that they would also have to be renewed ; in fact, four out of six broke in halves as we lowered them to the deck. The insides of the yards were like so much sawdust, and one could push a marling spike easily half-way into the wood. Most of the original crew, myself included, were invalided home with malaria in 1918, and since then I have lost track of her.

Yours faithfully,

RICHARD WILSON WHITFORD.

Kearsney.

Stiffening Model Sails

DEAR SIR,—I have been trying to find a suitable medium for stiffening up sails, having tried the following two methods without much success :—

(1) Cellulose, which made my sails and flags transparent.

(2) Thin glue sprayed on while hot, I found very messy, as it gets on rigging and deck, and hangs in blobs.

I decided to make up a solution of my own, as follows : ½ pint of water to ½ oz. of isinglass heated up in the same manner as glue, with a knob of gum arabic crushed up and added.

The sails were laid across the top of an empty box and allowed to sag as required, the corners being fixed by pins. The solution was then sprayed on while warm (as it cools, it thickens), by means of a syringe fitted with a glass container (purchased at the local well-known stores).

The sails, when dry, are as stiff as parchment and have no sign of discolouration or transparency.

I hope the above may prove of interest to fellow ship-modellers.

Yours faithfully,
Forest Gate.   KENNETH O. JONES.

The " Calvados "

DEAR SIR,—In your June issue, you give, in reply to " E.P.H.," that the s.s. *Calvados* of 1878 was originally built for the L.B. and S.C. Railway, and sold in 1911 to London owners. As it is of importance that history should be correctly recorded, I point out an error that has arisen, no doubt due to two boats having a similar name. In 1894, the L.B. and S.C. Railway had built, at Denny's, the T.S.S. *Calvados* and *Trouville* for their Newhaven-Caen service, and to be followed in 1896 by the *Prince Arthur*, all three being sister ships. As this service did not prove remunerative, the three boats were disposed of. The *Calvados* was sold to the G.S.N. Company and re-named *Alouette*, and ran to Ostend ; she was not lost in 1913, as stated, and as late as 1923 was still running' A new *Alouette* has since taken her place. The *Trouville*

and *Prince Arthur* were sold to the S. E. & C. Railway and re-named *Walmer* and *Deal* respectively. In part payment of the two latter boats, the L.B. and S.C. Railway took over the screw boat *Paris*, which was built in 1878 by Scott and Co., Greenock, for the L.C. and D. Railway and re-named her *Calvados*. The other boat was the old L.C. and D. Railway *Roubaix* ex *Calais*, and re-named her *Trouville*, a boat built in 1874 by J. and H. Dudgeon. These two steamers have long since been sold. If you care to publish a photo of the *Prince Arthur*, I can let you have a copy. I would again like to state my appreciaiton of your most interesting publication.

Yours truly.
Lewes.   FRANK BURTT, M.I.L.E.

Nautical Photographs

DEAR SIR,—I should be obliged if you could spare me a small space in your " Ship's Mail." I should be interested to know if any of your readers have any photographs of any type of vessel or steamship postcards that they do not want or would care to exchange.

I have a collection of about 800 steamship postcards and am anxious to add to it.

Yours faithfully,
JOHN W. DODDRIDGE.
25 Diamond Avenue, Plymouth.

(We publish this inquiry, but would suggest that readers desiring to arrange the sale or exchange of photographs or models should make use of our " Sale and Exchange " column, where announcements can be inserted at a very modest cost.—ED., S. AND S.M.)

The " Foudroyant "

DEAR SIR,—The " Ship's Log," in the June issue, under the heading Information Wanted, question No. 7 requires data of the *Foudroyant* (1790), and the following may be of interest —

H.M.S. *Foudroyant*, named after the French prize taken in 1758, was launched at Plymouth in 1798 She

Mr. L. G. Maynard's Model Four-Masted Barque.

was Lord Keith's flagship, and afterwards Lord Nelson's, in the Mediterranean in 1799-1800. She was sold
out of the Service in 1892, and purchased by a German shipbreaker, from
whom she was repurchased by the
late Mr. J. R. Cobb, F.S.A. He
brought her to the Thames and had
her re-masted, and the upper works
rebuilt in accordance with the original
sheer draft. He rigged and armed her
with the greater part of her original
armament obtained from Woolwich.
He then turned her over to his son,
Mr. G. Wheatly Cobb to maintain.
During a visit to Blackpool, the
Foudroyant was caught in a violent
gale. One of her cables parted, and
she dragged her other anchor and was
driven ashore, where she became a
hopeless wreck. £30,000 had been
spent on her, but her wreck was sold
for £200.

To take the place of the lost
Foudroyant, Mr. Cobb acquired a
frigate, H.M.S. *Trincomalee*, a 26-gun
vessel launched at Bombay in 1817, a
sister ship to Broke's famous *Shannon*.
He renamed her *Foudroyant*, and
equipped her with the guns and what
gear could be salved from the wreck,
and moored her in Falmouth harbour,
where she carried on as a holiday
training ship for boys from various
schools and organisations.''

Yours very truly,
Westcliff-on-Sea.   B. Lavis.

What Ship is This ?

Dear Sir,—Can any of your readers
assist me in the following matter ?
The enclosed photograph is of a model
of a four-masted barque, which was
recently purchased at a sale in Ipswich.
No names appear on the model. I
am wondering whether it represents
any ship that actually existed. If
so, I should very much like to ascertain her name.

I have enjoyed your Magazine from
the first number, and have recommended it to my friends.

Yours truly,
Ipswich.   L. G. Maynard.

The " Golden Hind "

DEAR SIR,—I enclose a photograph of a *Golden Hind* model made from the blue prints you supply.

One or two notes may be of interest.

The sails are of unbleached calico, stitched to represent the cloths, and stiffened with cellulose solution. The flags were made from tracing-cloth. This was boiled to remove most of the starch, dried, cut to shape, painted with water colours and doped as the sails.

The painting was done with artists' oil colours, made up with copal varnish as a medium and with a little turpentine added to quicken drying. This worked quite well, but on another occasion, for such small work, I shall use water-colour.

The guns were cast in lead, appropriately enough obtained from shrapnel bullets. I used a plaster-of-paris mould made to a brass pattern. This stood up to the repeated casting perfectly well. The only precaution to take is to see that the mould is *perfectly dry*. This is done by warming it until it no longer dims a mirror when held against it.

For the deadeyes I adopted a different method to Mr. Rogers. He cuts them from chipwood ; by this method, the thickness is uniform, but it is difficult to get the shape identical every time. I took a piece of dowelling and planed it until the section was the shape of the deadeye. I then grooved each one and cut it off, thus getting the *shape* uniform, which to my mind is more important.

Mr. Owen H. Wicksteed's Model "Golden Hind."   [*From S. & S.M. Blueprints.*

Drawing by]   **The S.E. & C.R. Paddle-Steamer "Myleta"**   *[Loftus P. Perkins*

One other point arises. The blueprints show the ensign as red St. George's cross with *blue* horizontal bands. Should not these be *green*?

Yours truly,
Darlington.   OWEN H. WICKSTEED.

The First Atlantic Steamer

DEAR SIR,—On account of the letter of your reader, L. McCormick-Goodhart, on page 310 of the June number of your periodical, I have the honour to draw your attention to the booklet, "The First Steamer to Cross the Atlantic," by Francis B. C. Bradlee, issued by The Essex Institute, Salem Massachusetts, in 1925, in which booklet the writer calls the *Curacao* the first steamer to cross the Atlantic Ocean.

Yours faithfully,
—. CANKRIEN, Librarian,
Nautical Technical Institute,
Rotterdam.

The P.S. "Alexandra"

DEAR SIR,—I notice, in your current issue, that one of our readers is desirous of obtaining information regarding a paddle-steamer named *Alexandra*.

Looking through my "Data Book," I find that a paddle-steamer of that name was built in 1879 and had a gross tonnage of 235. She was sold to British breakers in January, 1931, for the sum of £350.

I regret that I have no further details of this ship, but trust that the above may be of interest.

Yours faithfully,
Thundersley.   JOHN W. LIMMER.

Steamers of 1878.

DEAR SIR,—In reply to your correspondent, I well remember the paddle-steamer *Myleta* (spelt with a "y"). She was a smart little packet and was owned by the old South Eastern and Chatham Railway Company. I made several trips along the coast on her in the year 1900.

In enclose a drawing prepared from my original sketch of this vessel.

It will be noticed that she had *two* masts and a high bell-topped funnel, and was, I think, a sister ship to the *Edward William, circa* 1893.

Yours faithfully,
Cricklewood.   LOFTUS P. PERKINS.

The " Winterhude "

DEAR SIR,—With reference to the remark of Mr. Wladimir V. Mendl about the cover design, the seeming mystery of the spanker is easily explained. A ship running before the wind, as she is obviously doing, would not have the spanker set, but furled, as also the cro'jack, in order to give the mainsail a chance.

I noticed also your reference to the barque *Winterhude*. She has arrived

The barque "Winterhude" at Ipswich.

at Ipswich, the enclosed photo showing her coming up the river. From Ipswich, I understand, she is bound for Middlesbro' in ballast ; from there she will go to East Africa with nitrates, and so back to Australia.

I have heard that the *Hougomont* is to be broken up at Sydney, a sad end for a fine vessel. At the rate they are going now, I am beginning to think that there will soon be no more left.

Yours truly,
Ipswich.   R. D. STILES.

Ship Measurements

DEAR SIR,—I should like to ask a very elementary question regarding dimensions of ships generally, but particularly sailing ships. These are usually given in the following order : Length × beam × depth, and the extreme beam is given as being greater than the depth. In most of the ships and models which I have examined, the depth from main deck to keel has appeared to me to be greater

than the beam, measured by the eye in both cases from the midship section.

Last Sunday I was extremely fortunate in being allowed to go on board the four-masted barque *Herzogin Cecilie*, by kind permission of the captain. The ship was in dry dock at Birkenhead, and again I was impressed by the great depth which appeared much greater than the beam.

This, after taking into consideration the fact that the *Herzogin Cecilie's* main deck is covered by another deck for the greater part of her length.

My question, to put it as briefly as possible, is : From which point is the depth measured, in order to arrive at figures in relation to breadth which make them so puzzling to a landsman's eye ?

If some reader will kindly come to the rescue I shall be greatly obliged.

Yours faithfully,
Bradford.   H. E. LONGDIN.

" Ashmore " and " Southern Cross "

DEAR SIR,—E.W.H.W. (Hendon) asks about the *Ashmore* in the February number.

The *Ashmore* was built in 1877 by Reid, of Port Glasgow, for J. Stewart and Co., of 2, East India Avenue, Leadenhall Street, London, E.C. She was an iron ship of 1,179 tons gross, and her dimensions were : 219′ 3″ × 35′3″ × 20′ 6″. By 1905 she had been converted to a barque and was sold previous to 1909 to Norway, being owned in Arendal. She disappears from the Register after 1918.

In answer to G. W. Munro's letter *re* flag of the *Southern Cross*, I find that the *Southern Cross* was a wooden schooner of 134 tons gross, built in 1890 at Street Harbour, Nova Scotia. She was owned by W. Mitchell, of Halifax, N.S.

This must be Mitchell's house flag.

Yours faithfully,
Rangoon.   E. A. WOODS, Captain.

Northern Notes—We regret Jason's Notes did not reach us in time for insertion.

SHIPS AND SHIP MODELS

A Magazine for all Lovers of Ships and the Sea

Editorial and Publishing Offices:

Single Copies, post free, 7½d.

Annual Subscription 7s. 6d.

66 FARRINGDON STREET

L O N D O N :: E. C. 4

Vol. I. No. 12.   **AUGUST, 1932.**   Price 6d.

The Ship's Log

Our First Voyage

WITH the present issue the first voyage of SHIPS AND SHIP MODELS ends, or, in other words, our first volume is completed. It has been a very pleasant voyage, made especially agreeable by the large number of friendly and approving letters we have received from readers in all parts of the world. It has also been an easy passage, through the kindly co-operation and practical help from so many contributors and correspondents. For these good wishes, and for this valued assistance we are very grateful. We did not expect entirely to escape criticism, for we realise that the world of ship lovers and ship modellers is composed of enthusiasts of all degrees of skill and knowledge, and of a very varied range of interest in the subject matter which appeals to them. But the occasional criticism we have received has been of a helpful and constructive character, and we have endeavoured to profit thereby. We regret that it has not been possible to comply with all the suggestions we have received, nor has it been possible to publish all the correspondence, or

to reply satisfactorily to all the queries. But, in spite of these limitations, there is abundant evidence that we have afforded pleasure and instruction to thousands of ship-lovers and have thereby filled the purpose we originally set out to achieve. Having proved that there is a large and appreciative public for SHIPS AND SHIP MODELS, we shall embark on our second volume with ample confidence in the future, and shall hope to enjoy a continuance of the friendly correspondence and co-operation from our readers which is not only so helpful to us in producing the magazine, but which makes it, in turn, of so much interest to all our other readers.

*   *   *

Binding Cases and Volumes

For the information of those who wish to preserve their copies of SHIPS AND SHIP MODELS in bound form, we may say that we can supply neat binding cases, in blue cloth, gilt lettered, post free for 1s. 8d. If readers have any difficulty in getting their volumes bound locally, we can undertake this work if they will send their year's copies to us. The inclusive cost is 5s. 3d. We shall have a few bound volumes for sale, the post free price being 9s. 3d. These prices are for the United Kingdom; readers abroad should add another 6d. to cover mailing costs.

Annual Subscriptions

May we remind our subscriber friends that renewals are now due, from those whose subscription dates from No. 1. The rate is 7s. 6d. for a year, post free anywhere. Those readers who experience any difficulty in procuring the magazine locally, will find a direct subscription a very convenient way of ensuring regular delivery of their copies.

*   *   *

The Forthcoming "M.E." Exhibition

Everything points to the Ship Model Section of the coming *Model Engineer* Exhibition being of the greatest interest, both in the number and the character of the exhibits. We would remind our readers that August 15th is the latest date for returning entry forms for the Competition Section. The actual models are not required till the day before the show opens. Entry forms are obtainable post free on application to the Editor of SHIPS AND SHIP MODELS. Although some good entries have already been received, we are anxious to see the work of our readers well represented. Every model is of interest to the public, however good or however modest in character it may be, and everyone who exhibits is doing something to further the ship-modelling hobby. We are still open to receive a few offers of additional ship models of interest for the Loan Section. The space available in this section is limited, but we have room for a few more models, if early offer is made, and any exhibit of real interest for this section will be cordially appreciated. The Exhibition opens at the Royal Horticultural Hall, on September 1st, for a period of ten days, and will be a splendid show of engineering and marine model making of every description.

The "Calvados"

Mr. Frank C. Bowen writes: "With reference to Mr. Frank Burtt's note on the *Calvados* on page 348 of the July number, while I must wear the white sheet of the penitent for making the ship 'built for the L.B. and S.C. Railway' when transcribing my answer to 'E.P.H.' for your column on the Ship Lovers' Association—my postal answer to him was correct—I must protest against the statement that 'the *Calvados* (of 1894) . . . was not lost in 1913, *as stated.* . . .' This was certainly not stated in my note, which clearly referred only to the *Calvados* of 1878 which was sold in 1911, as stated, re-sold to Joseph Constant, and foundered in a gale in the Sea of Marmora on March 1st, 1913, when carrying 200 passengers. The *Calvados* of 1894, about which I was not asked and which I did not mention, was broken up at Rainham in the Spring of 1924."

*   *   *

Our Supplement Plate

We have to express our indebtedness to Mr. R. H. Penton for the admirable drawing of a Nova-Scotian timber ship which forms the subject of our plate this week. It is a beautiful example of Mr. Penton's marine draughtsmanship, and will, we think, make a very acceptable addition to any collection of records of the days of sail. The originals of Mr. Penton's drawings are available if any of our readers would like to consider purchase.

*   *   *

Information Wanted

Replies to the following queries would be appreciated by correspondents: (1) Wanted lines, elevation, and deck-plans of the North German Lloyd ship *Cassel* in service in 1911. Is this ship still in service to-day? (2) Information regarding owners, date, port of registry, etc., of steamers *Guthrie* or *Airlie*, built by Doxford. Clipper bow, two masts, single funnel and screw propulsion; length, 313'. Presumably passenger ships in China trade.

Sail Training in the Royal Navy

By B. LAVIS

A GREAT deal of interest has been aroused by the recent utterance of the First Lord of the Admiralty that the re-introduction of sail training for officers and men of the Royal Navy is being considered.

In view of the Admiralty Fleet Order issued a short time ago, asking for executive officers, petty officers and men who have had experience in sea-going sailing vessels, to volunteer for sailing training ships, some remarks on the system which existed in the Navy from the '80's up to the beginning of the present century, may be of interest.

Fifty years ago the famous Training Squadron was the principal feature in the training of officers and men of the Royal Navy. It comprised such ships as the *Active* and *Volage* of 3,080 tons, the *Calliope* and *Calypso* of 2,770 tons, the *Champion* and *Cleopatra* of 2,380 tons, the *Boadicea* 4,140 tons, and the *Raleigh* 5,200 tons. In length these vessels varied from 235′ of the

Calliope to 280′ of the *Raleigh*. Usually, the squadron consisted of four ships under a commodore, each vessel being commanded by a captain.

Midshipmen and boys, on leaving their shore training establishment, were embarked for a cruise of six months or more, thus receiving a thorough training in ship routine and work aloft under practical conditions. This was considered by the authorities to be the best practical method of instilling in the young bluejacket resource, smartness and the various qualities that go to the building up of the nerve and presence of mind.

During these cruises, the squadron visited a number of ports and so showed the British Flag in various parts of the world. Many international friendships were formed in this way, for the Navy proved willing and ready to help in numerous cases of need.

A supplementary and more economic method of training, which continued

Photo by]   **H.M.S. "Volage" of the Training Squadron**   *[Nautical Photo Agency*

for a few years after these training squadrons had been abolished in 1899, was the training brigs attached to the harbour training ships.

These harbour training ships were obsolete vessels, the better preserved of the surviving wooden two- or three-deckers.

A typical example was H.M.S. *St. Vincent*, launched in 1816 as a first rate 120 gun ship. After a period of active service, she was permanently moored in Portsmouth Harbour and fitted with everything suitable for training the embryo seaman, including spars and sails, and 22 guns for instruction.

Boys who had completed nine or twelve months' schooling in such a ship, going aloft for spar and sail drill under ideal conditions, were sent away in one of the sailing tenders attached to their ship to receive practical experience in life afloat.

One of the best known of these tenders was the brig *Martin*, of 508 tons, attached to the *St. Vincent*. In charge of a lieutenant, she had a complement of 30 officers, instructors and ratings.

Others to be met with in the Channel were the *Liberty* and *Pilot* of 501 tons, attached to the *Impregnable* at Plymouth, the *Seaflower*, 454 tons, and the *Sealark*, 311 tons, attached to the *Boscawen* at Portland. Although these vessels did not undertake the long voyages of the training squadron, they were considered a valuable asset in the early training of the young seaman.

The controversial point about sail training seems to be that a knowledge of royals, topgallants and stuns'ls is useless in these days of modern merchanised vessels, and that it is a waste of time training a lad to learn all about sails when so much technical and highly scientific knowledge has to

Photo by]   **H.M.S. "Implacable" in Falmouth Harbour**   *[Nautical Photo Agency*

Photo by]   **H.M. Training Brig "Martin"**   *[Nautical Photo Agency*

be crammed into his brain before he is fit to take his place in a modern vessel. With this argument most advocates of sail training will readily agree. The principle value of this form of training, however, is that it develops in the youngster at the most impressionable age resource, initiative and self-reliance. It strengthens the nervous system and moulds the body to physical fitness and healthy activity. Up on the yards in a gale of wind, a youngster has to think for himself, and others, and quickly, too! He gains a clear understanding of the true meaning of discipline and smartness in a way that cannot possibly be taught in a shore establishment or modern vessel.

In spite of the advance of sciences the introduction of ingenious safety devices, etc., it has not yet been found possible to mechanise the elements. Weather and sea are just as treacherous, and it seems strange that any doubt should exist that it is necessary for executive officers and ratings to receive practical instruction in the essential art of seamanship.

At the present time the financial question weighs heavily with all undertakings. It seems, therefore, appropriate to put forward a suggestion that is both practical and economical.

The old *Implacable*, for many years a familiar sight in Falmouth Harbour and now moored in Portsmouth Harbour, would make an ideal harbour training ship. She is lent by the Admiralty to a committee, who maintain her as a holiday training ship for boys from various schools and societies during the summer months. She has accommodation for 250 boys at a time. If suitable arrangements could be made for her to be fitted out on the same lines as the *St. Vincent*, elementary instruction in seamanship and sail drill could be given to a large number of midshipmen and boys under ideal conditions.

Photo by]   **Another view of H.M. Training Brig "Martin"**   [*Nautical Photo Agency*

During the time this preliminary training is being undertaken, it should not be difficult nor expensive to acquire two or three small tenders, fitted out as brigs or barques, capable of accommodating those cadets and boys who have made sufficient progress to be drafted to sea for practical experience.

As the scheme progresses, similar training vessels could be established in other ports.

In this way suitable sail training could be obtained which cannot but have a beneficial and lasting influence on the minds and bodies of England's future seamen.

Drawing by]   **The Coaster**   [*Harold A. Underhill*

Model Sail Making

By C. C. WALKER [Taunton, Mass.]

JUST what is the reason of so many "bare poled" models? Sails are as much a part of a ship as the spars, and characterise her nautical completeness. Why do we accept such a model as finished, for unfinished it certainly is. From what little I

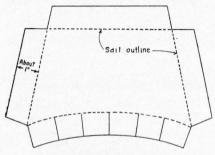

Fig. 1. Lay-out of rigging

have been able to learn may be two fairly good reasons. Instruction and information regarding sails not having kept pace with hull and sparing, and the more delicate and painstaking

work necessary, together with some 50% more blocks to be made. How many model builders know the general belaying-pin plan of pin and fiferail? Why should I and some others know it while the majority do not?

It is perhaps more a matter of what you will and wish to know, as all this information is to be had in both countries, in England by the tub full, as by the bucket full here. I doubt if, in citing American rigging practice, I vary greatly from English, as in almost any case rigging had to be an art rather than a science. In general, rigging ran about the same in each type of ship, varying in detail as did masting and spars.

Rigging, therefore, had to be laid out by the rule of common sense rather than by a draughtsman. But for ship model work, use all the draughtsmanship you possess, and if you do not possess any, try and acquire some. All of the writer's work is laid out on the drawing board before anything is commenced. On a sheet of paper draw extreme height of mast from deck to truck. Draw short cross line from lower cap and longer one for lower top. Same for t.m. cap and crosstrees, as per Fig. 1, and add length of yards at proper height.

Presuming the yards to have been made, the upper width or head of each sail is a wee bit short of jackstay length to allow for stretch. The lower

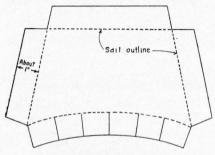

Fig. 2. Allowance for hem

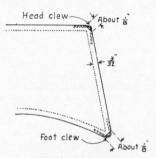

Fig. 3. Fitting Clews

width at clews is a bit shorter than distance between sheet sheave holes. Height of topsail roach is from yard to edge of top. Height of t.g. roach is from yard to crosstrees. Height of royal roach is from yard to t.g. head. Height of clew above yard at A equal to dia. of yard at that point.

For $\frac{1}{2}''$ scale or less, unless you can do a good job with a bolt-rope, it is much better to use a $\frac{3}{32}''$ hem which is about as narrow as the average good sewing-machine worker is able to handle. Allow a $1''$ margin, as per

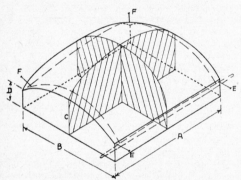

Fig. 4. Form for filling sails

Fig. 2, to allow of easy handling on sewing-machine. Fold over on dotted sail outline, cutting about four slits in foot tab so that roach may be easily folded on a curve. Now press under damp cloth with hot iron. You are now ready to hem. Hem may now be run $\frac{3}{32}''$ from edge *but never to it at corners*. (See Fig. 3.)

Excess of tabs may now be cut off close to hem with fine embroidery scissors. Short pieces of rope laid line are now dyed rope colour, and after cutting off corners of sail, as shown in Fig. 3, are inserted between hem and edge, as shown, and sewn in position with fine thread. This gives you head and foot clews. On lower sails small rings may be sewn in, in place of rope at foot clews for clew-irons.

On sails with reef points, draw parallel pencil lines for reef bands on both sides of sail. Then draw vertical lines to represent stitching (canvas width), taking care not to draw through reef bands. Sew two cringles at each end of reef band, upper one to take reef earring when stretched taut by reef tackle, lower block of which is hooked to lower cringle. Remember that all square sails are roped (hem turn here) on after side, and all fore and aft sails on the port side. Jibs, staysails and spanker are made in the same way.

Regarding wind filled sails, the writer has tried most ways, but finds the air blast method a rather messy and unreliable method. Clew lines on one side and buntlines and leach-lines on the other—yes, and reef points too—seem to make it a battle. Here is my method.

Using a soft porous wood, cut a block as in Fig. 4, with A dimension about $\frac{3}{4}''$ wider than width of lower course, and B about $\frac{1}{2}''$ longer than depth of course, making D what your judgment calls for a good rounded depth. The A side is straight to take the head of the sail. Round over, as shown, making other two sides like C side, and finish smooth. This will also take the single topsail. One smaller is made to take t.g. sail and royal. Warm block in oven or on back of stove whilst melting a dish of paraffin (candle composition). When melted and hot, apply to top of form with brush, working it into the wood. Rub excess paraffin off with cloth while warm; finish with smooth gloss.

Have sail attached to yard jackstay and lay yard on A side of form with jackstay at break of edge, as shown in broken lines, using pins EE to keep yard in place while sail is stretched snug and smooth by drawing and pinning clews with pins FF. You may now apply thin starch solution or whatever you choose, for stiffening and, when dry, your sail will probably fall off of the form, looking as a full sail should, as you were the " doctor " in cutting the form. A form will have to be made for the spanker; one will take all head sails, and one take all staysails.

The High Speed Cross-Channel Packet

By E. P. HARNACK

PROBABLY one of the reasons why the cross-Channel packet appeals to such a large number of ship lovers is because of its high speed. In this connection, it is interesting to note that, of all the merchant ships of the world classified in Lloyd's Register of 20 knots and over, well over 40 per cent. are those engaged in cross-Channel services around the British Isles. The fastest vessels are to be found on the shorter sea routes, mostly operated by day, for in the case of the longer routes, chiefly operated by night, the arrival at the terminal port is usually timed at a convenient hour, and no useful purpose would be served by expediting the service by the employment of ships of exceptional speed. The distinction of owning the fastest ships belong to the London Midland and Scottish Railway, with their Holyhead - Kingstown packets, *Scotia*, *Cambria* and *Hibernia*, though the Southern Railway are close rivals, with their Newhaven-Dieppe packets *Worthing*, *Versailles* and *Paris*.

These ships are amongst the fastest merchant vessels afloat, and the following are some particulars concerning them : The *Scotia*, *Cambria* and *Hibernia* are sister ships, built by Denny, of Dumbarton, in 1920-1921. They have a gross tonnage of 3,460, and with their geared turbine engine developing 16,000 s.h.p., they are capable of a speed of 25 knots. On trials, the *Scotia*, the last of this class, exceeded this figure, and was slightly faster than the Southern Railway Company's *Paris*. Originally, there were four vessels comprising the class, which were built for the then London and North Western Railway, when that company succeeded in wresting the Irish mail contract from the City of Dublin Steam Packet Co., but the *Anglia*, the first one to be placed in service, was withdrawn in 1925, and has been lying up at Barrow ever since. The *Hibernia* and *Cambria* have recently had their passenger accommodation altered and modernised, and part of their awning deck has now been enclosed with glass windows for a distance of 54 ft. at the forward end, whilst the *Scotia* is now undergoing the same treatment at the hands of her builders.

With regard to the *Worthing*, *Versailles* and *Paris*, the Southern Railway claim that, at full speed, these vessels can steam at 25 knots. On her trials,

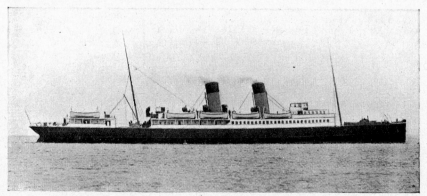

The R.M.S. "Hibernia" on the L.M.S. Holyhead-Kingstown Service

the *Paris* crossed from Newhaven to Dieppe in 2 hours 35 minutes, at an average speed of 25.107 knots, making a slightly faster passage than her French rival, the *Versailles*, which made her fastest crossing in 2 hours 38 minutes, at an average of 24.83 knots. All three ships have geared turbine engines driving twin screws, whilst other particulars concerning them are as under :—

Worthing : Tonnage 2,288 ; s.h.p., 14,500 ; year built, 1928 ; builders, Denny, Dumbarton.

Versailles : Tonnage, 1,903 ; s.h.p., 15,000 ; year built, 1921 ; builders, Chantiers and Ateliers de la Mediterranee Havre.

Paris : Tonnage, 1,774 ; s.h.p., 14,000 ; year built, 1913 ; builders, Denny, Dumbarton.

The *Paris* and *Versailles* had their awning deck enclosed with glass windows in 1929, thus bringing them more into line with the newer *Worthing*. The *Paris* is now being re-boilered and converted to burn oil fuel, whilst the *Versailles* is also being converted to burn oil fuel, and it is possible that the speed of both ships may be increased thereby. An order for a new steamer, similar in most requests to the *Worthing*, has recently been placed with Denny's of Dumbarton, by the Southern Railway.

Next in order of speed are the Belgian Government's Dover-Ostend packets, which are all rated at 23½-24 knots. Four new steamers—*Princesse Astrid, Prince Leopold, Prince Charles* and *Princesse Josephine Charlotte*— have been added to the fleet. These vessels are of 3,000 tons gross, and have geared turbines developing 15,400 s.h.p. It will be noted, that without exception, all the ships previously mentioned are turbine driven, and it is, therefore, of particular interest that the Belgian Government has adopted Diesel engines for their new ships, an order for which has been placed recently with Cockerill's of Hoboken. This vessel, which will have approximately the same dimensions as the newer steamers of the fleet, is to have two sets of two-stroke, single acting

Sulzer engines installed, developing 15,400 b.h.p. and a maximum of 17,000 b.h.p. with supercharge. These are intended to drive her at a maximum speed of 23½ knots, which will make her the fastest motor ship in the world.

In the matter of speed, it is interesting to note that little advance has been made in its application to the cross-Channel packet during the last 30-odd years. The City of Dublin Steam Packet Company's famous Holyhead-Kingstown packets *Ulster, Munster, Leinster* and *Connaught*, of 1896-1897, all reached a speed of over 23 knots on trials, the last named attaining the high figure of 24.15 knots. These ships were amongst the fastest merchant vessels of their time, and even to-day, they would still rank high in the same category. They were of 2,650 tons gross, and had triple expansion engines developing 9,100 i.h.p. Their builders were Laird's of Birkenhead. The fastest cross-Channel packet ever built was the turbine steamer *Ben-my-Chree*, of 2,651 tons, built in 1908, by Vickers of Barrow, for the Isle of Man Steam Packet Co. She had turbines of 14,000 s.h.p. driving triple screws. During a 6-hour run on trials, she easily maintained a speed of 24½ knots, attaining 25½ knots for part of the time. It is recorded that, at times, she actually exceeded 26 knots in service. Unfortunately, she was lost during the late war whilst on Admiralty service as a seaplane-carrier, being sunk by a concealed Turkish battery off Kastelorizo Island, Asia Minor, in July, 1917.

Eyre, Evans and Co.'s Ships

Mr. C. W. Moore writes :—" May I ask, through the medium of your columns, if any of your readers can give me information of any description concerning the ships of Messrs. Eyre, Evans and Co., of Liverpool—*Barcore, Indore, Pajore,* etc., and in particular, *Mysore* Advice as to sources from which I could obtain such information would be appreciated.

A Model of H.M. Aircraft Carrier "Glorious"

A New Addition to the Series in the Royal United Service Museum
By NORMAN OUGH

WHEN I was asked by the Secretary of the Royal United Service Institution in 1931 to make a model of the Navy's most recent aircraft-carrier, H.M.S. *Glorious*, for their Museum, I realised that the task would be formidable.

Of all warships, an aircraft carrier is, from a model maker's point of view, the most complex. The great height and freeboard of the hangar means greater weight above the water-line, so that in order to preserve stability the structure must be as light as possible and large sections of the ship's side outboard of the hangar left unplated. The effect is to leave much of the interior visible, and modelling such a vessel, one is, in a sense, working in four dimensions— length, breadth, height and "inside." Previous experience with more normal ships, such as battleships and cruisers, was found to count for little, and it was only after about a month's work on drawing out the necessary details of the ship deck by deck that I understood enough of the arrangements to be sure of success. I would like to pay tribute to the members of the Admiralty Staff in the aircraft carrier section for their great help in explaining things to me. Without their assistance I should have been lost in the maze of unfamiliar and uncomprehended detail.

The Hangars

The *Glorious* and her sister ship, the *Courageous*, were originally built, in 1917, as large light cruisers, and had an armament of four 15″ guns. She was converted to an aircraft carrier in 1930. The *Glorious* has two hangars and two flight decks, one above the hangars which occupy about three-quarters of the length and a shorter one on the level of the upper hangar deck over the forecastle. Aircraft can "take off" from either, but can "land" only on the upper flight deck. The hangars occupy most of the internal space on and above what was the forecastle deck of the original ship, and consequently all the ventilation trunks from below, the boats and boat-hoisting gear and guns are crowded to the ship's side clear of them. The hangars run fore and aft, one above the other, the upper being about 80′ longer than the lower, and approximately 56′ wide, the lower being about 49′ in width through most of its length. Two lifts, large enough to take an aeroplane, with wings spread, carry aircraft from both hangars to the flight deck. The funnel uptakes are trunked round underneath the lower hangar and up the starboard side to the funnel round which are situated the navigating and signal bridges, chart and plotting rooms, R.A.F. control position, and the sea

Model of H.M. Aircraft Carrier "Glorious"—Starboard Side

cabins of the captain and navigating officer.

The Flight Deck

The flight deck proper is about 60' above the water line: it is 100' wide and about 600' long overall, although not the whole of this length is available as landing space. It is ramped up over part of its length to 4' higher forward than aft. It has to be very strong yet very light, and its construction is one of the many marvels in this wonderful ship. Along each side are nets to accommodate the crews engaged in landing aircraft, while palisades are rigged over part of the length to prevent an aeroplane from pitching overboard in case of a bad landing.

and the second wireless office. The marines' mess deck is also situated on it, and recreation and lecture rooms. The deck is extended outboard on the starboard side as a walking platform, to allow a passage fore and aft round the funnel uptakes—a unique feature in a warship.

The Upper Hangar Deck

The upper hangar deck, below the upper gallery deck, is continuous with the flight deck over the forecastle, on to which it gives through great

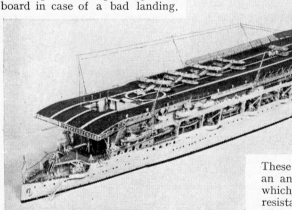

doors, wide enough to pass aircraft with wings spread. These doors, when closed, form an angle projecting forward which helps to lessen the wind resistance made by the ship when under way. Aircraft, when in the hangar, are parked along both sides with

View Aft, showing Flight Deck

Both upper and lower flight decks carry windscreens to protect aircraft while they are stationary. These are cleared away for flying by lowering them flush with the deck. On the lower flight deck are two large derricks for embarking seaplanes, which stow against the ship's side when not in use.

Immediately below the flight deck is the upper gallery deck, about halfway down the upper hangar. This, on the port side, is open for much of its length and the internal arrangements of the ship at this level can be seen, among them being the large air trunks that ventilate the boiler rooms

their wings folded back, and the hanger itself is divided at intervals transversely by fireproof curtains. On this level, externally, are two 35' R.A.F. motor boats with their hoisting gear, on shelves on the ship's quarters opposite the after lift, where they are in a convenient position for lowering into the water in an emergency. Below the upper hangar deck is the lower gallery deck, which carries the boats and winches for running them out and lowering them over the side. Each boat has three winches, one for hoisting, and two for traversing outboard along beams (instead of davits) under the upper hangar deck, which

Model H.M. Aircraft Carrier " Glorious "—View Forward

latter support the lifting tackle. There are 16 boats, the largest being the two 35′ motor pinnaces, and the smallest the 16′ skiff dingheys. The lower gallery deck is not continuous, except through the R.A.F. mess spaces which are part of it, but consists mainly of small winch platforms and frames for the boat chocks. Below it is the deck of the original ship, now called the lower hangar deck, and this, for modelling, is the most complex of all. Forward it carries the anchors and cables, capstans, paravane gear and winches, while along both sides are scores of hatches leading below, ventilation trunks leading from the flats and cabins on the upper and main decks through it and up the hangar bulkheads, gun sponsons and 4.7″ A.A. guns and mountings, ammunition lockers and hoists, funnel uptakes and boiler room vents, and the transverse bulkheads, most of them covered with ladders and ventilation pipes, which divide the guns and boats from each other. Being a " weather deck," it is planked from end to end, and extends from the extreme bow to about 30′ from the stern, where it ends in a projection giving on to a ladder-way leading to the upper deck. The latter is a small part of the original quarter deck, and is still so used.

At the present moment the aircraft carried in the *Glorious* consist of

flights of torpedo bombers, fighters and reconnaissance machines. The torpedo bombers are of the Blackburn Ripon type and carry an 18″ torpedo. The fighters are, at present, of the single-seater " Flycatcher " type, while the reconnaissance machines are Fairey III F, 570 h.p. three-seaters.

In spite of unusual features, the design of the ship is, from the point of view of appearance, exceedingly impressive. The vast bulk is so well proportioned that it does not overshadow the lines of power and speed, which are greatly enhanced by the superb " flare " of the bows, and the towering mass of superstructure and funnel.

Building the Model

The model was built to templates taken off the drawing of the transverse sections, the hull being carved first from the joined planks of American whitewood, and the superimposed hangars and flight decks added afterwards in convenient sections. The flight deck itself is made of veneer laid over beams in the upper hangar. This deck, with its nets and palisades and windscreens, was one of the most complicated parts to make, the overhanging portion at the after end alone requiring over 400 pieces in its construction. The after lift is shown part way down, which renders some of the hoisting gear visible, and also the structural detail underneath the lift itself, and the well into which it houses on reaching the lower hangar deck.

The main armament of 4.7″ A.A. guns in this model proved a formidable item, as there are 16 of them. The Mark XII guns carried in the *Glorious* and *Courageous* are very complicated weapons, since nearly all the elevating, training and director gear is exposed to view. In order to work out an effective convention to show the principal features, I made a detailed model to the scale of $\frac{1}{8}$″ to 1′ from a $\frac{3}{4}$″ scale drawing, and afterwards repeated it on the scale of the model of the ship ($\frac{1}{16}$″ to 1′), leaving out such detail as would disappear on approaching the limit of visibility of ordinary eyesight.

The model was made to be uniform with the rest of the series in the Royal United Service Museum, of which it now forms part, and which includes a battleship, the *Queen Elizabeth*, a 10,000-ton cruiser, the *London*; a destroyer, a minesweeper, and one of the " O " class submarines. Like all the others, the ship is represented at anchor, with lower booms out, accommodation ladders down, and the attached drifter alongside to give an idea of her huge proportions.

The time taken in building was about 3,600 hours (approximately 13 months), or nearly three times as long as the battleship in the same series. There is more work in one side of an aircraft carrier of this size than in a whole battleship model, and the work is much more troublesome owing to the inaccessibility of many parts of the structure. But, although modelling such a vessel is both difficult and tedious in places, it is also of enthralling interest, and one has always the satisfaction of knowing that every stroke of work done will produce a visible result, and that it will record for the student of the future the details of one of the most important ships of the present day.

Certifying Ship Models

The new " badging " scheme of the Ship Model Society

By "JASON"

WHAT is a correct model and who is to judge it ? Will a certified model be enhanced in value ? What is probably more important, will such a model be accepted by the world at large ?

These questions are prompted by the announcement of the Ship Model Society, better known to many by its former name of the Merseyside Model Ship Makers' Club, that they are now ready to receive models seeking the award of the Club Badge. Several models have arrived already, and others have been notified to the Secretary as due to arrive very shortly.

I have before me, as I write, the rules regarding the award of the Badge. It is only to be expected that they are very searching. Broadly they may be regarded as placing the onus upon the model maker of proving the correctness of his model. Thus we come to the first question, Is it worth while to seek such an award ?

Rule 1 reads : " The bestowal of the Club Badge . . . signifies that the accuracy of detail and the quality of craftsmanship so displayed, attains a very high standard and has met with the full approval of the Officers and Committee of the Club. The Officers and Committee shall seek, when necessary, the benefit of expert advice outside the Club membership."

The objective herein is a worthy one, and no seriously minded model maker has any other aim in his work. It cannot be denied that many models, especially some period models, contain glaring mistakes, not in tiny detail work, but in the major items of rigging or sparring or other important matters. Not a few of the books published as "guides" to model makers contain serious errors. In their favour some of these authors wrote their works a dozen or more years ago, since when research work has brought to light much evidence, not previously known. The last quarter of a century, for example, has multiplied our knowledge of Tudor and Stuart times a dozen fold. This is not due to any one person or body, but rather to the thousands of workers throughout the world. Prominent in welding and sifting this mass of evidence is the Society for Nautical Research. By caution and critical analysis truth has been established step by step.

Quite rightly, then, the Ship Model Society attach importance to the research work performed by an applicant. It would seem that they favour the group model, by which is meant that a model has been made by a group of workers, each one specialising in a part of the work. Rule 5, for example, asks for the names of those responsible for research work, drawings and plans, hull, deck fittings, masts and spars, rigging, sails, armament, machinery, painting and finish, and the case for the model. Many model makers may shudder at the thought of no less than eleven persons working on one model, yet this is an age of specialisation. The idea is not new. Many museum staffs already subdivide the work. So also do many model makers of international repute. One model in course of construction on the Mersey has no less than four in the group and probably more will join the group later.

There is an obvious advantage in the group system which can be summed up in the simple adage : "Two heads are better than one."

The same Rule 5 states that the following particulars *must* be declared, viz., period and type of vessel represented, and scale size of model. This eliminates the purely decorative model no matter how well finished and "pretty" it may be. It may not be out of place to interpolate a suggestion here. If a craftsman is able to make a decorative model, he should also by a little additional research work turn out a correct model. The decorative model of the past has given many headaches to present-day research workers.

Rule 7 is very important but optional in its scope. Obviously, if the details asked for are supplied, the applicant scores heavily. At the same time he narrows down his lattitide considerably. It is better to give the items in detail, viz. :—

(a) Name of ship.
(b) When built.
(c) List of authorities (in detail) referred to in the compilation of data.
(d) Original plans, drafts, and sketches (if any) used.
(e) If by personal service in the vessel, what means (if any) have been used to check possible errors of memory.
(f) Has the model been copied from another model ; if so, give particulars.
(g) Has model been copied from actual craft in existence ? If so, where and when.

This experiment of certifying a model will be watched with interest throughout the country. The Society, as a whole, are fully conscious of the responsibility they have undertaken.

One thing is certain. This badging business has had a tremendous effect upon the members of at least two of the new model making clubs, the Liverpool and Manchester Clubs. The *standard* of work has been heightened appreciably in striving for the Badge. Let us hope that, in due course, it will be a much coveted honour.

Notable Ships, Past and Present

No. 6.—THE WHITE STAR M.V. " GEORGIC "

BRITAIN'S largest motor liner, the *Georgic*, belonging to the White Star Line, and built by Messrs. Harland and Wolff, Ltd., of Belfast—the birthplace of the White Star ships —started on her maiden voyage from Liverpool to New York on June 25th.

The *Georgic* is of particular interest just now, for her design provides luxurious accommodation for travellers of moderate means. The popularity and success of this type of ship has well been proved during the last two years by the sister ship *Britannic*, and it may safely be said that of all the ships engaged in the North Atlantic passenger service she is one of the most successful.

The *Georgic*, although a sister ship to the *Britannic*, differs in many important respects, and in her design it will be found that the developments which were incorporated in the *Britannic* with such marked success have been carried a step further.

In outward appearance she has a straight stem, a cruiser stern, two low broad funnels, and perhaps most striking of all is the curved bridge front, which produces a streamline effect. The *Georgic* has the following dimensions :—

Length, b.p., 680′.
Breadth, moulded, 82′.
Depth, moulded, 43′ 9″.
Gross tonnage, 27,000 approx.
Load, draft, 34′ 3½″.

The ship is sub-divided into 13 watertight compartments, and there is a continuous double bottom arranged to carry fresh water, water ballast and oil fuel. She has nine complete decks and eight cargo holds for the carriage of dry and refrigerated cargo.

Accommodation

The accommodation provides for 1,632 passengers in cabin, tourist and third class, and this accommodation is slightly greater than in the *Britannic*.

The most striking room in the ship is the cabin smoking room, where in an endeavour to get away from the customary imitation of a period room ashore, an original note is obtained by panelling the room in horizontal flat sections of lacquer work in black and vermilion suggestive of the construction and quality of a steel vessel of to-day. It is an artist's abstract impression of engineering surroundings. Other noteworthy features are the swimming pool, tennis courts and elevators in the cabin class, the children's playrooms and elevators in the tourist, and children's playrooms in third class accommodation.

The principal public rooms are on the promenade deck, on which there is a new feature which will be much appreciated—the spacious palm court arranged for dancing, lounging and promenading, undisturbed by bad weather. This palm court is also an observation room with glass windows all round.

The " B " deck cabin class entrance has been arranged as the centre of the " business " side of the passenger life, and all the essential services are grouped together ; the purser's, chief steward's, inquiry, mail and baggage, master's and wireless offices are here on the port and starboard sides, with an effectively arranged shop on modern lines near the lift. An arched recess contains a fireplace and recesses for settees and chairs complete the scheme on this deck.

Two beautiful altars have been built, so that the passengers may have facilities for religious worship. The altar in the cabin class is a magnificent peice of work, and is placed behind a folding screen in the lounge which, with its slender classic pillars and soft lighting, gives some aspects of a cathedral.

The tourists' smoking room represents a room in a 16th Century English

[Stewart Bale]

The New White Star Motor Vessel "Georgic."

Photo by]

farmhouse, while that of the third class is like a village inn, with oaken rafters and old-fashioned settees for seats.

One of the two funnels of the vessel is a dummy, and in this has been built a spacious smoking room for the ship's officers.

The Main Engines

The propelling machinery consists of two 10-cylinder double-acting 4-cycle motor engines of Harland-B. and W. type, concentrating maximum power per cylinder in a compact space. The clinders are cooled by fresh water and the pistons are oil cooled, while all the auxiliary machinery is electrically driven. The two main engines are of air injection type but have not attached compressors, these being arranged in the compartment forward of the main engine room. One small steam driven emergency compressor is also fitted. The injection air supply is maintained by four independent compressors, each driven by a 4-cylinder trunk type engine of H. and W. type and of a design which with very little modification would make an ideal power station unit. These units also supply air to four reservoirs for manoeuvring purposes.

There are two Clarkson thimble tube exhaust gas boilers for the main engines on the *Georgic*, also two smaller boilers for the auxiliary machinery—one boiler for the generator engines and one for the compressor engines. This comprises the largest marine waste heat installation afloat, and follows on the Clarkson installation on the *Britannic*, which up to the present has been the largest.

Two main engine exhaust gas-fired boilers will generate steam at sea ; also two auxiliary engine exhaust gas-fired boilers and two cylindrical single-ended boilers, oil fired only, are available for generating steam in port and at sea for heating and cooking purposes.

Auxiliary Machinery

The *Georgic* has a powerful electrical installation for auxiliary and " hotel " work, the supply for which is taken from four Diesel driven generators having a combined output of 2,000 kw., situated in a separate compartment forward of the main engine room. All the engine room auxiliaries, of which there are over 70, are electrically operated, the individual horsepower for driving the pumps varying from 100 down to $2\frac{1}{2}$, while the extent of the lighting may be gathered from the fact that there is an equivalent of over 7,000 30-watt lamps installed throughout the ship. There is also a 75 kw. Diesel driven emergency generator situated on the upper deck for supplying lighting and power for all essential services, if for any reason the main sets are out of action.

The refrigerating installation is of J. and E. Hall type, designed to operate on the CO_2 and brine system, and consists of two vertical twin compressors, each coupled direct to an electric motor ; the usual condensers, evaporators and electrically driven brine and water pumps are provided.

Ventilation requires a total of about 85 electrically driven pressure fans, ranging in size from 10″ to 60″ in diameter. Over 43 of these fans are fitted with heating elements, by means of which the vessel can be kept comfortably warm in the coldest weather which may be experienced *en route*. These air heating fan units are supplemented by electrical heaters distributed throughout the accommodation, and in the engine room there are special heaters for use in New York in the winter months.

The hatchways are served by 16 electric winches and derricks capable of dealing with loads up to 10 tons. The deck machinery includes, in all, 18 silent electrically driven winches for cargo handling and warping, and 20 for handling the lifeboats' steering gear, four large capstans and two large windlasses.

Every care has been taken to combine efficiency in navigation with the safety of passengers ; the equipment of the vessel includes gyro compass, submarine signalling apparatus, direction-finding gear and motor lifeboats fitted with wireless telegraphy.

How I Make My Ship Bottle Models

By JOHN MITCHELL

(Concluded from page 335)

Now take the mizzen royal yard and tie a piece of thread round it exactly in the middle, then tie the yard to the mizzen t'gallant mast in the position it would normally occupy when hanging in its lifts. Take a piece of thread, tie it to one yard arm, pass the end through the appropriate hole in the mast, and tie it to the other yard arm. This makes the lift. The end of the thread when the masts are set up will be passed round the main

slot to hold knitting needles behind which are passed shrouds and back-stays, C the hole for knitting needle which passes through screw eye in bottom of model, and D the holes for knitting needles which pass through screw eyes in board—and a small screw eye screwed into the top of one of them. Now screw into the board at one end four No. 000 screw eyes about 6″ apart, and pass two knitting needles through the two lower

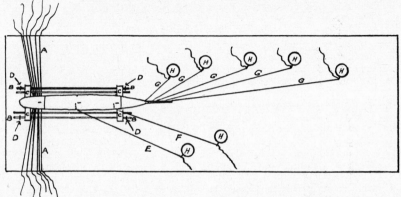

Fig. 6. Showing method of arranging shrouds and stays.

mast and made fast to the other yard arm, thus making the mizzen royal braces (see Fig. 7). The other yards are rigged in a similar manner. Rig the main and foremast the same way, only the topsail and main braces lead to the deck.

When I started to make these models I found great difficulty in setting up the masts and rigging, so I made what I call the "stocks," on which the model is placed to set up the masts and rigging. It consists of a piece of board about 18″ long and 6″ wide; 5 small screw eyes, Bassett-Lowke's, No. 000; 5 knitting needles, and 2 small blocks of wood, $1\frac{1}{2}″ \times 1″ \times \frac{1}{2}″$. Holes are cut in the blocks (see Fig. 5). A is the screw eye for spanker sheet, B the

holes in the blocks, and through the screw eyes. This holds the blocks in position, and they may be set according to the length of the model. Two knitting needles are passed through the slot. A large screw eye screwed into the bottom of the model, which is placed on the blocks, and the fifth knitting needle passed through the middle hole in one block, then through the screw eye in the model, and through the hole in the other block. Small wedges are then inserted between the bottom of the ship and the blocks, which will make it firm and ready for rigging. Cut nicks in the edge of the board with a penknife to take the shrouds and back stays; screw into the board seven large screw eyes about $\frac{1}{2}″$ in diameter to take the stays

The Rigging set for hauling taut.

which lead out from the bowsprit and side of model (see Fig. 6.) A are the shrouds and back stays passing behind upper needles and pulled into nicks in board, B the knitting needles holding blocks C to board, D the screw eyes, E the mizzen and mizzen topmast stays led out through side of ship, F the main and main topmast stays let out through side of ship, G are the stays leading out through bowsprit, and H the large screw eyes.

I found it absolutely necessary to set the model up in this manner, otherwise it is very difficult to get the correct rake of the masts and get the proper tension on all shrouds and back stays. Now take the spanker sheet and pass it through the small screw eye on top of the block, and make it fast to the side of the board ; then take the mizzen and mizzen topmast stays and pass them through the hole in the deck abaft the main mast, and twist them round the appropriate screw eye. This will hold the mast in position fore and aft. Now take the shrouds and back stays on one side and pass them behind the knitting needle, which is resting in the slots in the blocks ; lead them to the side of the board and pull them into the nicks already cut ; deal with the shrouds on the other side in a similar manner. The main mast is dealt

similarly, only be sure the mizzen royal and mizzen t'gallant stays are rove through the holes in the main mast, thus forming the main and main topmast stays. These threads are continued through the hole in the deck abaft the foremast. The main royal and main t'gallant stays are rove through the foremast, and from there through the bowsprit. When the masts are in position the two knitting needles resting in the slots

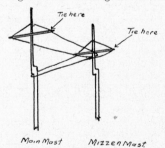

Fig. 7.   The Mizzen Royal Braces.

should be moved under the model and wedged in position. This brings the shrouds and back stays against the side of the ship, where they can be spaced out before sticking with seccotine. Now make the braces fast, putting a small spot of seccotine on each knot, and when you are sure everything is taut, stick the shrouds and back stays to the side of the model. The ship is now rigged, but before inserting it in the bottle it is necessary to make the sea and the land for the village, etc., inside the bottle. These are made from putty, and the sea can be coloured by mixing a little green paint with the putty. This is put into the bottle with a piece of tin

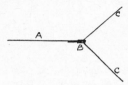

Fig. 8.   The brace pennant.

and smoothed out as required. If houses, etc., are to be put into the bottle, these should be inserted now. Take the piece of wire with the needle soldered to the end ; stick the needle into the side of one of the houses and place it where required. When all the houses, etc., are in position slack back the rigging of the ship, fold down the masts and cockbill the yards ;

then stick the needle into the stem, push the ship through the neck of the bottle, and with the aid of the piece of wire place it where required. The bottle should now be put away for a few days until the putty hardens, care being taken to see that none of the threads rest on the putty. When the putty is hard, take away the blocks and knitting needles from the board, and put the bottle in their place, then haul on the threads, and with the piece of wire guide the masts into their slots, making the threads fast on the screw eyes. As soon as everything is taut, put a drop of seccotine on each stay where it leads out through the bowsprit and the sides of the ship, and, when dry, cut off short.

The blocks shown on the model illustrated are made from fine needle heads. The brace pennant A (Fig. 8) being rove through the eye of the needle B and stuck back on itself ; C is the brace.

The anchors, which should not be attached until the ship is rigged, are made out of needles cut with pliers to the proper length, a piece of bent

The complete model before insertion in the bottle.

wire stuck on the end with seccotine for the flukes, and a small piece put through the eye for the stock.

I should recommend a barque for a first attempt, as the rigging of the main and mizzen braces on a full-rigged ship is rather complicated.

Be sure and put a spot of seccotine on each knot immediately it is tied, as the silk is inclined to slip back, and it is possible that something may slip after the model is in the bottle, which of course would be impossible to rectify.

A Model of a 130-ton Dumb Barge
Made by A. Smith

WE have pleasure in recording another instance of the fraternity which exists amongst model makers. A visitor to our last *Model Engineer* Exhibition, Mr. A. Smith, came into our office there and inquired if we would like to have on show in the Loan Section a model of a barge which he had made. He explained that he had so much enjoyed the show that he felt a desire to contribute an exhibit which was out of the usual in the way of models and might be instructive. We gladly accepted Mr.

Smith's kindly offer and placed on view his model dumb barge. It certainly is instructive, as it shows the details of construction of an actual barge, and further, being the work of a professional barge builder is accurate. There is also much of interest connected with the inception and reasons for making the model, as will be discovered from the message to our readers, in which Mr. Smith relates the pleasure and benefit he has found in model making. As usual with true craftsmen, he is very

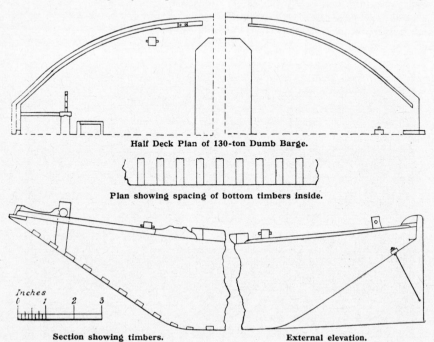

Half Deck Plan of 130-ton Dumb Barge.

Plan showing spacing of bottom timbers inside.

Inches
0 1 2 3

Section showing timbers.

External elevation.

A Model of a 130-ton Dumb Barge.

modest and disinclined to be put into publicity, except that he wishes to be helpful and encouraging to other model makers.

An open, or dumb barge, as the correct designation is, floating on a river, black, and to the undiscerning an uncouth object, may not seem to be a desirable object to model. But the photographs we publish of Mr. Smith's model, and particularly to those who viewed the model itself, indicate, that a large amount of interesting and nice work is involved by the construction of a model barge accurate and true to scale. A barge is designed and built to serve a particular purpose. Various parts are known in the trade by special terms, the floor boards, for example, are known as the " ceiling." There are many special details, such as " lave holes " at the back of the aft bulkhead, and timber holes at each side and down ends to the lave holes. If built to Port of London requirements, there is a cabin fitted with a floor, bench and stove. In a specification for a 250-ton open dumb barge, lent to us by Mr. Smith, there are 43 clauses describing the making, fittings and materials to be used. In an actual barge the bottom is usually Danzic fir, bottom and side chines of English oak, also gunwales, bollards and bits. The wales are $3\frac{1}{2}''$ thickness by $4''$, the skin averages $2''$ thickness, joints of skin rebatted and set with a composition made of three parts tar to one of pitch and coir. Registered tonnage would be rated as three-fifths the actual tonnage capacity on account of dock dues.

The model was made about the year 1900, at home, in spare time, as a hobby. It was also intended, partly, to serve as a demonstration model or exhibit in possible law actions. Mr. Smith's employer was frequently engaged as an expert in disputes and arbitrations. On one of these occasions it was the means of obtaining a successful decision. It has also been used to instruct apprentices in their work and as an assistance in making drawings. Its construction

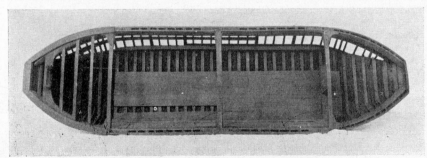

Plan view of Model showing internal structure

occupied about three years of spare time; Mr. Smith had only simple tools and often had to make a needle drill for drilling holes to take the trenails. It is built of pear wood; he recommends this kind to amateurs for similar work, as it yields readily to cutting tools. The length of the model is 29″ overall, 8¼″ beam, and 3¼″ depth at the midship section. The scale is ⅜″=1′; the dimensions of the actual barge would be 77′ 6″ length, 21′ 8″ beam, 7′ 6″ depth amidships. The model is very nicely made, the workmanship being excellent; there is no painting, the wood being left bare, various parts removable,

pleased to help with information to any fellow model makers.

Mr. Smith's message to our readers is as follows :—

" What inspired me to take up modelling as a hobby? I suppose the answer is because it fascinated me. At any early age I used to watch my father building boats, and I often found myself with a piece of wood and knife trying to imitate his vessel, and I now look back and think what crude methods I must have adopted. Later on I became apprenticed to barge-building, and I was more eager than ever to know how to build a barge to help me learn my trade. By

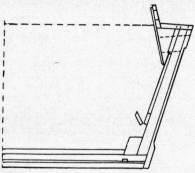

Half-cross-section forward.

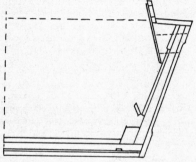

Half-cross-section aft.

and the timbers left exposed, as shown by the photographs, for demonstration use.

We append Mr. Smith's message to our readers and feel assured that his sentiments will be appreciated. He has made several model sailing cutters and bawleys; he was a member of the Alexandra Model Yacht Club at Victoria Park. When about 15 years of age he copied the late King Edward's famous yacht *Britannia*, for which he was awarded a 1st prize at the Edinburgh Castle Mission, Limehouse also for his first model at Battersea Baptist Chapel. We hope that he has not yet finished with his hobby, but will make more models, and perhaps exhibit them at future *Model Engineer* Exhibitions. We are sure he would be

devious methods of measuring what I saw by day I tried to model by night, but to make an accurate object I found it very perplexing, surmounting all obstacles such as finding the necessary tools, materials, etc., presented no mean effort. I have seen many beautiful models in different places I have visited, and I think, in conversation with different builders of many kinds of models, we agreed that the hobby is very educative, interesting and much pleasure derived from it. At the same time, it shows how to build the original article or show full details in construction in case of damage. If one would like to kill many weary hours on their hands, take up modelling of their calling, and they will find it is more instructive than one imagines."

A Model of H.M.S. "Bounty"

By COMMANDER E. C. TUFNELL, R.N.

IT is only through an accident of History that some particular little ship has fame thrust upon her, and for this reason it is often difficult in after days, if not impossible, to obtain any accurate details of her appearance, rig, etc. Had not Columbus sailed to America the *Santa Maria* would never have been heard of, and had not a certain event occurred on April 28th, 1789, there is little doubt that the *Bounty* would have been a mere name in some forgotten register.

As it is, one of the most famous mutinies in history came to a head on that day and so inscribed her name on the Scroll of Fame.

The *Bounty*, a ship of 215 tons, was on her way to Tahiti, whither she had been sent to try the experiment of transplanting bread fruit from there

to the West Indies. For this purpose the after part of the main deck had been converted into a "garden" with racks holding some 700 flower pots. The ship must have been more than usually uncomfortable owing to this further limitation of the already cramped space, and the officers' cabins had been placed under the "garden" in the bowels of the ship, so that the Tropics must have tried them severely. When to these discomforts is added a commander of the—to say the least of it—difficult nature of Lieut. William Bligh, it is hardly a matter for surprise that the crew went on strike. A further example of this officer's lack of tact when, as Captain Bligh, he was made Governor of New South Wales some years later, caused the Colonists to emulate the example of the men

A model of H.M.S. "Bounty"

of the *Bounty* and cast their Governor forth, only this time there was to be no punishment for the mutineers.

I do not propose writing a historical treatise on the mutiny; those interested can obtain the details from Bligh's narrative of the mutiny, published in 1790, or from " Bligh of the *Bounty*," by G. Rawson, or numerous other books on the subject. Bligh's own personal log of the voyage is in the Public Record Office, it having been handed to him by one of the mutineers as he left the ship.

Concerning the model, I was lucky enough to find that very excellent plans of the ship were in existence in the Admiralty Curator's office. The question of the figurehead was uncertain, and I have drawn on my imagination and fitted a Ceres carrying a Cornucopia, which seems to me a very probable design.

The dimensions of the *Bounty* were : 91' length and 24' 3" beam, and she was armed with four 4-pounders and ten swivel guns. In the model I have only shown the pedestals for these.

On either side of the centre line, on the upper deck, are rows of bollards or rollers, and these are, presumably, to keep warping lines clear of the wheel, hatches, etc., the lines passing though ports in the stern.

The model, which is to a scale of 6' to the inch, is planked with mahogany veneer glued on brown paper to prevent splitting—this, when polished, gives a very nice finish. In the photograph, all the rigging appears white owing to my not very clever lighting arrangement, which also makes the white running rigging appear to be heavier than it is.

Before concluding, I wonder if any of the readers of this magazine can give me any information concerning the design of the *Dove* and the *Ark*, the two ships that conveyed the Papists and other assorted sects to Maryland ? If so, I should be more than grateful for it.

The Ship's Mail

Information Wanted.

DEAR SIR,—May I seek the assistance of your readers to answer a few queries of shipping interest ?

(1) At Oddicombe Beach, Torquay, is an old and very battered figurehead, apparently of a female figure with its head missing. Upon its breast is the name " *Bonaccord*," and a local sailor told me that it came from a sailing vessel of that name which was rammed by a steamer " some years ago." Could any reader give me date of wreck and any other information ? Were the crew saved by the old Torquay life-boat ?

(2) The keel-piece and two boilers of a steamship lie buried in the beach at the Portland end of the Chesil Beach. What vessel ? What date of wreck ?

(3) An old steamer, the *Earl of Erne*, was mentioned in the July SHIPS AND SHIP MODELS. Is she any relation to the *Countess of Erne* which was bought by the Bristol Steam Navigation Company about 1890 and broken up soon afterwards ? What date brought to Bristol ? What date broken up ?

Yours faithfully,
Bristol.   G. E. FARR.

Capt. Cook's " Endeavour "

DEAR SIR,—Your most interesting little magazine provides most useful and absorbing information to one who practices the art of model ship building in the back blocks of the Australian Bush.

I am anxious to build a series of the vessels used by our early explorers. Perhaps some of your readers could supply details—or a source of reference—particularly as regards rigging—of Capt. Cook's *Endeavour*.

Yours faithfully,
Merredin, W.A. ALICE M. CUMMINS.

The "Adelaide"

DEAR SIR,—I recently purchased a water colour painting of a brigantine, the *Adelaide*, the name being on the bow and also on a large blue pennant with red edge. As the picture is obviously that of an actual vessel, I am wondering if any of your readers could give me any information about her port of registry, etc. On looking through the Register of Small Fry in Mr. Basil Lubbock's "Last of the Windjammers," Vol. I, I can only find one brigantine, the *Bella Rosa* of Brixham.

The man who sold me the painting, in Plymouth, said he thought she was a Brixham boat. I am wondering if it is possible that the name was changed at any time.

The "Winterhude" at Stockton

I must add how much I enjoy your little Magazine, which I have had from its inception.

Yours truly,
Callington. MARTIN BODY.

Double Spankers

DEAR SIR,—Recently I visited the barque *Winterhude*, lying at Stockton. I noticed that she has a double spanker, upper and lower. The upper was bent, but furled to the mast, and the

The "Passat" in the River Tees

lower was unbent. The second officer, who showed me round, informed me that this is a German idea. Personally, I've never seen it before.

I enclose two photographs, taken recently, one of the *Winterhude* and one of the *Passat*, both now flying the Finnish flag and owned by Capt. Erikson, but both built in Germany, the *Winterhude* in 1898 and the *Passat* in 1911.

Is this a peculiarity of German barques?

The photographs distinctly show the two gaffs used in this type of sail.

Yours truly,
A. P. CUMMING,
Darlington. Lieut.-Comdr. R.N. (ret.).

Stiffening Model Sails

DEAR SIR,—*Re* my letter on "Stiffening Model Sails," I would like to point out that the quantities should read " $\frac{1}{2}$ pint of water to $\frac{1}{4}$ oz. of isinglass." This is important, as a too-thick solution would leave a crystalline deposit on the sails, also it would be too thick to spray on in a satisfactory manner (hence the gum arabic to " body up " solution).

In reading through the rest of The Ship's Mail, a correspondent gives the past history of the P.S. *Alexandra*, and states that she was sold to be broken up, but I believe that she was saved from that fate and has a new lease of life, running on the Thames as the *Show Boat* this year and seems to be doing well. " There's life in the old (sea) dog yet ! "

Yours faithfully,
KENNETH O. JONES

We are indebted to several other correspondents for similar information regarding the *Alexandra*.

Ed. S. & S. M.

Old-time Blocks

DEAR SIR,—With reference to the 15th and 16th Century blocks described by Mr. Sam Svensson in the June Number, it may be interesting to know that similar blocks are still in daily use in Holland.

The accompanying poor sketches try to give an idea of these blocks.

A is used as a lower " katteval " block and B is the top block.

A is also used as a jib downhaul and, in small inland craft, such as scows, for a main sheet and spritsail-brails.

A " katteval " is the tackle used in Dutch inland craft to scandalise the

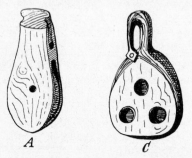

A—Katteval lower Block.   C—Deadeye.

mainsail. As the blocks belonging to it dangle constantly against the lower mast, I presume that these mediaeval blocks kept their place so long against the modern ones, strapped with iron, as they give the least chafe. Of blocks, strapped with iron, Dutch craft carry a large assortment, of which C and D are specimens. C is a deadeye, as used to set up the

shrouds in a small boejer yacht, and D is a throat-halliard block of a small tjalk. Blocks of a similar shape as D are also used for leeboard tackles and rudder lifts.

B is turned on a lathe and comes also with a single knob and hole to replace A.

Blocks like C and D in Mr. Sam Svensson's article are used to set up the rigging in the model of a Spanish caravel, found lately at Mataro, near Barcelona, and now in the Rotterdam Maritime Museum.

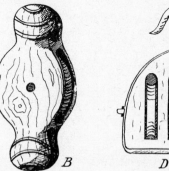

B—Katteval top Block.   D—Throat-Halliard Block.

In the article by Capt. E. Armitage McCann, in the May Number, is a sketch of this model, on page 269. A full description of this model, by the Director of the Rotterdam Museum, may be found in the *Mariner's Mirror* of October, 1931.

This Spring, I repaired six models of fishing craft for the firm of Hoogendijk, at Vlaardingen. One of these, a hooker, made in 1878, has a main tie-block with four sheaves resembling A. The last hooker was built at Vlaardingen in 1866.

I quite agree with Capt. Armitage McCann's article on the *Santa Maria* What does he think of the full-sized model of Hudson's *Halve Maen*, given by the Dutch in 1909 to New York, and of the *Halve Maen* model made by Mr. G. C. E. Crone, as described in his book of 1926 ?

Yours truly,
Rotterdam.   CAPT. DIRK VERWEY.

Ships' Measurements

DEAR SIR,—It is assumed that Mr. H. E. Longdin is not acquainted with the technical literature relating to ships, as most books give the information he seeks in varying detail. The following is from Campbell Holm's " Practical Shipbuilding " :—

" Depth, moulded, is measured amidships from the top of the keel (or intersection of the outside of the frame with the centre line) to the level of the top of the upper deck beam at the gunwale (or of the second deck in the case of shelter or awning-deck vessels).

" Breadth, moulded, is the greatest breadth of the hull, measured to the outer surface of the frames."

The statutory deck line may be found cut in the ship's side, a broad mark 12″ in length and 1″ wide, at a distance immediately above the 12″ circle, denoting the vessel's summer load line in salt water.

Mr. A. Campbell Holm's treatise on " Practical Shipbuilding " is in two volumes, price £3 7s. 6d. Volume II contains 115 large plates of constructional detail that would be of real value to model builders. The scaled drawings cover every phase of construction on the different systems in modern use. The detail covers work on the scrieve board, framing, plating, stern frames, rudders, ventilation, rigging plans, boat systems, and other matter too voluminous to mention.

Within the writer's experience, the book is unique.   Yours, etc.,

London, N.W.1.   W. H. HAMM.

P.S. " Mileta "

DEAR SIR,—In answer to Mr. Hammond's letter, I well remember the above passenger steamer, for I enjoyed a trip in her from Ramsgate to Dover. To me she always seemed a very steady boat, and she hardly ever rolled, especially when going round the South Foreland.

However, I fear I do not know the name of her builders, etc., but I thought the enclosed photo, which I took in Ramsgate Harbour in 1904, may interest Mr. Hammond and some of your readers.

During the winter the *Mileta* was kept in Folkestone Harbour, and perhaps the authorities of that port may know what eventually became of her.   Yours faithfully,

Fleet.   A. SIDNEY MARSH.

The P.S. " Mileta " in Ramsgate Harbour, 1904

The Ship Modellers' Scrap Book

(Continued from page **346**.*)*

Derrick

An appliance for lifting weights on shipboard. In a sailing ship it was generally rigged when wanted by utilising a spare spar, most weights and cargo being lifted either with the yard-arms or else with a span between the masts or yards on which a gin was suspended.

In steamers and motor ships the derrick is one of the most important items of equipment and most modern ships are very plentifully supplied with them for working their cargo.

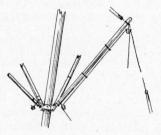

A Derrick

In their simplest form they are a spar with a gin block at one end used as a crane, but nowadays they are very often very elaborate, their weight-lifting capability varying according to their duty and the part of the ship in which they are placed. The heel is hinged either to a mast or to a sampson post, to which the lift leads. In the old days of narrow ships, masts were the most popular supports for the derricks and the four-masted rig was popular ; nowadays the sampson post is more generally used, for it can be placed near the side of the ship, which gives the derrick a very much bigger span. Most modern derricks have the winch, either steam, motor or electric, fitted at their foot. The Navy also uses derricks for hoisting boats, which would interfere with the fire of the guns if they were all placed under davits round the ship's side.

Donkey

An auxiliary boiler in a steamer, but in sail the small engine and its boiler, sometimes portable, which was fitted in the later ships for working cargo and, occasionally, the anchor and halyards. First introduced in Donald Mackay's *Great Republic.* British sailing ships were generally more backward in this important particular than Continental, especially French and German, which often had a very fine steam equipment, which saved its cost many times over by reducing their time in port, etc., and lightening the labour of the crew.

(To be continued.)

Books to Read

Forty-eight Days Adrift. The Voyage of the *Neptune II*, from Newfoundland to Scotland. By her Captain, Job Barbour. London : Simpkin, Marshall, Ltd. Price 7s. 6d. net.

Among the many tales of endurance which have been recorded, none can surpass that of the forced voyage across the Atlantic of the Newfoundland trading schooner, *Neptune II*.

Fitted solely for local trade, the vessel was engaged in short voyages between Newtown and St. Johns, Newfoundland. When on a return passage to Newtown, a distance of about 100 miles, on November 29th, 1929, she was caught in a severe storm and blown out to sea.

Having no navigating instruments and no knowledge of deep water sailing, the crew of this little vessel were at the mercy of the elements. They drifted about the Atlantic, experiencing storm after storm without a break, until with her canvas worn threadbare, her ropes all frayed, bulwarks and boats stove in, she eventually brought up off Ardna-murchan Point, North Scotland, at the worst but only possible place on the coast there was to anchor, on January 15th, 1930.

There were eleven people on board, including passengers, one of which was the bo'sn's wife, who joined the ship at the last moment, expecting to reach her home in St. Johns the following day. She was taken sea-sick the first day out, and was taken to her bunk, where she remained for 48 days. Considering the privations she endured, the lack of food and drink, it is not a little surprising that she lived through it all.

As the days wore on, anxiety regarding the food increased. Eyes were ever more eagerly scanning the horizon for the sight of a vessel or land. " . . . about 8 o'clock in the morning we saw a steamer coming towards us. We signalled, and she came alongside. She stopped for a while. We asked for course for nearest port. We put up our signal boards for her to read. She could see that we were unmanageable. We held a cup to our mouth, meaning we wanted water, but it made no differ-ence in the least, and away she went out of our sight."

Such an experience, in addition to the appalling hardships, is indeed a test, but none of this gallant company lost heart. Trusting wholly to Provi-dence to guide them through, they again proved truth to be stranger than fiction, for the circumstances of their eventual rescue are as remarkable as their tale of endurance.—" Chips."

The Ship Lovers' Association.

WHILE the regular meetings and dinners among the London members at the Admiral's Cabin Restaurant are suspended for the summer months, river outings of various sorts are being arranged as opportunity offers. A thorough in-spection of the new P. and O. liner *Strathaird* at Tilbury, at which a large number of members and their friends attended and which was thoroughly enjoyed. A fortnight later, thanks to the kindness of Commander Gordon Steele, V.C., the captain-superintend-ent, members were invited to hold a meeting on board H.M.S. *Worcester* at Greenhithe. After being shown all over the ship and being entertained to tea, a meeting was held in the games' room of the ship, when all the cadets listened to the three papers presented as eagerly as the members and, by their questions to the speakers after-wards, showed how very carefully they had been following.

Members in London and the home counties will be notified of these events in the ordinary way* as it proves possible to arrange them, and members from the provinces and abroad will always be welcome whenever one coincides with their visit to London.

Members' Questions and Answers

N.B.—Only those of more general interest are reprinted here.

F.S.B. (Bournemouth).—The *Belgian Prince* of 1885 had a very curious history. She was built by Armstrong, Mitchell and Co., as the *Hajeen* for the Bedouin S.N. Co., who sold her to Black, Cowen and Co., of New-castle, in 1898. Later she went to Spain and was re-named *Berriz*, but in 1907 was taken over by the Wallsend Slipway Co. for a debt. As they had no facilities for running ships, she was put under the management of Knott's Prince Line and, by them, was re-named *Belgian Prince*. She is not to be confused with the other *Belgian Prince* which was so much discussed, for she was sold to Norway in 1911 and re-named *Normanna* for whaling work. She was torpedoed by a German submarine off the Scillies in February, 1917.

E.P.H. (London).—The Great East-ern Railway Co.'s *Chelmsford* of 1893 was built by Earles of Hull. She went to the Great Western Railway as the *Bretonne* in 1910 for £8,500, but two years later was sold to Greece for £7,000. Under the Greek flag she has twice been *Esperia* and twice *Syros*, bearing the latter name at the present time under the ownership of the National S.N. Co.

E.A.W. (Rangoon).—The end of the wooden full-rigged ship *Anglo-India*, built in 1877 by Hilyard Bros. of Portland, N.B., for David W. Roberts, of St. John, N.B., was on January 6th, 1889. She was wrecked on the coast of Formosa and nine of the crew landed in one of the boats. They were immediately set upon by the natives, and the 14 men who remained accordingly put out to sea instead of risking the same treatment, and were never heard of again.

H.S. (Preston).—The original owners of the *Lady Louth* (1906) were the Dublin and Glasgow Sailing and Steam Packet Co. In 1908 she became the Burus' *Tiger* and, finally, the *Lairdsforest*.

Northern Notes

By "JASON"

Certified Models

ELSEWHERE in this issue will be found an article dealing with the question of the certification of models. The Ship Model Society (formerly The Merseyside Model Ship Makers' Club) have already commenced their task of scrutinising models for the Society's Badge. I was fortunate enough to be present at one of the committees in session. There are different committees for each group or type of vessel. The majority of the members work in, or belong to, that particular group under discussion, and no person may sit in judgment on his own model. As the Committee have been previously notified regarding the model under discussion, most of the members were well prepared for their jury work. Pictures, photographs and reference books were produced during the session. It is worthy of note that professional sailors were challenged on some details. It is well known, too, that the rigging of a ship may alter from time to time. Many scores of the clippers and the windjammers received drastic alterations in rig and sail plan during their half-century of existence.

Overloaded Models

While it will not be disputed that serious technical errors cannot be overlooked, yet I gather that it is possible for the Badge to be awarded to a model containing mistakes. These errors, however, will be noted in the Committee's report. Where details have been omitted, this would not be regarded in an unfavourable light unless the amount of detail omitted detracted from the value of the model. This is as it should be. There are many models which have been overloaded with tiny items sometimes out of scale.

3/- Model Competition

Full particulars are now available regarding the Three Shilling Model Competition being organised in connection with the First Annual Exhibition of the Ship Model Society of Liverpool, October 3rd-8th, 1932, at the Bluecoat School, Liverpool. The secretaries of the four model makers' clubs in the North will gladly supply information :—

H. Owen, Esq., Ship Model Society, 18, Greasby Road, Wallasey.

T. Sheppard, Esq., The Director of the Municipal Museums, Hull.

W. F. Hemmingway, Esq., "Withens," Littleboro', Nr. Manchester.

R. Macmenemy, Esq., 35, Bellwood Street, Glasgow.

There are valuable prizes and the conditions are simple. The model may be of any period, and it must not be more than 20″ overall. The cost of the materials used must not exceed 3/-. Get into touch with your nearest society and enter.